Precarious jobs in labour market regulation:
The growth of atypical employment
in Western Europe

Precarious jobs in labour market regulation: The growth of atypical employment in Western Europe

Edited by Gerry and Janine Rodgers

International Institute for Labour Studies
Free University of Brussels

ISBN 92-9014-452-1 (hard cover)
ISBN 92-9014-453-X (limp cover)

First published 1989

Copies can be ordered from: ILO publications, International Labour Office, CH-1211 Geneva 22 (Switzerland).

Preface

This book consists of selected papers presented at a seminar on precarious and vulnerable forms of work, held at the Université Libre de Bruxelles from 26 to 28 September, 1988, and jointly organised by the *Institut du Travail* at ULB and the *International Institute for Labour Studies*, Geneva. The seminar was built around an exchange of views among a small number of specialists, for its organisers believed that the state of existing research could be most effectively reviewed by a small group, in which individual contacts and exchanges could be dense and fertile. A general conference with numerous participants might appear more spectacular, but such meetings are generally less fruitful. I believe that the following pages amply confirm this point of view.

An earlier seminar was held at the headquarters of the International Labour Organisation in 1986, on the subject of labour market flexibility[1]. This seminar provided a benchmark for collaboration between the Institut du Travail and one of the most prestigious of international agencies; the scope of its scientific contributions clearly demanded a follow-up in order to consolidate this collaboration, a follow-up which would be of value both in synthesising the findings of current research and in developing new methodological avenues.

The 1986 seminar was devoted to employment issues in a broad sense, and in addition to the organisers it primarily involved economists and jurists. In his preface to the proceedings, ILO Director-General Francis Blanchard underlined the necessity to "define more precisely the concept of flexibility and to assess its impact...to better understand the way in which the market operates, so as to wage a more effective battle against unemployment and job insecurity, to prevent the negative effects of technological change, to devise and implement new employment policies, new institutional frameworks in the service of the international community".

These concerns remain as relevant today as then. In striving to address them the aim has been to enlarge further the analytical perspective, shifting focus from employment to work, from legal and policy issues to practical outcomes (and practices), from the formal to the informal. This widening of the scope also corresponds to the perspective of our Institute, which has in the course of time become more open to the methods utilised in the sociology and the psychology of work.

This interdisciplinary focus was reflected in the seminar held at ULB in September 1988, and differentiates it from other, narrower seminars which have in the past been held around the theme of precarious work.

---

1. Many of the papers were published in a special joint issue of *Labour and Society* (Vol. 12, No. 1, Jan. 1987) and *Cahiers Economiques de Bruxelles* (No. 113, 1st trim. 1987).

Indeed, the chapters which follow document the diversity of points of view presented in the seminar, from the broadest macro-economic perspective to the finest analysis of the feelings of the actor at the centre of our concerns, the worker.   Beyond the presentation of these diverse viewpoints, as representatives of the different social sciences involved in the analysis of labour issues we need to understand each other and to collaborate. And it is precisely this understanding and collaboration, which, alongside the particular conclusions reached, constituted the crucial dimension of our seminar.

I would like to thank all those who contributed to the organisation of the seminar. First of all, I would like to recall the role of Mrs Meulders, of Mr Rodgers and of Mr Wilkin, who so well organised the 1986 seminar. Their contribution at that time laid the groundwork for the 1988 meeting, which could not have been as successful if we had not been able to count on the capacities, as both organisers and researchers, of my colleagues Rodgers and Salengros. I would like to thank them here for their efforts and for the quality of their work.

I would also like to add a personal dedication in remembrance of the deeply regretted Deputy Director-General of the ILO, Elimane Kane, who was taken from us much too early, and who initiated this seminar while he was still Director of the International Institute for Labour Studies.

Professor A. Godart
President,
Institut du Travail,
Université Libre de Bruxelles.

Acknowledgements

In addition to the authors and seminar participants, the editors would like to thank several others who have contributed to the completion of this book:

For much of the typing and formatting: Françoise Weeks.
For checking and correcting bibliographical references: Maryse Gaudier.
For the design of the cover: Ximena Subercaseaux.
For editorial support: Françoise Charpentier and RoseMarie Greve.
For initial translation into English of chapter 4: Michael Bell.
For initial translation into English of chapters 7, 8 and 10: Ann Williams.

Gerry Rodgers
Janine Rodgers
Geneva, July 12, 1989.

Table of contents

1 Precarious work in Western Europe: The state of the debate

Gerry Rodgers[1]

Precarious forms of work have rarely been absent from systems of wage employment. The contemporary problems are most acute in developing countries, where a large fraction of jobs are insecure, low paid, and vulnerable to many forms of abuse. Western European countries have, in contrast, made significant progress towards eliminating or marginalising these phenomena. Forms of labour market regulation built around regular, protected jobs have come to dominate their industrial systems, especially during the phase of steady economic growth between the end of the Second World War and the mid-1970s. The "standard employment relationship", which developed under the aegis of legislation or collective agreement, incorporated a degree of regularity and durability in employment relationships, protected workers from socially unacceptable practices and working conditions, established rights and obligations, and provided a core of social stability to underpin economic growth.

And yet the debate about precarious work has re-emerged. Over the last decade or two, there has been increasing awareness of the persistence and often growth of "atypical" or "non-standard" forms of work. Atypical work is more easily defined by what it is not than by what it is; it covers a host of forms of work which deviate from the standard, and this book covers temporary, casual and part-time work, various forms of disguised or illegal wage employment, homeworking and moonlighting, self-employment and outworking. This heterogeneity makes generalisation dangerous; in particular, it implies that "atypical" does not necessarily mean precarious. Many authors have in fact argued that there is increasing dissonance between the "typical" employment relationship and the needs of the industrial system and of its actors, so that atypical jobs respond to new needs. But while many would agree that employment relations should change to reflect changing social and economic needs, the changes which can be observed appear diverse, fragmentary and responsive to partial interests. Many seem to create new vulnerabilities, or to renew old ones. These issues are the subject of an increasing literature, attempting to assess whether there is a move away from the standard, regular, permanent job, and what consequences this might have for workers and enterprises.

---

1. International Institute for Labour Studies, Geneva.

The present volume brings together contributions from authors who have participated in this debate from several perspectives, and sets their work within a comparative perspective. It includes factual material on changing forms of work – the trends in different types of "non-standard" jobs and their variation across European countries; assesses these changes within broader models of labour market functioning, identifying the groups most affected, the consequences for labour market vulnerability and the roles played by atypical jobs in different labour market mechanisms; and investigates a number of specific themes in the analysis of labour market precariousness. Chapters 2 to 7 take the broad national or international perspective, although each develops a particular angle in detail. The chapters by Caire for France (ch. 4), by Büchtemann and Quack for the Federal Republic of Germany (ch. 5), and by Marshall for five countries (ch. 2), focus primarily on *wage* labour, and within wage labour mainly on part-time and temporary work; Rubery for the UK (ch. 3) covers a wider range of atypical work forms, exploring their precariousness and their economic and social content; Bettio and Villa examine *non-wage* work in Italy (ch. 6), and the variety of forms it can take; and Meulders and Tytgat (ch. 7) provide some of the basic statistics at the level of the European Community.

The remaining chapters are built around more specific themes. Salengros and colleagues (ch. 8) and Burchell (ch. 9) focus on the individual: the perception of precarious status and its effects on health, welfare and motivation in Belgium and the UK respectively. Alaluf (ch. 10) assesses trade union responses in Belgium. And the chapters by Mückenberger (ch. 11) and Ricca (ch. 12) are concerned with the State: Mückenberger in terms of its legislative strategies in the FRG, and Ricca in terms of the broader political economy.[2]

Some overlap between chapters was inevitable, and could not be eliminated without undermining the structures used by the authors. But there is virtue in this necessity, for different perspectives on the same issue emerge from different chapters as a result. More serious problems can arise at the conceptual level: concepts and vocabularies vary, in part reflecting theoretical differences, in part linguistic origins.[3] Some of these differences are of little import – in this book, the terms "atypical" and "non-standard", for instance, should be regarded as close substitutes. Others merit more discussion. The most obvious such issue is the conceptualisation of precarious work.

---

2.   Subsequent references to these authors refer to their chapters in this volume unless otherwise indicated.

3.   The papers in this volume originate partly in French, partly in English (a French edition, with a slightly different selection of papers, will be published shortly); moreover, much of the source material for chapters 5, 6 and 11 is in German or Italian. Such heterogeneity inevitably gives rise to differences of terminology and perception, some of them obvious, others rather subtle; see inter alia the discussion of "regulation" in the last section of this chapter.

I. The concept of precarious work

What makes work precarious? There is a tendency to regard regular, permanent wage work as secure, and to consider other forms of work as precarious insofar as they deviate from this norm. But there are several dimensions to precariousness. First, there is the degree of certainty of continuing work. Precarious jobs are those with a short time horizon, or for which the risk of job loss is high. Irregular work should be included here too, insofar as there is uncertainty as to its continuing availability. Second, there is an aspect of control over work – work is more insecure the less the worker (individually or collectively) controls working conditions, wages, or the pace of work. Third, protection is of crucial importance: that is, to what extent are workers protected, either by law, or through collective organisation, or through customary practice – protected against, say, discrimination, unfair dismissal or unacceptable working practices, but also in the sense of social protection, notably access to social security benefits (covering health, accidents, pensions, unemployment insurance and the like). A fourth, somewhat more ambiguous aspect is income – low income jobs may be regarded as precarious if they are associated with poverty and insecure social insertion. The elements involved are thus multiple: the concept of precariousness involves instability, lack of protection, insecurity and social or economic vulnerability. Not that this eliminates ambiguity; an unstable job is not necessarily precarious. It is some combination of these factors which identifies precarious jobs, and the boundaries around the concept are inevitably to some extent arbitrary.

The extent to which different forms of "atypical" work are precarious in these senses varies a great deal. Temporary wage work, which is perhaps the archetypal non-standard job, is a good example. In countries where a great deal of administrative and legal protection is given to permanent wage jobs (e.g. France; see Caire, ch. 4, Marshall, ch. 2), growth in temporary forms of work arguably reflects a desire of employers to facilitate lay-offs. Workers in these types of jobs are therefore more liable to unemployment, virtually by definition. But temporary work takes many forms: fixed-term contracts; agency work; casual short term work; and so on. There is evidence (e.g. Rubery, ch. 3) that agency and contract work grows in areas of relatively low unemployment, perhaps reflecting a preference among workers for short term jobs with higher returns; a fair proportion of fixed-term (but not "casual") work appears to be linked to training and apprenticeship (Belgium, Salengros et al, ch. 8; FRG, Büchtemann and Quack, ch. 5; U.K., Dale and Bamford, 1988; but the evidence is less convincing for France, Caire, ch. 4), and so probably contributes to career development; and case study evidence suggests that, in some occupations at least, many short term workers are motivated and do not regard themselves as particularly precarious (Salengros et al). These case studies indicated that there were greater problems of stress and fatigue among temporary workers because of work intensity. On the other hand the degree of social protection accorded to these different forms of temporary work is systematically less than for regular, permanent work (Büchtemann and Quack; Marshall), because of gaps in legislative coverage or because of long qualifying periods for employment protection or social insurance. Qualifying periods are particularly important for entitlement to fringe benefits; as a result, despite theoretical equality of treatment, temporary workers often fail to obtain paid holidays, bonuses and the like. And of course longer term security is always absent, by the nature of the fixed time horizon, while many temporary workers suffer intermittent periods of unemployment between short-term jobs. An indirect indicator of the precariousness of this form of work is provided by the proportion of those with temporary jobs who are seeking permanent work; Marshall cites evidence that this proportion is large.

There is also a somewhat more theoretical problem. In some countries the rights of permanent workers are much more solidly established and defended than in others. As a result, the degree of differentiation between temporary and permanent workers also varies. In France, for instance, dismissals of permanent workers are subject to greater legal constraint than in the UK. If you can dismiss permanent workers, then there is little reason to create a class of temporary workers. As a result, fixed term contracts, fairly widespread in France, are relatively rare in the UK (except in the public sector, where there has in the past been a greater assumption of security of tenure); see Rubery. Of course, the situation is more complicated than this. Trade unions play an important role in differentiating permanent from temporary workers, and rights to, say, redundancy payments rise with the duration of employment in the UK. But it does suggest that a dualistic model, distinguishing secure from precarious workers, may in some situations be less useful than a more general concern with degrees of precariousness and vulnerability which will vary from one group of workers to another, or may affect the labour force as a whole.

There are similar conceptual problems with part-time work, probably the most widespread "atypical" form of work, so much so that "atypical" is not the most appropriate adjective. Such work frequently lacks adequate social protection. In the UK, 35% of part-time workers receive no sick pay in 1980 (against 13% of full-timers), and only 9% belonged to a pension scheme (53% of full timers). In the FRG and France part-time workers appear to be better protected, and there has generally been some increase in legislative protection, which however often fails to cover those working very short hours (chapters 2 to 5). Wage agreements or guarantees are often inoperative. Legal or social restrictions on dismissal tend to be weaker, and there are various other disadvantages; see e.g. Büchtemann and Quack, and Rubery, who also notes high variability in hours worked among part-time workers in the UK. Another indicator of precariousness among part-time workers is the overlap between this category and other forms of atypical work. Temporary employment, for instance, is from two to five times as frequent among part-time workers in the UK as in the work force as a whole, and correspondingly a high proportion of temporary workers are part-timers (ch. 2).

Nevertheless, much part-time work is clearly regular and stable; Büchtemann and Quack report that 60% of part-time workers had tenure of 5 years or more in the FRG, almost as high a percentage as for full-time workers. Surveys of part-time workers also regularly report a substantial fraction of *female* (not male) part-time work as voluntary, in the sense that many workers claim that this is the type of work they are seeking. Marshall (ch. 2) argues that much of the "voluntary" nature of part-time work is fictitious, in that women on the labour market will be forced to consider only the types of jobs that are available; that is, some "voluntary" part-time work should be regarded as conceptually similar to the "discouraged worker" effect of drop-out from labour supply in the face of unemployment. Nevertheless, part-time work is clearly not *necessarily* precarious. A substantial fraction is stable and to a reasonable degree protected. On the other hand, the German data in chapter 5 show around one-third of part-time work to be "marginal", tending to be found in low income households, to be irregular, subject to wage discrimination and with less social protection; thus a large minority of part-time workers can legitimately be regarded as precarious.

Some homeworking has characteristics similar to those of part-time work, but – in the UK at least – this tends to be irregular and very poorly paid, and home-workers have difficulty to obtain social security status, so that the tendency for homeworking to be precarious is easier to establish (Rubery). Bettio and Villa (ch. 6) likewise show Italian homeworkers to be underprotected and often in the "degenerative" segment of the economy, which they associate with pauperisation and underdevelopment. They also identify several related categories of non-wage workers whose employment is liable to be precarious.

The broader self-employment category is usually included in typologies of atypical work, but the self-employed are very diverse (Rubery). Among those classified as self-employed we certainly find many workers who are in some sense precarious, some undertaking irregular, marginal or illegal forms of work, others sub-contracting their labour in disguised forms of wage work which by-pass most forms of social protection (Bettio and Villa). But the instability or insecurity of some types of self-employment is not necessarily perceived as a major disadvantage. Contract workers are a particularly difficult case to judge. Dombois and Osterland [1987], referring to ship-building work in Northern Germany, comment: "The assumption that skilled contract workers can be classified together with marginal, deprived groups is inaccurate...Their earnings are usually higher than those of the permanent workforce in the company where they are employed... On the other hand... social safeguards are minimal and the risk of dismissal is high" (p. 238). Yet it would be important to distinguish the precariously self-employed from stable, productive own-account workers. Possible techniques include an income criterion, a capital criterion, a skill criterion and an hours worked criterion – perhaps a combination of all four. Alternatively, a categorisation in terms of economic function is possible, as in Bettio and Villa's "novel", "functional" and "degenerative" segments (ch. 6).

So the identification of precarious forms of work is by no means straightforward. The simple dichotomy between secure, regular jobs and precarious atypical jobs may be misleading. In practice, an equally important issue may be the security and protection of regular jobs, if these are threatened; and although atypical jobs tend to be more precarious than regular jobs, this is not universally so. Nevertheless, trends in the incidence and characteristics of atypical work are clearly major determinants of trends in precariousness overall; and their growth would constitute prima facie evidence that labour market conditions have deteriorated, even if there were not still more compelling evidence in the form of persistent high unemployment. Chapters 2 to 7 examine the evidence on trends in some detail, so only a brief section is needed here to note the main conclusions, before we go on to review some of the underlying economic and social mechanisms.

II. Patterns and trends

Differing typologies of atypical work are developed in succeeding chapters, e.g. by Rubery, by Caire for wage work, and by Bettio and Villa for non-wage work. Here we briefly summarise some of the aggregate patterns which are developed in more detail in individual chapters.

1. Temporary work

In the mid-1980s, temporary work of various sorts accounted for between 3 and 10% of all wage work in the countries of the EEC (ch. 7), and probably a somewhat higher percentage of self-employment. Of course, this is not really comparing like with like, for the definitions vary, and even the conceptual basis of the statistics is not uniform. For instance, if formal apprenticeship contracts are included, the figures rise, especially for the FRG (Büchtemann and Quack). Still, it is striking that the figure is not a particularly large proportion of the work force overall. In terms of labour market functioning, though, it is important at the margin, disproportionately affecting new labour market entrants and those re-entering work after unemployment (Marshall). Thus the rate of temporary employment for those aged less than 25 tends to be at least double the average, and about half of temporary work is found in this group. It is particularly important for unskilled work; in France in 1986 over 80% of unskilled workers were recruited with fixed term contracts (Caire). In the FRG the distribution is bi-modal (ch. 5), with relatively more temporary work in the lowest and highest skill categories.

Trends in temporary work vary a great deal from country to country. In France there has been a pronounced increase since the mid 1970s in both interim and fixed term contracts, apart from a period from 1981 to 1984 when policy controls were important (Caire; Marshall). This shows up in the labour market, for instance in reasons for entry into unemployment – the end of a short term contract was the reason in 42% of cases in 1987, against 25% in 1979 (and this was probably already significantly higher than the early 1970s). The fastest growth in the 1980s has been in very short term contracts. In the Federal Republic of Germany the trend has been in the same direction, but weaker (Büchtemann and Quack; Marshall). In the UK the evidence is unclear; there has probably been some increase in the 1980s, but this is subject to interpretation of ambiguous figures.

2. Part-time work

There has been widespread and substantial growth in part-time work in Europe in recent years, mostly of women;   chapters 2 to 5, and 7 document the trends in some detail, for this is one "atypical" form of work for which data are good.   In Northern Europe, from 10 to 25% of all employment was part-time in the mid-1980s, although the figures were much lower in Southern Europe (ch. 7). 80 to 90% of part-time work concerned women in Belgium, France, the UK, FRG and the Netherlands (Marshall), so that up to 50% of female employment was part-time. "Part-time" tends to mean half-time, for there is a clustering of hours worked around 20, although there is a significant group working much shorter hours. The work tends to be disproportionately found in low skill, tertiary activities (FRG, ch. 5).

The growth, although widespread, has not been uniform. In France, the share of part-time work rose from 4.6% to 11.4% from 1971 to 1987; in the UK from 15.4% in 1971 to 23.4% in 1986. Italy, on the other hand, did not share in this growth, and the proportion of part-time work has stayed low. In the FRG, most of the growth was earlier – during the 1960s and early 1970s – with a slower increase between the mid-1970s and late 1980s (ch. 5).   Marshall in fact argues that the earlier phase of growth was associated with high labour demand in a tight labour market, while the more recent growth may more resemble a form of disguised unemployment.

3. Homeworking and other forms of outwork

The evidence on homeworking and outwork tends to be anecdotal, since much of it by its very nature escapes official statistics. Estimates of the numbers of home-based workers for England and Wales at the beginning of the 1980s gave about 7% of the labour force (Rubery). However, this included a variety of categories, working at home or from home, for one employer or many; many of these would be better classed as self-employed. A little over half were working for a single employer, a situation which frequently reflects disguised wage employment. The Italian data (ch. 6) also show how homeworking is conceptually related to other forms of disguised employment, with over 15% of total employment "disguised", and perhaps a fifth of this homeworking; but the boundaries with family work and self-employment are again ill-defined.   Including both hidden and open homeworking, around 4% of the labour force might be concerned. Wages are often very low, and homeworkers tend in practice not to be effectively covered by labour legislation, although in Italy there is a subgroup of relatively skilled and well-paid homeworkers. In all these dimensions, female homeworking tends to be more precarious than male.

The UK evidence suggests that there has been some rise in homeworking since the late sixties, but the figures from different years are difficult to compare. In France the number of homeworkers declined during the 1970s, though this trend may have been reversed in the 1980s.

4. Self-employment and related activities

The proportion of non-agricultural self-employment in Western Europe is generally less than 10% of the labour force (but 25% in Italy); it seems fairly stable in France, FRG and the Netherlands but has been growing significantly in the UK and Italy (a 50% increase in the UK between 1979 and 1988). Self-employment has an ambiguous position in non-standard work typologies, since much of it is stable and remunerative. But the recent UK growth seems to reflect some increase in subcontracting, free-lancing and franchising, and it consists largely of own account workers without employees, suggesting that this is at the low end of the self-employment spectrum, more a response to unemployment than dynamic small businesses [Lindley, 1986]. Rubery notes that short working hours are more common in self-employment than in wage employment in the UK, and regards this as an indicator of underemployment (though the majority of the self-employed work very long hours). But the links between self-employment and unemployment are complex. There is a widespread view that the unemployed engage frequently in self-employment, largely in the black economy (so as not to prejudice unemployment benefits). However a European Commission study [1987] has shown that this is incorrect – the unemployed tend not to have the requisite skills for self-employment, and are concentrated in regions where the market for their potential services is limited, thus limiting their access to the black economy (Rubery).

Labour contracting, on an organised basis, is on the other hand much more frequent in the black economy. Dombois and Osterland's [1987] study on northern Germany indicates that labour contracting in several industries is largely illegal – in construction illegal labour contracts outnumber legal by 9 to 1 (and make up 20-50% of the work force). Bettio and Villa's disguised employment category accounts for 30% of all self-employment in Italy, and includes a variety of illicit or semi-legal activities.

5. Who are the atypical workers?

The characteristics of atypical workers vary greatly from one form of work to another; chapters 2 to 7 in particular present and analyse the patterns. But three characteristics stand out: they tend to be women; they tend to be young; and they tend to be less educated and skilled than the population average for their age-sex group. These tendencies are probably stronger, the more "precarious" is the work concerned. The feminisation of atypical work is most apparent for part-time work and homeworking; relative youth clearest for temporary work. Temporary work disproportionately affects the young, of course, because it is an important means of initial labour market access; difficult access to jobs may also result in frequent disguised, illicit or irregular work among children and youths (cf. Bettio and Villa, ch. 6). Immigrants are vulnerable too: they are over-represented among temporary workers (ch. 4, 5) and notably in disguised and illegal employment in Italy (ch. 6). Since these are the most common forms of non-standard work, their characteristics dominate those of atypical work overall.

These aggregate patterns, however, need to be interpreted cautiously. Some non-standard work forms, notably self-employment and contract work, are more frequently found among men, and older workers (ch. 3); this is particularly true of moonlighting (ch. 6). The patterns are also complicated by a distinct tendency to bi-modality; that is, in any particular "atypical" category a small but significant percentage will be in relatively skilled, well paid work, even if the majority is precarious – and the characteristics of the better off group will be different: more often male, older, better educated. This applies to self-employment and contract work, to homeworking (see Burchell, ch. 9), to certain forms of temporary work, and, in lesser degree, to some types of part-time work. Nor are individual characteristics, in terms of age, sex or education, necessarily good predictors of perceptions of precariousness. Psychological studies (ch. 8) show that the attitudes, behaviours and responses of precarious workers depend on many other factors, some personal, some structural and social.

III. Interpretation

The evidence therefore supports the proposition that precarious forms of work have been growing in several European countries, although the growth is far from uniform across countries and does not affect all atypical forms of work. A great deal of intellectual effort has gone into exploring why this should be so. Is the deterioration in employment conditions merely a concomitant of recession, or are there longer term structural changes in progress? What are its consequences for the economic relationships and individuals involved? Who have been the principal actors, and what have been their responses?

The papers in this volume approach these questions from a variety of angles, and there are several groups of issues which need to be considered: the role of current labour market conditions; changes in industrial and enterprise structures; the institutional framework, including the changing role of the State and of labour market organisations; and the status of individuals, in terms of new labour supply patterns and responses.[4]

1. Labour market conditions

The most obvious explanation for growing labour market precariousness is the deterioration in labour market conditions over the last 15 years or so, reflected most clearly in persistent high unemployment. This weakening of the position of job seekers makes it possible for employers to offer less attractive jobs, if it is in their interests to do so (a point which is

---

4.   This breakdown is primarily based on that used by Rubery in chapter 3.

developed below). Some of the evidence suggests a fairly direct link between rising unemployment and the growth of precarious work – for instance the growth of low-income self-employment in the U.K., or very short term temporary jobs in France (Caire). As noted above, part-time work has also grown in parallel with unemployment. Marshall discusses the evidence in some detail. But there are also longer term trends, notably towards part-time work, which may have other causes. And many of the practices which are attracting attention today, such as homeworking, labour contracting and the like, are long established and have persisted through periods of labour shortage as well as surplus, so that factors other than labour market conditions are clearly involved. Rubery (ch. 3) and Alaluf (ch. 10) also note that adverse labour market conditions may well render all jobs more precarious, rather than intensifying dualism.

Another important way in which labour market conditions might affect the growth of precarious forms of work is in the mechanisms for job access. In a slack labour market, employers would have a greater possibility to screen new recruits by prefacing any permanent job offers with a probationary period; thus new jobs would tend to be temporary. This would certainly explain the tendency for the growth in temporary jobs to be concentrated among the young, and for such jobs to have a significant training component. In the FRG (ch. 5), about one third of temporary contracts are reported as being followed by permanent contracts in the same enterprise. However, opinions are divided about the importance of this mechanism. Marshall (ch. 2) is sceptical.

2. The industrial system and enterprise structure

There are many elements in the industrial system where one can search for sources of precarious work: changing industrial and sectoral production patterns, patterns of technical change, increasing competition on product markets because of international integration. But the liveliest debate has revolved around the issue of enterprise structure, especially with respect to the model of the "flexible firm". In this model, firms follow a strategy of employing a secure group of core workers and a periphery of temporary and casual wage workers, outworkers or sub-contractors. The precarious workers provide a labour reserve, permitting the enterprise to rapidly adapt labour use to production needs, without having to bear the costs of a permanent labour force large enough to meet peak production. Such models, developed for instance by Atkinson [1987], have their roots in the work of Piore and others on dualistic labour market structures [Doeringer and Piore, 1971].

The important point about the flexible firm model is that it provides a framework for explaining why enterprises would wish to create precarious types of jobs. For it is by no means obvious that precarious work is in the interests of enterprises. There is reason to doubt that insecure, short-term workers would be highly productive. Most jobs, even if apparently unskilled, require some degree of training, raising costs in proportion to labour turnover; supervisory costs are likely to be high; and motivation is likely to be weak unless there are prospects for permanent work. It is true that there are certain types of activities – fast food retail outlets, some types of construction, office cleaning – where a casual, low skill labour force with high turnover is the norm; presumably there is little scope for skill acquisition in such jobs and the other costs are offset by very low wages. But for the mainstream of the labour market the use of precarious employment has a cost in terms of labour productivity, which may or may not be compensated by lower direct wage costs. Marshall discusses these issues. The flexible firm model suggests that there are additional benefits for employers. Nevertheless, the extent to which it is in the interest of firms to create dual structures seems likely to vary considerably with the product, the production techniques, labour market conditions and so on, and in practice in the UK (where the flexible firm model has been influential) little empirical evidence has been produced that the practice is spreading (Rubery).[5] Büchtemann and Quack comment that fixed-term work in the FRG is concentrated in industries with short term fluctuation in labour demand. It may well be that in the majority of industries there are sharply diminishing returns to use of precarious forms of labour beyond a relatively small fraction of enterprise employment.

3. The institutional framework of the labour market

Two aspects of the institutional framework are particularly interesting in the debate on precarious work: the role of the State, and the responses and attitudes of collective organisations in the labour market. The State can in turn be seen to play two roles: as actor and as legislator.

There is in fact a case that the public sector, as employer, has played a more active role than the private in the development of atypical forms of work. For instance, the public sector appears to play a leading role in promoting the growth of part-time work in the U.K., Belgium, the Netherlands and France; for instance, in France 63% of the growth in part-time work from 1982 to 1987 was accounted for by the public sector (Marshall; Caire; Ricca). Such work is probably less precarious than most of the other categories discussed here, but there is also evidence of the State playing an active role in the development of fixed-term contracts, and also – – through privatisation and the contracting out of various public services – of some forms of contract labour and short term temporary work (Ricca). And of course some government make-work and retraining programmes for the unemployed fall in the precarious work category. Caire illustrates how the introduction of multiple schemes of this sort in France has fragmented the labour market and led to the creation of precarious jobs, alternating only with unemployment.

An important factor stabilising the "standard employment relation- ship" has been its progressive incorporation in labour legislation (albeit less

---

5. Although the fairly large numbers of homeworkers and other outworkers in the U.K., and some indication of a growth in their numbers, would be consistent with the model.

in the UK than in other European countries), as measures of protection have become guaranteed by the State and the boundaries of possible employment contracts narrowed. Mückenberger (ch. 11) shows how in the FRG this has led to State-defined criteria which determine the degree of protection granted to an employment relationship, and thus exclude some groups from protectection at the same time as they include others. He argues that current moves towards deregulation may weaken further the protection of "atypical" employment relationships more than undermining standard ones, at least in the short term; and while the State may not be the prime mover in the shift towards precarious employment relationships, its legislative retreat helps to accelerate the process.

The attitudes and roles of employers and trade unions in the growth of precarious jobs are perhaps too easy to stereotype: the employers are for and the unions against. As Caire illustrates for the case of France, for the employers the issue is one of flexibility in labour use; the precariousness of atypical jobs is a side-issue, and one which can be resolved by the creation of employment through economic growth. Trade unionists have adopted diverse strategies, but a typical trade union view, in the U.K. and Belgium at least (Rubery; Alaluf) would be that precarious work is only the tip of the iceberg; that the major long term issues are the erosion of protection of regular jobs, in terms of rights and wages, and the growth of a low wage segment among regular workers. The position of the CGT in France would be similar (Caire). Precarious work is then one aspect of this larger issue, rather than the primary concern in its own right. Indeed, many trade unions regard the precarious work issue as essentially conjunctural, and one which will resolve itself with a return to full employment. As a result there is a tendency for trade unions to concentrate their attention on defending the rights of those in standard jobs. They may oppose the extension of non-standard employment where it replaces standard jobs, but acquiesce in this extension if this helps to protect the core workers (Rubery). This strategy is itself precarious: Alaluf sees in current developments threats to the effectiveness, solidarity and legitimacy of the trade union movement, although if it succeeds it has the potential to prevent atypical jobs from becoming the new norm. In the meantime, as Caire points out, collective relationships and negotiations are becoming more differentiated and fragmented.

4. The consequences for individuals and their responses

Do "precarious" jobs correspond in some way to new needs, as systems of social reproduction change? It is widely argued that increases in part-time work among women, homeworking, and even casual and temporary work reflect a change in labour supply patterns, and correspond to the types of jobs which some labour force entrants at least are seeking. To assess the validity of this position, labour supply patterns need to be set within the overall income needs and labour market strategies of households and individuals; see in particular Büchtemann and Quack. Much of the non-standard work we have been discussing refers to secondary work in households where there is also a regular worker – e.g. work by spouses of a regular worker and first-time labour market entrants. One consequence of this is that employers can impose wages, working conditions and employment discontinuities which primary earners could not accept. This does not mean that there are no primary earners in precarious work; there are no doubt serious problems for specific social groups, such as women bringing up families alone, or those unable to obtain regular work after a long duration of unemployment. Nevertheless, precarious jobs are no doubt a much smaller proportion of all jobs for primary than for secondary workers.

There have been changes in patterns of social reproduction, but whether these are enough to account for changes in the observed patterns of work seems doubtful. Steadily increasing female economic activity rates point to a changing domestic division of labour in most European countries, but whether this would have led to the same expansion of part-time work in a tight labour market is not at all obvious; it is worth noting that the extent of part-time work in the U.K. has ceased to increase since unemployment rates started to fall. The growth in unemployment of primary earners has no doubt been partly responsible for the growth of labour supply to precarious jobs – not necessarily of the household member who is unemployed, but of other household members attempting to make up the income shortfall.[6] This is consistent with Büchtemann and Quack's finding that marginal part-time work is found in households where other earning members of the household have low incomes, whereas regular part-time work is associated with high incomes among other household members.

The presumption remains, then, that a substantial fraction of atypical jobs are primarily associated with inadequate labour market insertion and inadequate incomes. Two chapters in this book try to directly explore the consequences for individuals: Salengros, van de Leemput and Mubikangiey in chapter 8, who look at several groups of temporary workers in Belgium; and Burchell in chapter 9, who looks more generally at the psychological consequences of temporary work and homeworking in the UK. Salengros and colleagues find a complex and differentiated situation. The psychological responses varied greatly, with many individuals able to adapt and find motivations in temporary and insecure situations, while others were stressed and discouraged. "Precarious" workers reject the idea that they are marginal, but many find their position difficult, both financially and socially. There were clear differences between occupations: interim teaching could be an access route to the profession, whereas temporary workers in fast food outlets clearly had no career prospects. Burchell stresses the importance of security and ability to plan; he finds that the mental health of the insecurely employed is as bad as that of the unemployed – and indeed the two populations overlap, since the insecurely employed suffer frequent periods of unemployment. The psychological consequences of homeworking are

---

6.   In the FRG in 1984, at least one household member was unemployed in 21% of multiple person households reporting part-time but not full-time employment; for similar households reporting at least one member employed full time there was only 4% unemployment [Büchtemann and Schupp, 1987].

quite different, and apart from problems of isolation may be primarily linked to low incomes.

IV. Towards new forms of labour market regulation?

A central issue in the debate on precarious work is whether there is a movement towards a new system of labour market regulation; in a sense this is the consolidation of the different issues addressed above and in the different chapters in this book. But the word regulation can be given several interpretations. At its most narrow it concerns only legislated rules; at its most broad,[7] it covers the entire range of economic, social and juridical factors involved in determining labour market outcomes. The problem derives in part, in English, from the linguistic origins of the term "regulation" in this context; in French the word means not rules (*réglementation* in French) but rather regulatory *mechanisms*, which can as readily be social as legal. To clarify the use of the term in relation to the labour market, it is helpful to distinguish *direct* (or legal and administrative) from *indirect* (or social and economic) regulation. By direct regulation we mean control over employment contracts or labour market structures that derives from legal statute, or is legally enforceable. This includes on the one hand, traditional labour legislation and administration, and the associated rights and patterns of social insurance; and on the other, legally enforceable rules governing trade union or employer activities and domains of control, obligatory patterns of collective organisation, negotiation or implementation of agreements and other similar explicit institutional structures. Indirect regulation encompasses firstly, voluntarist working procedures and patterns, based on consensus or agreement rather than enforceability; secondly, customary, habitual or normative patterns of behaviour – socially reinforced norms and responses; and thirdly, the underlying economic mechanisms and social institutions – so that economic necessity and various forms of subordination are also elements of indirect regulation. In this book, Mückenberger concentrates on direct regulation, and within this mainly on its legislative component. Rubery is concerned with both direct regulation and what she calls the voluntary system of regulation; in the UK the scope of legally enforceable, direct regulation is limited and the first component of indirect regulation correspondingly more important. Marshall too considers both direct and some aspects of indirect regulation. In using the word in the title of this book, the intention has been to maintain a broad meaning, so that "regulation" should here be interpreted as including the indirect as well as the direct. The advantage of the broad interpretation is that it makes explicit the links between the legislative, the economic and the social; "deregulation", as Mückenberger's reasoning shows, necessarily involves "re-regulation" because labour relationships imply a reference point of social institutions, within which the overt and legislated may be only a small part.

---

7.   As used by the "regulation school": Aglietta [1976]; Boyer [1986].

Current trends in the system of labour market regulation can be interpreted in various ways. One possibility, which has generated much debate, is in terms of labour market flexibility [Standing, 1986; Boyer, 1986; Tarling, 1987]. The basic argument, which is related to that concerning the "flexible firm", discussed above, revolves around whether a loosening of the framework of rules and collective agreements which constrain hiring, firing and working arrangements would promote flexibility and adaptability in enterprises. Since these rules are largely designed to give measures of security or protection to workers, the likely outcome is growth in atypical forms of work. There are several possible explanations why pressures for flexibility should be more widespread today than in the past, if they are. One is that competitive pressures on firms have intensified, and this is reflected in their labour market practices when they are unable to adapt through other means. A second is that a growing structure of rules and constraints has limited the adaptability of firms which use only regular wage labour. A third is simply that the desire to avoid labour legislation is not new – it is just easier now because of high levels of unemployment and weaker trade unions.

But while the flexibility debate clearly overlaps with that on precarious work, the overlap is only partial, for the route to flexibility does not necessarily involve precarious jobs, while atypical forms of work are found in many situations where they have little to do with a search for flexibility by enterprises. In the long term, the issues posed by precariousness in the labour market are more fundamental, for if the "standard employment relationship" is no longer to be the reference point, this calls for the remodelling of labour institutions – or the design of new ones.

The chapters in this book do not systematically try to build up such a new framework. But by comparing national experiences and relationships it is possible to identify elements of the regulatory framework, both direct and indirect, which may have desirable or undesirable effects. Marshall, for instance, points to the lack of protection for very short-time workers in the UK and the Netherlands (and therefore lower labour costs) as an important reason for the relative frequency of this type of work in those countries. The dangers of fragmentation arising from ill-considered state intervention can be seen, from different perspectives, in Caire's chapter on France and Mückenberger's on the FRG. Büchtemann and Quack also illustrate the discrimination implicit in much of the regulatory system in the FRG, because it remains structured around the standard employment relationship, while Ricca argues that the differentiation which this implies may often be deliberate State policy.

Several authors highlight the importance of underlying social and economic mechanisms in determining the impact and coverage of formal regulation, which suggests that indirect regulation may condition the direct. This comes out particularly clearly in the chapters dealing with non-wage work (Rubery; Bettio and Villa), but it also applies to wage labour. Direct regulation which is contrary to prevailing economic incentives and power structures will generate countervailing or distorting patterns of social and informal behaviour, which need also to be managed if effective overall regulatory structures are to be designed. Indeed, several of the chapters show how the interaction of direct and indirect forms of regulation tends to concentrate disadvantage among specific groups of workers, in the absence of a unifying institutional frame.

Whether the latter will be generally recognised as a desirable goal, and if so, whether it will be feasible, is not yet clear. It would have to provide a coherent framework for increasingly fragmented forms of labour, in order to achieve appropriate forms of social insurance and protection for differentiated situations, while responding to equally diverse patterns of need. It would involve not only the State (Mückenberger, Ricca) but also other social forces and organisations, among them trade unions – Alaluf's argument, that the trade union movement needs to maintain a project for society as a whole, rather than adopting a case-by-case, pragmatic approach, is pertinent here. Whether moves towards international economic integration within Europe will be accompanied by attempts to construct such unitary labour institutions, or whether the task will be one of creating a pluralist structure which can encompass different forms of work and the needs of different categories of worker, remains an open question.

References

Aglietta, M. (1976): *Régulation et crises du capitalisme.* Paris, Calmann-Lévy.

Atkinson, J. (1987): "Flexibility or fragmentation? The United Kingdom labour market in the eighties", in *Labour and Society* (Geneva, IILS), Vol. 12, No. 1, Jan.

Boyer, R. (ed.)(1986): *La flexibilité du travail en Europe.* Paris, La Découverte.

Büchtemann, C.; Schupp, J. (1987): *Socio-economic aspects of part-time employment in the Federal Republic of Germany.* Berlin, WZB (mimeo).

Dale, A.; Bamford, C. (1988): "Temporary workers: Cause for concern or complacency?", in *Work, Employment and Society* (London), Vol. 2, No. 2, June.

Doeringer, P.; Piore, M. (1971): *Internal labor markets and manpower analysis.* Lexington, Mass., Heath.

Dombois, R.; Osterland, M. (1987): "New forms of flexible utilisation of labour: part-time and contract work", in Tarling, R. (ed.): *Flexibility in labour markets.* London, Academic Press.

European Commission (1987): *Le travail au noir: Etat de la recherche – débats.* Brussels (mimeo).

European Foundation for the Improvement of Living and Working Conditions (1988): *New forms of work: Labour law and social security aspects in the European Community.* Luxembourg, Office for Official Publications of the European Communities.

Lindley, Robert (1986): *New forms and new areas of employment growth in France, Germany, Italy, the Netherlands and the United Kingdom: a comparative study,* Study No. 85397. Brussels, Commission of the European Communities.

Standing, G. (1986): *Labour flexibility: Cause or cure for unemployment?,* Public Lecture No. 25. Geneva, IILS.

Tarling, R. (ed.) (1987): *Flexibility in labour markets.* London, Academic Press.

2   The sequel of unemployment: The changing role of part-time and temporary work in Western Europe

Adriana Marshall[1]

I. Introduction

The interest in forms of wage employment which diverge from the typical wage employment relationship – characterised by a direct, permanent contract for full-time regular work – has been rapidly expanding, first in Western Europe and later in other parts of the world. The names given to those practices, such as the more neutral denominations of "non-standard" and "atypical" work, and the less euphemistic labels of "precarious" and "vulnerable" employment have permeated an important fraction of the Western European labour market literature. Interest in these practices has been growing in parallel with their diffusion across the economic structure, and awareness of the detrimental aspects that these forms of employment have – as much for the workers who are employed under non-standard contractual conditions as for labour as a whole – has increased. In particular, there is a growing concern among trade unionists about non-standard forms of employment.[2]

Non-standard forms of employment include a variety of situations ranging from clearly defined wage employment to casual self-employment, and the many ambiguous situations where the legal classification does not necessarily coincide with the economic content of the employment relationship. There is considerable superposition among non-standard employment practices, and this fact should be borne in mind while looking at the dimensions of non-standard employment and its impact.[3] Most of these

---

1. Consejo Nacional de Investigaciones Científicas y Técnicas, Buenos Aires; IILS consultant.

2. [This issue is discussed by Alaluf in chapter 10 - eds.].

3. Non-standard employment as a whole is not equivalent to the sum of all its modalities: although part-time employment is predominantly regular, permanent work, many part-time workers are in temporary positions (in 1985, 22.6% of part-time workers in Belgium, 9.1% in France, 15% in the Netherlands and 16% in the UK had a temporary job; OECD, 1987). Conversely, many temporary workers are in part-time jobs: according to labour force surveys,

practices have long coexisted with standard wage employment; some of them had even dominated certain industries at earlier stages in the development of capitalism. Their specific modalities, though, have been changing along with economic and social transformations and changes in labour legislation. While in the "golden" post-war period of Western Europe's economic affluence non-standard employment might have had some appeal for specific sectors of the workforce, with today's unemployment it is becoming the only option for many workers. Although some forms of atypical work continue to be overwhelmingly dominated by particular groups of the labour force (e.g. women in part-time employment), they have spread to a much wider range of economic activities, and thus to new categories of workers. In contemporary Western Europe, non-standard employment has been assigned a new labour market role.

The features of diverse forms of non-standard employment have been studied, but large *lacunae* in knowledge persist, and there are substantial disparities across countries in this respect. Using official statistics as well as ad hoc surveys, attempts have been made at appraising how widespread is non-standard employment, what role it plays in the labour market in theory and in practice, what groups of the labour force are particularly affected and why, what is their prevalent situation in regard to earnings, social benefits and social protection, what are the reasons that lead enterprises to use non-standard forms of employment, the global conditions that have favoured their expansion, and the unions' response. In this chapter I will focus only on two of the *wage* employment practices[4] that have deserved the denomination of non-standard employment: part-time and temporary work. I will review and discuss statistics and findings, concentrating on five Western European economies (Belgium, France, the Netherlands, the United Kingdom [UK] and the Federal Republic of Germany [FRG]), and paying particular attention to the 1980s.[5]

II. Part-time employment

Part-time employment is the most "standard" and best studied of non-standard employment practices. It is the most important in terms of its share of the labour force. Its definition varies from country to country,

---

11% of the wage earners with temporary jobs in the FRG, 27% in France, 29% in Belgium, 51% in the UK (1986) and 44% in the Netherlands (1985) had part-time positions [Eurostat, unpublished data]. Many outworkers and most homeworkers, too, are employed only part-time and for short periods alternating with lack of work.

4.   Non-standard *wage* employment means that the part-time and temporary self-employed, employers and unpaid family workers are disregarded. The emphasis is on employment practices in the capitalist firm and the public sector, thus excluding other workers often classified as wage labour, such as those in household services.

5.   The balance of evidence discussed reflects both the extent of research in the countries concerned and my access to relevant publications.

as it does over time within same country. Part-time employment admits a variety of situations: working part of the day, part of the week, and even part of the month. It generally refers to regular employment, but in several countries irregular work is also included, explicitly or merely because it has not been excluded explicitly. While some countries have a *legal* definition of part-time employment, others have only a *conventional* definition, not always consistently applied, used for data collection purposes; others have several definitions, each one linked to a specific collective agreement or economic activity [Baroin et al., 1981].

Whatever the definition, in actual practice most part-time employment is concentrated around 20 hours per week (table 1). More precisely, in the FRG the most common situation among women in part-time employment is regular half-day work: about 50% of part-time employees worked between 20 and 25 hours per week [Loos, 1981; Büchtemann and Schupp, 1986]. In the United Kingdom, the mean basic hours worked by adult women in part-time employment in 1982 was 19.2 in manual occupations and 20.1 in the non-manual jobs [Robinson and Wallace, 1984]. The highest concentration was in the 16-21 hours per week class, followed by 8-16 hours. In France, 63% of women and 68% of men part-time wage earners worked between 15 and 29 hours per week [*Enquête sur l'emploi*, March 1987].

Table 1:   Wage earners in part-time employment: usual number of hours worked per week, 1985 (% distribution)

	Number of hours					
	1-10	11-20	21-24	25-30	31+	All
Belgium	11.7	54.6	11.3	12.8	9.7	100.0
FRG	11.1	48.4	11.5	24.6	4.4	100.0
France	12.5	44.4	9.7	20.4	13.0	100.0
Netherlands	25.9	41.0	8.3	16.6	8.2	100.0
UK	26.1	41.3	11.6	15.1	5.9	100.0

Source: Eurostat [1987a].

In the countries where part-time employment continued to expand while total employment tended to stagnate, or where manufacturing employment declined, growth of part-time work coincided with a feminisation of wage employment. Part-time jobs are taken overwhelmingly by women, and part-time work is increasing its share in total female employment. In 1985 women had 87% of all part-time wage employment in Belgium, 85% in France, 78% in the FRG and in the Netherlands and 90% in the United Kingdom. Between 23% (Belgium) and over one-half (the Netherlands) of employed wage-earning women had a part-time job [Eurostat, 1987a]. The majority of women working part-time are over 25 years old, married and generally with children.[6] With a husband who provides the main household income and children to take care of, part-time employment appears at least acceptable, and sometimes positively attractive. The other labour force group likely to be employed part-time are older workers [Eurostat, 1987a, table 42], often already retired.

1. Choice or constraint?

According to conventional wisdom, a large fraction of workers employed part-time, most of them women, "prefer" this form of employment, i.e. they are employed part-time on a "voluntary" basis. It is argued that this feature of part-time work differentiates it from other forms of non-standard employment, as if "voluntariness" could make it less precarious. In reality, little has been published about the proportion of "voluntary" in total part-time employment in Western Europe. Instead, the case of the U.S. is widely cited: 65% of part-time workers are "voluntarily" in part-time employment [U.S. Bureau of Labor Statistics, 1986]. Unpublished results from labour force surveys tend to confirm the voluntary character of part-time employment (not for men). On the one hand, the proportion of interviewees who were in part-time jobs because they could not find a full-time position is generally small – 10% or less in the FRG, the Netherlands and the UK [Eurostat, unpublished]. Belgium is an exception, with involuntary part-time employment reaching 35% in 1985 (a recent study also found that half the women working part-time would actually prefer a full-time job; Tollet and Vanderwalle, 1987). On the other hand, the proportion who did "not want" a full-time job is very high in the UK and the FRG, and considerable in the Netherlands and Belgium; this is not true for men, however (table 2). Other reasons (training and studying, illness and disability, family problems, etc.) given for working part-time by some 30% of part-timers (60% in the Netherlands) in fact amount to a constraint which makes such part-time work also in a sense voluntary. By contrast, part-time work is less appealing for the unemployed: in 1987, only 10% were seeking preferentially permanent part-time employment in France, 1.9% in the case of men, 16% for women [*Enquête sur l'emploi*, March 1987]. These proportions have been quite stable over time, at least during the 1982-1987 period, but the proportion of unemployed workers that would accept part-time employment if unable to obtain a full-time job has been increasing rapidly, from 27% in 1982 to 46% in 1987 [*Enquête sur l'emploi*, ibid.; Letablier, 1986], indicating that part-time employment is often becoming the only option given limited employment opportunities. In the United Kingdom, in 1981, few of the registered unemployed were seeking part-time work, but more than half of non-registered unemployed were doing so; the majority of the latter being women [Garnsey, 1984]). A survey by Martin and Roberts, cited in Garnsey

---

6.   In 1985 married women represented 78% of all part-time employment in the FRG, 63% in France, 56% in the Netherlands, 70% in Belgium and 75% in the UK [Eurostat, 1987a].

[1984], showed that 43% of the unemployed women interviewed were looking for a job part-time. In any case, the argument that the voluntary nature of part-time employment differentiates it from other non-standard practices contains a basic flaw. Even when part-time employment is voluntary, it generally means that these workers *cannot* opt for full-time work because of their household constraints. They are therefore forced to accept part-time work as it comes, with its disadvantages.

Table 2: **Wage earners in "voluntary" part-time employment, as a percentage of all part-time wage earners, 1983-1986**

	1983	1984	1985	1986
Belgium				
- all	39.5	46.0	42.1	19.5
- males	5.7	1.2	10.6	6.5
FRG				
- all	-	61.7	62.3	63.6
- males	-	19.9	24.1	22.5
Netherlands				
- all	28.8	-	27.6	-
- males	10.6	-	12.0	-
UK				
- all	71.7	62.7	60.2	60.6
- males	33.1	27.3	24.8	22.0

Source: Unpublished tables with data from labour force surveys, kindly supplied by Eurostat.

2. Low wages and restricted protection

Part-time work is undoubtedly at the bottom of the wage scale. This does not necessarily deter workers from taking up part-time employment if they only provide the household with supplementary income. Lower pay is basically due to the nature of the jobs, their location in the occupational hierarchy, and to the fact that even if part-time workers are not "discriminated" against, they normally receive only the guaranteed minimum or basic wage rate without any fringe benefits. Part-time employment also implies a greater vulnerability to economic and biological "risks". In Western Europe some part-time workers (e.g. with wages lower than a certain stipulated minimum, or working fewer hours than a stipulated threshold), experience disadvantages vis-à-vis those employed full-time, either because they have been explicitly excluded by the legislation from entitlement to social benefits, or simply because their status has been left ambiguously or vaguely defined, so that eventually entitlement to benefits has to be determined casuistically, and in practice only a tiny minority of these part-time workers do take their cases to court.

In some countries, part-time workers have been restricted in their access to the *minimum hourly wage* but, by the early 1980s, they had the legal right to receive the hourly wage agreed through collective bargaining on the same basis as full-time workers in the FRG, France and Belgium, and/or the national minimum wage in France and Belgium. In the UK the right to the minimum wage was restricted to part-time workers covered by Wage Councils or similar bodies, and in the Netherlands, to those working more than 13 hours per week. In France, the law stipulates that part-time workers have full rights to the collectively agreed conditions, but in other countries there are few rules governing their access. However, in some specific agreements their access has been regulated (e.g. in the Netherlands and the FRG), generally applying the rule of pro rata to the rights of full-time workers [Baroin et al., 1981].

Substantial restrictions apply also to part-timers' access to social benefits and social security systems. In the early 1980s, part-time workers had the right to holidays on a pro rata basis in the FRG, France, Belgium, and the Netherlands; in the UK the entitlement was subject to restrictions similar to those for the minimum wage. In the UK, the FRG, Belgium and France limitations in terms of minimum number of hours worked per week and/or minimum wage applied to the reimbursement of expenses incurred for illness and maternity (or the access to free medical care). There was also a threshold in terms of minimum number of hours worked and/or minimum wage for access to the retirement pension scheme (except in Belgium and in the Netherlands for the general state scheme). Similar or stronger limitations applied to benefits from the unemployment insurance system in all five countries [Baroin and al., 1981]. In the FRG, France, Belgium and the Netherlands family allowances are independent of the type of activity, but in order to receive this supplement in the UK at least 30 hours per week (in the case of a family head) or 24 hours (in the case of households with only one parent) should have been worked. In the case of the UK, rights such as redundancy payment and maternity pay have not been extended to part-time employees working less than eight hours per week, have been granted to those working between 8 and 16 hours only if they have been employed with the same firm for at least five years, and to those working 16 hours or more only if they have been with the same firm for at least two years [LRD, 1986].[7] Part-time workers in the UK fare worse in terms of access to protection than their counterparts in the advanced Western European economies [ibid.].

To encourage part-time employment with the intention of reducing the high level of unemployment, the 1985 Employment Promotion Act in the FRG relaxed restrictions on the use of temporary employment and guaranteed to all part-time workers the same protection as full-time workers .."unless there are objective reasons to justify different treatment" [*SLB*, 1985/3-4]. In France, the legal reform of 1981 and 1982 intended to provide

---

7.   By 1986 it was proposed to raise the statutory threshold for part-timers from 16 to 20 hours per week in order to qualify for unfair dismissal rights, supposedly to encourage the growth of part-time employment [Deakin, 1986].

part-time workers with rights similar to those of full-time employees, though the unions argued that the reform was insufficient. Part-time work was defined in legal terms as an average working week of 32 hours or less, and the ordinance decreed, inter alia, that pay of part-time workers should be pro-rated according to hours worked, on the basis of full-time workers' pay in a similar grade, with the same length of service, and who perform equivalent jobs [*EIRR*, 1982].

Exclusion from social benefits and lack of a guaranteed minimum wage means that these workers are in a more vulnerable situation, and that there is a strong incentive to business to keep hours and wage rates below the threshold beyond which part-time employment would raise labour costs. It is not surprising, in this context, that in the Netherlands – where the minimum wage is guaranteed only to those working at least 13 hours a week – and in the UK – where social rights have practically not been extended to those working fewer than 8 hours a week – the proportion of part-time workers employed for fewer than 10 hours a week is much larger than in the other three countries (table 1). Nevertheless, working fewer than the threshold hours per week might be based on some consensus between worker and employer. Some workers might prefer keeping down hours and wages so that no social security deductions would encroach on an already meagre salary, particularly if they are anyway covered by their spouse's social security scheme. The fraction of the workforce left out of social protection, although varying from one country to the other, may thus be considerable. In the UK, in one instance,[8] the proportion of female part-time workers not covered by the main employment protection legislation (excluding those working very irregularly) reached 40% in 1980, as compared with 33% for full-time employees. Some 35% (as compared with 13% of the full-time employees) were not entitled to sick pay, and 34% (as compared with 18% among full-time workers) did not belong to an employer pension scheme although the employer had one. Moreover, only 9% of part-time workers belonged to a pension scheme, as compared with 53% of workers employed full-time. According to Schoer [1987], in the UK nearly 30% of part-time workers are excluded from the National Insurance Scheme. But in the FRG, only 11% of part-timers are not covered by the social security system.

The obverse of the underprivileged position of part-time workers vis-à-vis full-time employees in terms of pay and access to social security benefits is that part-time employment implies lower labour costs to business. On the one hand, many part-time workers get only the guaranteed minimum wage or even less. On the other, employers' social security contributions, though generally calculated on a pro rata basis of the contributions due for full-time jobs, often start to be paid only above a stipulated wage threshold. As some inter-country comparative studies have demonstrated, it is not accidental if in the United Kingdom, where the wage threshold for employers' contributions is the highest, the share of part-time in total employment is one of the largest [Schoer, 1987; Garnsey, 1984]. Nor is it a

---

8.   The findings are from a study by J. Martin and C. Roberts, *Women and employment: a life time perspective* (London, Department of Employment, 1984), cited in Garnsey [1984].

pure coincidence that in the other country with a high ratio of part-time work, the Netherlands, the minimum wage has not been guaranteed to workers employed fewer than 13 hours a week.

3. Size and trends

By 1985, the Netherlands had the largest share of part-time in total wage employment (22.6%), followed by the UK (21.8%).[9] In the FRG, France and Belgium, part-time employment represented a much smaller fraction of total wage employment – 12.3%, 10.5% and 9.3% respectively (annex table A). The share of part-time work in female wage employment was markedly higher (but the differentials between countries were wider), ranging from 51% in the Netherlands to 21% in France. In the UK or the Netherlands part-time employment could hardly be labelled as "non-standard" in the case of women. Various factors explain inter-country differentials in the relative size of the part-time labour force: the weight of the tertiary sector (in particular of some of its components) in total employment; female labour force participation rates; the relative position of the threshold above which employers are taxed with contributions for the social security system [Garnsey, 1984; Schoer, 1987]. But other factors, of a social and cultural nature, also affect the behaviour of labour supply in relation to part-time work. Certain labour force groups, e.g. married women with children, have been socialised so as to perceive part-time employment as the only feasible – even desirable – option; this is reinforced by the absence or sparsity of state child-care facilities and by economic barriers limiting the access to private child care.

In Western Europe, part-time employment is not a new phenomenon; its origin was associated with the relative labour scarcity of the early 1960s, and the need to attract women, particularly married women, into the labour force. Part-time work expanded side by side with the growth of female labour force participation rates. Its differential diffusion since that time has probably been influenced by the availability and functionality of alternative labour sources. The volume of part-time employment has been expanding fast in the late 1970s and during the 1980s, but it is less clear whether its share of total employment has been rising as fast. The weight of part-time in total employment has been increasing partly as a result of the stagnation (or decline) of full-time employment, and partly as a consequence of its own dynamism. Massive substitution of full-time by part-time jobs has not taken place (although it did occur locally). While economic activities characterised by full-time employment, such as manufacturing, were stagnating, sectors where part-time work is typical expanded steadily. The result is clearly illustrated by the trends in total and part-time employment in the UK and France (see figure 1). There has also been some diffusion

---

9.   We must recall here that definitions of part-time work differ in scope in the different countries.

Figure 1: Trends in total and part-time wage employment – France and the UK

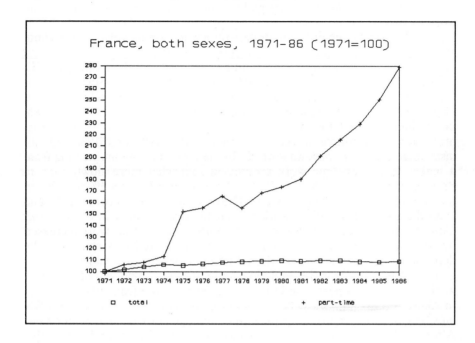

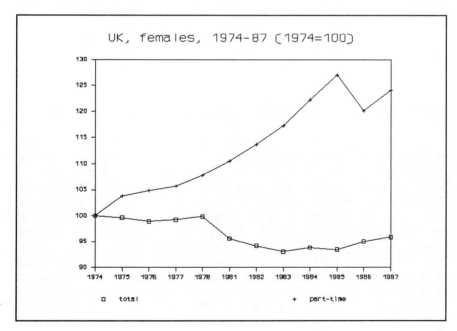

Note: No data are available for 1979 and 1980 on part-time employment in the UK.

of the practice of part-time employment to activities where it had not been usual in the past, reinforcing the global tendency for the share of part-time work to rise.

In France, the diffusion of part-time work is relatively new [Michon, 1987], and has been quite fast. The proportion of part-time in total wage employment was only 4.6% in 1971 but had reached 11.4% by 1987 [INSEE, 1987].[10] The proportion of men in part-time employment was still very minor (3.2%) though it had more than doubled between 1971 and 1987. The share of part-time work among wage-earning women, much higher than for men, more than doubled too, from 10.6% to 22.3%. Progress in the social protection of part-time workers in France after 1981 and 1982 did not discourage the use of part-time work. In the United Kingdom, starting from a higher level, part-time work progressed somewhat more slowly than in France, rising from 15.4% in 1971 to 23.4% in 1986 (from 4.3% to 7.2% in the case of men, and from 33.5% to 43.3%, of women). Between 1983 and 1986 the share of part-time work tended to stabilise [data in *Employment Gazette*]. In the Netherlands too, the proportion of part-time work increased but the "jump" between 1979 and 1983 might be linked to a change in the definition of part-time work. Excluding employment in social workshops and in the public sector (i.e. excluding an important component of part-time work), the share of part-time in total employment rose from 19.8% in 1981 to 23.8% in 1984 [*Statistical Yearbook of the Netherlands*, 1985]. In the FRG and Belgium the expansion of part-time employment has been rather slow. After 1983 its share of total employment remained fairly stable, declining slightly in 1983-85 in the FRG while rising slightly in Belgium [OECD, 1987, table 1.3]. The share of female part-time employment followed this overall trend, but its increase (in Belgium) and decrease (in the FRG) between 1983 and 1985 was more marked than for the total share of part-time employment.

4. Users: The importance of the public sector

Did part-time work extend through an intensified use of this practice by "traditional" users of part-time work (within both the private and the public sector) or through its diffusion to new spheres? That the pace of part-time employment growth in the 1980s might have been faster in the public than in the private sector cannot be overlooked. Though the importance of part-time work in some government activities has been mentioned in the literature, little attention has been paid to the role of the state *qua* employer in the recent diffusion of this form of employment. Between 1983 and 1985 the share of part-time in total employment increased more in public administration than in any other sector in Belgium and in France (in this case it was followed by "other services" which include the public sector social services; OECD, 1987, table 1.5). In the United

---

10.   Some of the increase from 1985 is due to the inclusion of part-time workers employed via the Travaux d'Utilité Collective [INSEE, 1987].

Kingdom, leaving aside agriculture, part-time work increased most in "other services" followed by public administration, and in the Netherlands, in "other services". In the latter country, the rapid increase in part-time employment after 1982 (the proportion of part-time employment, now including the public sector, rose from 23% in 1981 to 32% in 1984) was apparently due, inter alia, to the impact of the introduction of the 32-hour week for young workers in the public administration [Bodson et al., 1985]. Although the global impact of part-time work in state activities depends on the relative size of public sector employment in each country, it seems that the state is taking the lead in "promoting" the diffusion of the practice. This is confirmed by more disaggregated data from France, where about 63% of the growth in part-time employment between 1982 and 1987 is explained by the expansion of part-time jobs in the public sector. While among wage-earners in the private sector (excluding household services) the share of part-time employment between 1982 and 1987 increased from 7.3% to 9.3%, in the public sector it rose from 8.1% to 12.6% in public administration, from 11.3% to 18.5% in local authorities, and from 4.5% to 6.3% in public services [*Enquête sur l'emploi*, May 1982 and March 1987]. In the United Kingdom, although important, part-time work in state employment has played a much less significant role than in France in the recent expansion of part-time employment as a whole. Some 37% of the labour force employed by local authorities (i.e. a part of total public employment), and 26.4% in the public sector as a whole, worked part time in 1987. Between 1981 and 1986 part-time employment under local authorities increased by some 80,000 while part-time work in the British economy as a whole increased by 454,000. But while between 1984 and 1986 part-time female employment in the economy actually declined by 70,000, in the public sector it increased by 40,000, and jumped by another 30,000 from 1986 to 1987.[11] In the second half of the 1980s it looks as if the public sector will have had a more important role, no doubt because of similar – cost-associated – determinants as in the private sector.

Within the private sector, part-time work "spontaneously" developed in some typical service sector activities, ranging from retail trade to banking, from hotels and restaurants to education and health care, in close association with the objective of reducing "fixed" labour costs in relation with the uneven distribution of daily and weekly consumers' demand. Some types of firms are more likely to resort to part-time work than others. In the United Kingdom "part-time using establishments"[12] are larger than average and disproportionately located in non-manufacturing sectors. But small firms (between 25 and 49 workers) show the highest shares of part-time workers in their workforce [Blanchflower and Corry, 1986]. In France, the proportion of part-timers in the workforce is higher in establishments with 10 to 49 workers, but the differential with larger establishments has tended to narrow

---

11.   On the basis of data in *Employment Gazette* and *Economic Trends*, various issues.

12.   Blanchflower and Corry [1986] define "part-time using establishments" as those that employ at least 25 part-timers or, if the establishment has less than 50 workers, those where at least 50 per cent of the workforce is part-time.

between 1975 and 1984, since the use of part-time employment has been increasing faster in the largest firms with more than 500 employees [Javillier, 1986; Garnsey, 1984]. As in the UK, part-time work is more widespread in tertiary activities (hygiene, retail trade, business services, private education, health, catering, hotels, etc.). Within manufacturing, only a few industries (such as leather, printing and publishing) have increased part-time employment [Garnsey, 1984]. Accordingly, part-time work has expanded among white-collar workers while remaining practically stagnant among manual workers, except among female manual workers where it rose rapidly during 1975-1984, probably because of cleaning and similar activities.

The motives for using part-time employment in the service sector are well known [Garnsey, 1984; Schoer, 1987] but its diffusion in the manufacturing sector is a more novel phenomenon, often of an experimental nature. Though its share in overall manufacturing employment is low (particularly in Belgium and France) part-time work has reached an appreciable share of female manufacturing employment in the FRG, the Netherlands and the UK [Eurostat, 1987a], probably in the clerical and cleaning occupations but not among operatives. A more systematic assessment of the benefits derived from using part-time workers has only recently been undertaken. Among the motives that would induce employers to "prefer" part-time workers the following can be cited: the small size of the establishment and the consequent indivisibility of labour; the variability of demand combined with the inability to store the product or service offered for sale; the need to maximise capital equipment utilisation and to ensure continuous operation, avoiding the extra costs associated with overtime or shiftworking of full-time workers; the relatively lower cost of part-time labour in general; and the fact that they are less likely to be unionised [Blanchflower and Corry, 1986]. However the evidence is insufficient as yet to permit an evaluation of their true impact [ibid.].[13]

5. Assigned role: From easing labour scarcity to "combatting" unemployment

The diffusion of part-time employment has been affected by its extensive use in the public sector. But the state has intended to accelerate its diffusion within the private sector too, resorting to a wide array of incentives in the hope of reducing massive unemployment. The incentives have included: (i) direct subsidies and removal of associated additional costs – if there had been any – so as to make part-time more attractive to employers; (ii) better protection and more equal pay to make it more attractive

---

13.   In relation to part-time work in labour-intensive manufacturing industries, where fluctuations in demand can be anticipated but not controlled, Robinson and Wallace [1984] emphasised, over any other consideration, the fact that it permits costs to be controlled by controlling the number of hours worked.

to workers; and (iii) several government-sponsored schemes.[14] Schemes such as "job-splitting", "job-sharing", on-the-job training and other apprenticeship schemes for the unemployed youth have proliferated. Generally, policies relying on incentives have had a very minor, sometimes negligible, impact and the numbers enrolled in government schemes have been quite small.[15] In the FRG, the Employment Promotion Act of 1985 included encouragement to part-time employment, but only one-third of the companies surveyed in a study conducted in 1985 had made use of this possibility, accounting for a mere 5% of recruitment; practically no full-time jobs were transformed into part-time positions and hardly any job-sharing contracts were signed [*SLB*, 1987/1]. In France, government aid through subsidy to employers who created part-time jobs, and "financial compensation" to unemployed workers who accepted part-time work, had very little success. Part-time employment increased independently of government incentives and their only impact was on economic activities traditionally employing part-time workers spontaneously [Bloch-London, 1987].

Encouragement to part-time employment had been an important component of the "active manpower policies" in the 1960s, when it was perceived as a crucial tool for enlarging the supply of labour, namely of married women. It has now become a central, though inefficient, instrument of labour market policy designed to reduce registered unemployment by "redistributing employment". But the impact of part-time employment growth upon registered unemployment is, to say the least, doubtful. Part-time work generally appeals to a labour force that, had these jobs not emerged, would probably have stayed out of the labour market altogether. Besides, to the extent that part-time employment is "forced" upon the unemployed via incentives and the absence of alternative opportunities, it merely transforms some fully unemployed into a larger number of partially unemployed. Such part-time employment creation policies transform open unemployment into underemployment, at the same time providing low incomes to many workers. Low income of household heads may foster labour market participation of other household members, who might then work part-time. Increased supply of labour and stagnant employment opportunities end up by offsetting the initial impact, if any, of the promotion of part-time employment on the level of unemployment. Job-sharing via part-time employment is the alternative to working time reductions but its cost falls on workers. While working time reductions as demanded by trade unions imply some kind of "job-sharing" but with no reduction of weekly earnings, part-time work means the redistribution of labour income among more workers, with lower earnings for each. Part-time employment appears as an alternative to income supplied by the state, thus by society as a whole, to the unemployed. This policy seeks to maximise labour's contribution to

---

14. For a complete analysis of government policy in this area in Western Europe before 1983, see Casey [1983].

15. On the latter, see detailed estimates in Eurostat [1987b].

the income maintenance of the unemployed, which is consistent with the
more general trend in labour market regulation.

III. Temporary work

Temporary employment has always coexisted with permanent
employment. Its function has been to satisfy seasonally regular labour
requirements and to respond to exceptional circumstances, ranging from
replacing absent workers to unexpected increases in workload. Temporary
contracts have been also associated with organised systems of international
labour recruitment. Since the late 1970s temporary employment practices
have been expanding in Western Europe, both spontaneously and fostered
by government incentives, either indirectly through a relaxation of the
conditions for using temporary labour or directly via government-sponsored
schemes, often associated with training programmes. The spontaneous
diffusion of temporary employment in a period of slowing economic growth
and of high and rising levels of unemployment has been linked with its
extension to *non-exceptional* circumstances. The rationale for using
temporary workers has partly changed, and temporary contracts have often
been used *instead of* permanent or open-ended contracts. Besides being
viewed as a complement to employment on a permanent basis, temporary
labour became an alternative to the recruitment of permanent personnel,
because contracts of different lengths facilitate a rapid adaptation to
fluctuations in economic activity without any durable and costly commitment
on the part of the employer. Temporary workers cannot claim lay-off
compensation if their contract, once terminated, is not renewed. Labour
legislation has sometimes followed behind the spontaneous development of
these forms of employment, regulating *faits accomplis*, but has sometimes led
the process of change by encouraging and reinforcing ongoing trends.

"Temporary" employment refers to a number of different contractual
modalities: direct fixed-term, seasonal and occasional contracts, and
temporary employment through specialised agencies (agency labour). It
encompasses diverse forms of purely casual employment, even on a daily
basis, as well as longer, e.g. two-year, fixed-term contracts. Legal (if present)
and conventional definitions of temporary employment vary across countries[16]
as does the combination of temporary employment forms and the relative
weight of each modality. In the UK, in 1984, about 12% of all temporary
workers had fixed-term contracts, almost 70% other direct contracts
including contracts for seasonal and casual work, 8% were temporary self-
employed and 6% agency-supplied labour [Potter, 1987]. In France, fixed-
term contracts (including seasonal labour) accounted for about 80% of
temporary contracts in the private sector, the other 20% being interim

---

16.   For definitions, see OECD [1987].

contracts, i.e. agency labour [INSEE, 1987].[17]   The latter represent a negligible proportion of the labour force in the FRG (about 0.15% in 1982) as against some 6% in the case of workers with fixed-term contracts [Daubler, 1983].   While being one of the most regulated among forms of temporary employment, the employment of agency labour is one of the least widespread. As reasons for "preferring" fixed-term contracts over agency labour, we can quote: lower labour costs, possibility for the employer to choose the workers to be employed, and possibility of a longer duration contract permitting on-the-job training [Coëffic, 1982].   The contractual conditions and the situation of temporary workers may vary with the form of temporary employment.

1. Temporary workers and their limited options

Though women tend to be disproportionately represented among temporary workers,[18] the difference between sexes is not as overwhelming as in the case of part-time work, and the pattern is not so uniform across countries. The economic structure of temporary employment, in particular the fact that temporary contracts are quite usual in manufacturing and in construction activities (and that seasonal work is widespread in agriculture) contributes to explaining the narrower sex differential. It is age rather than sex that typifies workers with temporary contracts: either "spontaneously" (because it is the only means to enter the labour market) or through some government-sponsored scheme, younger workers are over-represented in some forms of temporary employment. In France, in 1987, 10.4% of the wage workers in the age group 15-24 years employed in the private sector had a fixed-term contract, while only 2.7% of all wage workers were in that situation [INSEE, 1987]. The proportions were quite similar for both sexes in that age group, 10.8% for men and 10.4% for women. Interim contracts were also more frequent among youths, but with much lower proportions (1.7% of the 15 to 24 year-old workers as against 0.7% of all workers). In the FRG, the proportion of workers aged between 15 and 24 in temporary employment (10.3%) was double that of the workforce as a whole [Rudolph, 1987]. In the Netherlands, 44% of the temporarily employed in 1983 were under 25 years old [Bodson et al., 1985]. And in 1985, the age group 15-24 had 47% of temporary wage employment in Belgium, 63% in France, and 51% in the UK, notably more than their share of total wage employment [OECD, 1987].

---

17.   The data refer to wage-earners only, and exclude wage-earners employed in the public sector. "Agency labour" does not include permanent employees of the intermediary agencies.

18.   In 1985, women's share in temporary wage employment was 55% in Belgium and the UK, and 41% in France, where they were under-represented in comparison with their share of total wage employment [OECD, 1987]. According to Eurostat figures, in 1981 women had 86.5% of "occasional" wage employment in the FRG, 78.6% in the Netherlands, 64.2% in France and 62.1% in the UK.

Temporary contracts have not been confined to manual workers, nor to unskilled labour, although they are over-represented in this latter category. In France, in 1986, 82.3% of recruitment of unskilled manual workers and 81.2% of hirings of unskilled white-collar workers were under fixed-term contracts, but still over one-half of the skilled manual workers (56.6%) and skilled white-collar employees (56.9%) were recruited in the same way. Only supervisors, technicians and especially *cadres* were less affected by temporary employment [Perreaux, 1987]. In all categories except unskilled manual workers the share of fixed-term contracts in recruitment was higher for women. A similar pattern is visible in the FRG where temporary employment is equally frequent among manual and non-manual workers [Rudolph, 1987]. In the UK, most temporary workers were in the least skilled occupations, but they were also over-represented in certain categories of highly skilled occupations such as teachers and nurses [Casey, 1987]. Temporary employment of non-manual workers occurs to a large extent in the public sector.

It has been argued that temporary work is sometimes "voluntary" [OECD, 1986]. However this claim has been put forward much less strongly and less often than for part-time work, and in contrast to part-time employment, several indications point to the "forced" nature of temporary employment. First, the proportion of wage earners who are in temporary positions because they could not find permanent employment visibly exceeds the proportion not wanting a permanent job in Belgium, the FRG, the Netherlands and, to a lesser extent, the UK (table 3).[19] Second, in several countries temporary employment is over-represented among formerly unemployed workers who had found wage employment [OECD, 1987]. Moreover, in France only a negligible 4% of the unemployed looking for a job were searching for temporary work (both full- and part-time). Similarly, only 3% of the employed active population looking for another position sought temporary employment. In neither case were the proportions higher for women [*Enquête sur l'emploi*, 1987]. Though often the only option available to those seeking employment, temporary work is seldom attractive. A further indication of the involuntary character of temporary employment is that many workers use it as a means to reach a permanent position. A survey of interim workers in France showed that 70% had hoped to obtain a permanent job at the end of a temporary assignment, but just about one-third had succeeded [*SLB*, 1987/4].

2. Size and trends

Various forms of temporary employment are believed to have increased in the 1980s, but information is sparse and there is no widespread

---

19. These estimates exclude temporary workers under training programmes, a varying but important proportion of all temporary workers (ranging from 20% in the UK to 48% in the FRG in 1986; Eurostat, unpublished), and temporary workers who did not specify or gave other reasons for temporary employment.

Table 3: Wage earners in "involuntary" temporary employment, 1983-1986 (%)*

	1983	1984	1985	1986
Belgium				
- all	87.5	94.5	58.6	53.4
- males	95.9	99.2	68.7	56.4
FRG				
- all	-	66.6	-	-
- males	-	68.7	-	-
Netherlands				
- all	78.4	-	81.0	-
- males	82.5	-	86.0	-
UK				
- all	52.6	60.2	56.0	57.2
- males	68.2	77.1	76.4	76.5

Note: * Percentage in relation to the sum of those who "could not find" and "did not want" a permanent position (i.e. excluding workers in training and those who did not state a reason).

Source: Unpublished tables with data from labour force surveys, kindly supplied by Eurostat.

supporting evidence. According to the OECD [1986], in countries where there are signs of increasing use of temporary workers, the phenomenon still remains marginal. For the share of "occasional" employment – a category used in the labour force surveys of the EEC in the late 1970s and early 1980s – in total wage employment, the Netherlands came top, with some 3% between 1977 and 1983, until 1981 when they were overtaken by the UK whose share of occasional workers jumped from 0.9% in 1977 to 4.6%. Both in France and in the FRG the figures were little above 1%, and in Belgium the proportion was negligible [Eurostat; Bodson et al., 1985]. According to OECD estimates (not comparable with the above), in 1985 the share of temporary in total wage employment was somewhat higher in Belgium (6.9%), in the Netherlands (7.5%) and in the UK (5.7%) than in France (4.8%), and in 1983 all except France (which had a smaller share) had a similar proportion of about 5.5%. France is usually perceived as *the* example of an important diffusion of temporary employment, but in fact it has remained less widespread there than in the other three countries and also than in the FRG, where temporary employment is close to 6% of the workforce [Rudolph, 1987].[20]

Statistical information on trends over time is insufficient except for France. In France, the expansion of temporary contracts was facilitated by a law enacted in 1979. Later, in 1982, the legislative reform that granted some protection to interim workers discouraged this form of temporary employment. In 1986 limitations on both fixed-term and interim contracts

---

20. Important differences in definitions used for data collection in each country should be taken into account in this context.

were relaxed. Changes in labour legislation induced some substitution between forms of temporary contract so that of the main forms of temporary employment in France, only one, fixed-term (including seasonal) contracts, has steadily expanded. The number of employees with interim contracts, including the permanent employees of the labour agencies, increased regularly between 1975 and 1979 to decline thereafter, rising slightly once again in 1986-87 after the new legislative reform. The number of labour agencies followed approximately the same trend. Not counting workers employed permanently by temporary-work agencies, the share of workers with interim contracts in total wage employment remained practically stagnant between 1982 and 1987, reaching 0.7% in 1986 and 1987.[21] In contrast, fixed-term contracts in the private sector expanded quite substantially between 1982 and 1987, though their share of wage employment still amounted only to 2.7% in 1987 [INSEE, 1987]. Despite its low global impact, this form of employment has been playing a considerable role in total new recruitment (a small total anyway), with almost 64% of all recruitment taking place via fixed-term contracts [Perreaux, 1987], and the number of establishments that made use of fixed-term contracts has been increasing. The proportion of establishments with at least ten workers that resorted to fixed-term contracts almost tripled between 1977 and 1983, rising from 12% to 31% [Michon, 1987]. While it is premature to speak of a restructuring of labour demand in France, temporary contracts certainly have an important role, at least "at the margin".

Concerning the UK there is some controversy as to whether temporary employment has been expanding rapidly or not. The OECD quotes figures that show very little expansion between 1983 and 1985: the share of temporary employment increased from 5.5% to 5.7%. The estimates of the UK Department of Employment on the basis of the Labour Force Survey (LFS) confirm the relative constancy of the share of temporary employment (including wage earners and self-employed): 4.1% in 1983 and 4.0% in 1985 for men, and 7.6% and 7.8%, respectively, for women [CSO, 1987]. However, considering a somewhat longer period, Hakim [1987] concludes that "...the most dramatic increase [in peripheral employment, AM] has been in temporary work. The numbers of temporary workers rose from 621,000 in 1981 (*including* some people on government schemes) to 1,314,000 in 1985 (*excluding* people on government schemes)....By 1985 there were also some 400,000 people on government-subsidised employment and training schemes." Taking these figures and those from the *Employment Gazette* into account, the share of temporary workers in total employment would have more than doubled, from about 3% in 1981 to over 8% in 1985, including temporary employment via the government schemes cited above. Hakim, as others, refers to Meager's study [1986] in support of the upward trend in temporary employment, but looking more closely into that study the information provided could equally bear the opposite interpretation: since 1980, 39% of the employers interviewed had increased the use of temporary

---

21.   The global figure hides two contrasting trends: a slightly rising share in the case of men and a somewhat declining share in the case of women [INSEE, 1987].

labour relative to total employment, 44% had not changed and 17% had reduced [Meager, 1986]. While it is true that more firms increased than reduced the use of temporary employment, over 60% of the firms did *not* increase it. For his part, Casey [1987] questioned a rising trend in temporary employment in the UK in the light of two studies of employers' use of fixed-term contracts, which indicated a negligible increase between 1980 and 1984 in the proportion of establishments using fixed-term contracts (from 19% to 20%), while an unchanging 7% of establishments had used fixed-term contracts in a proportion that at least equalled 5% of their workforce both in 1980 and 1984. In brief, while the number of temporary workers has been expanding, it seems that their share of total employment has remained quite stable, or had risen before 1983.

In West Germany temporary employment arrangements seem to have been expanding fast during the 1980s. Though some believe it to be the consequence of the Employment Promotion Act (1985), which inter alia eliminated some restrictions on the use of temporary contracts, a study quoted by Dombois [1986] showed that the proportion of temporary hirings in relation to total job vacancies had jumped upwards before the law was enacted, from 5.9% in 1980 to 15.7% in 1983, and stayed at that level during 1983-1985.[22] A rising share of temporary recruitment in total hirings was also reported in a local labour market, with a jump from 27% in 1982 to 53% in 1985 [Dombois, 1986]. This is confirmed by a larger study which showed that after 1985, 50% of the new recruitment undertaken by the firms surveyed in sixteen industrial sectors had been under fixed-term contracts [*SLB*, 1987/1].

No information on trends in fixed-term contracts seems to have been published in Belgium and the Netherlands. But agency labour has been decreasing after 1980 in both countries, even in absolute numbers in the Netherlands. In both it represents, in any case, a tiny fraction of employment: 0.3% in Belgium, 0.7% in the Netherlands [Bodson et al., 1985].

3. Users and rationale

Some economic activities could be regarded as "traditional" users of temporary contracts, namely those facing seasonal peaks in demand: agriculture, services such as hotels, some manufacturing industries (e.g. food processing and clothing), and often the construction sector. Temporary contracts are more frequent in these economic activities where they do not constitute a "novel" phenomenon. Across countries, the activities with above-average shares of temporary in total employment have varied over time [OECD, 1987, table 1.8]. Manufacturing is consistently an important

---

22. These data are inconclusive, because we do not know the evolution of job vacancies. The use of agency labour also increased before the Employment Promotion Act: according to the Federal Employment Institute agency workers increased from 140,000 in 1975 to 380,000 in 1981. In 1985, man-hours provided by agency labour were four times the 1975 level [Bosch and Sengenberger, 1986].

temporary contract user, although temporary employment is more wide-spread in other sectors. In the UK, the Netherlands, Belgium and the FRG, the proportion of temporary workers in manufacturing employment is below average [OECD, 1987; Rudolph, 1987]; in France it is close to average, and the share of fixed-term contracts in total recruitment by manufacturing has been above average [Perreaux, 1987]. Somewhat in contradiction with the above estimate, according to a 1984 survey of 175 employers in the UK, 78% of employers in the manufacturing sector had made use of temporary workers, a higher level than in all service activities [Meager, 1986]. A survey in the FRG found that after promulgation of the 1985 Employment Promotion Act, 50.6% of recruitment in the metal processing industry had been under fixed-term contracts [*SLB*, 1987/1]. A number of case studies in the Netherlands also show the importance of temporary labour in manufacturing, as much in seasonal industries (fruit and vegetable processing, soft drinks) as in the publishing industry. The use of temporary labour increased between 1982 and 1985, each individual plant surveyed having opted for one preferred practice: holiday casual labour, on call labour, fixed-term contracts or agency labour [*EIRR*, 1987].

As in the case of part-time work, temporary employment in France, Belgium and the UK seems to have been progressing more rapidly in the public than the private sector. Between 1983 and 1985, the increase in the share of temporary employment in public administration and "other services" (including social services) was above average in France, Belgium and the UK [OECD, 1987, table 1.8]. In the UK its growth has been noted in local authorities (white collar temporary staff grew by 47.5% over a year in the Severn Trent Water Authority; Potter, 1987)[23] and in the Post Office [IDS, 1985]. In addition, a 1984 survey covering 2,000 establishments in all economic sectors revealed that the proportion of public sector establishments (particularly in education) that used temporary workers was practically double the average, i.e. 39% against 20% [Casey, 1987]. In the FRG, Dombois [1986] also singled out the significant role played by the public sector in the diffusion of temporary contracts. In 1982 temporary recruit-ment represented 47% of all public sector hirings in a local area, and 45% in 1985. In the Netherlands, too, labour "on call" has been employed in public hospitals, partly because of continuing cuts in public expenditure [*EIRR*, 1987]. The rapid expansion of temporary employment in the public sector in Western Europe is explained mainly by the self-imposed freeze on recruitment for permanent positions in government institutions, aimed at curtailing state expenditures, and often, at reducing the level of taxation, but the rationale for its use in the public sector requires further investigation.

Many of the "traditional reasons" for employing temporary workers are shared by the whole spectrum of economic activities. These reasons cover cases explicitly allowed by labour codes and refer to "exceptional" situations. They include replacement of personnel (during holidays, sickness, etc.), exceptional expansion of activity, seasonal peaks and other exceptional

---

23.   See the same article for details on why temporary employment in the UK public sector has seldom been acknowledged.

needs. Despite the process of change which has taken place in the 1980s, these traditional reasons still seem to dominate, at least according to the declared motives, independently of whether temporary employment had been increasing. But in the UK firms where the use of temporary labour had been rising, "new" reasons have acquired significance: 38% of employers mentioned the need to avoid permanent recruitment because of uncertainty, and 18% the wish to avoid future redundancy costs [Meager, 1986]. Lower labour costs (other than lay-off compensation) were seldom mentioned.[24] The "new" reasons were more important in manufacturing firms than in service sector activities. The diffusion of temporary employment, particularly in manufacturing, was an effect of the economic recession (manufacturing was one of the hardest-hit sectors) and of uncertainty about the duration of the recovery. According to Meager [1986] it has not been a well planned strategy but merely the result of ad hoc adjustments, facilitated by ready labour availability in the external market. The main reasons for using fixed-term contracts given by German employers confirm the relative balance of traditional (still dominant) and new factors: "seasonal character of labour requirements" was mentioned by 60.5% of employers while "uncertainty about trends in economic activity" was mentioned by 34.3% (survey of the German Confederation of Employers' Associations, in *SLB*, 1987/1).

Little is known about the relationship between overtime working and some kinds of temporary contracts, but it seems that the latter have not increased at the expense of overtime work. In the UK the use of overtime in manufacturing at times of economic expansion has been fairly constant in the long term, including the 1980s, in terms of both the proportion of all operatives doing overtime and the average hours of overtime worked; the latter, moreover, increased somewhat after 1984.[25] It is not clear whether some forms of temporary employment have been fostered by a reduction in overtime working in the FRG. The voluntary reduction of overtime has been encouraged by the German government, and the total volume of overtime has been falling since 1970. A survey of 1450 manufacturing firms in 1986 found that overtime was not the preferred means to cope with seasonal variations. At the same time 79% considered overtime as a "necessary flexibility cushion", but during 1980-1985 two-thirds of the firms had taken steps to reduce overtime [*SLB*, 1987/1]. According to Dombois [1986] overtime continues to have advantages over temporary contracts since labour requirements can be met by the permanent workforce without additional training costs. But a decrease in use of overtime as an adjustment mechanism is not likely to have been due to its cost; rather, the limitations imposed by labour regulations on overtime work and, more recently, the specific incentives implemented in some countries to curtail the volume of

---

24.   The employers surveyed explained that the advantages of being able to match manning levels precisely to workloads, and the extra flexibility gained from being able to adjust the size of the workforce rapidly without incurring major severance costs, exceeded any advantages due to lower wage and non-wage costs.

25.   Data for 1964-87 in *Employment Gazette* (Historical Supplement No. 1, Aug. 1984, and Jan. 1988).

overtime with a view to reducing unemployment, have prevented its more intensive use or have stimulated its decrease. At times of economic uncertainty, the amount of allowable overtime being in a sense "fixed", hiring temporary labour becomes the adaptive mechanism, given the potential costs of dismissal associated with employing new permanent workers.

It has been argued [OECD, 1986] that temporary contracts are sometimes a means of "screening" workers before final commitment, thus not necessarily bringing about more employment instability.[26] "Screening" implies that a positive selection is confined to a few who obtain a stable position, while the rest return to the labour market. According to a survey of temporary workers in France (with interim contracts), out of a million temporary workers entering the labour market each year, 17% find a permanent job within six months, and only one-third of these with the employer they had been working for under a temporary assignment [SLB, 1982/4]. Comparing the share of fixed-term contracts in hirings and in quits it has been estimated that, in 1986, no more than 22% of workers with fixed-term contracts could have obtained an open-ended contract, and that a fraction of those might still be in employment, not as a result of having benefitted from a transformation of their contract from temporary into permanent, but merely because they had a longer fixed-term contract [Perreaux, 1987]. Similarly, in a survey from the UK that analysed the rationale for using temporary workers, "screening" was mentioned by only 15% of the employers interviewed [IDS, cited in Potter, 1987]. Although in his study of a local labour market in the FRG Dombois [1986] found that in many companies the use of temporary contracts as a "probationary" period to assess workers' suitability to the job had become "common practice", a broader survey in Germany reported that no more than a quarter of the firms investigated were planning to offer permanent employment to those recruited under a fixed-term contract [SLB, 1987/1]. In brief, temporary employment seldom constitutes a direct entry path to a secure position.

This leads to an inter-related question: to what extent is temporary work linked with continued employment instability? Has a pattern of alternating periods of unemployment and of temporary employment become characteristic of the "temporary worker's" life? Are temporary positions a step on the road to permanent employment or, rather, a step in a "career" of successive temporary jobs? Prospects look particularly bleak for young workers, who are over-represented in temporary positions, and whose chances of securing a permanent job in the context of slow employment growth seem to be confined to "natural" replacement. The available evidence, very sparse and short term, does not describe one homogeneous, single pattern. A considerable proportion, about one-third to one-half, occasionally even more, of workers with temporary employment continue in that situation at least in the immediate future, but the number of workers that have been able to obtain a permanent contract is not negligible. Even so, 70% of temporary workers with interim contracts in France that wished

---

26.   One-third of all workers who in March 1983 had fixed-term contracts in France were still in the same job in March 1984 with a contract of indefinite duration [OECD, 1986].

to move into permanent employment had not been able to do so, and about 36% and 47.5% of workers who in 1979 had interim and fixed-term contracts, respectively, still had the same type of contract a year later [Coëffic, 1982, tables 1 and 2]. According to a longitudinal study of Dutch temporary workers [cited in OECD, 1987] 56% of workers with temporary employment in 1985 had a permanent contract one and a half years later (although not necessarily with the same employer), i.e. the remaining 44% had not obtained any permanent position. Moreover a substantial fraction of workers in Belgium, France, the Netherlands and the UK, who were in temporary positions in 1985, had been either unemployed or inactive a year earlier, and of those who had been in wage employment (a much lower proportion than in the case of the workers with permanent employment in 1985), an unknown part might have been in a temporary position. Termination of temporary employment is an important cause of unemployment - 25% of the unemployed workers in France, 22% in the UK (1987) and 6% in the FRG (1986) – although straight dismissal continues to be the major single factor contributing to unemployment – 34%, 33% and 31%, respectively [*Enquête sur l'emploi*, 1987; *Employment Gazette*, 1988; Eurostat, unpublished].

Anyway, temporary employment implies instability; even if many temporary workers later obtain a permanent contract, it is seldom in the firm where they had had a temporary assignment. Moreover, temporary employment is often associated with periods of unemployment.

4. Access to social protection: Law and practice

In agreement with the "new" role assigned to temporary employment by governments and business, changes in the regulation of temporary employment have concentrated on removing obstacles to its diffusion rather than on improving the situation of temporary workers (albeit with some important exceptions). On the whole, temporary workers tend to have the same rights as permanent personnel,[27] and employment through labour agencies has been subject to many specific regulations.[28] In spite of legal equality, however, the "normal" limitations on qualifying for various social benefits (such as a minimum length of uninterrupted service with the same employer), which apply to all workers, temporary and permanent alike, are easily overcome by the latter, but become a persistent cause of exclusion from coverage for many temporary workers. Instability of employment is not only dramatic in itself, but also brings about other forms of vulnerability.

In the case of agency labour, responsibility for a worker's social protection tends to lie with the agency and not with the user firm, and the

---

27. Except in the case of a fixed-term worker dismissed before the expiration of his contract.

28. On the regulation of fixed-term and interim employment in the early 1980s, see Javillier [1983] for France, Vogel-Polsky [1983] for Belgium, Daubler [1983] for the FRG, and Napier [1983] and Leighton [1986] for the UK.

interim worker generally has similar rights to those of a permanent worker. In France, since the 1982 ordinance on interim contracts via specialised agencies, interim workers have a right to a written contract, to wages equal to those of permanent workers performing the same tasks, to a precise knowledge of the duration of their assignment, to an instability allowance and an indemnity instead of paid leave, and to access to staff facilities in the enterprise [*SLB*, 1985/1].[29] This is the general rule too in the UK since 1973, but in a few cases interim workers lacked social protection because they were regarded as having no employment relationship with the agency, and categorised as "self-employed" [Leighton, 1986]. In Belgium, collective agreements ruling in the user firm cover interim workers [Bodson et al., 1985]. In the Netherlands, there is no legal difference in pay and social protection between interim workers and permanent employees [Bodson et al., 1985].

Legally speaking, for workers with fixed term contracts, a written contract and equality of pay, social security coverage and working conditions are the rule in all countries. To some extent since 1979, but particularly after 1982, such workers in France also have a right to an end-of-contract indemnity, i.e. a sort of wage supplement that depends on the duration of the contract and the wage rate, but should not be below a stipulated minimum level [*SLB*, 1982/2]. Since the 1986 decree, fixed-term and interim employees should have the same working conditions as permanent workers with the same qualifications, in relation to pay, severance payment and other matters [*EIRR*, 1986].

In practice, however, the prerequisite of a minimum period of unbroken service with the same employer appears as the main obstacle to obtaining social security benefits and other rights. If, in principle, fixed-term workers in France have the same rights as permanent workers, in actual fact this is often restricted by collective agreements which stipulate some minimum length of service in order to qualify for certain social benefits [Javillier, 1986]. In the Netherlands, interim workers often do not qualify for unemployment insurance [Bodson et al., 1985]. In the UK, too, many employment rights are granted only after minimum periods of continuous employment with the same firm, such as two years to qualify for unfair dismissal procedures, redundancy payments and maternity rights, thirteen weeks to have the right to a written statement of terms and conditions of employment, three months to be entitled to statutory sick pay, and four weeks to have the right to a minimum period of notice. Workers under longer-term contracts are in a privileged position vis-à-vis workers with short-term, seasonal and casual contracts [Potter, 1987] who, according to Leighton [1986], are often excluded from entitlement to benefits by the "contribution record" rules. The proportion of temporary workers with no access to

---

29.   Collective agreements have also been signed which concern temporary workers' rights and which include social security provisions.

various benefits depends on their distribution in relation to the types and duration of contract.[30]

As is the case with part-time employment, the right to equal pay may guarantee nothing more than equality of the basic agreed wage rate, so that many temporary workers, not earning any fringe benefits and with no seniority rights, in practice do not have the same hourly earnings as their permanent counterparts. Sectors with considerable contingents of temporary workers may constitute an exception if collective agreements encompass special provisions related to temporary workers' situations (e.g. fixed-term workers in the public sector or in banking and finance in the UK; Leighton, 1986). In the Netherlands the interim agencies' organisation signed agreements with trade unions about hours of work, pay, advance notice of lay-off, etc. [Bodson et al., 1985] but in the FRG agency labour tends to have worse pay and working conditions than permanent workers, as well as more restricted social security rights, because, on the one hand, they are excluded from the scope of the collective agreements in the user firm and, on the other, the number of collective agreements directly signed by agencies is small [Kravaritou, 1986].[31]

Therefore, temporary contracts are particularly attractive to business which sees in them diverse advantages: the absence of costs associated with the termination of employment, lower wage (due to fewer or no fringe benefits and seniority rights) and non-wage labour costs. Their adaptability to economic fluctuations with no severance costs outweighs any other advantage or even disadvantage such as extra administrative costs, however [Leighton, 1986; Meager, 1986]. Furthermore, many recent government schemes have provided firms with subsidised labour by means of payroll and other tax exemptions or rebates, while the employer has had no obligations beyond a minimum stipulated period of employment.

5. A tool of labour market regulation

Some modalities of temporary employment have undergone a changing role on the labour market. At times of near full employment, temporary contracts were used inter alia to meet labour requirements with workers recruited beyond national borders. The "threat" of temporariness (i.e. expulsion from the host country) was always present in the *Gastarbeit*

---

30. In the UK, seasonal, casual and other directly employed labour, excluding workers with fixed-term contracts, constituted as much as 70% of all temporary workers in 1984; this may give an approximate notion as to the maximum size of the group with less or no protection. However, many seasonal and casual workers have the possibility of making contributions while not working so as to preserve the necessary contribution record for qualifying for benefits [Leighton, 1986].

31. There are examples of the reverse situation as well. A Dutch survey found that "on call" workers in catering and hotels are paid above the hourly rate, agreed collectively, but they do not have a written contract nor a guaranteed number of hours of work, and the firm does not even keep a record of their employment. In public hospitals "on call" labour received pay and allowances determined in the collective agreement [*EIRR*, 1987].

system, enhancing labour discipline, though in practice, temporary contracts were often renewed and many foreign workers stayed permanently on the job. At times of high unemployment the diffusion of temporary employment is regarded by the state as a tool for reducing, albeit during a short period, the number of registered unemployed workers who require income maintenance and by business as an attractive option – precisely because there is massive unemployment – for coping with economic uncertainty. To that effect governments not only eliminated barriers to the diffusion of temporary employment,[32] but also implemented several government-sponsored temporary employment schemes.[33] In any case, the impact of temporary employment on the level of unemployment seems to have been very limited, as have been the effects of the growth of part-time employment.

IV. Non-standard employment and labour market regulation

Non-standard employment and unemployment have been increasing *pari passu* both in France and the UK (see figure 2).[34] In the context of high unemployment (annex table A), workers are not faced with many employment options, and the few available ones are often non-standard types of employment. The basic reason why the latter are available instead of regular full-time positions is their relatively lower cost: temporary workers do not qualify for dismissal compensation at the end of the contract; part-time work may imply fuller utilisation of equipment, thus lower unit costs; or may simply be less expensive because only a few hours of daily work are really needed. At times of "tight" labour markets these advantages were outweighed by the high cost of rapid turnover of workers who could opt for better employment opportunities. With massive unemployment, workers try to keep their jobs, and except in very specific cases, there is no need to offer costly benefits to retain them in the firm. How vulnerable permanent workers are is evidenced by unemployment trends. Dismissal continues to be the main single cause of unemployment, and the current (proposed or enacted) relaxation of the rules restricting lay-offs will produce more unemployment.

---

32.   See, for instance, the relaxation of rules in the 1985 Employment Promotion Act in the FRG (cf. Mückenberger, chapter 11), and the 1986 Act in France that eliminates the requirement for authorisation before hiring temporary workers and extends the maximum duration of temporary contracts [*SLB*, 1985/3-4 and 1986/3-4].

33.   [Such schemes in France are discussed in more detail by Caire, chapter 4 - *eds.*].

34.   The R squared for the association between unemployment and part-time employment rates is 0.95 (t=17.91) in France (1971-1987) and 0.86 (t=7.75) in the UK (female part-time employment and total unemployment rate, 1974-1987; no data available on part-time work for 1979 and 1980). Own estimates with data from INSEE [1987] and *Employment Gazette*, several issues.

Figure 2: Unemployment and part-time work – France and the UK

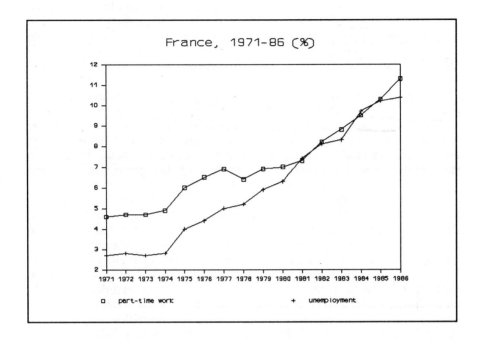

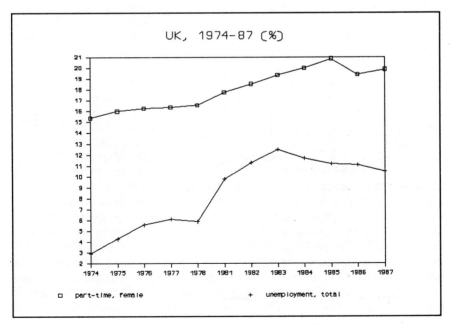

In actual fact non-standard employment in the private sector did not increase spontaneously *that* much. Its importance has been enhanced more by the lack of full-time, permanent job creation than by a marked "jump" in the growth trend of non-standard employment. The growth rate of part-time work and of temporary employment indeed accelerated in the 1980s, but for part-time employment the rate did not depart much from the regular trend that had started long previously (see figure 1), and moreover, both forms have been promoted directly (government-sponsored schemes) and indirectly (incentives to workers and employers) by the state. In addition, the state as employer makes an increasing use of both part-time and temporary employment within its institutions, accounting for an appreciable segment of temporary and part-time work growth. It has been sufficiently important to explain over 60% of the growth in part-time employment in France between 1982 and 1987.[35]

As instruments of state labour policy, these two forms of non-standard employment have been assigned an important role in labour market and social security regulation. In the past they had been mechanisms to increase labour supply within the framework of labour scarcity, now they have been turned into instruments to "combat" high unemployment. These features in a way differentiate temporary and part-time employment from other non-standard forms of employment, with the exception of self-employment which is actively promoted, at least in some Western European countries, as another convergent "solution" to the unemployment problem. In the fifties and sixties, self-employment was viewed as a "labour reserve" and some "active manpower policies" put forward during that period were designed precisely to encourage self-employed workers to leave their positions and move into wage employment. At present, the opposite policy prevails: a wide range of incentives is offered to workers to encourage them to become self-employed and set up their own business.

State encouragement of non-standard employment in the private sector has so far shown limited results. The share of some non-standard practices (other than part-time employment) has not yet risen alarmingly and is still lower than unemployment rates. However, the sum of non-standard employment practices and unemployment, added to the much broader policy designed to consistently reduce social transfers to labour and undermine employment security, is having a more dramatic impact. Not only has recruitment under non-standard employment practices increased, often with low pay and little social protection, but unemployment levels are high too. In addition, benefits for both the permanently employed and the unemployed have been curtailed, and restrictions on discretionary firing have been relaxed. Deregulation both in the private and the public sector is underway. And, more generally, there is reduced state intervention in boosting aggregate demand. These processes have jointly created conditions of greater insecurity for labour at large – and not only for the workers in non-standard employment. Current policies have also undermined a pillar

---

35.   Whether part-time and temporary workers in the public sector fare better and are less vulnerable than in the private sector still remains to be investigated.

of the "welfare state", i.e. income transfer from capital to labour, in the expectation that the other source of support, income redistribution *within labour*, will suffice to ensure the continuity of social benefits. A contradiction of this policy is that while the expansion of part-time and temporary work might contribute to decreasing the number of unemployed drawing income maintenance, at the same time it implies reduced revenues for the social security system, creating an additional source of financial strain.

Seen in a historical perspective, non-standard employment practices have an important role (and indeed a changing role according to the global labour market situation) "at the margin". Their role is comparable to that of other mechanisms of labour market regulation, such as imports of labour. But as for immigration, it does not necessarily follow that labour would have been better off had "atypical" employment not expanded. In any case, the effects of the diffusion of non-standard employment would be less adverse for labour if temporary, part-time and irregular (and immigrant) workers became the object of active trade union protection. The global impact of the progression of non-standard employment is clearly independent of whether such forms of employment are taken "preferentially" by certain groups of the labour force or not. Once again, the problem may be set in the same terms of analysis as the imports of labour in the past. No doubt migrant workers were very willing to be employed in low-paid occupations, in shift-work, in non-protected jobs lacking social security benefits and with undesirable working conditions, and in temporary positions. This did not prevent labour imports from having more global effects, ranging from their impact upon the evolution of wages, unemployment and labour demand, to changes in the economic structure.

The diffusion of each form of non-standard employment is governed by legal, institutional, market and labour supply characteristics prevailing in each country [Deakin and Rubery, 1986]. The role played by labour costs, in particular social security costs, in the propagation of non-standard employment requires more investigation. It is worth noting that one of the countries with the largest rates of part-time employment, the UK, actually has the lowest proportion of non-wage in total labour costs (annex table A), but this proportion has risen the fastest before stabilising, as in the other four countries, during the 1980s. Differences between countries in the degree of diffusion of and trends in part-time employment are much more noticeable than in the case of temporary forms of work, suggesting that part-time work has been the most affected by differences in legal and socio-economic settings. The incidence of temporary employment is much more uniform across countries, indicating on the one hand that its use might be still dominated by a "traditional" rationale, and, on the other, that differences between countries in its "relative advantage" are not substantial. The exhaustive analysis of the factors that determine inter-country differentials in the ratio and pace of these (and other) non-standard employment practices remains to be undertaken.

Annex table A: Unemployment, temporary and part-time employment, and non-wage labour costs (percentages)

	Belgium	FRG	France	Netherlands	U.K.
Unemployment rate, 1986					
- all	12.3	9.0	10.4	12.0	11.9*
- female	17.9	10.5	13.1	12.3	9.1*
Temporary wage employment as % of total, 1985					
- all workers	6.9	(6.0)	4.8	7.5	5.7
Part-time wage employment as % of total, 1985					
- all	9.3	12.3	10.5	22.6	21.8
- female	23.2	29.1	21.0	51.0	44.5
Non-wage labour costs, as % of total labour costs, 1983	44.9	44.4	44.4	44.0	26.5

Notes: * 1985.
Sources: OECD [1987], Eurostat [1987a], ILO [1987], INSEE [1987], Rudolph [1987].

References

Baroin, D.; Loos, J.; Ouazan, J.M. (1981): *Changement en matière de durée du travail. La situation juridique et la couverture sociale du travail à temps partiel dans six pays membres de la Communauté Européenne.* Brussels, European Commission, EC-V/1398-81.

Blanchflower, D.; Corry, B. (1986): *Part-time employment in Great Britain*, Research Paper No. 57. London, Department of Employment.

Bloch-London, C. (1987): "Les aides au développement du travail à temps partiel et à l'aménagement du temps de travail", in *Bilan de l'emploi 1986, Dossiers statistiques du travail et de l'emploi*, Supplément au *Bulletin Mensuel des Statistiques du Travail* (Paris, Ministère des Affaires Sociales et de la Solidarité), Nos. 34-35.

Bodson, D.; Nyssen, B.; Spineux, A. (1985): *Les travailleurs précaires dans les pays industrialisés à économie de marché: Belgique-Pays-Bas.* Louvain-la-Neuve, Université Catholique de Louvain, Institut des Sciences du Travail (mimeo).

Bosch, G.; Sengenberger, W. (1986): *Employment policy, the state and the unions in the Federal Republic of Germany* (mimeo).

Büchtemann, C.F.; Schupp, J. (1986): *Zur Sozio-Okonomie der Teilzeitbeschaftigung in der Bundesrepublik Deutschland*, Labour Market Policy Discussion Paper 86-15. Berlin, Wissenschaftszentrum, IIM.

Casey, B. (1983): *Governmental measures to promote part-time working*, Labour Market Policy Discussion Papers 83-26. Berlin, Wissenschaftszentrum, IIM.

—— (1987): "The extent and nature of temporary employment in Great Britain", in *Policy Studies* (London, Policy Studies Institute), Vol. 8, No. 1.

Central Statistical Office [CSO] (1987): *Social Trends* (London, HMSO), Vol. 17.

Coëffic, N. (1982): "L'ampleur des emplois précaires", in *Economie et Statistique* (Paris, INSEE), No. 147.

Daubler, W. (1983): *Crise, maintien de l'emploi et partage du travail*, Rapport allemand. Geneva, Université de Genève, Centre d'études juridiques européennes (mimeo).

Deakin, S. (1986): *Deregulation, social legislation and positive rights*. International Working Party on Labour Market Segmentation, VIIIth Conference, Cambridge (mimeo).

Deakin, S.; Rubery, J. (1986): *Typology, dimensions and regulation of homework in the UK*. Cambridge, Department of Applied Economics (mimeo).

Dombois, R. (1986): *Flexibility by law*. International Working Party on Labour Market Segmentation, VIIIth Annual Conference, Cambridge (mimeo).

Employment Gazette, various issues. London, Department of Employment.

Enquête sur l'emploi, various issues. Paris, INSEE.

European Industrial Relations Review (London) [EIRR] (1982): "France, part-time work law reform", No. 100, May.

—— (1986): "Decree on 'peripheral work'", No. 153, Oct.

—— (1987): "Netherlands: flexible working survey", No. 160, May.

Eurostat (1987a): *Labour Force Survey of 1985*. Brussels.

—— (1987b): "Schemes with an impact on the labour market and their statistical treatment in the member states of the European Community", in *Population and Social Conditions*. Brussels, ECSC-EEC-AEC.

Garnsey, E., in collaboration with Dahan, J.; Napier, B.; Scott, B. (1984): *The provision and quality of part-time work: The case of Great Britain and France*. Cambridge, Department of Applied Economics (mimeo).

Hakim, C. (1987): *Home-based work in Britain*, Research Paper No. 60. London, Department of Employment.

Incomes Data Services Ltd. [IDS] (1985): "Post Office – Terms agreed on new technology", in *IDS Report* (London), No. 449, May.

Institut National de la Statistique et des Etudes Economiques [INSEE] (1987): *Population active, emploi et chômage depuis 30 ans*. Paris, La Collection de l'INSEE.

International Labour Office (1987): *Yearbook of labour statistics, 1987*. Geneva.

Javillier, J-C. (1983): *Crise, maintien de l'emploi et partage du travail*, Rapport francais. Geneva, Université de Genève, Centre d'études juridiques européennes (mimeo).

—— (1986): *Les travailleurs précaires en France*. Bordeaux, Université de Bordeaux (mimeo).

Kravaritou, Y. (1986): *Formes nouvelles d'emploi: Leurs effets en droit du travail et de la sécurité sociale dans les Etats-membres de la Communauté Européenne*, Rapport général, Fondation Européenne pour l'Amélioration des Conditions de Vie et de Travail. Dublin/Thessaloniki (mimeo).

Labour Research Department [LRD] (1986): *Part-time workers*. London.

Leighton, P. (1986): "Atypical employment: The law and practice in the United Kingdom", in *Comparative Labour Law Journal* (Philadelphia, University of Pennsylvania), Vol. 8, No. 1.

Letablier, M-T. (1986): "Les dynamiques de diffusion du travail à temps partiel aux Etats-Unis et en France", in *Travail et Emploi* (Paris, Ministère du Travail), No. 30.

Loos, J. (1981): "Situation juridique et couverture sociale du travailleur à temps partiel en R.F.A.", in Baroin, D. et al. (1981): *Changement en matière de durée du travail. La situation juridique et la couverture sociale du travail à temps partiel dans six pays membres de la Communauté Européenne*. Brussels, European Commission, EC-V/1398-81.

Meager, N. (1986): "Temporary work in Britain", in *Employment Gazette* (London, Department of Employment), Vol. 94, No. 1, Jan.

Michon, F. (1987): *Work force flows, non-standard unemployment, non-standard employment.* International Working Party on Labour Market Segmentation, IXth Conference, Turin (mimeo).

Napier, B. (1983): *Crise, maintien de l'emploi et partage du travail*, Rapport anglais. Geneva, Université de Genève, Centre d'études juridiques européennes (mimeo).

Organisation for Economic Cooperation and Development [OECD] (1986): *Employment Outlook, 1986.* Paris.

—— (1987): *Employment Outlook, 1987.* Paris.

Perreaux, P. (1987): "Les mouvements de main-d'oeuvre en 1986", in *Bilan de l'emploi 1986, Dossiers Statistiques du Travail et de l'Emploi*, Supplément au *Bulletin Mensuel des Statistiques du Travail* (Paris, Ministère des Affaires Sociales et de la Solidarité), Nos. 34-35.

Potter, T. (1987): *A temporary phenomenon: Flexible labour, temporary workers and the trade union response.* London, Low Pay Unit.

Robinson, O.; Wallace, J. (1984): *Part-time employment and sex discrimination legislation in Great Britain*, Research Paper No. 43. London, Department of Employment.

Rudolph, H. (1987): "Befristete Beschäftigung – ein Uberblick", in *Mitteilungen aus der Arbeitsmarkt- und Berufsforschung* (Stuttgart), Vol. 20, No. 3.

Schoer, K. (1987): "Part-time employment: Britain and West Germany", in *Cambridge Journal of Economics*, Vol. 11, No. 1.

Social and Labour Bulletin [SLB], various issues. Geneva, ILO.

Tollet, R.; Vandewalle, V. (1987): *L'emploi à temps partiel de 1973 à 1985.* Brussels, Ministry of Economic Affairs, Planning Office, May.

U.S. Bureau of Labor Statistics (1986): *Employment and Earnings.* Washington, D.C., Oct.

Vogel-Polsky, E. (1983): *Crise, maintien de l'emploi et partage du travail*, Rapport belge. Geneva, Université de Genève, Centre d'études juridiques européennes.

3　Precarious forms of work in the United Kingdom

Jill Rubery[1]

I. Introduction

This paper is concerned with "precarious work" in the UK. There is no precise definition of this concept in the UK on a statistical, legal or economic basis. Moreover there is no clear distinction between precarious non-direct employment and other non-standard work forms such as part-time work. Nevertheless, there is a widely-held belief that "precarious" work has been increasing in the UK since the 1970s, based on apparent evidence of increasing incidence of various types or forms of working. These include non-direct employment such as homeworking, self-employment and work in the black economy, as well as other, more direct forms, such as temporary or contract working and part-time working. To assess the validity of this belief it is necessary to address three issues: first to examine the empirical evidence on the incidence of these employment forms; second to assess the quality of the available evidence; and third, to consider the extent to which it is justifiable to consider these employment forms to be "precarious".

II. Precarious work: the empirical evidence

As there is no statistical category "precarious work", the only way in which we can investigate precarious work is to look at the employment forms which are expected to be in some sense precarious. We will concentrate on five, potentially overlapping employment forms: temporary or contract work, homeworking, self-employment, irregular work in the black economy and part-time work. This last form is usually direct, regular employment; it is also the most important form of non-standard work and is often included in the category of precarious work. The tax incentives available for part-time working in the UK mean that it may be in practice equivalent to more irregular employment forms in other countries when these are used explicitly for tax avoidance purposes.

1.　　Department of Applied Economics, University of Cambridge.

1. Temporary and contract work

Temporary and contract work is taken to include all types of casual, seasonal, temporary, short- or fixed-term contract work. The expressions "temporary" and "fixed-term" in practice define this work to be in some sense precarious, and thus necessarily within the precarious work category.

The main source of information on temporary workers is the Labour Force Survey. This survey of individuals allows respondents to select between "permanent jobs", "seasonal, temporary or casual jobs" and jobs done "under contract or for a fixed period of time". There is in fact no precise legal definition of temporary work, and in practice many temporary workers are found to be employed on open-ended contracts; the temporary nature of their job was simply made clear to them at the point of hiring. These LFS data have been extensively explored in three articles [Casey, 1988; Dale and Bamford, 1988; King, 1988]. The survey results reveal a modest increase in temporary working in the 1980s, but consistent time series data are only available since 1983. Moreover this increase only follows a decrease at the beginning of the 1980s, so that temporary working is now probably only back to the level of the 1970s. These data cast doubt, therefore, on the wilder predictions of the "flexible firm" model, backed up by surveys of personnel managers mainly in manufacturing firms [Meager, 1986], which heralded a large growth of temporary working the 1980s. In 1986 there were 1.3 million temporary workers (or 1.6 if those on government schemes were included), that is less than 6% of the employed population [King, 1988].

The LFS data also reveal considerable overlap between temporary and other forms of precarious working. Sixty per cent of temporary jobs were part-time and 13% of casual workers and 23% of contract workers were self-employed, compared to 11% of permanent workers. Taking temporary work as a whole, the majority of temporary workers were women (54% in 1984, compared to a 41% female share of the labour force). However men were in the majority among contract workers, which in turn account for around 25% of all temporary workers in the survey. Contract working was more common in the more skilled occupations and professions, while casual work was most common in low skilled service sector jobs. Moreover, contract work and particularly agency work was also found to be associated with areas of high employment, indicating a response by firms to labour shortage [Casey, 1988]. Levels of temporary work were not particularly related to unemployment rates, but the extent of *involuntary* temporary working (i.e. those who take a temporary job because they cannot find a permanent one) was higher in areas of high unemployment [Casey, 1988]. However, by this definition, involuntary temporary working was found to be much greater among men than women workers.

The most comprehensive data on the use of temporary work by firms are from the Workplace Industrial Relations Survey (WIRS). This survey again found no evidence of an increase in temporary working between 1980 and 1984; nor did it find support for the "flexible firm" hypothesis that temporary work would be found more in large firms which could adopt a sophisticated personnel approach. This finding was further supported by the Warwick IRRU company-level industrial relations survey covering companies with over 1000 employees. No change in employer policy towards temporary working was found in the majority of companies [Marginson et al., 1988]. Temporary work is found in unionised as well as non-unionised establishments. Indeed the most striking difference between types of firms was the overwhelming dominance of the public sector in the use of short, fixed-term contracts [Millward and Stevens, 1986]. One explanation is the greater assumed permanence of public sector jobs, especially for professionals, when open-ended contracts are given, coupled with the restrictive government policy towards public expenditure. The public sector has also been active in expanding the use of contract labour through the privatisation of services such as catering and cleaning in hospitals. These are "permanent" jobs which have been turned into temporary or casual work through a change of employer [Coyle, 1986a and 1986b; Potter, 1986].

These findings suggest that there are very different employment practices under the umbrella title of temporary employment. There are many jobs which fit the traditional typology of temporary, casual and seasonal jobs in distribution, catering, tourism and so on, but there is also a wide range of jobs which are temporary not because the demand for labour is *known* to be short-run but because firms need to retain flexibility to reduce labour quickly should further expenditure cuts or a downturn in demand occur. These "temporary jobs" may in practice involve permanent employment through a series of renewable temporary contracts or through an open ended but always precarious contract. Such work is then potentially rather than necessarily precarious and thus differs from explicitly seasonal or casual work.

2. Homeworking

Since the 1970s there has been a major growth in research on homeworking, initially largely relying on case-study data but culminating in two large-scale national surveys in the 1980s. The first investigated the use of homeworkers and freelancers by employers as part of the Workplace Industrial Relations Survey, carried out in 1980 and 1984 [Hakim, 1985]; the second was a follow-up survey to the 1981 Labour Force Survey of a sample of those who said they worked at or from home [Hakim, 1985; Hakim, 1987a]. However, the publication of the results of these surveys has not ended controversy over the extent, nature and implications of homeworking in the UK.

Most of the results from both case-study and national surveys have indicated a rising incidence of homeworking, but as all surveys use different questions and terminology, the strength of the upward trend remains uncertain. The first survey to cast doubt on this upward trend was the 1984 Workplace Industrial Relations Survey which found a fall in the share of establishments using freelancers between 1980 and 1984 from 22 to 14%. But as these surveys only covered establishments with over 25 employees,

and many homeworkers are known to work for the expanding small firm
sector, these results do not settle the issue.

The 1981 National Homeworking Survey aroused controversy by
revealing a quite different picture of the typical homeworker than that
revealed by the case-study material [Hakim, 1987a]. The majority of
homeworkers were, as predicted, married women, but they were much more
likely to be doing non-manufacturing work than manufacturing work. They
were better educated and more likely to be homeowners than the average
for the labour force as a whole. This picture contrasted sharply with that of
women homeworkers in traditional manufacturing industries in inner city
areas, belonging to ethnic minority groups, who have been the subject both
of specific studies of homeworking and the target for political campaigns to
improve the position of homeworkers. The Department of Employment,
which undertook the 1981 survey, has been accused of bias in its sampling
and survey procedures by those concerned to press the case of the ethnic
community homeworkers, and has in turn suggested that researchers have in
the past been misled by the narrow range of homeworkers and small sample
numbers that they have studied.

A more promising approach might be to see merit and value in both
types of research, and to draw on both sets of results to develop a full
picture. It is very likely that representative national samples will always
under-represent and understate the importance of ethnic minorities, with the
consequence for these surveys of also partly downplaying the role of
manufacturing. It remains that there are a very large number of homeworkers that do not fit the standard stereotype, except insofar as they are
women and often have children. The potential importance of homeworking
in information technology industries has been emphasised in some studies
[Huws, 1984] although in practice it is often the same handful of firms that
are cited. The 1981 survey, however, reveals a much wider range of non-
manual employment than that strictly related to information technology.
Overall there may have been a process of divergence in the trends in
homeworking, with a general increase in the importance of non-manual work
coinciding with an increase in the intensification of use of homework in
manufacturing in certain inner city areas and industries.

Using the 1981 national survey, homeworking accounted for over
257,000 workers or 230,000 excluding child-minders. Of those working at
home (excluding child-minders) about 45% worked for a single employer and
55% for 2 or more employers. Women accounted for 82% of the former
group and only 56% of the latter. Thus not only is homeworking a
predominantly female employment form but men who work at home are also
much less likely to be dependent on one employer than women.

Homeworking is not an employment form which is either precisely
defined or distinct from other precarious forms such as temporary work or
self-employment. There is no general legal definition either of homeworking
or of whether or not homeworkers should be considered employees or self-
employed. Many are very confused about their employment status. After
detailed questioning in the 1981 survey it appeared that only 21% considered
themselves to be employees and 44% to be self-employed, with no less than

35% in a grey area. This grey area can exist partly because many home-workers do not have to define their status for tax purposes, as their earnings fall below the threshold for national insurance. Moreover the status of employee is not precisely defined in the UK. It is possible for homeworkers to obtain the status of employee and thereby benefit from employment protection if they are continuously in receipt of work, even if for tax purposes they are treated as self-employed [Leighton, 1983]. The 1981 survey suggests that most homeworkers would have difficulty claiming this status, as breaks in the continuity of work flow are the norm rather than the exception. This also suggests that homeworking in some sense normally belongs to the category of precarious work, as individuals bear the risk of fluctuations in work levels even if they work on a long term basis for individual employers. Indeed labour turnover in homeworking jobs appears to be slightly below that for the labour force as a whole [Hakim, 1987a], but stability of labour supply does not guarantee stability of employment. One third of homeworkers had worked for the same employer for six years or longer and a further third for between two and five years.

Whatever the individual homeworkers' view of their employment status, the terms and conditions under which they are rewarded are not those of a direct employee. Most receive no holiday pay, sickness pay or any guarantees of minimum weekly pay. All surveys have found homeworkers to be low paid, absolutely and relative to their qualifications or skills, and often relative to the pay received by inworkers of the same firm for identical tasks.

3. Self-employment

The one employment form associated with precarious non-direct employment that has expanded unambiguously over the 1980s is self-employment. There are now over 2.8 million self-employed in their main job, compared to 1.9 million in 1979 [*Employment Gazette*, 1988; Storey and Johnson, 1987]. There has also been a marked increase in both the percentage of those in employment who have a second job, and some slight increase in the share of those who are self-employed in their second job. Creigh et al. estimate that in 1984, 2.6 million were self-employed in their main job, but a total of 2.79 million were engaged in self-employment. However, confusions in people's perceptions of their employment status (because as for homeworking there is often no reason to define employment status if earnings fall below the national insurance contribution threshold), imply that these estimates do not refer to a precisely defined employment form. Even this large increase in self-employment has still left the UK with a relatively low incidence of self-employment by EEC standards, the low share of agriculture providing only a partial explanation [Creigh et al., 1986].

The characteristics of the self-employed population are different from those of the employed population: the majority are men (75% compared to 59% of employees), the majority are middle-aged, with a higher share of over-60s than employees, and a higher percentage work full-time.

These characteristics have changed slightly over recent years, with a greater than average increase in youth, female and part-time self-employment. There has also been an increasing tendency for the self-employed to be own account workers, without employees: around 80% of the recent growth in self-employment (1981-84) was in own-account employment. These changes do provide evidence that the growth of self-employment may be more to do with an expansion of precarious forms of employment than evidence of "rebirth of the entrepreneurial spirit". The likelihood that the self-employment category increasingly includes precarious work is enhanced by examination of the hours of work. Proportionally more self-employed than employees work very short hours (less than 9 per week), particularly women. The inclusion of precarious and variable work within the self-employed category should not, however, deflect attention from the excessively long hours of the majority of the self-employed: 20% work more than 60 hours per week, compared to only 2% of employees. These long hours may reflect another type of "precariousness" associated with employment, that is the need for long hours of labour time to secure the viability of a business. Nevertheless the majority of the self-employed are firmly engaged in full-time employment.

Another argument has been put forward, that the new self-employed have in fact taken over directly the jobs of employees, with employers encouraging or forcing direct employees to switch to self-employment status. This could be considered a change to precarious work mainly because the "employees" would bear the risks of demand fluctuations and overheads more than the employer. Evidence from the Labour Force Survey does not support the idea of widespread transfer of status with the same employer. Seventeen per cent had become newly self-employed between 1984 and 1983 but only 7.7% of all self-employed had been employees one year previously, and most of these had changed occupation or the organisation they worked for (62 and 88% respectively). These data on flows into self-employment also indicate the potential importance of non-employment as a source of recruitment to self-employment. Only 3.3% of all self-employed had been unemployed one year earlier, but a further 6.2% had been economically inactive. Thus there is some evidence of a flow from non-employment into self-employment, a movement encouraged by the government through the Enterprise Allowance Scheme.[2] The relatively low share of increases in self-employment with own employees, the high share of own account self-employment and the continued importance of construction and services in self-employment suggests that these trends are not evidence of a revival of small-firm, dynamic entrepreneurship. They are more likely to be associated with the *decline* in opportunities for full-time direct employment, the *increase* in the proportion of women seeking some form of paid employment, and a possible increase in the share of individuals seeking direct control over their

2.   This scheme allows the unemployed who set up in business to carry on receiving unemployment benefit up to a much higher level of earnings than applies to those entering direct employment.

own tax returns, because of the considerable opportunities for evasion available to the self-employed [Pahl, 1988].

4. The black economy

Precarious, non-direct employment is often assumed to be synonymous with work in the black economy. But in Britain much precarious work may fall outside the scope of the national insurance and income tax systems, and thus would not be subject to tax, whether declared or not. Estimates of the earnings from casual, part-time and non-direct employment are not therefore very relevant to estimates of the size of the black economy in the UK. Moreover, tightening up by the Inland Revenue on the taxation at source of casual and temporary workers may even mean that these workers pay more tax than is necessary, at least in the short term.[3] A much more important source of tax evasion is self-employment, either through under-reporting (for those who are self-employed in their main job) or not declaring their earnings at all (probably most common for those self-employed in a second job). Female part-time self-employed workers may also fall into the second category, but many may not be liable for tax if they did declare their earnings. Estimates, therefore, such as those by Pahl [1984], that up to 5% may be working in the black economy, may be a large overestimate of those actually evading tax [Pahl, 1988]. Moreover, wilder estimates of the share of the black economy derived from studies of national expenditure or cash levels must be discounted because of the extreme variations in levels and trends which these estimates yield and the implausibility of some of the assumptions on which they are based. A particularly implausible assumption is that most of those operating in the black economy are the unemployed. Pahl argues convincingly that this is increasingly unlikely; all the evidence suggests that the unemployed are the least likely to have the personal skills, the capital equipment or the contacts, or to be located in the right geographical areas, to be able to participate in the black economy. As the problem of unemployment becomes increasingly one of long term unemployment, the exclusion of the unemployed from even black economy activities is likely to increase. Black economy activities are often related to particular occupations such as firemen [Edgell and Hart, 1988], which provide training for workers in useful skills (e.g. driving), and offer non-standard working hours so they are available for work in the daytime. These types of black economy activities have probably been relatively stable over time, although there has been some increase in second jobbing. If there has been a substantial increase in the black economy in Britain, and there is no direct evidence for this [Thomas, 1988], it is the result primarily of the growth in self-employment. Tax evasion by the self-employed is both more common and more socially acceptable than "fraud" by unemployment benefit claimants [Pahl, 1988].

---

3.   Temporary workers are now to be taxed as if they are working permanently over the whole tax year and they will thus need to reclaim tax.

5. Part-time employment

Part-time work is *usually* regular direct employment and thus by definition could be said to fall outside the scope of the paper. However, part-time working could be said both to overlap with and in many respects to substitute for forms of precarious non-direct employment which may be more prevalent in other countries. It has been argued that relatively large thresholds before either income tax or national insurance contributions are paid for *direct* employees in Britain[4] explain the high incidence of part-time working [Schoer, 1987], and suggest that part-time *direct* employment may offer similar advantages to those of black economy workers or temporary workers in other societies.

Part-time working is by far the most important non-standard work form in the UK, and has continued to increase absolutely and relatively in the 1980s [Rubery and Tarling, 1988]. Direct part-time employees may be more subject to bearing the cost of fluctuations in demand than full-time permanent employees. Some evidence suggests that part-timers may be more liable to be laid off, and more importantly subject to variable hours according to levels of demand. Firms in Britain may thus be able to gain most of the advantage of precarious work forms through part-timers; they can vary workloads, avoid employment taxes and pay even lower wages than for full-time female employees (through for example the exclusion of part-timers from bonus or from grading schemes, in addition to providing lower fringe benefits; Horrell, Rubery and Burchell, 1989). However, the majority of part-timers are female, and employed only in female-typed occupations. Most of the growth of female part-time employment has been associated with structural change towards service sector employment, where part-time work offers particular labour cost advantages; even here there has been little *direct* substitution of female part-time workers for full-timers and even less direct substitution for men. Thus this employment form is used in specific types of occupations and industries and firms may be forced to have recourse to other employment forms to meet their needs for precarious employment in other areas.

6. Conclusion

Table 1 summarises the current state of knowledge of the different forms of employment associated with the twin notions of precarious work and non-direct employment. There is no overwhelming evidence of a significant expansion in this type of employment in the 1980s. The only employment forms for which the evidence of expansion is unambiguous are self-employment and part-time employment. The latter is in any case primarily both permanent and direct employment, and the former, self-employment, is primarily a form of continuous full-time employment,

---

4.   In May 1988 both employers and employees are exempted from payment of national insurance contributions if weekly pay is less than £41.

although more precarious than direct employment in the sense that the individual worker bears more of the risks of discontinuities. Temporary and contract work, homeworking and black economy work fall more squarely within the concept of precarious work, although even here large areas of semi- or fully permanent employment are found. These, however, are the employment forms where expansion appears to have been at best modest. Nevertheless within *each* of the employment forms discussed, there is evidence of an increasing share of very precarious and low-paid work – the growth of contract working in catering and cleaning, of homeworking in inner city areas, of part-time and own account working among the self-employed – and thus of increasing inequality within the overall employment system.

III. The relative incidence of "precarious" work forms: a framework for analysis

Comparative analysis of the relative importance and the pattern of incidence of precarious work forms within and, more especially, *between* countries requires consideration of four sets of conditions: the system of labour market regulation; industrial structure and organisation; labour market conditions; and the system of social reproduction and income maintenance.

1. The system of labour market regulation

The legal and economic significance of permanent employment status within the employment system will determine the incentives for employers to use "precarious" employment forms and the incentives for workers to secure permanent status [Deakin, 1986; Mückenberger, 1988]. Table 2, column A summarises the economic and institutional arrangements which may underpin the distinction between precarious and permanent, distinguishing between legal or directly regulatory factors and those which derive from collective or organisational influences.

One of the major reasons for the use of the various employment forms we have been discussing is to avoid the designation of an individual as an employee. Employees may have legal or regulatory rights which impose costs on employers; these range from employment taxes, contributions to social security or health insurance, rights to specific terms and conditions of employment and rights to employment protection, including restrictions on lay-off or redundancy. The *level* of these costs will influence the extent to which employers may seek to avoid employee status; eligibility conditions for employee status will influence the work form chosen. In the UK the *level* of costs associated with employee status is comparatively low. Employment taxes and social security contributions are relatively low and even low paid "permanent" employees are exempt from these contributions.

Table 1: Precarious work – Summary of empirical evidence

	Temporary or contract work	Homeworking	Self-employment	Black economy	Part-time work
Main data sources (National estimates) + key survey articles	LFS [King, 1988; Casey, 1988] WIRS	1981 National Homeworkers Survey WIRS [Hakim, 1987a]	LFS [Creigh et al., 1986]	None [Pahl, 1988]	LFS [Schoer, 1987; Rubery and Tarling, 1988]
No. of individuals involved	1.3m* (<6% of employment) + 0.5m on government schemes	0.25m (c. 1% of employment)	2.8m (12%** of all employment	not available but 5% probably too high	4.3mφ (20% of all employment) (women only) +.9m men
Recent trends	Increase in 1980s, following decrease late 1970s, early 1980s No real trend growth.	Increase in 1970s; some evidence of decrease 1981-84	Increase from 1.9m 1979++ associated with growth of self-employment + second job holding (3.4%)	Increase in tax evasion +++	Steady increase from 3.8m 1979 (women only)
Share of women	54%+	70%+	24%***	Mainly *men* as high share self-employed + many women's earnings too low for tax	83%φ (men's share increasing)
Overlap with other "precarious" forms of work	13% of casual and 23% of contract workers are self-employed* 60% of all temporary are part-time	44% self-employed (minimum estimate) 83% part-time	19% part-time*** (52% female self-employed are part-time)	Associated with all forms of precarious work but part-time work often not subject to tax	16% temporary* 12% self-employed+

	Temporary or contract work	Homeworking	Self-employment	Black economy	Part-time work
Nature and extent of "precariousness"	Limited contracts or expectations of lay-off; exclusion from employment protection and some employer benefits	Variations and discontinuities in work flow; exclusion from employment protection and most employer benefits	Bear risks of changes in demand but mainly full-time employment	No employment protection or employer benefits; one-off jobs to full-time self-employment	Some variation in hours and lay-offs; if work <16 hours excluded from employment protection; fewer employer benefits than full-timers
Occupations/industries where concentrated	*Industries** *Casual workers* Other services (39%) Distrib., hotels (33%) *Contract workers* Other services (52.5%) (often public sector) Construction (15%) *Occupations* *Casual workers* Catering, cleaning (26%) Clerical (17%) Selling (15%) *Contract workers* Professional, education (28%) (mainly teaching)	*Industries* Other services (30%) Other manuf. (23%) Insurance/fin. (22%) Distribution, hotels (16%) (=75% services) *Occupations* Processing, making, repairing (19%) Clerical (17%) Professional, education, health (15%) Literary, artistic, sport (15%)	*Industries**** Distribution/ Catering (28%) Construction (20%) Agriculture (11%) Other services (10%) *Occupation* Managerial (33%)	As for self-employed	*Industries♦♦* Other services (28%) Distribution, hotels, etc, (19%) Metal goods industries (12%) Other manufacturing (11%) (women 85.5% services) (men 55.1% services) *Occupations* (women only) shop assistants (14%) cleaners (14%) other clerks (11%)

Notes: LFS: Labour Force Survey; WIRS: Workplace Industrial Relations Survey.

Sources:

Temporary or contract work: * 1986 data [King, 1988]; + 1984 data [Casey, 1988].

Homeworking: ** 1981 National Homeworking Survey estimates.

Self-employment: *** 1987 data, *Employment Gazette;* ++ 1979 data [Storey and Johnson, 1987, p. 130]; 1984 data [Creigh et al., 1986].

Black economy: +++ 1985 data; see Pahl [1988].

Part-time work: ♦ 1988 data (unless otherwise specified), *Employment Gazette;* * 1986 data [King, 1988]; + 1984 data [Casey, 1988]; ♦♦ 1983 data [Schoer, 1987].

Table 2: Factors influencing precarious work

A. *Labour market regulation*	B. *The industrial system*	C. *Labour market conditions*	D. *Social reproduction and income maintenance*
Legal and fiscal 1. Protection for employees 2. Definition of employee status 3. Level and coverage of employment taxes 4. Income tax collection system	*Demand* 1. Level of aggregate demand 2. Variability of demand *Industrial structure* 1. Size composition of firms 2. Sectoral distribution 3. Vertical/horizontal integration 4. Geographical concentration of industry 5. Extent of family agriculture	*Labour demand conditions* 1. Level of unemployment 2. Bottlenecks and labour shortages	*Household demand for precarious work* 1. Role of informal economy in supplementing or substituting for formal economy goods or services 2. Extent of cash versus reciprocal arrangements in informal economy
Voluntarist 1. Strength of trade unions, collective agreements, custom and practice and organisational systems in protecting non-precarious employment status within plants. 2. Attitudes of trade unions etc. to precarious work 3. Opportunities to generalise protection to non-union plants, etc.	*Employer policy and competition* 1. Technological and product market requirements for integration/flexibility 2. Importance of labour costs in competition 3. Political and social conditions influencing employer strategy and managerial ethos	*Recruitment, screening and training systems* 1. Precarious work as a route into permanent employment	*Supply of labour for precarious work* 1. System of family income pooling or state income support for those not in permanent employment (unemployed, housewives, students, elderly, etc.) 2. Regulations on paid work for those in receipt of state benefits 3. Social attitudes to participation by women, etc. 4. Demand for more flexible employment patterns by households/individuals 5. Social networks for childcare arrangements, etc.

There is no link between employee status and health insurance contributions and there is a very restricted framework of individual rights at work. For example there are no general minimum wage laws[5], no restrictions on hours of work or holiday entitlements. Most of the benefits of employee status relate to entitlement to maternity leave, redundancy pay and protection against unfair dismissal. However even here *eligibility* restrictions are quite stringent so that many employers can take on individuals with full employment status and still avoid these costs. For maternity leave and unfair dismissal two years continuous employment is required, while redundancy pay is related to years of service and at one week per year of service cannot be considered a major constraint.

This set of legal or directly regulatory constraints on the employment contract are not, in international comparative terms, very onerous to employers, and thus the direct incentives to use employment which evades the standard employment relationship are limited. However, conversely the incentives to individuals to ensure that they are granted employee status are also weak: employee status is not required, for example, for access to free health care, and there are few employment rights associated with this status. Those that were established in the 1970s, such as unfair dismissal protection, have been considerably reduced in the 1980s. Thus there may be fewer problems for UK employers in persuading individuals to take on non-regular work, and self-employment may seem an attractive proposition to individuals because of the opportunities to reduce or delay their tax payments. However, the incentive for individuals to become temporary workers has been considerably reduced through the tightening up of Inland Revenue regulations, requiring even temporary workers to be taxed through the Pay As You Earn system as if they were to be employed for 52 weeks, with tax only refundable at the end of the year. It is not, however, necessary for individuals to accept non-employee status to avoid national insurance and income tax because of the exemptions that also apply to low paid and usually part-time but direct employees.

The absence of strong directly regulatory controls on employment is not the whole picture. Custom and practice, organisational and motivational issues as well as the impact of trade union organisation and collective bargaining will also determine the sets of incentives towards the use of these forms of employment. Individuals may be employed as homeworkers, temporary workers or self-employed because direct employees have customary expectations of regular work, holiday pay and payment of the rate for the job, and not because of legal constraints on these practices. These aspects of the voluntary system of labour market regulation are probably extremely important in determining the incidence of particular types of non-regular employment. Fixed-term contract employment is most common in the public services [Milliard and Stevens, 1986] and the explanation may be related to the image of the public sector as a good

---

5.   Some low paying industries are covered by wages councils which set legal minimum wages, but under 21-year-olds are exempt from the legislation. Some wages council regulations extend to "non-employees" such as homeworkers.

employer offering *permanent* employment, unless it is explicitly stated from the start that the job is temporary or fixed term.

Where there are much weaker expectations of continuity of employment the need to *define* a job *ex ante* as temporary is much reduced. Empirical research has found that many individuals who state that they are in temporary jobs are in fact on open ended contracts so that the temporary status of their job derives not from a formal or contractual position, but because they were either verbally informed that they would be laid off, or gained this impression from the practices of the firm [Casey, 1988]. It should also be noted that, in the UK, employment status is determined by *practice* and not by contract, so that even homeworkers can be deemed to be employees with employment rights if in practice they work on a regular basis for one employer [Leighton, 1983].

It is not only the employers that respond to voluntary collective organisation and the establishment of good employment practices by the creation of "peripheral jobs". Trade unions may also cooperate in the development of core/periphery distinctions in order to protect the employment of the core workers. For example, tenure has been defended strongly in universities (albeit ultimately unsuccessfully) while temporary fixed-term contracts have multiplied. Examples can also be found of trade unions attempting to incorporate homeworkers within the scope of a collective agreement with the prime aim of formalising the system whereby home-workers are the first to lose employment in the downturn [Deakin and Rubery, 1986]. On the other hand the acquiescent attitude by trade unions towards the expansion of *part-time* employment in the UK has meant that employers have, to some extent, been able to incorporate a more flexible, cheap and subsidised employment form within their main labour force, thereby reducing the need for recourse to subcontract and casual labour. Thus both the fiscal and the trade union regimes in the UK have favoured the incorporation of "flexible" or "atypical" and subsidised employment within the mainstream category of employees.

Equally, fiscal policy may be a very important factor in explaining the other main growth of "atypical" or "precarious" employment besides part-time work, namely self-employment. The very comprehensive PAYE system in Britain means that the only effective means of tax evasion is through self-employment, and tax avoidance opportunities may help explain favourable attitudes towards and growth in self-employment. Nevertheless the general reduction in tax rates should reduce the fiscal incentives for self-employment in the UK.

To summarise: the regulatory system will both shape the definition and determine the importance of the distinction between permanent and precarious work. This regulatory system includes the system of legal employment rights, the taxation system and the system of voluntary or collective regulation. Distinctions between permanent and precarious work will be stronger, the more developed the systems of either legal or voluntary protection for core employees. However the greater the opportunity for divisions within the *core* labour force (for example between part-time and full-time jobs because of the system of tax subsidy to the former) the less the significance of the division between direct employment and other employment forms. Trends in recent legislation in the UK have been to reduce legal distinctions between permanent and precarious work through the general erosion of individual rights for all, but to increase the importance of distinctions arising from voluntary regulation. Industrial relations legislation restricts the opportunities for unions to generalise employment protection to non-unionised firms and to individuals in precarious forms of employment, thereby increasing the importance for individuals to secure direct employment in unionised firms.

2. The industrial system

The demand for labour services through the various employment forms associated with "precarious" work arises out of the system of industrial organisation and production. Table 2, column B summarises the different elements determining the structure and level of demand for precarious work; these include the level and variability of product market demand, the size structure and composition of firms, the industrial, occupational and regional pattern of employment demand and the degree of horizontal and vertical integration. These industrial characteristics are important because of their potential significance for firms' employment practices and their demand for "precarious work". If this demand is simply related to "flexibility" in the organisation of production and labour costs it might be expected to be higher the greater the variability of demand, the higher the share of small firms, the greater the decentralisation of industrial production, and the greater the importance of labour costs in competition. However the predictions become more complex if other factors are introduced: for example precarious work may not be strictly related to variations in demand for labour if it is the larger firms which are more able or more willing to introduce flexible employment systems, with the aim of either reducing labour costs or developing greater specialisation within their own direct employment systems. Thus employer power and employer policy must be added to the other economic and technical characteristics of firms which are associated with greater use of precarious work.

This framework for analysis of the incidence and level of precarious work can be applied to the UK situation. The evidence found in Section 1 of some increase in the incidence of precarious work in the 1980s was probably related to the collapse of demand in 1979-81, and the uncertainty with which any recovery has been viewed since. The relatively low overall *level* of precarious working is probably associated with relatively high degrees of industrial integration [Marsden, 1987], and in particular with the absence of well developed local industrial districts [Pyke, 1987].

Shifts in the occupational distribution of precarious work, in particular in the incidence of homeworking, can be explained in part by the overall shift out of manufacturing towards services. But this collapse of manufacturing has also led to a further intensification of labour exploitation in particular industries, such as clothing, arising from the twin forces of high unemployment amongst ethnic minority communities and the intensification of competition in these industries [Mitter, 1985]. There has not been any straightforward switch from manufacturing to services; those employed in precarious work in the service sector are likely to be different people, often with higher qualifications, than those who previously undertook, for example, manufacturing homework, and even within this latter sector there seems to be evidence of increasing importance of ethnic minority groups in inner city areas.

A similar pattern of analysis may be used to explain the incidence and increase in self-employment. This development is associated with the expansion of service sector activities, including business and personal services. Consideration of the relationship between demand for services by private individuals and the growth of self-employment will be postponed until Section 4 below. The growth of self-employment within the business service sector is related both to an increase in the use of subcontracting by firms (to reduce overheads and enhance opportunities to use specialists), and to an apparently increased enthusiasm for self-employment by individuals, possibly related to the tax advantages or as a response to the so-called "enterprise culture" fostered by the Tory Government [Pahl, 1988]. Most of the growth of self-employment is "own account" workers without employees, so that there is relatively little correlation with the growth of small firms [Creigh et al., 1986; Pahl, 1988]. However, again in the inner city areas growth of self-employment may be associated with the increase in small businesses among the ethnic communities in traditional industries such as clothing [Storey and Johnson, 1987].

Explanations of changes in incidence of precarious work cannot only rely on changes in the industrial composition but must also consider changes in employer policy by types of firm or industry, related to changes in markets, technologies or political and institutional conditions. In Britain much of the discussion about precarious work has focused on micro-level changes in employer policy with the so-called development of the flexible firm [Atkinson, 1985], and the industrial composition arguments have been largely ignored [Rubery, 1988a]. However, there has been relatively scant evidence to support the hypothesis of major changes in employer policy within the private sector overall [Atkinson and Meager, 1985; Pollert, 1987; Rubery et al., 1987]. Even the protagonists of the flexible firm hypothesis admit that the approach has only been adopted in a piecemeal way within most of the firms they have studied [Atkinson and Meager, 1986]. Moreover, where major changes in employment practices have taken place these have mainly affected the *core* labour force (through changes in job demarcations, manning levels, working-time arrangements, etc.) and have not resulted in use of precarious work forms.[6]

The major exception to this pattern of relatively little change has been the public sector, where major changes in employer practices have occurred, spurred on by the government policy of cash limits, together with

---

6.   See for example the much publicised changes in the printing industry, in the ferry industry, television, coal mining, etc.

changes in industrial relations legislation *and* the provision of large sums for investment in new technologies and patterns of work organisation to prepare industries for privatisation [Burns et al., 1985; Ferner, 1985; Ferner and Terry, 1985]. Again the main effects of these policies within nationalised industries has been on the core workforce, but in more service provision sectors there has been a direct impact on the extent of precarious working through the privatisation of catering, cleaning and other service activities. Contract cleaning and catering firms have taken over, offering much more unstable and precarious employment than was the case for direct employees in the public service [Coyle, 1986a and 1986b]. This precariousness arises from the public sector switching between contractors as well as from firms only offering temporary jobs. The main effect of this contracting out is probably to lower wages and increase work effort, with most workers still being relatively permanently employed. Some employees may be part of the black economy; cases of employment of underage school children and the like have been cited, but for the majority who are married women working part-time, no tax or national insurance contributions are required.

The other main involvement of the public sector in the development of precarious work is through the use of fixed-term contracts to differentiate explicitly between permanent and temporary jobs [Millward and Stevens, 1986], which employers in the private sector feel less obliged to do because the right to *permanent* employment has never been so firmly established.

Most of the changes within the public sector in employment practices which have encouraged the growth of precarious work are explicitly related to institutional and political change (including here the financial constraints imposed on public sector managers, as these are politically and not market determined). It has also been argued that trends towards precarious work reflect fundamental changes in both technology and market conditions which reduce the need for permanent, integrated and stable employment patterns [Clutterbuck, 1985; Handy, 1984]. The technological argument relates particularly to the opportunities for distance working offered by information technology [Huws, 1984]. These factors are important for some of the growth of freelancing and outwork amongst non-manual employees, but there is a danger of overstating their importance. For most jobs direct communication with other colleagues at the place of work is essential; moreover these types of outwork are not necessarily precarious or unstable, as high levels of firm-specific skills may be required. The argument about the impact of changing markets is even less tenable. Increasing emphasis on quality in competition suggests that stability of employment is likely to become more rather than less important for key employees. Apparent increases in the use of temporary or precarious work are unlikely to reflect permanent changes in *product market* conditions. Instead they may reflect the failure of UK firms to adjust to new market conditions through the development of quality production, so that the share of firms which compete through labour cost cutting increases as this is the only form of competition open to UK firms [Rubery et al., 1987]. Alternatively they may reflect the undermining of employment standards through the exploitation of high levels of unemployment. Thus changes in employ-

ment practices cannot be taken as indicators either of changes in requirements for long term competitiveness or as reflections of changes in *technical*
and *product market* conditions without consideration of the impact of *labour
market* conditions on employment practices.

3. Labour market conditions

Labour market conditions and practices will structure the opportunities for and the consequences of precarious work forms. Table 2, column
C provides a summary of the main factors to be considered. Firstly, the
level of demand relative to the supply of labour will influence the number
and the types of people willing to take on precarious work [Fevre, 1986].
Excess labour supply may also encourage employers to offer only precarious
work in circumstances where permanent, regular employment would be
offered if labour market conditions were tight. It does appear highly
probable that in Britain the growth of various forms of precarious work has
been associated with high levels of unemployment, coupled with the
structural, political and institutional conditions already discussed. An
example which provides some evidence of labour market effects is the
different incidence by region of the Youth Training Scheme (a form of
temporary employment). In areas of high labour demand firms have to offer
young people "proper jobs", thereby countering the argument that permanent
changes had taken place in the demand for youth labour, so that a period
of subsidised training would be required before they could be integrated into
the labour force [Ashton et al., 1988].

The growth of precarious work is not confined to areas of high
unemployment, nor is it universal in its incidence. A more complex
explanatory framework is required. Indeed the relatively low incidence of
precarious work in the UK, despite the high levels of unemployment, suggest
either that the important factors in determining the nature of employment
are the organisational and technical conditions of production, or that the
social security system precludes the combination of precarious work with
unemployment [Pahl, 1988]. The latter factor is explored in Section 4 below.

The association of precarious work with areas of lowish unemployment can be explained in various ways. Firstly, the high level of labour
demand allows for multiple job holding, and many of the precarious jobs are
second jobs for either directly employed or self-employed workers. Secondly,
firms facing labour shortages in key occupations may make use of subcontract or agency labour to supplement their labour supply, as they are
either unwilling or unable (possibly because of national pay scales or
divergences in house prices) to raise wages sufficiently to attract new
permanent recruits from other areas [Casey, 1988].

The second labour market factor which must be considered in any
comparative analysis of the incidence of precarious work is the relationship
between involvement in precarious work and periods of both unemployment
and permanent employment. The significance of an increase in precarious
work for labour market inequalities cannot be assessed without knowing

whether precarious work is usually just an interlude between spells of unemployment, or a means of gaining access to permanent employment.

There is some evidence in the UK for both propositions. Employment in temporary work, especially as one's first job, has been found to be associated with multiple spells of unemployment [Casey, 1988], but temporary work is also likely to be a stepping stone out of unemployment or non-employment. Similarly there is evidence that a high share of those entering self-employment in the early 1980s did so because they had become unemployed or feared redundancy [Storey and Johnson, 1987]. This role of self-employment as a route out of unemployment has been institutionalised by government schemes to help the unemployed enter self-employment. However, the percentage of the unemployed who have the appropriate skills, equipment, contacts and opportunities are still relatively insignificant [Pahl, 1984]. Certain forms of precarious work may thus only be available to individuals who have already had some experience of permanent employment, through which they acquired skills which they can sell on the market. The motivation for the decision to sell labour services instead of seeking direct employment may be either the expectation of a higher price or the lack of opportunities for direct employment. Some forms of general skill or qualifications are usually required for this type of work activity, but individuals with only firm-specific skills may not be excluded if their previous employers seek to retain access to these skills after they have interrupted their labour market participation for domestic reasons. Homeworkers are often ex-employees of the industry or firm they work for, with industry or firm-specific skills [Rubery and Wilkinson, 1981].

There are also forms of precarious work that are used not to capitalise on an existing skill but to gain the experience necessary for access to permanent employment. This function of precarious work is most common for the young but is less the case in the UK than in other advanced countries as there is still more a system of direct recruitment into permanent employment for the young [Marsden and Ryan, 1986]. However, the widespread introduction of the Youth Training Scheme has to some extent broken that system and employers are now keener to screen potential new recruits through employment on YTS or other training schemes before making a final selection.

4. The system of social reproduction and income maintenance

The specific organisation of social reproduction within an economy, and in particular income support for all individuals, will have a very marked effect on both the demand for and the supply of labour for precarious work [Deakin, 1988]. Table 2, column D summarises these influences.

Taking first the *demand* for precarious labour, where the society relies on the provision of services to households on an informal basis, as essential supplements to goods and services purchased from the formal economy, the demand for precarious labour is likely to be high. However, not all exchanges of informal services are paid for, and many may be provided on a reciprocal or intra-family transfer basis [Pahl, 1988]. Research suggests that, in the UK, the monetary value of services provided in this way is relatively low as a share of GDP, although the volume of services actually exchanged is much higher because of systems of reciprocity, among other reasons.

Turning to the *supply* side, the system of social reproduction and income maintenance will influence both the quantity and the type of labour available for precarious work. The first factor is the system of family income pooling and state income support for those not fully in the labour market or who do not find permanent employment. The comparatively comprehensive system of state income support for the unemployed in the UK, combined with the comparatively rigid rules restricting benefit recipients' involvement in the wage economy, is probably a major factor in limiting the availability of labour for precarious work [Pahl, 1988]. But some groups are excluded from access to benefits, mainly women who have not been participating in the labour market in the recent past[7], and these differences in access to income support help explain the importance of women in the most precarious forms of work, that is homeworkers and temporary and casual workers, and the comparative absence of prime-age men, except in full-time self-employment categories.

A second factor is the system of providing support for non-labour market participants, that is the retired or sick, those involved in housework and childcare and those undertaking education or training. Again Britain has relatively well-developed and comprehensive systems of *state* income support for these groups except for housework and childcare. The grant system for students in higher education is particularly important in reducing the supply of students outside the vacation periods for precarious work. The requirement to complete degree courses within three years is a further disincentive to combining study with precarious work. School children and students in other forms of further education do, however, take on temporary and precarious work [McLennen et al., 1985; Pahl, 1988] as there are no income subsidies for education except for those on degree-type courses. Retirement and sickness pensions are relatively comprehensive, but fairly generous earnings allowances (compared to the restrictions faced by the unemployed on topping-up benefits) allow retired people to take on part-time and sometimes precarious work. However, the lack of income support for housework and childcare, or for those trying to re-enter the labour market does generate a supply of labour for precarious work, consisting both of married women and married men seeking second jobs to "top-up" their household income, in order to alleviate the life cycle problems of highest consumption demands and lowest income during the period of childbearing. Societies with more income pooling between generations than in the UK may provide alternative means of bridging these income/consumption gaps.

---

7.   Married women who opted prior to 1975 not to pay national insurance contributions may still be excluded from unemployment benefit. This option is no longer available to married women who entered the labour market after 1975.

Social attitudes to employment and participation will also affect the supply of labour for precarious work. The increasing permanence of women's participation in the UK [Dex, 1984] will tend to reduce the acceptability of precarious work[8], but the continuation of the practice of quitting the labour force for childbearing and child care, albeit for a shorter time, may still force them to use precarious work as a way back to employment. There is also discussion of new attitudes to employment, based on a demand for more flexible employment patterns to provide for a more equal division of domestic labour and more leisure time for both males and females. But there is little hard evidence of such attitudes being put into practice: the long work hours of the self-employed suggest that the growth of self-employment cannot be explained by a demand for more leisure or even more control over working hours. The growth of homeworking is sometimes interpreted as evidence of a demand for integration of home and work, but there is evidence that this integration may in some cases cause more and not less stress for working women [Huws, 1984]. Perhaps more important is the involvement of ethnic communities in homeworking because of strong attitudes against women working outside the home.

Consideration of the development of precarious work forms thus requires analysis of the precise mechanisms by which such a labour supply is generated. In Britain there is relatively restricted scope for individuals who seek to cover their full reproduction costs, and/or those of their families, through wage employment to become involved in precarious work. There are two main exceptions: those taking on precarious work as a second job, and full-time self-employment. The low share of agriculture in the UK restricts the numbers who work in industry or services as supplements to family agricultural production, and thus second jobs have to fit around permanent and mainly full-time wage employment. They tend to be most common for workers in jobs with non-standard working-time arrangements [Edgell and Hart, 1988]. Full-time self-employment is only precarious in that individuals have continually to sell their labour to a range of clients. These opportunities only exist for a limited range of occupations in the UK, partly because of the absence of industrial districts with widespread subcontracting networks.

The generation of a labour supply for precarious work, even among those not seeking to cover full costs of reproduction, is not necessarily straightforward. For example, further research is required to discover how women taking temporary jobs mobilise childcare arrangements at short notice, in a country where family networks are relatively restricted. Recent expansions in the labour supply for precarious work may also have hidden costs for other family members, not only those who take on childcare. Unpaid family helpers are commonly used to support self-employed male workers, and even, to a lesser extent, homeworkers. Family helpers are less

---

8. Collinson [1987] shows that an important factor maintaining employment opportunities for women in areas of high male unemployment may be their availability for precarious work contracts, and the opportunity for establishing strong managerial control systems in female-dominated types of work.

common in the UK than elsewhere in Europe but the increase in self-employment has increased their importance and exacerbated the opportunities for "self" or "own family" exploitation through self-employment. The development of the Youth Training Scheme has also conferred both a precarious and a low pay status on young workers and forced families to increase their subsidies to young people, both directly through income provision and by postponement of the age at which they leave home. It is still probably the case that UK families provide or at least expect to provide less financial help to their young adult members than in several other advanced countries. Nevertheless, changes in government policy, coupled with high unemployment, have forced families to extend the period in which they provide financial support for their children.

IV. Conclusion

The diversity of factors which influence the level and pattern of non-standard and precarious employment forms must cast doubt on simplistic notions concerning the presence of universal trends towards flexible employment [Atkinson, 1985; Hakim, 1987b; Bolle and Gabriel, 1988]. There are major differences even between advanced EEC countries, in their industrial systems, in their systems of labour market regulation, and in their systems of social reproduction and income maintenance. These differences influence the incidence and significance of non-standard and precarious work [Rubery, 1988a]. Thus, evidence of similarities in levels and trends between countries may be the outcome of different combinations of circumstances which have by chance resulted in similar net overall changes. Moreover, current demand for precarious work may not reflect long term trends in the organisation of markets and technology, but short term responses to uncertainty or variability in product markets or over-supply in labour markets. There are three common factors experienced in most EEC and other industrialised countries which may account for evidence of some general upward trend in non-standard work. These are the universal recessionary conditions, the continuing rise in the participation rate of women, who have always been one of the least protected segments of the labour force, and the general shift towards services. There is much less evidence to support any strong or universal movement, in the UK or elsewhere, towards irregular, precarious employment forms associated with new technologies or new competitive conditions.

The problems with universalist explanations of the development of precarious or flexible work become even more apparent when particular countries or particular employment forms are studied. In the UK there is unambiguous evidence of growth only for self-employment and part-time work: the former is still primarily associated with male full-time work, albeit without guaranteed earnings, while the latter is primarily associated with female direct employment, mainly of a regular or permanent kind. The evidence for a general growth of other precarious work forms such as temporary, contract or homework is much less strong. Where there is evidence of an increase it is primarily within the public sector, in response to political factors. This change in policy cannot be simply taken as a proxy for market forces within the public sphere, as other countries have not introduced such sweeping changes in employment law and employment protection, even where the initial level of protection at the onset of the recession was higher.

However, perhaps the most important difference between countries is neither the incidence and level of precarious work, nor the differences in the contingent factors accounting for recent trends, but the differences in the significance and meaning of the very distinctions between precarious and non-precarious work. The generally low levels of protection for direct regular employment in the UK, and the recent erosion of such protection, both legal and voluntary, has effectively further reduced the significance of these different employment structures. The main interest in the growth of non-standard employment forms arises from the increasing share of low paid and vulnerable workers within these categories. The more significant divisions in the employment sphere in the UK may not be between categories of employment contract but between employment in unionised or non-unionised establishments [Rubery, 1987] or simply between full-time and part-time jobs [Horrell et al., 1989]. The focus of research into the restructuring of the labour market should therefore not be exclusively or mainly on different contractual arrangements but also include the potentially much more significant transformations in employment conditions for those within the regular, but increasingly unprotected labour force.

References

Ashton, D.; Maguire, M.; Spilsbury, M. (1988): "The youth labour market in the United Kingdom and the 1979-82 recession: The effects of cyclical and structural change", in *Labour and Society* (Geneva, IILS), Vol. 13, No. 4, Oct.

Atkinson, J. (1985): "Flexibility: Planning for an uncertain future", in Atkinson, J. (ed.): *Manpower Policy and Practice*, Vol. 1. Aldershot, Gower.

Atkinson, J.; Meager, N. (1985): *Changing working patterns*. London, NEDO.

—— (1986): "Is flexibility a flash in the pan?", in *Personnel Management* (London), Vol. 18, No. 9, Sep.

Bolle, M.; Gabriel, J. (1988): *New forms of employment: Trends, patterns and conflicts – a comparison of the FRG, the UK and the US*. International Working Party on Labour Market Segmentation, Xth Conference, Porto (mimeo).

Burns, A.; Newby, M.; Winterton, J. (1985): "The restructuring of the British Coal industry", in *Cambridge Journal of Economics* (London), Vol. 9, No. 1, Mar.

Casey, B. (1988): "The extent and nature of temporary employment in Britain", in *Cambridge Journal of Economics* (London), Vol. 12, No. 4, Dec.

Clutterbuck, D. (1985): *New patterns of work*. Aldershot, Gower.

Collinson, D. (1987): "Picking women: The recruitment of temporary workers in the mail order industry", in *Work, Employment and Society* (London), Vol. 1, No. 3, Sep.

Coyle, A. (1986a): *Dirty business*. Birmingham, West Midlands Low Pay Unit.

—— (1986b): "Going private", in Feminist Review (eds.): *Waged work: A reader*. London, Virago.

Creigh, S.; Roberts, C.; Gorman, A.; Sawyer, P. (1986): "Self-employment in Britain", in *Employment Gazette* (London), Vol. 94, No. 5, June.

Dale, A.; Bamford, C. (1988): "Temporary workers; Cause for concern and complacency?", in *Work, Employment and Society* (London), Vol. 2, No. 2, June.

Deakin, S. (1986): "Labour law and the developing employment relationship in the UK", in *Cambridge Journal of Economics* (London), Vol. 10, No. 3, Dec.

—— (1988): *The comparative structure of labour law systems: State systems of regulation and the harmonisation of labour standards in the EEC*. International Working Party on Labour Market Segmentation, Xth conference, Porto (mimeo).

Deakin, S.; Rubery, J. (1986): *Typology, dimensions and regulation of homework in the UK*, report prepared for the EEC Commission. Cambridge, Department of Applied Economics.

Dex, S. (1984): *Women's work histories; An analysis of the Women and Employment Survey*, Research Paper No. 45. London, Department of Employment.

Edgell, S.; Hart, G. (1988): "Informal work: A case study of moonlighting firemen", in *Salford Papers in Sociology and Anthropology* (University of Salford), No. 6.

Employment Gazette, various issues. London, HMSO.

Ferner, A. (1985): "Political constraints and management strategies: The case of working practices in British Rail", in *British Journal of Industrial Relations* (London), Vol. 23, No. 1, Mar.

Ferner, A.; Terry, M. (1985): "The crunch had come: A case study of changing industrial relations in the Post Office", in *Warwick Papers in Industrial Relations* (University of Warwick, Industrial Relations Research Unit), No. 1.

Fevre, R. (1986): "Contract work in the recession", in Purcell, K.; Wood, S.; Watson, A.; Allen, S. (eds.): *The changing experience of employment*. Basingstoke, Macmillan.

Hakim, C. (1985): *Employers' use of outwork*, Research Paper No. 44. London, Department of Employment.

—— (1987a): *Home-based work in Britain*, Research Paper No. 60. London, Department of Employment.

—— (1987b): "Trends in the flexible workforce", in *Employment Gazette* (London), Vol. 95, No. 11, Nov.

Handy, C. (1984): *The future of work*. Oxford, Blackwell.

Horrell, S.; Rubery, J.; Burchell B. (1989): "Unequal jobs or unequal pay", in *Industrial Relations Journal* (Nottingham), Autumn.

Huws, U. (1984): "New technology homeworkers", in *Employment Gazette* (London), Vol. 92, No. 1., Jan.

King, S. (1988): "Temporary workers in Britain", in *Employment Gazette* (London), Vol. 96, No. 4, Apr.

Leighton, P. (1983): *Contractual arrangements in selected industries – A study of employment relationships in industries with outwork*, Research Paper No. 39. London, Department of Employment.

Marginson, P. et al. (1988): *Beyond the workplace*. Oxford, Blackwell.

Marsden, D. (1987): *Small firms and labour markets in the UK*. Geneva, International Institute for Labour Studies (mimeo).

Marsden, D.; Ryan, P. (1986): "Where do young workers work? Youth employment by industry in various European economies", in *British Journal of Industrial Relations* (London), Vol. 21, No. 4, Mar.

McLennan, E.; Fitz, J.; Sulivan, J. (1985): *Working children*, Low Pay Pamphlet No. 34. London, Low Pay Unit.

Meager, N. (1986): "Temporary work in Britain", in *Employment Gazette* (London), Vol. 94, No. 1., Jan.

Millward, N.; Stevens, M. (1986): *British workplace industrial relations 1980-84*. Aldershot, Gower.

Mitter, S. (1985): "Industrial restructuring and manufacturing homework: immigrant women in the UK clothing industry", in *Capital and Class* (London), No. 27, Autumn.

Mückenberger, U. (1988): *Before the completion of the internal market: Laws concerning labour market segmentation in Germany, the UK and France*. International Working Party on Labour Market Segmentation, Xth Conference, Porto.

Pahl, R.E. (1984): *Divisions of labour*. London, Basil Blackwell.

—— (1988): *The black economy in the UK*. European Commission on the Black Economy in Europe, Brussels (mimeo).

Pollert, A. (1987): "The 'flexible firm': A model in search of reality or a policy in search of a practice?", in *Warwick Papers in Industrial Relations* (University of Warwick), No. 19.

Potter, T. (1986): *Temporary benefits: A study of temporary workers in the DHSS*. Birmingham, West Midlands Low Pay Unit.

Pyke, F. (1987): *Industrial networks and modes of cooperation in a British context*. University of Manchester, North West Industry Research Unit.

Rubery, J. (1987): "Flexibility of labour costs in non-union firms", in Tarling, R. (ed.): *Flexibility in labour markets*. London, Academic.

—— (ed.) (1988a): *Women and recession*. London, Routledge and Kegan Paul.

—— (1988b): "Employers and the labour market", in Gallie, D. (ed.): *Employment in Britain*. London, Blackwell.

Rubery, J.; Wilkinson, F. (1981): "Outwork and segmented labour markets", in Wilkinson, F. (ed.): *The dynamics of labour market segmentation*. London, Academic.

Rubery, J.; Tarling, R.; Wilkinson, F. (1987): "Flexibility, marketing and the organisation of production", in *Labour and Society* (Geneva, IILS), Vol. 12, No. 1, Jan.

Rubery, J.; Tarling, R. (1988): "Women's employment in declining Britain", in Rubery, J. (ed.): *Women and recession*. London, Routledge and Kegan Paul.

Schoer, K. (1987): "Part-time employment: Britain and West Germany", in *Cambridge Journal of Economics*, Vol. 11, No. 1.

Storey, D.; Johnson, S. (1987): *Job generation and labour market change*. Basingstoke, Macmillan.

Thomas, J. J. (1988): "The politics of the black economy", in *Work, Employment and Society* (London), Vol. 2, No. 2, June.

4 Atypical wage employment in France

Guy Caire[1]

Casual work, odd jobs, precarious work, special forms of work, peripheral work – there is no lack of terms to designate this vague concept which embraces the emerging forms of a new type of employment. The very variety of vocabulary in use illustrates the difficulty of delimiting these forms of employment, which depart from the standard employment contract as defined by law and which give rise to ambiguous situations, sometimes straddling employment, unemployment and inactivity.

We shall use "atypical employment"[2] as a generic term to designate all these different forms of work. *A contrario*, the term refers to "typical" employment, defined as wage work which is performed within a formalised employer-employee relationship (i.e. under a statute or a contract of indeterminate duration concluded within the framework of a collective agreement), is stable (possibly offering career prospects), is full-time (thus a basis for participation in collective life and social identity), provides the essential part of the family income, depends on a single employer, is performed at a specific workplace and is specifically assigned to the individual concerned.[3] "The conventional model of full-time employment in the service of a specific enterprise has been treated as the 'to be or not to be' of labour legislation" [Dupeyroux, 1981, p. 486]. On this basis Pélissier [1985] has defined the different employment relationships as follows:

> A non-clandestine activity performed for an indefinite period, full-time, in a service or production activity, for the benefit of the employer: such is the typical employment relationship. Any employment relationship which does not have all these characteristics may be considered as atypical. Thus the term "atypical employment relationship" embraces clandestine employment (a concealed employment relationship), contracts of limited (as opposed to indeterminate) duration, work done at home (as opposed to work performed on the premises of the enterprise), work done for an enterprise which is not in law the employer of the worker concerned (as opposed to a situation in which the beneficiary of the work and the employer are one and the same) and part-time (as opposed to full-time) work. [p. 531]

---

1.   Centre de Recherches en Sciences Sociales du Travail, Sceaux, France.

2.   Expression used in the July-August 1981 issue of *Droit Social*, which devoted a special issue to the subject.

3.   These are the essential features of the relationship as seen by Puel [1981]. Lyon-Caen [1980] offers a similar definition, but includes a collective dimension to enhance understanding of the concept.

Many factors make for more widespread recourse to atypical employment: technological advance, which gives a new lease of life to homeworking; management practices seeking less costly or less constraining forms of employment; and so on. It is difficult to bring out any unequivocal pattern in this propagation of atypical forms of employment, since it not only includes survivals of old forms of wage work but also retrogression in labour legislation or in aspirations to achieve new forms of organisation of working time.

I. The multiple forms of atypical employment

There is wide variety in the forms of atypical employment, corresponding to heterogeneous situations. The available statistics do not always make it possible to follow the evolution and changes affecting each of them over the years. It is thus useful to adopt a classification. We shall consider, firstly, the traditional forms used by firms seeking greater flexibility, and secondly, the new forms which owe their origins to government action relating to categories of persons who experience difficulties in the labour market [Elbaum, 1988].

1. Traditional forms of personnel management

These forms, older or more recent, are mostly characterised by the ways firms use them. During the 30 years of expansion which followed the end of the Second World War, firms had an interest in institutionalising typical employment and in developing internal labour markets to promote stability in their labour forces. Atypical employment was then resorted to only in emergencies and in four types of situations: (i) for seasonal or casual work; (ii) to facilitate the entry of new groups of potential workers into working life; (iii) to secure workers with skills in short supply in the labour market; and (iv) to mobilise labour at relatively low cost. The onset of the recession led firms to change their practices; in their endeavours to achieve greater flexibility they developed a new interest in atypical forms of employment.

A. Part-time employment

In 1971 there were 1,200,000 persons in part-time employment. By 1977 the figure had risen to 1,700,000. In March 1986 there were 2,500,000 such workers (2,100,000 of them women) – i.e. 23.1% of all women, and 3% of all men with jobs. Most of them (83%) were wage and salary earners; but a not insignificant proportion were not (and of these, 72% were family workers). This group overlaps to some extent with that of trainees in enterprises; in March 1986, 115,000 part-timers, 97,000 of them women, were undergoing training. The proportion of wage-earners working part-time has changed little among men, for whom the practice of part-time employment is still very marginal. On the other hand, it has increased considerably among women, rising from 6.5% of all women employees in 1975 to 11.8% in 1984. During the years 1982-86, 550,000 part-time jobs were created – 4 out of 5 being for women. It is this which enabled female employment to increase during the period under review. The increase in part-time employment having taken place in parallel with a decline in full-time employment, the explanation for the expansion of women's employment since 1982 is to be found in the fact that four part-time jobs have been created for every full-time job abolished.

Of all the forms of atypical employment, this is probably the one in which personal choice is most important; but caution is necessary in formulating any judgement here, for "the people who dream of part-time employment are not those who work part-time ... In practice it seems to be taken up ... only under compulsion. Short-time working seems to a significant extent to be a form of underemployment which is accepted because of a lack of alternative opportunities" [Lucas, 1979, pp. 111, 130].   A great variety of situations are found among part-time workers, as regards both patterns of working time and constraints [Bue and Cristofari, 1986], and a distinction should be made between part-time work of a "social" character, mainly reflecting the desires of workers, and that of an "economic" character, deriving from the needs of the enterprise concerned [Lehmann, 1985].

When we examine the situation of women workers[4] by age group, we observe a steady increase in the proportion of part-timers in the private sector among both manual workers and salaried employees over age 40. This may result from many women dropping out of employment after the birth of children, and subsequently taking up part-time work when opportunities for a return to full-time work are restricted.   Among women employees in the public service "there is no significant discrepancy between the 25-40 and the 40-55 age groups; transfers to and from part-time or full-time employment and inactivity are possible without any risk. This is the only category in which working part-time rather than full-time results from a free choice on the part of practically all the women concerned... Part-time work does not mean the same for a civil servant adapting her working time patterns to the school calendar as it does for a woman employed by a contract cleaning firm, who works five days a week after office or factory hours" [Belloc, 1986, pp. 46-49].

Among men, part-time work is often transitional. It may represent a stage between full-time work and inactivity among non-wage-earners (and in particular elderly farmers); it may be a first step towards conventional full-time employment for a young worker; it may follow the end of

---

4.   In earlier times, it was argued that part-time work enabled married women to reconcile the two elements of their dual role [Hallaire, 1970]. However, recent analyses have shown that "the strategies of women in dealing with time worked turn on three axes – activity and employment, work, family – and not, as analyses based on the concept of reconciliation of roles would have us assume, on two (work and family). The structure is not static; it changes with time, with developments within the family itself (upward mobility of the husband or its absence, births, number of children, sharing of household chores), as well as with developments in the labour market and in social relationships" [Kergoat, 1981].

conventional full-time employment for retired persons, or persons approaching retirement. The number of men between ages 25 and 40 working part-time is steadily rising – probably for want of better opportunities, as can be concluded from a comparison between the proportion of unemployed persons seeking part-time work (17% of women and 3% of men) and that of unemployed persons who are forced to accept part-time jobs (40% of men and 50% of women).

The regulations in force are conducive to the development of part-time work. The Ordinance of 31 March 1982 and the Act of 11 January 1984 offer public service employees a wide range of opportunities to work part-time. The Ordinance of 26 March 1982, which supplements the Act of 28 January 1981, provides better safeguards for part-time employees and sets a ceiling for part-time working (four-fifths of the duration of full-time working); in addition, it gives enterprises more flexibility with regard to social security contributions and statutory obligations. Two decrees, promulgated on 5 March 1985, were designed to promote part-time work and at the same time to reduce unemployment. One of them provides for compensatory payments to certain job seekers (particularly persons over age 50) willing to accept part-time work at a level of remuneration below their unemployment benefit. The other offers financial incentives to induce firms to engage certain categories of job seekers (in particular the long-term unemployed) in part-time jobs.

B. Temporary employment

During the period under review the legislation concerning interim employment was amended several times – in 1982, 1985 and 1986. Two very different work philosophies were successively applied. The first was restrictive and had as its explicit objective "a reconstitution of the working collectivity". In contrast, the second and more flexible approach, although it did not go to the extent of deregulation, at least sought to loosen the rigidities in the labour market and to enable it to function in a more flexible manner.

Though available statistics often vary considerably with regard to magnitudes, they agree on structural changes. There is a seasonal peak of activity in July and August. We notice that the slight economic recovery which took place in 1976 induced a strong increase in the activities of temporary labour agencies, and also that during the period of slower growth (1977-79) those agencies continued to expand steadily and at a faster rate than economic activity in general (table 1). Their expansion slowed down in 1981 and levelled off in 1983-84, but resumed in 1985 and was further stimulated by the legislative changes introduced in 1986.

The volume of temporary work can be measured in work-years – i.e. the equivalent in full-time permanent jobs. This indicator, after a period of steady rise (it was multiplied by a factor of 2.4 between 1975 and 1980), subsequently fell back to its pre-crisis level before rising again during the last quarter of 1987 (the multiplier rose again to 1.98). This figure gives a daily average of the number of temporary workers and is less than the number of persons who passed through temporary work agencies during the whole year.

Table 1: Temporary work contracts and their equivalent in full-time permanent jobs

Year	Individual contracts concluded with user establishments	Adjusted for cases of non-reply	Equivalent in full-time permanent jobs
1974	502,674		
1975	1,004,824	1,148,910	97,819
1976	1,369,062	1,686,170	140,150
1977	1,479,652	1,900,252	158,438
1978	1,669,836	2,240,097	189,657
1979	2,073,002	2,561,119	205,176
1980	2,374,230	2,809,178	237,782
1981	2,189,271	2,436,622	198,098
1982	2,046,938	2,295,639	142,157
1983	2,139,729	2,356,189	113,425
1984	2,220,904	2,353,306	101,988
1985	2,776,473	2,904,498	123,585
1986	3,314,480	3,436,402	120,479
1987	4,003,421	4,150,513	183,603

Source: Ministère du Travail, Paris.

A sample survey undertaken in 1981 threw light on the principal characteristics of temporary (interim) workers: more often men than women, younger than workers in "permanent" jobs, more often foreigners than French nationals.

C. *Fixed-term contracts*

Marginal in terms of absolute numbers, this form of atypical employment is involved in the majority of labour market movements. In 1985, fixed-term contracts accounted for between 2.6 and 2.9% of wage work (2.0% in industry and 3.5% in commerce and services). Their average duration is very short: between 2.3 and 2.6 months for all sectors of activity in 1985. During the same year, 43.5% of the fixed-term contracts were concluded for periods under one month, and four out of five for periods of three months or less. The work involved is unskilled; the persons concerned are usually young, and a high percentage of them are women.

The number of fixed-term contracts is rising sharply. They accounted for 12.1% of all recruitment in 1984 (8.7% in industry and 13.0% in commerce and services) and 13.5% in 1985 (9.6% in industry and 20.0% in commerce and services)[Corbel, Guergoat and Lauhle, 1986]. The Ordinance of 5 February 1982 sought to restrict their use; their numbers did in fact fall slightly [Poulain, 1982]. However, this was only a pause in a trend towards increasingly widespread use of this form of contract. An Ordinance dated 11 August 1986 fleshed out the legislation governing this form of atypical work. It is now permissible to conclude contracts for intermittent work, without a fixed duration, to fill permanent posts in which the nature of the work is such that periods of activity alternate with periods of inactivity – but only in occupational sectors where a collective agreement contains a provision to that effect. If the parties concerned are not careful, this type of intermittent work contract could – even where the reference texts contain some safeguards – become a major contributory element to a process of precariousness should it become a standard form of recruitment [Belier, 1987].

The Act of 25 July 1985 "introducing various provisions of a social nature" and the Ordinance of 11 August 1986, which amended the legislation concerning interim employment and added an item to the list of situations in which it is permissible (for a specific, precisely defined task of short duration), brought into line the legislation concerned with interim employment and fixed-term contracts. It thus would be necessary to consider all forms of atypical employment and of precariousness of employment together. The new texts will probably lead to increased use of these forms of employment. Previously, fixed-term contracts were considered as a complement to interim employment. Recourse to both types of employment had varied directly with the size of the establishment concerned; but at the same time an increasingly widespread tendency to resort to this form of labour force management was observed among small and medium-sized enterprises (31% of establishments were doing so in 1983 as against 12% in 1977). Unlike interim employment, this process of precariousness affected more women than men and more the tertiary sector than industry. These differences will tend to lessen inasmuch as, the needs being roughly the same, the decisive factor in the choices made by entrepreneurs will essentially be relative cost considerations. A further consequence may be anticipated; since these forms of employment will become more frequent, they will constitute a larger proportion of the reasons for becoming unemployed, thus accelerating a trend which has already become apparent.

D. Self-employment

Self-employment is spreading to new sectors of economic activity. For many years it was a marginal form of employment; but today it is used as a management tool by large economic entities. Statistics show that self-employment is growing in: (i) ancillary services mainly supplied to enterprises; (ii) auxiliary services in the finance and insurance sectors; (iii) legal services; and (iv) services related to the construction sector where employment is stagnant. This trend is at times ambiguous. For instance, the setting up of a private consultancy office may offer an alternative to unemployment to young graduates who cannot find salaried employment corresponding to their skills, and thus constitutes a temporary refuge [Trogan, 1984]. But having made a virtue out of necessity and turned his back on employee status, the person concerned, fascinated by the liberal aspects of his situation and intoxicated by a feeling of freedom, may feel that he has attained a more enviable social standing. An enterprise will see in this form of self-employment a means of simplifying its structures and lowering its break-even point while benefitting from increased flexibility. In this way big companies can externalise some of their functions and concentrate on the substance of their activity. To identify such "self-employed persons with a single employer" it would be necessary to seek converging evidence, such as non-payment of social security contributions, legal sub-ordination, lines of authority, the nature of the contracted service, the degree of economic dependence and the exclusive character of the relationship.

Some professions offer more favourable conditions than others for the development of self-employment:[5] tax consultancy and advisory services, management and financial consultancy and human resource auditing. Hostesses, interpreters, journalists and press attachés working on a freelance basis also fall within this category, as do engineers, designers and architects employed by engineering companies and computer specialists working for data processing companies. At lower levels in the occupational hierarchy we find managers of petrol stations and franchisees in the distributive trades; and lower still there are lorry and taxi drivers, agricultural piece-workers, lumberjacks and workers in the building sector – where besides traditional subcontracting we find work on own account, formerly encountered during periods of economic difficulties, but today systematically organised by groups of skilled craftsmen handling particular types of work (painting, roofing, plumbing). "There is a logic underlying this sudden profusion of unusual situations. In each case the objective is for firms to trim their management budgets and to externalise accessory jobs. In the context of economic crisis, it looks as if the enterprise is protecting itself and shifting the burden of economic risk – and subsequently that of social risk – on to the last link in the chain, namely the worker. The latter bears the risk, but, paradoxically, often accepts it freely. The considerate manner is to be satisfied with the organisation of a network of subcontractors. The cynical way is to get rid of all 'normal' wage employment" [Lebaube, 1988a, p. 7].

E. Clandestine employment

Clandestine employment – which may be defined as "sole or secondary gainful, non-casual occupation that is carried out on or beyond the fringes of the law or the terms of regulations and agreements" [de Grazia, 1980, p. 549] – is a long-established practice. Its extent is difficult to estimate, particularly as it is frequently confused with the underground economy, which exists on a different plane [Barthélemy, 1982]; however, the number of clandestine "regular" workers is estimated at between 800,000 and 1,500,000 [Vitek, 1977]. The bracket is wide because it is not easy to draw a borderline between clandestine and "official" work; "clandestine work is more than just atypical; it is illegal. But it is difficult to prosecute it, because it is the ultimate extreme in a wide range of situations, linked through infinitesimally small graduations to do-it-yourself work and giving a friend or neighbour a hand – and also because the sociological ramparts protecting it are breached only rarely" [Fossaert, 1981, p. 499].

The term "clandestine work" covers a variety of situations.[6] From

---

5.   *Tableaux de l'état physique et moral des salariés de la France.* Paris, La Découverte, 1988.

6.   J. Fau, in his report submitted to the government in November 1988, established a classification of a fundamentally legal character.

the economic standpoint, three types can be distinguished.

> 1) The first type is encountered in the fallow areas of the market, which have been abandoned by artisans or enterprises because they are not profitable enough. If there were no illegal work these activities would be handled by the non-monetary sector; this is an area in which the customers are individuals.
>
> 2) A second type is found in industry and crafts, in low-return areas which in many cases are not adapted to market requirements. It enables many small craftsmen to survive. The products pass through commercial middlemen, and the arrangement takes the form of a "speciality" or single-product subcontracting agreement. Work of this type becomes genuinely competitive only when exchanges reach a substantial volume.
>
> 3) The third type is organised on a market system where smaller employers are all clandestine. It is not often found in France. One example is the Sentier workshops. [Debordeaux, n.d., p. 15].

Clandestine work is by its very nature ambivalent; for some it is a form of unfair competition, while for others it is a means of survival. It takes a variety of forms; it may be completely regular or highly intermittent; and it may be highly specialised or highly polyvalent. The rates of pay for this kind of work vary considerably on account of the room for manoeuvre left by non-payment of social charges or of VAT.

Opinions are sharply divided on the subject. The public authorities are divided between a desire for collective regulation and the need to promote labour market flexibility.[7] The employers' organisations, while trying to suppress it, nevertheless distinguish between clandestine workers who are doing no harm to anybody, those who are poaching their customers and those who are trying to set up on their own account and to whose activity a blind eye will be turned provided it has a time limit. Workers with an official status (that of employee or artisan) commit minor and relatively inconsequential breaches of the law; but those who have no such status are trapped in a vicious and almost inescapable spiral of illegality.

Lae [1987] describes four typical clandestine workers:

(i)   the artisan who is on the brink of indebtedness and can only keep his declared official activity going thanks to this extra income, which represents 18% of his total income (1,700 francs per month out of 9,700);

(ii)   the employee with a wage of slightly over the minimum wage (SMIC)[8], who obtains 32% of his disposable income (1,920 francs per month out of 7,136) – and an opportunity to learn a new employable skill – from clandestine work;

(iii)   the unemployed person who occasionally does clandestine work, which provides him with 50% of his income (2,310 francs per month out of

---

7.   In the light of a series of reports submitted to the Economic and Social Council or the government (Antoni in 1950, Soupa in 1971, Fau in 1980, Delorozoy in 1980, Ragot in 1983) the relevant legislation has been amended several times (Act of 11 October 1940, Act of 11 July 1972 and Act of 27 January 1987, which redefines the offence of clandestine employment and extends its coverage).

8.   SMIC = Salaire Minimum Interprofessionnel de Croissance.

4,690) and thus enables him to survive economically;

(iv) the "all black", a former artisan without a licence, riddled with debt, who obtains 80% of his income (5,640 francs per month out of 7,015) from clandestine work.

2. New forms of social management of unemployment

The policies of the public authorities have sought to integrate both young people and the long-term unemployed into working life. A variety of programmes – some of them involving training elements, others not – have been implemented for specific target groups. In the vocational training context the generic term of *stages* (in-firm practical training periods) embraces a complex range of schemes on which it is difficult to report comprehensively. "The general framework was established by an agreement between the social partners on 'alternating training' (alternation of work and training). That agreement defines the three forms of training which enterprises can finance out of their contributions to vocational training, namely skill-acquisition contracts, adaptation contracts and *stages* of induction into working life (of three or six months' duration). These arrangements began to be resorted to on a large scale from 1986 onwards when, under the Séguin plan, hirings through or following alternating training gave rise to exemptions from social charges" [Elbaum, 1988, p. 312]. The measures taken by the public authorities – which were designed to improve the employability of target groups and to promote job creation outside the scope of the conventional labour market – form an extremely complex whole on account of the wide range of facilities offered, the great variety of statuses encountered among the individuals concerned, the terms of remuneration of the latter and the changes continually being made in the regulations:

- The *"future for youth" plan*, launched during the second half of 1981, was primarily concerned with training and the search for better integration into working life. It strengthened the role played by *stages* designed to facilitate integration in training of the most disadvantaged young persons. It was a transitional scheme.

- The *plan for the 16-25s*[9] was implemented in three stages. Firstly, the Ordinance of 26 March 1982 established the programme of integration and skill-acquisition courses of the sandwich type for young persons between ages 16 and 18, and also the network of reception, information and guidance centres (PIAOs) and of local units. Secondly, in June 1982 the government adopted the plan for the 16-25s establishing a new structure for the occupational and social integration programme, comprising three principal orientations – training (provision of additional facilities by the educational system, *stages* for the age groups 16-18 and 18-25); integration into employment (reforms of the apprenticeship and training-cum-employment contracts for the 18-25s);   and

---

9.   This plan is based on the report by Bertrand Schwartz, which demonstrates that factors of social selectivity operate in the labour market against young people with working-class backgrounds and poor school records and stresses the need to establish special induction facilities for young people with problems in these groups, and to ensure individual monitoring of their progress along their respective paths to their ultimate entry into employment.

participation in the promotion of social life (training periods spent with social and educational associations as "young volunteers"). Thirdly, negotiations on alternating training for young persons in enterprises took place at the interoccupational level, leading to the agreement of 23 October 1983 and subsequently the adoption of the Act of 24 February 1984.

– The *"action for employment" plan* dated 26 September 1984 completed the arrangements made for the integration of young persons. To promote alternating training, it introduced relief from the 0.1% apprenticeship tax and from the 0.2% continuous training tax, so that the use of these amounts, which were paid to the State, reverted to the enterprises and the social partners. It also provided for the development of "intermediary enterprises" and for experiments with manpower training associations (AMOFs) to facilitate the integration of the most disadvantaged young people through work. Finally, it established the "work of general utility" scheme (TUCs), which enabled young persons under age 21 (or age 25 if they have been registered with the National Employment Agency [ANPE] for over one year) to work part-time in jobs of social utility. The persons concerned must not be in full-time employment or training. They work 80 hours per month for a period of between three months and one year; the Decree of 26 July 1985 allowed a six-month extension, and that of 20 March 1987 raised the maximum duration to two years. The persons concerned enjoy the status of vocational trainees; their social security contributions are paid by the State, which also pays them a remuneration of 1,250 francs per month; the association concerned may pay them an additional 500 francs. In quantitative terms, this is the most important programme; since its establishment it has involved 830,000 young persons.

– The Ordinance of 17 July 1986 introduced *emergency measures to facilitate the recruitment of young persons in the 18-25 age group* – a group in which the unemployment rate was 2.5 times the national average. The provisions were designed to associate training and access to employment; they added considerably to the complexity of the social protection system in that they offered relief from social security contributions at the rate of 100% to enterprises organising training (alternating training, apprenticeship, skill-acquisition or adaptation contracts, etc.), 50% to enterprises hiring young persons who had recently completed training of one of the types mentioned or been a *"tucist"* and 25% to enterprises taking on any new employees in the age group concerned during the period covered.

– The programme of *assistance for job seekers creating or taking over enterprises* is designed for job seekers still receiving benefits and certain categories of persons entitled to benefit but not yet receiving it. The assistance given varies according to the duration of unemployment preceding submission of the application; it is increased if one or more additional jobs are created within the six months following its award. The State provides social security coverage during the first six months. Between 1979 and 1984, 170,000 persons received assistance under the scheme; in 1985 the number was 70,000 and in 1986, 71,500.

– The *departmental fund to promote youth initiatives* has been set up for persons aged 18-25, either individually or in groups, without any requirement of registration with the ANPE. It also caters for certain categories of long-term unemployed, irrespective of whether they are receiving unemployment benefit or not.

– The *local initiatives programme* is designed to promote job creation within the framework of the modernisation and development of small and medium-sized enterprises. Assistance is provided for one year but must be repaid if the job is abolished within two years of its creation.

– *Local integration programmes* are designed for long-term unemployed persons over 25 and receiving solidarity benefits. The persons concerned do not have the status of employee but that of trainee; however, they may retain the amount of social benefits received by the unemployed if that level is more favourable. The maximum duration of a training course is six months, but a single extension involving 80-120 hours of training per month is permissible.

- *Local programmes for the integration of women living alone* are designed to enable women over 40 and without resources to return to working life. They are trained for periods not exceeding nine months.

- Under the *local supplementary resources schemes*, persons aged over 25 and not receiving any income as employees, trainees or unemployed persons can obtain half-time work, for which they receive a remuneration of 2,000 francs per month.

- *Sandwich-type reintegration contracts* (CRAs) are for long-term job seekers (whether receiving unemployment benefit or not) aged over 26; they involve alternate employment and training for at least a two year period, and the beneficiaries are assured of an employment contract.

- *Alternating in-firm training for reintegration* (SRA) is designed for persons over age 26 who have been unemployed for more than two years. Training lasts for 5 months and the beneficiaries have the status of trainees.

- Under *intermittent employment contracts* (authorised by the Ordinance of 11 November 1986) periods of work may alternate with periods not worked.

- The purpose of *intermediary associations*, authorised by the Act of 27 January 1987, is to organise loans of workers by hiring unemployed persons and subsequently making them available to employers. As with interim employment, the system involves on the one hand a contract of employment with the beneficiary, who thus has the status of employee (for either an indefinite or a fixed term or for part-time work), and on the other a supply contract with the user. The fields in which these associations may operate are restricted by law to "activities which in the economic circumstances prevailing locally are not carried on either by private enterprise or by public agencies or bodies receiving public resources"). The function of intermediary associations of this type is to assist and support unemployed persons. Although they are profit-making, they are nevertheless treated as non-profit-making associations for taxation purposes. They are totally exempted from payment of social security contributions for work done by the beneficiary up to 200 hours per quarter and partially exempted for 200 to 233 hours.

Between July 1981 and December 1985, under all these different schemes, young persons benefitted from 75,200 practical training courses; 328,930 *stages* for persons in the 16-18 age group and 207,240 for persons in the 18-25 age group; 309,350 employment-cum-training contracts [Goupil and Termouille, 1982]; 568,250 apprenticeship contracts; 42,000 "young volunteer" courses; 24,250 alternating training courses; 49,800 enterprise-based induction courses; 324,000 TUCs; and 13,000 *stages* for the long-term unemployed.

To illustrate qualitatively these schemes, one may take the example of the best-known of them – the TUCs. The scheme is undergoing continuous adjustment, and a number of its features are to be found in other types of training schemes or in occupational situations preceding stable employment. The TUC scheme is a crossbreed between situations which are *a priori* incompatible or derived from different logics. TUC projects take after both training and employment and comprise elements of both social and productive work in varying proportions. They are supposed to be a step in a process of integration into working life; but many young people merely go through projects and no further. Users treat the scheme as a convenient way of obtaining abundant, cheap and relatively unskilled labour without entering into any commitment concerning employment contract or promises of recruitment; the actual training is not compulsory either for the trainee or for the user. Individual projects are sometimes used as a means of

Table 2: Beneficiaries of schemes for the social management of unemployment

	1984	1985	1986
Creation and safeguarding of employment			
- Unemployed persons creating enterprises (1)	16,000	32,000	34,000
- Locally sponsored employment initiatives	5,500	3,500	4,000
- Reorganisation and reductions of working time	2,000	3,000	3,000
- Other assisted forms of work	39,000	41,400	40,000
- TUCs (3)	1,000	188,000	198,000
Alternating training (4)	197,000	201,000	314,000
- Apprenticeship	114,000	115,500	122,400
- Skill adaptation	83,000	82,500	172,800
- Skill acquisition	-	3,000	19,200
- Induction courses (SIVPs) (5)	-	20,000	70,000
Vocational training			
- Young persons (other than SIVP courses)	6,000	66,000	42,000
- Job seekers (long-term unemployed)	9,000	54,000	40,000
- Adults	72,000	71,000	71,000
Incentives to withdraw from work			
- Early retirement (ages 55 - 59)	296,000	289,000	267,000
- Guarantee of resources and retirement at age 60	535,000	530,000	530,000
- Cessation of work at age 55 or over	831,000	819,000	797,000
- Assistance with reintegration	1,000	15,000	9,000

Notes:

(1) Estimate of the number of jobs created by the scheme. The calculation involves an assumption concerning the proportion of new jobs created at the expense of pre-existing ones. During 1986 a total of 71,500 persons benefited from the scheme.

(2) Estimate of the number of jobs created or safeguarded.

(3) The average duration of TUC *stages* is 7 months. The total number of beneficiaries during 1986 was 364,000.

(4) The figures given for apprenticeships, employment-cum-training contracts and skill acquisition and adaptation contracts relate to starts during the year concerned. There are no figures concerning the number of beneficiaries at the end of a year.

(5) Practical courses of induction into working life.

Source: INSEE, *Bilan de l'emploi 1986*, Dossiers statistiques du travail et de l'emploi, special issue, Paris, October 1987.

selection or as probationary periods; they are concerned mainly with four types of activities primarily related to service functions – maintenance, renovation and installation (32%); administration (27%); personal services (23%); and technical assistance (5%). All in all,

> the TUC scheme shows that, during periods of high unemployment, when one has no training and no connections to help in the search for a job, it is as though it were necessary to start working in order to obtain training later on (a different logic from that of attending a training course first in order to be hired afterwards, even if training

is a lengthy process which prepares you for entry into the labour market at some future date); but the work is performed under conditions different from those applicable in a production environment or in conventional dependent employment. Thus initial approaches to a labour market develop along the same lines as in the associations, in which two trends - an endeavour to promote the general interest and the pursuit of economic rationality - run in parallel; but it is impossible to measure exactly the importance of or the trend in these forms of employment, which reflect how the "flexibility" of TUC projects and the uncertain and changing statuses of young people vis-à-vis gainful employment do adjust. It would appear that at least as much importance is given to the acquisition of occupational and social experience (so as not to depend solely on diplomas or evaluations of similar types) as to being able to derive benefit from beginner's work (even if relatively unskilled work) and to attribute a value to "youth", in particular in an labour market where unemployment is rife [Schmidt, 1988; see also Villalard, 1985].

The majority of young people are increasingly undergoing an "initiation into working life" consisting of short-term, precarious jobs, before they can obtain access to regular jobs in line with their training. These new methods of induction into working life allow for an intensified selection in the recruitment process by sometimes giving more weight to personality factors (discipline at work, mental flexibility, etc.) than to technical competence in the strict sense of the term. This transitional period between leaving school and entering regular employment is comparable in some respects with the apprenticeship system. But today traditional apprenticeship is replaced by "apprenticeship through instability" [Partrat, 1979].

II. The economic implications of atypical employment

The picture which emerges from the above description of the different forms of atypical employment is not well defined. It is true that some forms of employment which constitute exceptions to general legislation existed before the onset of the recession, but the latter increased their incidence and gave rise to other forms. The characteristic feature of the current period is not so much the novelty of the departures from the standard model of employment as the scale on which they are now being encountered. The responsibility for this situation is shared by workers, whose choice is restricted by difficulties in the labour market; by employers, who are being forced to seek increased labour flexibility in a context of increasing competition and growing uncertainty; and public authorities, who are seeking to organise the social treatment of unemployment in the most effective manner possible.

1. Consequences from the statistical standpoint

The statisticians' descriptions of labour market trends are affected in two ways. The development of these atypical forms of employment increases labour flows; and at the same time the concepts with which statisticians are accustomed to work are losing clarity. "The visible effects of the development of intermediate situations on the functioning and the regulation of the labour market are complex... The dividing lines between situations which were previously distinctly differentiated – employment, unemployment, inactivity – are becoming blurred... through successive selection processes new segmentations are appearing between a wide variety of situations, ranging from unemployment to integration into a stable job" [Elbaum, 1988, p. 313].

Two forms of atypical employment contribute particularly to the increasing volatility of the labour market: fixed-term and interim contracts (table 3). These two categories together accounted for 47% of all new cases of unemployment in 1987 compared with 31% in 1979. The increase is due entirely to an increase in the numbers of fixed-term contracts (25% in 1979 and 42% in 1987). But other forms of atypical employment have also contributed to the fluidity of the labour market by giving rise to transfers to inactivity or training. Even among persons without employment, immediately available and seeking full-time employment of indeterminate duration, secondary movements could be seen affecting the labour market during the first quarter of 1988 and supporting the statement that "precarious employment and recurrent unemployment are becoming a characteristic of the labour market, a management tool for enterprises and – unfortunately – one means of integration for the long-term unemployed" [Lebaube, 1988b, p. 60].

Table 3: Reasons for becoming unemployed

	1986	1987	1988 (Jan.-Apr.)
Dismissal for economic reasons	14.4	14.7	15.5
Dismissal (other reasons)	8.4	8.3	9.3
Resignation	6.2	5.8	6.1
End of fixed-term contract	39.7	42.3	41.2
End of interim employment	5.1	5.1	5.3
First entry on the labour market	15.0	13.5	9.4
Re-entry on the labour market	7.6	6.6	8.4
Other cases	3.6	3.7	4.6

Source: Ministère du Travail, Paris.

Demarcation lines between statistical categories (employed, inactive, unemployed) are not only constantly shifting; they have also become much less clear. "Employment and unemployment have never been homogeneous categories... but the heterogeneity in forms of employment and forms of unemployment has increased, and intermediate situations have developed" [Lebaube, 1988b, p. 85]. The measuring of unemployment now results from the aggregation of responses to the employment survey [Cezard, 1986]. In March 1986, 2,518,000 persons declared themselves as unemployed, but not all of them fell within the statistical category of unemployed; conversely, a number of persons who did not initially state that they were unemployed did fall within that category. In addition, a number of the persons seeking employment (2,691,000 in March 1986) did not fall within that category. It will be recalled that, according to the definition adopted by the ILO in 1982, an unemployed person must:

–   meet the following criteria: be seeking a job and taking steps to find one, be available for work and not have engaged in any occupational activity during the reference week. In March 1986, 2,242,000 persons met those criteria and formed the group of unemployed persons seeking employment (PSERE);

–   be available in the sense that they are currently unemployed but have found a job which will begin later (206,000 persons in March 1986). Thus there were in all 2,448,000 unemployed persons according to the international definition.

But around this central core of unemployed persons there is a grey area of unemployment with all kinds of shadings. Three categories of persons declared as unemployed are not job seekers: those who have given up trying to find work; those who have found jobs which do not begin immediately; and those who worked during the week preceding the inquiry and are thus classified as active and occupied under the ILO definition. Conversely, there are three categories of job seekers who are not registered as unemployed – school pupils, students and persons called up for military service; other inactive persons (mainly women); and persons classified as working at the beginning of the questionnaire but classified as inactive according to the ILO definition (in particular in-firm trainees). The last-mentioned category offers a number of examples of the confusion which arises at the margins of the definitions used by statisticians. In March 1986 there were 407,000 trainees in firms receiving a remuneration; but one-fifth of them (for instance, persons receiving training under the auspices of the AFPA), although remunerated, had no occupational activity. Conversely, other trainees (for example, trainees in TUC projects) are deemed to have an occupational activity; but 5% of all trainees (youths in programmes for the 16-18 age group or adults being retrained for new jobs) are classified as unemployed according to the ILO definition. It should also be borne in mind that more than half of the 298,000 trainees who are classified within the active and occupied population (and in particular the TUC trainees) are in part-time employment. Wages in this category are very low: 59% receive less than 2,000 francs per month and 20% between 2,000 and 4,500. It may be concluded that "trainees (i.e., undergoing practical training in an enterprise) cannot be considered as being employed by the enterprise in which they work, because they have no employment contract, they receive no remuneration and enjoy none of the guarantees generally offered to employees; finally, enterprises have no obligations towards them at the end of the training period. They cannot be treated as being in education in the customary sense of the term (and consequently inactive) inasmuch as they are integrated into the enterprise and contribute to its output with a greater or lesser degree of skill. Finally, they cannot be treated as unemployed, since they are not registered with the ANPE" [Colin and Espinasse, 1979].

Table 4: Numbers of persons unemployed in March 1986 ('000)

Category	Declared unemployed	Students and conscripts	Other inactive	Declared active	Total
Declared unemployed	2,518				2,518
less those who					
- have found jobs (ILO)	- 81				- 81
- have found jobs not starting immediately	- 132				- 132
- are not seeking work	- 133				- 133
plus					
- other persons seeking work but not forming part of the active occupied population		+ 152	+ 307	+ 61	+ 520
Total job seekers	2,170	152	307	61	2,691
less					
- persons not available	- 115	- 107	- 24	- 27	- 263
- persons available who have not taken any steps to find work	- 50	- 12	- 107	- 7	- 176
Net total unemployed (PSERE)	2,006	3	176	27	2,242
plus					
- persons available who have found jobs not starting immediately	+ 132		+ 35	+ 28	+ 206
Total unemployed (ILO definition)	2,138	33	21	55	2,448

Source: Economie et Statistique (Paris), Nos. 193-194, Nov.-Dec. 1986.

The combined effects of the recession and the development of atypical forms of employment are casting doubts on the relevance of the definitions used and the stability of estimates in time and space. This situation suggests that a diversification of the statistical definitions and instruments in use is desirable. In 1986, the director of the National Statistical Institute (INSEE) [Malinvaud, 1986] proposed to add to the three basic concepts – activity, employment and unemployment – three complementary ones – visible underemployment, employment-cum-training situations and discouraged workers – in order to take into account the increasing variety of employment situations and the multiplication of cases in which employment is associated with training or is not as full-time as the persons concerned would wish.

The measurement of underemployment depends on the definitions and assumptions on which it is built. For the ILO any person in employment, whether remunerated or not, and whether at work or absent from work, is in a state of visible underemployment if he/she is involuntarily working less than the number of hours customary in that activity and if during the reference period he/she was seeking additional work or was available for such work. For the purposes of determining whether a person is in a state of visible underemployment, normal working hours in a given activity should be determined in the light of national circumstances, the relevant legislation or current practice, or form the subject of a uniform agreed standard. For the INSEE [Thelot, 1986] a person is deemed to be underemployed if he/she is (i) working part-time and seeking a different, full-time, job, or (ii) working full-time and seeking a different full-time job but had worked less than usual during the reference week. One possible variant consists of not specifying the nature of the employment sought and to include everyone who is seeking employment, whether full-time or not. This approach gives a substantially different estimate – 483,000 persons in March 1986, instead of 380,000. On the basis of these conventions, 1.8% or 2% of all active and occupied persons were underemployed, and underemployment represented 0.8% or 1% of the potential hours of work of the labour force (i.e., assuming that there is no underemployment or unemployment). In either case, the proportion has doubled during the last four years. Underemployment is frequently of short duration, either because it alternates with periods of unemployment or because it constitutes a transition from unemployment or inactivity towards full-time employment. It is particularly frequent among young women (at managerial, intermediate and manual worker levels). In the youngest age groups, underemployment is concentrated among those who have just begun work; one-third of the boys and girls hired less than a year previously by the public service or a non-commercial organisation were underemployed. The situation of young persons recently hired by an enterprise is somewhat similar, although to a lesser degree; they are more often underemployed than the other employees.

2. Economic consequences

A number of structural factors promote the use of these forms of atypical employment. These are:

– population trends, which have given rise to growing imbalances between labour supply and demand and have weakened the bargaining position of the workers;

– sociological changes, which have brought into the labour market new groups of persons and new social categories (young people, women), with different aspirations and needs and, as a consequence, new attitudes to work;

– changes in the production system, which have reduced the importance of the manufacturing sector (in which "standard" employment had come into being and developed) and increased that of the service sector, in which more appropriate forms of employment have emerged.

In addition, the depressed condition of the economy has encouraged enterprises to develop still further the use of atypical forms of employment.

"The use of these special forms of employment is situated in the framework of cost minimisation, not so much by reducing wage rates as by endeavouring to keep staffing levels strictly in line with the workload. As a short-term tool, it makes it unnecessary to maintain surplus staff, hired specifically to ensure regularity in production (in order to face absenteeism, peak workloads, unexpected orders, etc.). Considered in a broader perspective, these different forms of employment have one common feature: they are a means of limiting the financial and institutional risks attached to statutory hirings. They thus serve as a instrument for the selection of staff, as a tool for anticipating possible falls in workload and also, to a certain extent, as a means of keeping the labour force under control through a differentiation of status. Finally, as an essential element within a context of economic uncertainty, those techniques, extremely flexible in their application, offer a means of recovering that freedom of manoeuvre which enterprises had lost on account of the increasing rigidity introduced in employment status" [Broudic and Espinasse, 1980].

From this standpoint, then, the development of atypical forms of employment is a component of the trend towards deregulation and flexibility which has been the object of an abundant literature [Boyer, 1986]. The recession has pushed unemployed workers and workers threatened with the loss of their jobs to accept any job going, however precarious or unstable. It has also put pressure on governments, concerned with the search for new ways of creating jobs or distributing the work available, to develop new and different forms of employment (employment-cum-training contracts, new forms of apprenticeship contracts, forms of early or gradual retirement involving part-time work, etc.).

The discussion is still continuing on the relationship between atypical forms of employment and unemployment. Some people argue, on the basis of unorthodox modes of analysing the functioning of the labour market, that, far from having reduced unemployment, they have actually increased it, in particular by having given rise to unemployment linked to high job mobility. Others, however, relying on a more neo-classical labour market analysis, consider that the new forms of employment cushion the effect of unemployment - and that, in any case, the reasons for their existence are not exclusively connected to unemployment.

To sum up, it is difficult to offer a fully satisfactory evaluation of atypical employment. By definition it cannot cover all forms of employment (and in particular clandestine employment). The figures given vary according to the sources used. The lines of demarcation between inactivity, unemployment and self-employment are not clearly drawn. The areas covered by the different forms of atypical work vary with the criterion selected: the nature of the contract, the place where the work is done, whether there is a single employer or several, the number of hours worked, etc. If the last-mentioned criterion is used to define "odd jobs" as activities with very short working hours or carried on for only very short periods, then the findings of the employment inquiry of March 1987 concerned approximately 1.2 million people, or 5.4% of all gainfully occupied persons if trainees and apprentices are excluded and 5.8% if they are included. These atypical forms of employment may be classified under four main categories, as shown in table 5 [Elbaum, 1986].

Table 5: Categories of atypical jobs

	Type of work	Numbers ('000)	Percentage of total	Percentage of active & occupied persons
1. Working hours normally less than 20/week	Short work-time	672.9	57.9	3.1
2. Working hours under 20 during reference week; no set schedule	Short & irregular work-time	172.4	14.8	0.2
3. Occasional activity; no set schedule; weekly hours under 39	"	31.4	2.7	0.2
4. Fixed-term contracts (FT) of one month or less or interim work for two weeks or less	Temporary odd jobs	35.8	3.1	0.2
5. FT of 1-3 months' duration and interim work of 2-4 weeks' duration	"	109.9	9.5	0.5
6. Temporary employment of at least 3 months' duration by State or local authority	"	23.7	2.0	0.1
7. At least 1 hour of work during reference period but no occupational activity	Marginal or casual activity	116.0	10.0	0.5
Total less trainees and apprentices		1162.1	100.0	5.4
8. Trainees and apprentices in one of the forms of employment mentioned above		80.2		

Source: Economie et Statistique (Paris), No. 205, Dec. 1986, p. 50.

All in all, the number of odd jobs increased during the period 1983-87 by 14.5% (18% if trainees are included). The biggest increase occurred in very short-term precarious jobs. In the short working-time sphere, three major socio-occupational groups predominate:

- persons providing services directly to individuals (domestic servants, mother's helps, child-minders);

- persons employed by the public service and in health or social welfare occupations;

- unskilled workers (the great majority engaged in cleaning).

There are clear majorities of married women in short working-time employment (553,000 out of 673,000); of young people and adult men in precarious jobs involving long hours; and of persons aged over 60 in occasional and casual work. Half of the people engaged in odd jobs have no formal qualification, or no qualification of a higher level than the primary school certificate (CEP). Higher levels of qualification are relatively rare; only 9% have certificates of upper secondary education and 8% higher education diplomas.

Partly based on the foregoing evaluation but introducing also other situations, the work of Marioni [1987] distinguishes the following categories:

- persons visibly underemployed (the situation of persons working, for reasons beyond their control, for less than normal hours and seeking additional work): 400,000-500,000. Measured in this way, under-employment doubled over a four-year period. The increase was primarily due to the expansion of employment schemes organised by the public authorities for the benefit of young people (of the TUC type);

- persons working part-time for less than 15 hours per week but not seeking any change: 300,000;

- persons engaged in odd jobs: between 100,000 and 500,000, according to the definition adopted. Of these, 116,000 had no regular activity but performed at least one hour of work during the reference week, 200,000 were active but were not working normal hours and 170,000 were in short-term jobs (FT or interim);

- job seekers registered with the ANPE but stating that they were employed: 150,000 (but the proportion of persons falling within this category was probably higher).

The foregoing evaluations are based on the number of jobs which are contractually limited in time, to which have been added situations which, by law, are not covered by employment contracts but which are considered as jobs under the ILO definition as interpreted in France. One can go beyond this institutional definition and define three categories of active and occupied persons, either on the basis of certain features actually present in the jobs themselves or by taking into account certain elements other than those relating to duration (fixed-term or indeterminate) in the contract of employment. These are: (i) underemployed persons, that is to say, persons working less than standard hours or (for specific reasons) less than usual and who at the same time declare that they are seeking another, full-time, job (this is not quite the ILO definition of visible underemployment but is very close to it). In March 1986 there were approximately 250,000 persons in this situation; (ii) persons seeking other jobs because their own are either under threat or considered by them as stepping-stones; in March 1986 these persons numbered approximately 200,000; (iii) persons seeking other jobs to improve their situation (better suited to their skills, more satisfactory conditions of work, more convenient location, higher pay) or who, without giving any specific reason, seem somewhat dissatisfied and can therefore be deemed to fall within the ILO definition of disguised underemployment; in March 1986 there were 650,000 persons in this category. If the definition of atypical employment is further widened to include persons employed part-time but who have not expressed a desire for change, an additional 2 million persons must be added to the figures for March 1986 given so far. Notwithstanding the great variety of the situations identified, all these forms of work have one feature in common – their numbers either remained constant or increased during the years 1984-86. The trend was fairly steady with the exceptions of in-firm trainees, whose numbers rose rapidly from 1984 onwards, and fixed-term and interim contracts, whose numbers followed a V shaped profile (mainly due to changes in the legislation governing these two types of employment). Meanwhile, the numbers of other types of employment fell from 18,340,000 in the spring of 1982 to 17,470,000 in the spring of 1986.

These different forms of employment do not affect the same individuals, the same sectors or the same categories of enterprises. The "institutional" forms (apprenticeships, in-firm training, fixed-term contracts) concern mainly young workers; the active persons seeking other jobs and those who have "chosen" part-time work are usually adults. Employees in trade and commerce, persons providing services to individuals or enterprises and unskilled workers are more affected by these special forms of employment than are managerial and supervisory personnel, persons in intermediate-level occupations and skilled workers, a very high proportion of whom are in standard types of employment. Atypical jobs are encountered principally in the "mobile" tertiary sector (distributive trades, services to enterprises or to individuals, hotels, cafes, restaurants), in which barely two-thirds of jobs are "normal" jobs. In the tertiary sector of "statutory" services (telecommunications, health, financial institutions, central and local administration, non-commercial organisations) practical training courses are particularly frequent, as are part-time jobs for women. In light industries (food processing, consumer goods, construction, public works, agriculture) apprenticeship for men is of considerable importance. Normal jobs are most frequent in heavy industry (intermediate and capital goods, motor vehicles, energy, transport) even though, in this sector, young workers are quite frequently found in precarious jobs. Finally, special forms of employment are encountered mainly in small establishments; the proportion of normal jobs in larger establishments is greater (but on the other hand, interim employment is more frequent).

III. The social consequences of atypical employment

1. The viewpoints of the actors concerned

What are the attitudes towards atypical employment? "Some observers regard the new forms of atypical employment as a threat to the survival of the principles that have shaped labour law. Others are worried about the growing number of workers not covered by the classical system of protection... On the other hand, there are those who see in atypical employment yet another sign of the vitality and responsiveness of labour legislation, which, confronted with the prolonged recession and changes in the structure of the labour market, has been able to extend its scope to include the new variants in contractual and *de facto* employment relationships" [Cordova, 1986, p. 641].

A. The positions of the employers

They were clearly spelt out in 1986 by Yvon Gattaz in the following terms:

> For many years it was thought that social progress consisted of security, rigidity, regulation and the immutability of acquired advantages. Today true social progress consists of the expansion of employment for which we must all unite. But the expansion of employment is blocked by rigidities. Employees generally have understood this. They are investing more and more of themselves in their enterprises; they are developing a better understanding of the goals of their enterprises; and in addition, they want for themselves increasingly individualised working conditions, atypical work schedules and pay differentials. The principal fields – but not the only ones – in which flexibility can help to create jobs are:
>
> – Freedom to adapt staffing levels. A controversy has broken out over whether the abolition of the prior permission from the authorities to dismiss workers on economic grounds will lead to the creation or the disappearance of jobs... There is no doubt in my mind; the abolition of the need for official authorisation to adjust staffing in accordance with levels of activity in the enterprise will lead to the creation of jobs – lots of jobs. For French employers this step is of the utmost priority, on a par with the freedom to set prices.
>
> – Flexibility in wages and salaries will enable us to pay priority attention to individual merit and to reward the qualities of those who devote their skills and energies to the service of the enterprise, thus promoting the interests of all its members... We must not neglect the "lesser trades" which create relatively little value added but have made a major contribution to employment in the United States during the last few years and which frequently offer transitional employment at momentarily lower rates of pay. The substantial increases made in the minimum wage (SMIC) were certainly a generous gesture; but they have adversely affected employment, and in particular that of young people.
>
> – Flexibility of working conditions includes flexibility of work schedules... all the forms of differentiated work and scheduling of work over long periods which we refer to as "annualisation". We are making very unsatisfactory use of this reserve of employment, and freedom is needed to make use of all these forms of differentiated employment – part-time employment, interim employment and fixed-term contracts.
>
> – Flexibility with regard to "social staffing thresholds" will also be an important factor promoting employment. Many employers are reluctant to employ more than nine or forty persons because of the avalanche of additional fiscal, social and administrative constraints which will overwhelm them once they pass those thresholds. [Gattaz, 1986].

This text is a true programme of action. It calls for a mobilisation of employers to secure greater flexibility, which justifies recourse to atypical forms of employment, and requests an extension of their use. The objective of the new employer strategies can be summed up in the words "adaptability and flexibility" [Germe, 1981].

B. The positions of the trade unions

The abusive practices to which clandestine employment has given rise in the textile and clothing sectors are well known. The French Democratic Confederation of Labour (CFDT) in particular has worked for the regularisation of the situation of such workers (Turkish workers especially) in the Sentier district of Paris. There is thus unanimous agreement that "black" labour is undesirable. However, the unions have to bear in mind, in making their case, that many workers are forced to resort to it by unemployment, and that opinion polls have shown that public opinion is somewhat tolerant towards this type of work. One inquiry [Klatzmann, 1982] revealed that in France the persons asked for their views considered that in their neighbourhood 18% of people were doing a lot of small jobs for which they were paid directly in cash and 53% were doing occasional odd jobs. In addition, 49% of the interviewees considered that clandestine employment was reprehensible but 36% thought it a good thing, while 14% thought that it was advisable for persons who could not find jobs to work clandestinely.

The workers' organisations have also denounced abusive recourse to fixed-term contracts, which they consider to be means of extending trial periods unduly and of selecting employees more strictly. They are also closely watching developments in the fields of homeworking and part-time employment; they see in the proposals to facilitate these forms of employment a danger of reverting to forms of exploitation which they had hoped had disappeared for ever. But the three-cornered employment relationship arising from the existence of temporary work agencies is viewed as the most controversial problem; however, even though they are hostile to the general principle, in most cases they endeavour to secure the protection of the workers concerned by negotiation. The viewpoints of the organisations differ in some respects as follows:

(a) The *General Confederation of Managerial and Supervisory Staff (CGC)* has a relatively open mind on the new practices being promoted by the employers. It has proposed negotiations, during which, among other things, the question of the diverse forms of differentiated employment could be examined. These negotiations would offer a means "of dealing with the problem areas one by one, giving priority to all matters relating to the reintegration of the unemployed into working life and the creation of secure new jobs... The employers must understand that in our view (i.e., that of the CGC) the reduction of the role of the State and of administrative constraints means that new fields become open to contractual agreement. In our view changing the nature of social protection does not mean to regulate retrogression, but to introduce the adjustments made necessary by changes in our society" [Mandinaud, 1985, p. 24].

(b) The *General Confederation of Labour (CGT)* prefers a global approach to the problems rather than a case-by-case approach. Its position is as follows:

> In actual fact the employers want to abolish all guarantees of stable, full-time work. For many years they have seen the development of interim employment as a means of

adjusting manning levels to the situation of the enterprise without needing to hire or fire. But today they are trying to do the same thing on a much larger scale – to adjust the numbers of employees solely on the basis of the needs of the enterprise and without being subject to any constraints whatsoever. They have only one objective: to secure a maximum return on capital. To achieve this they will try anything:

- straightforward dismissal, with or without an FNE[10] contract;

- partial unemployment, for which the system of benefits has just been weakened as far as the minimum benefit is concerned...

- the conversion of full-time jobs into part-time ones... The people primarily affected by these underpaid jobs are women; in some enterprises the employers subject them to direct or indirect pressures to induce them to go over to part-time work. Part-time work is acceptable only if a genuine choice is offered to the persons concerned, with guarantees of a return to full-time employment and of identical social protection, particularly with regard to social and trade union rights;

- the conversion of jobs of indeterminate duration into fixed-term jobs; the Decree of 3 April 1985 allows this where the person concerned has been unemployed for over 12 months;

- the use of courses of induction to working life (SIVPs) as a means of obtaining cheap labour by refusing to subsequently hire the young trainees and, in some firms, maintaining a constant 'float' of young SIVP trainees. In this way they save on wages and social charges and, in some cases, manage to keep below the thresholds for trade union representation.[11]

(c)   The *CFDT* has a more open mind towards new and fashionable ideas; it has not refused to examine new approaches and specific forms of employment which might reduce unemployment, meet the new aspirations of workers and satisfy needs which a consumption-orientated society cannot meet. This attitude has enabled its general secretary to write:

In a mobile and changing economy there must inevitably be a certain amount of short-term unemployment caused by the adjustment process of labour supply and labour demand. Setting a target of zero unemployment today implies an affirmation that, apart from this "frictional" unemployment, it is possible to enable every registered unemployed person and every potential job seeker to escape from unemployment and social exclusion by taking part in a socially useful activity, even if that activity is performed under new conditions which constitute departures from the generally accepted rules. The principal "reserve tank" of new jobs today is among small enterprises. However, artisans and small firms are reluctant to take on additional employees, even if they cannot cope with their workload; sometimes, without even doing their sums, they fear that new hirings will be too costly. It is possible and necessary – without causing any prejudice to workers – to organise assistance to management, to find ways of simplifying administrative procedures, flat-rate methods of calculating social charges and fiscal measures apt to facilitate hirings and to impart a lasting job creation momentum to enterprises. French society is organised in such a way that important needs are not met even where they give rise to significant creation of activities and jobs. For example, we have observed the substantial proportion of TUC projects devoted to environmental protection. Assisting with the social integration of an unemployed person may also be beneficial to the collectivity. In our market-orientated society there is a sharp dividing line between employment and unemployment, depending on whether the work performed yields a full return or not. However, there are all kinds of opportunities for

---

10.   Fonds National pour l'Emploi.

11.   "Les faces cachées de la flexibilité", in *Le Peuple*, 13 June 1985.

useful activities which partly pay for their costs and which have hitherto remained unexplored or been left to the black economy. This is the case with personal services provided in the home. Upkeep of dwellings, domestic services, looking after children or old people who want to go on living in their own homes: all these activities demand a different social organisation of daily life, with appropriate taxation and social arrangements which call for imagination and require practical proposals and negotiated agreement. The yawning gulf separating the active from the inactive must also be bridged. Many pensioners and people who have taken early retirement want useful work to do. In addition, there is a potential demand for part-time work among active persons which can be helped to find expression, in particular by offering the persons concerned appropriate guarantees regarding career development [Maire, 1986].

These theoretical debates have had practical outcomes. For instance, the CFDT and the CGC are actively participating in a programme which seeks to encourage unemployed persons to set up on their own account by establishing their own enterprises; however, the CGT and Force Ouvrière (FO) consider that converting employees into heads of enterprises is not a matter for the unions. There is a wide range of evaluations of atypical forms of employment. A pessimist is tempted to see in them only a deterioration in the conditions of normal employment and a weakening of labour legislation. An optimist will find in them a means of coping as well as possible with the current difficulties in the labour market. An utopian will see in them the beginnings of the development of an new type of economy.

C. The positions of the public authorities

A wide range of differing views is to be found among public authorities as well. Philippe Séguin, while Minister of Labour, said in 1986:

There are three possible interpretations. First: these jobs are precarious and consequently open to criticism. Second: they are antechambers of working life, particularly for young people. Third: they correspond to new needs. The first interpretation seems to me to be out of date, since it is based on a dichotomy between market-oriented employment and unemployment which is obsolete. The second is borne out by inquiries into the employment of young people; let me remind you that one out of every three TUC participants gets a job on completing his project. The third will become increasingly valid, as service sector undertakings create jobs.

On the basis of the foregoing the policy to be followed involves

an approach in three stages. Priority must be given to non-material investment and to research and development, as well as to capital productivity in sectors where competition is fierce. Unemployment assistance must be reorganised into a system which encourages the resumption of activity; thus it should be possible to receive a remuneration and partial unemployment benefit simultaneously. We should – and in the longer term we shall have to – encourage the development of employment in services... by freeing the people who want to create jobs from statutory and social constraints, and ourselves from the obsession of a dual society, which is more of a threat because of the crystallisation of acquired rights than because of the creation of these new jobs. [*Revue Française d'Economie*, 1986].

The public authorities are facing a dilemma. Either they can leave the social partners to deal with the situation, taking measures *post facto* and providing safeguards to prevent serious abuses and undesirable developments; or they can regulate the matter carefully, reserving each type of employment for a particular area or a particular category of persons for which it is particularly suitable. The hesitation between the two alternatives is reflected in the misadventures experienced by interim work. Three periods of different lengths may be distinguished:

(a) Between 1972 and 1982 there were regulations governing interim work, but the firms concerned were frequently ill-informed of their provisions. The Act of 3 January 1972 defined interim work, specified the cases in which it could be resorted to and stipulated that (subject to exceptions) a contract could not exceed three months in duration. The economic crisis gave rise to radical changes in methods of personnel management and thus to a considerable increase in precarious employment, and particularly in interim employment. Between 1975 and 1979 the number of temporary work agencies increased by 106% and the average number of persons on interim assignments daily by 110%.

(b) In 1982 a reform, designed to have far-reaching effects, was introduced. Ordinance No. 82-131, dated 5 February 1982, sought at the same time to reduce the numbers of precarious jobs by restricting them to cases justified on economic grounds, and to improve the situation of the workers concerned with regard to both their individual and collective rights, while strengthening the enforcement machinery and stiffening penalties. It left problems relating to sickness benefits, occupational organisation, industrial health and safety, and compensation for layoffs caused by bad weather to be dealt with by collective bargaining.

(c) These rules were soon relaxed in order to revert to practices more in line with the wishes of the temporary work agencies and of the firms using their services; the legislative framework was amended by the Act of 25 July 1985 and the Ordinance of 11 August 1986. The 1985 Act was designed to achieve three objectives: (i) to satisfy certain specific economic needs that enterprises experienced by establishing two new types of cases in which interim contracts could be resorted to; (ii) to bring the existing regulations concerning fixed-term and temporary employment contracts respectively into line with one another, particularly with regard to the cases in which they could be used, the duration of contracts and the rules governing the renewal and the succession of contracts; (iii) to improve the system of occupational integration of certain categories of job seekers. The obstacles encountered by enterprises in making use of temporary work agencies were to be removed, without, however, thereby increasing precarious employment or threatening the social situation of the employees concerned. The new Ordinance dated 11 August 1986 was also designed to attain three objectives, namely (i) to safeguard the social situation of the interim workers concerned by granting them social rights identical to those enjoyed by other employees in the enterprise concerned; (ii) the elimination of rigidities, arising from the fact that the freedom to conclude interim contracts was no longer restricted by a list of cases where recourse to interim workers was allowed (thus an enterprise could use interim workers for the performance any temporary, specific task) and also that prior administrative authorisations had been abolished and that the maximum duration of interim contracts had been raised; and (iii) to ensure that there was no increase in precarious employment by providing that interim contracts could be concluded only for the performance of temporary tasks and could not be used to fill on a long-term basis a job forming part of the normal and continuing activity of the enterprise concerned.

2. The impact on industrial relations

Atypical forms of employment have a wide range of effects. They give rise to divisions between workers, which segmentation theories represent analytically. In the sociological sphere, it is permissible to speak of fragmentation of the labour class, the term "fragmentation" having a twofold significance – first, the workers are divided into categories which have some degree of difficulty in living side by side; and secondly, the ability of the workers thus fragmented to act collectively is considerably reduced. In addition, the multiplication of different individual statuses, sometimes accompanied by a high degree of uncertainty concerning the question of whether an employment relationship still exists, creates "grey areas" in the field of labour legislation corresponding to those surrounding unemployment. From the purely legal standpoint, it might be said that labour law is disintegrating.

(a) The condition of workers is affected from the economic standpoint. In developing new forms of employment in considerable numbers the employers are seeking greater efficiency – which can be defined in neo-classical terms as the maximum conversion of fixed labour costs into variable labour costs, or in Marxist terms as the attempt to reduce to the greatest possible extent the "pores" in the working day so as to exploit human labour more effectively. This objective underlies the different forms of "independent" work, in which the workers manage their own time, with the result that absenteeism is reduced and at the same time output increases. It also underlies the increase in part-time work, which increases productivity while reducing a certain number of cost elements. Where workers in different legal statuses are placed in competition with one another, the same result ensues: an interim worker who is placed at the head of an assembly line will help to speed up the pace of work of all the workers; a worker on loan, or under subcontract, has a level of productivity which can be more closely controlled, if only because when production so requires he can be laid off; a worker on a fixed-term contract saves the slack time which characterises a period of notice; the fragmentation of production through setting up subsidiaries breaks up routine patterns of organisation and revives the spirit of initiative and problem-solving among managers. Innumerable examples can be given of the economic implications of atypical forms of employment.

(b) The social consequences of the development of atypical forms of work. The most striking observation to be made here is that:

each group of employees so differentiated has its own statute which is governed by the laws, regulations and agreements applicable to the employer company, with the result that within the user establishment under consideration the staffing structure resembles a mosaic, with as many different statutes as the number of employer companies represented at that work place, this notwithstanding the fact that their conditions of work are identical, their occupational skills and the tasks they perform are similar and there is only one management - in reality that of the user, who, more or less openly and directly, has in his hands the essential prerogatives of head of enterprise and of employer vis-à-vis the personnel detached to him by other enterprises" [de Maillard et al., 1979, p. 323].

The repercussions are many: the hiring procedures become more selective (interim and fixed-term contracts serve as a means of selecting the most suitable persons); the danger of becoming unemployed increases (for some of these forms of atypical employment give rise to repeated returns to the labour market); there is more frictional unemployment; the vulnerability of those who are trapped in a recurrent employment-unemployment cycle is heightened; and in addition conditions of work (particularly from the safety and health standpoint) may deteriorate.[12]

(c) Ideological implications. Only a few elements need to be mentioned here. Precarious employment breaks up workers' solidarity and arouses individualism. The mobility undergone may, by a process of occultation and internalisation of the values proclaimed by the system, become adorned with the virtues of individual accomplishment. More generally, the multiplication of statuses departing from common law tends to call into question the general provisions of law governing the contract of employment as a normative reference point: "the employment contract of indeterminate duration, which has hitherto provided the general legal basis of employment, is keeping its value as a reference but is tending to become the exception rather than the rule. It is being insidiously called into question, and its salient features... are gradually being whittled away... The argument is advanced that it grants exorbitant privileges in comparison with the risks incurred by a self-employed worker, the head of an enterprise, a shopkeeper or a member of one of the liberal professions. As the recession continues, the criticisms levelled at it are becoming harsher" [Lebaube, 1988b, p. 33]. By marginalising one category of workers, atypical forms of employment exercise a depressing effect on their living and working conditions.

(d) Prejudicial effects on collective relationships. According to Broudic and Espinasse [1980]:

> The introduction of greater precariousness into work status makes it extremely difficult to organise a fraction of the wage-earners' collectivity. This is all the more serious as the workers concerned are precisely the ones who enable adjustments to be made at the margin and consequently bear a crucial part of the running costs of the system.

---

12.   According to Thille [1981], occupational accidents are more numerous and more serious in temporary work enterprises than in the principal branches of industry. In addition, the organisational structure of occupational medicine is inappropriate for three-cornered relationships, since the firm lending the worker has no knowledge of the workplace to which he is assigned, while the user firm has no knowledge of his record. Finally, in relationships of this kind the user firm is exonerated from all liability in the event of an accident, since it is neither the employer nor a third party; and since the accident will not be included in its own accident record, it has every interest in engaging temporary workers.

From the union standpoint this means that part of the workforce is less willing to give them a hearing; this compounds the organisational problems which arise from the separation of the legal negotiating partner (the employer company) from the centre where economic decisions are actually taken. These difficulties have emerged at a time when economic problems and fears of job losses make it difficult to present comprehensive platforms of demands and have thus tended to weaken the effectiveness of trade union action [pp. 12-13].

The public authorities, in an effort to "reconstitute the labour collectivity" [Auroux, 1981], have endeavoured to extend all collective rights to the workers concerned, though they may be subjected to special regulations concerning the methods of exercising them.

(e) Atypical forms of employment threaten the unity of labour legislation and social security. The indeterminate duration of the contract and the existence of a single employer are the two yardsticks used by lawyers to define the typical job, as developed over the years by industrial relations systems [Rettenbach, 1979]. Since the contract of indeterminate duration is the norm, it will be used as a basis for the classification which follows.[13]

(i)   The nature of the wage-employment relationship: the form of employ-
       ment furthest from the norm is that of clandestine work, in which there
       is no contract at all. Work of this type has become much more
       frequent in recent years and has contributed to the development of the
       underground economy;   some forms of homeworking resemble
       clandestine work in many respects. In a second group of cases the
       nature of the contractual relationship is unclear; is a work contract for
       a non-established position a commercial contract with a self-employed
       person or an employment contract with an employee? The different
       forms of atypical employment devised within the framework of national
       agreements (practical training periods in enterprises, employment-cum-
       training contracts, apprenticeships) do not in the majority of cases
       provide for employment contracts, hiring (and consequently trial
       periods) or dismissal (and consequently periods of notice and
       termination benefits); in practice the employer exploits the confusion
       between employment and training. In the field of interim employment
       the assignment contract established by the Act of 3 January 1972 is
       closer to the norm, although it involves departures from general
       legislation (for example, the precarious employment allowance excludes
       any entitlement to notice). The fixed-term contract (Act of 3 January
       1979) – whether it takes the form of a contract with starting and
       finishing dates or of one for a predetermined period between dates not
       yet set – comes still closer to the norm, although the new provisions
       call into question earlier case-law, which specified that in the event of
       any confusion concerning the date of completion of the contract, or if
       it was extended more than once, it automatically became of indeter-
       minate duration. Thus between the absence of any contractual status,
       at one extreme, and the "typical" status, characterised by the stability

---

13.   For another typology of atypical employment see for example Broda [1976].

of the relationship between employer and employee, which has shaped all the labour legislation (especially with regard to individual or group dismissals) at the other, there is a wide range of practices by means of which the employer "with his hands free" [Lyon-Caen, 1980] intends to have at his disposal an hiring policy without having to bear the overhead costs of employment as described above.

(ii)   The status of employer: one has to deal not only with this increase in the range of unstable individual situations, but also in certain cases with the problem of determining who is the employer - and thus who is the accountable person to whom the employee should turn [Vaccarie, 1980]. As things now stand, it is possible to encounter a wide range of different legal situations which, because employment or work are increasingly externalised, lead to a breaking up of the legal unity of the work force. For instance, in a single establishment with 500 employees Magaud [1975] found as many as 10 different employers (an association of economic interests, a service company, a catering company, a security company, a cleaning contractor, a temporary work agency, etc.). The bilateral relationship typical of standard employment contracts is replaced by a triangular relationship in which, as Lyon-Caen put it, the real employer has "dropped out of sight". The transfer of responsibility from the "real" or the "economic" employer can take a variety of forms. In a subsidiary company, the general manager is only the delegate of the parent company, which is the real employer; in a subcontracting relationship, the subcontractor (i.e. the legal entrepreneur) depends on the principal; in interim employment, the temporary work agency acts only in a context of delegation of personnel management functions. The variety of possible legal and economic situations becomes even greater where, for example, a large firm can set up a temporary work agency of its own, or where it distances itself from the employment relationship twice over by setting up a service company or a sub-contractor company with the status of a subsidiary which subsequently establishes a temporary work agency as its own subsidiary. Thus one can have a production unit using a labour force of which it is not the employer, or an employer whose labour force is controlled only by delegation, or whose work is organised by an external production unit.

With regard to social security legislation, atypical employees may be in an even more delicate situation, in relation not only to the financing of the institution but also to the entitlement to benefits. For instance, in the triangular relationships encountered in interim work, there may be some problems in determining to which insurance scheme occupational injury contributions should be paid. In part-time employment, not only are the general rules not applied when their application would have unfavourable consequences for the employer (particularly with regard to social security contributions) but in addition the law now contains provisions designed to give enterprises substantial flexibility with regard to personnel management. We have also seen how, within these new forms of employment, the person liable to pay contributions may be the worker, the employer or the public authorities, and how the amounts of the contributions may vary according to whether the individual concerned is employed, unemployed or undergoing training. The situation would probably become even more complex if certain proposals concerning the establishment of a separate social protection scheme for these "new wage-earning groups" [Dalle and Bounine, 1987] were to be adopted. As for benefit entitlements, the situation is as tricky. The reason is that

> social security – particularly with regard to coverage of the risks related to old age, invalidity and death – requires by definition relatively long periods of employment and contributions; consequently only persons who have been employed and have contributed for the requisite periods are entitled to benefits or can pass on this entitlement to their survivors. In practice many atypical employees who have only contributed to social security intermittently, occasionally or for limited periods find themselves within the scope of the scheme for purposes of payment of contributions but excluded for purposes of entitlement to benefits. Social security is based on actuarial calculations and is unable to effect the analogies and assimilations which have been introduced in labour legislation; for many of its branches were designed to cover the risks affecting typical employees working full-time and continuously. This gives rise to problems when attempts are made to extend the scheme to atypical workers [Dalle and Bounine, 1987].

IV. Conclusions

In the context of economic fluctuations, atypical jobs constitute, depending on the terminology used, a regulator or a buffer between workers in active service and the industrial reserve army; they form a device used by employers to restore to wages the character of variable cost which had been partially lost. At the structural level, the constitution of a "second working class" may be considered as the contemporary form of the "general mobilisation" concept [de Gaudemar, 1979] on account of the greater control it gives over labour mobility. From the standpoint of the more general questions raised by the increasingly widespread use of atypical forms of employment, the problem may be defined in terms of whether these new forms constitute "a retrograde step or the development of a new type of wage relationship" [Boyer, 1981]. It is already clear how the development of these new forms of employment constitute one means of coping with the rigidities of Keynesian regulation; but discussion is still continuing on whether or not, in the current climate of recession, they highlight the realities of an emerging neo-liberal type of regulation.

References

Auroux, J. (1981): *Les droits des travailleurs*. Paris, La Documentation Française.

Barthélemy, P. (1982): "Travail au noir et économie souterraine: Un état de la recherche", in *Travail et Emploi* (Paris), No. 12, Apr.-June.

Belier, G. (1987): "Le contrat de travail à durée indéterminée intermittent", in *Droit Social* (Paris), Nos. 9-10, Sep.-Oct.

Belloc, B. (1986): "De plus en plus de salariés à temps partiel", in *Economie et Statistique* (Paris), Nos. 193-194, Nov.-Dec.

Bichot, J. (1987): "L'insertion professionnelle des jeunes", Rapport au Conseil Economique, in *Journal Officiel* (Paris), No. 13, 23 June.

Boyer, R. (1981): *Les transformations du rapport salarial dans la crise: une interprétation de ses aspects économiques et sociaux*. Paris, CEPREMAP, Feb.

—— (ed.)(1986): *La flexibilité du travail en Europe*. Paris, La Découverte.

—— (1987): "Labour flexibilities: Many forms, uncertain effects", in *Labour and Society* (Geneva, IILS), Vol. 12, No. 1, Jan.

Broda, J. (1976): *Problématique de la sous-traitance et du travail temporaire, analyse d'un cas: La zone de Fos et le système Solmer*, thèse de 3ème cycle. Université d'Aix-en-Provence.

Broudic, P.; Espinasse, J.M. (1980): "Les pratiques de gestion de la main-d'oeuvre", in *Travail et Emploi* (Paris), No. 6, Oct.

Bue, J.; Cristofari, M.F. (1986): "Contraintes et rythmes de travail des salariés à temps partiel", in *Travail et Emploi* (Paris), No. 27, Mar.

Cezard, M. (1986): "Le chômage et son halo", in *Economie et Statistique* (Paris), Nos. 193-194, Nov.-Dec.

Colin, J. F.; Espinasse, J. M. (1979): "Les subventions à l'emploi, un essai d'analyse", in *Travail et Emploi* (Paris), No. 1, June.

Corbel, P., Guercoat, J.C. and M.C. Laulhe (1986): "Les mouvements de main-d'oeuvre en 1985: Nouvelle progression des contrats à durée déterminée", in *Economie et Statistique* (Paris), No. 193-194, Nov.-Dec.

Cordova, E. (1986): "From full-time wage employment to atypical employment: A major shift in the evolution of labour relations?", in *International Labour Review* (Geneva, ILO), Vol. 125, No. 6, Nov.-Dec.

Dalle, F.; Bounine, J. (1987): *Pour développer l'emploi*, Rapport au Ministre des Affaires Sociales et de l'Emploi. Paris.

Debordeaux, J. (n.d.): "Travailler au noir, les pratiques d'alternance entre le travail salarié, le chômage et le travail au noir", in *Bulletin de Recherches et Prévisions de la C.N.A.F.*, No. 10.

Dupeyroux, J.J. (1981): "Et maintenant?", in *Droit Social* (Paris), Nos. 7-8, July-Aug.

Elbaum, M. (1986): "Les 'petits boulots': Plus d'un million d'actifs en 1987", in *Economie et Statistique* (Paris), No. 205, Dec.

—— (1988): "Petits boulots, stages, emplois précaires: Quelle flexibilité pour quelle insertion?", in *Droit Social* (Paris), No. 4, Apr.

Fossaert, R. (1981): "Pourquoi et comment normaliser le travail atypique?", in *Droit Social* (Paris), Nos. 7-8, July-Aug.

Gattaz, Y. (1986): "L'emploi, l'emploi, l'emploi", in *La Revue des Entreprises* (Paris, C.N.P.F.), Mar.

de Gaudemar, J.P. (1979): *La mobilisation générale*. Paris, Editions du Champ Urbain.

Germe, J.F. (1981): "Instabilité, précarité et transformation de l'emploi", in *Critiques de l'Economie Politique* (Paris), Nos. 15-16, Apr.-June.

Gollac, M.; Seys, B. (1984): "Les professions et catégories socioprofessionnelles: Premiers croquis, les indépendants", in *Economie et Statistique* (Paris), No. 171-172, Nov.-Dec.

Goupil, N.A.; Termouille, F. (1982): "Le contrat emploi formation en 1980: Un processus de sélection et d'adaptation de la main-d'oeuvre âgée de 16 à 26 ans", in *Travail et Emploi* (Paris), No. 13, July-Sep.

de Grazia, R. (1980): "Clandestine employment: A problem of our times", in *International Labour Review* (Geneva, ILO), Vol. 119, No. 5, Sep.-Oct.

Hallaire, J. (1970): *Le travail à temps partiel dans l'emploi des femmes*. Paris, O.E.C.D.

Kergoat, D. (1981): "Les femmes et le travail à temps partiel: Une relation multiforme et complexe au temps travaillé", in *Travail et Emploi* (Paris), No. 21, Sep.

Klatzman, R. (1982): *Le travail noir*. Paris, P.U.F.

Lae, J.F. (1987): *Travailler au noir*. Colloque européen sur le travail non salarié, vol. V, C.G.P., E.E.C., Dec.

Lebaube, A. (1988a): "L'entreprise atomisée", in *Le Monde des Affaires* (Paris), 26 Mar.

—— (1988b): *L'emploi en miettes*. Paris, Hachette.

Lehmann, A. (1985): "Le travail à temps partiel de 1978 à 1983, pratiques des employeurs et conditions d'emploi des salariés", in *Travail et Emploi* (Paris), No. 26, Dec.

Lucas, Y. (1979): "Le travail à temps partiel", in *Pour une politique du travail 2 – Le travail*. Paris, La Documentation Française.

Lyon-Caen, G. (1980): "Plasticité du capital et nouvelles formes d'emploi", in *Droit Social* (Paris), Nos. 9-10, Sep.-Oct.

—— (1983): "Le recours au travail limité", in *Droit Social* (Paris), No. 1, Jan.

Magaud, J. (1975): "L'éclatement juridique de la collectivité de travail", in *Droit Social* (Paris), No. 12, Dec.

de Maillard, J. et al. (1979): "L'éclatement de la collectivité de travail, observations sur les phénomènes d'extériorisation de l'emploi", in *Droit Social* (Paris), Nos. 9-10, Sep.-Oct.

Maire, E. (1986): "Le chômage peut être vaincu", in *Le Monde* (Paris), 20 Aug.

Malinvaud, E. (1986): *Sur les statistiques de l'emploi et du chômage*. Paris, La Documentation Française.

Mandinaud, J.L. (1985): "La voie étroite", in *Cadres et Maîtrise* (Paris, CGC), Mar.

Marioni, P. (1987): *Les petits boulots*. Colloque européen sur le travail non salarié, vol. V, C.G.P., E.E.C., Dec.

Partrat, M. (1979): "Evolution récente et caractéristiques actuelles du chômage des jeunes", in *Travail et Emploi* (Paris), No. 1, June.

Pelissier, J. (1985): "Travail à durée limitée et droits des salariés", in *Droit Social* (Paris), No. 1, Jan.

—— (1985): "La relation de travail atypique", in *Droit Social* (Paris), Nos. 7-8, July-Aug.

Poulain, G. (1982): "La réforme du contrat à durée déterminée", in *Droit Social* (Paris), No. 4, Apr.

Puel, H. (1981): "Emploi typique et représentation du travail", in *Droit Social* (Paris), Nos. 7-8, July-Aug.

Rettenchach, B. (1979): "Diversité des formes juridiques de travail et restructuration des enterprises", in *Travail et Emploi* (Paris), June.

Revue Française d'Economie (Paris) (1986): "Entretien avec Philippe Séguin, Ministre des Affaires Sociales et de l'Emploi", Summer.

Schmidt, N. (1988): *Les travaux d'utilité collective, des tâches multiples dans un dispositif mouvant*, dossier de recherche No. 20. Paris, Centre d'Etudes de l'Emploi.

The European Omnibus (1978): *Chômage et recherche d'un emploi: Attitudes et opinions des publics européens*, étude 78/31.

Thelot, C. (1986): "Le sous-emploi a doublé en quatre ans", in *Economie et Statistique* (Paris), No. 193-194, Nov.-Dec.

Thelot, C. (1987): *Les formes particulières d'emploi en France*. Conférence internationale sur les nouvelles formes d'emploi, E.E.C., June.

Thille, P. (1981): "L'entreprise éclatée", in *Liaisons Sociales* (Paris), documents, 5 Feb.

Trogan, P. (1984): "L'emploi dans les services: Une croissance quelque peu ambiguë", in *Economie et Statistique* (Paris), No. 171-172, Nov.-Dec.

Vacarie, I. (1980): *L'employeur*. Paris, Sirey.

Villalard, J. (1985): "Les TUC: Dans quels organismes, pour quels travaux?", in *Travail et Emploi* (Paris), No. 26, Dec.

Vitek, J. (1977): *Le travail au noir... un frein à l'emploi*. Geneva, ILO (mimeo).

5 "Bridges" or "traps"? Non-standard employment in the Federal Republic of Germany

Christoph F. Büchtemann and Sigrid Quack[1]

I. Introduction

Until the mid-1970s, paid work conforming to the "standard employment relationship"[2] had not only been growing in the FRG, but had also been the pattern of gainful employment upon which most labour legislation and welfare state regulations were centred. Other types of gainful employment, such as self-employment, part-time work and casual labour, were regarded as diminishing phenomena of peripheral importance, and were accorded little attention. It was not until the unprecedented loss of jobs in key industrial sectors of most Western European countries in the mid-1970s, and the persistent general slowdown in employment growth since the beginning of the 1980s, that "non-standard" forms of employment have attracted much attention from labour-market researchers and policy-makers [Münstermann and De Gijsel, 1981; Dahrendorf et al., 1986; Lindley, 1986; Cordova, 1986].

In the 1980s the proportion of workers engaged in a "standard employment relationship" (henceforth SER) has declined, and growing attention has been paid to the detrimental effects that non-standard forms of employment may imply for the individual worker as well as for labour as a whole. A dominant view, not only held by trade unionists, is that non-standard employment is "precarious" in that it endangers the worker's legal protection and social security, since most welfare state regulations focus on the dominant model of the SER [Bosch, 1986; Möller, 1988].

Non-standard forms of employment thus raise a series of important questions to which answers are still rather scarce. In the present paper we shall focus on the implications of those forms of employment for the social and economic well-being of the workers involved as well as for their social protection. In doing so, we shall "test" the notion frequently put forward by

---

1. Labour Market and Employment Research Unit, Social Science Centre Berlin (WZB). Data in tables in this paper are copyright WZB/AMB 1988.

2. That is, work involving permanent, full-time and dependent employment. See Mückenberger [1985], Leighton [1986], Puel [1980].

critics of non-standard or atypical work that such forms of employment are in any case precarious compared to SER employment.

Non-standard forms of work, indeed, are frequently associated with a lesser degree (or in some cases even absence) of social protection. Many forms of non-standard work may thus be regarded as precarious. In as much as this lesser degree of social protection implies advantages in terms of labour costs and flexibility for the firm, it may act as an incentive for employers to substitute non-standard for standard employment. Furthermore, the erosion of uniform standards that is caused by the growing diversity of work patterns may complicate collective representation of workers in standard employment as well. On the other hand, the relatively unprotected status of many workers in atypical jobs may act as an additional safeguard for the core workforce in standard employment in that employment hazards such as job loss, low pay, and exclusion from fringe benefits are concentrated among those in non-standard employment. Finally, with the persistent shortage in employment opportunities of the standard type, individuals may be forced to accept non-standard employment over longer periods; in those cases non-standard forms of work may, indeed, turn out to be "traps" with respect to the employment and income perspectives of the workers involved.

However, non-standard employment does not necessarily imply an individual "trap". In some cases non-standard forms of work may conform more to the individual's actual life situation and personal preferences than a SER would. Therefore, any treatment of the socio-economic implications of the growth of non-standard forms of work should also take into account ongoing structural changes on the supply side of the labour market, such as the differentiation of socio-biographical patterns and the growing diversity of social roles, life-styles, and work preferences. Thus, on the background of increased female labour force participation, part-time or casual work may well act as a "bridge", enabling women with young children to keep in touch with the labour market rather than temporarily withdrawing from work altogether. For students and school leavers temporary job arrangements may function as a "bridge" into regular employment, especially when firms are reluctant to recruit personnel from the external labour market but prefer to select candidates through informal recruitment channels. In any case, the degree of precariousness inherent in non-standard forms of work depends not only on their relative protection within the context of existing welfare state regulations, but also on specific individual circumstances under which they are pursued. Given the broad spectrum of both life situations and job arrangements covered by the term non-standard employment, it seems worthwhile to discuss the alleged precariousness of non-standard forms of work in more detail in order to assess to which extent they can be considered as "bridges" or rather as "traps" in the labour market.[3]

---

3.   Our analysis is based primarily on two data sources – the annual official population survey (Mikrozensus) and the "Socio-Economic Panel", a population-wide longitudinal survey that has been conducted since 1984 and which provides data for cross-sectional as well as longitudinal analysis (for greater detail, see Hanefeld, 1984).

II. The relative importance of non-standard forms of employment

Non-standard employment has increased considerably in recent years in both absolute and relative terms (figure 1). Among the major categories, *self-employment* accounted for 7.7% of all gainfully employed persons outside agriculture in 1985. While the numbers have been growing recently (by 6.7% between 1982 and 1985 alone), they remain well below the levels of the 1950s and 1960s. A part, but only a part of the recent growth may be regarded as precarious [Büchtemann and Gout, 1988]. Around 14% of all persons in dependent employment (excluding apprenticeship and military conscripts) during the reference week were in *part-time employment* in 1987 (18% of all persons who were employed for at least some time during the year). This type of work began to expand in the 1960s, stagnated from 1976 to 1980, and then grew again (by some 15%) between 1980 and 1986. It is concentrated in services, and in the public sector. Among forms of *temporary work*, *agency work* has also grown significantly over the last 15 years, but it remains marginal (0.3% of the dependent workforce). *Fixed term employment*, on the other hand, accounted for 7% of wage and salary earners in 1987 (14% including apprentices and trainees). The numbers grew significantly between 1983 and 1986, but the trend was reversed when the economy weakened in 1987 [Büchtemann and Höland, 1989].

Figure 1: **Structural change in the labour market and "atypical" forms of work in the Federal Republic of Germany, 1976-1985/6 (in '000 and percent)**

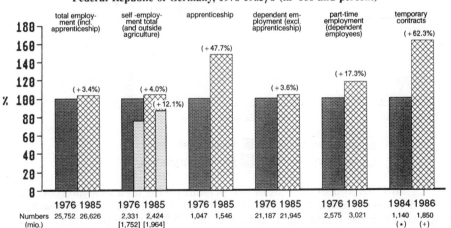

Sources: Mikrozensus 1976-85 except: * EEC-LFS Survey, 1984; + FORSA [1987].

Despite these trends, the SER has remained the predominant type of paid work on the West German labour market. According to the German annual official population survey, 65% of the gainfully employed population was dependently employed in a permanent, full-time job in 1987 (table 1).

The attention paid to non-standard forms of employment, as well as the hopes and fears attached to them in the current debate on employment policy, cannot be explained solely by their net growth. It is rather explained by the overall decline in the number of wage and salary earners and the decrease of full-time jobs which has taken place since the 1970s. In the mid-1980s, there were approximately one million fewer full-time jobs than in the early 1970s and one million more part-time jobs [Brinkmann, Kohler and Reyher, 1986]. By contrast, comparable growth rates of part-time work in the 1960s were accompanied by an expansion of full-time work and overall employment. The integrative capacity of the guiding socio-political notion of SER was not shaken until there coincided an increase in non-standard employment, a decline in standard employment, and persistent high unemployment. Moreover, the significance of non-standard forms of employment for labour market dynamics is revealed when the perspective is shifted from all persons employed at a particular point in time to labour market movements (figure 2).

Figure 2: Patterns of employment seen from different perspectives, FRG, 1984/5 (%)

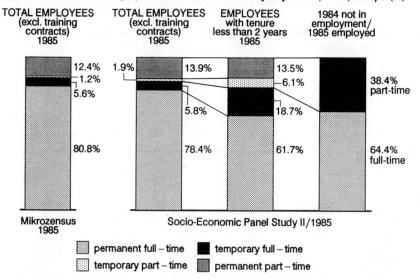

In 1985, almost one out of two persons taking up a new job (coming either from outside the labour force, from unemployment or from another employer) entered a non-standard type of job. Whereas immediate changes of employer take place largely (80%) within the sphere of standard work, 32% of all first entries and almost 60% of all re-entries into the labour market lead to non-standard forms of employment (table 2). Non-standard forms of employment obviously have developed into an important bridge into the employment system. Thus, from the point of view of individual working careers, too, the integrative capacity of the SER seems to be gradually declining.

Table 1: Changing patterns of the labour force in the Federal Republic of Germany, 1976-1987 (in '000 and per cent)

	April/May 1976	May 1980	June 1984	June 1985	May 1986	March 1987*	Percentage change 1976/84	1984/87	1976/87
All persons in the labour force	25,752	26,874	26,608	26,626	26,940	27,073	+ 3,3%	+ 1,7%	+ 5,1%
	100.0%	100.0%	100.0%	100.0%	100.0%	100.0%			
Self-employed in agriculture/forestry	579	505	502	460	436	434	+ 13,3%	-13,5%	-25,0%
	2.2%	1.9%	1.8%	1.7%	1.6%	1.6%			
Self-employed outside agric./forestry	1,752	1,810	1,928	1,964	1,967	1,997	+ 10.0%	+ 3.6%	+ 14.0%
	6.8%	6.7%	7.2%	7.4%	7.3%	7.4%			
Family workers	1,180	924	896	712	718	658	- 24.1%	-26.6%	- 44.2%
	4.6%	3.4%	3.4%	2.7%	2.7%	2.4%			
Apprentices/on temporary training contract	1,047	1,380	1,678	1,546	1,461	1,674	+ 60.3%	- 0.2%	+ 59.9%
	4.1%	5.1%	6.3%	5.8%	5.4%	6.2%			
Permanent full-time[1] employees	18,412[4]	19,550[4]	17,606[5]	17,357[5]	17,500[5]	17,646[5]	- 0.4%	- 0.2%	+ 2.3%
	71.5%	72.7%	66.2%	65.2%	65.0%	65.2%			
Temporary full-time[1] employees			881	1,194	1,320	1,193		+ 35.4%	
			3.3%	4.5%	4.9%	4.4%			
Permanent part-time[2] employees	2,544	2,705	2,666	2,677	2,625	2,792	+ 15.0%	+ 4.7%	+ 20.3%
	9.9%	10.1%	10.0%	10.1%	9.7%	10.3%			
Temporary part-time[2] employees			259	261	286	268		+ 3.5%	
			1.0%	1.0%	1.1%	1.1%			
Other (compulsory military/community service//no answer)	238	–	192	455	627	411	- 19.3%	+114.1%	+ 45.2%
	0.9%	–	0.7%	1.7%	2.3%	1.5%			
Total	100.0%	100.0%	100.0%	100.0%	100.0%	100.0%			
Sum: Part-time[2] employees[6]	2,544	2,705	2,952	3,013	3,098	3,123	+ 16.0%	+ 5.8%	+ 21.8%
	9.9%	10.1%	11.1%	11.3%	11.5%	11.5%			
1-20 hrs. usual working time	1,213	1,459	1,589	1,664	1,743	1,752	+ 31.0%	+ 10.3%	+ 44.4%
	4.7%	5.4%	6.0%	6.2%	6.4%	6.5%			
Sum: employees on fixed-term contracts	(no data available)	(no data available)	1,140	1,455	1,606	1,461	(–)	+ 28.2%	(–)
			4.3%	5.5%	6.0%	5.4%			
Sum: agency workers[3]	17	37	33	49	70	73	+ 94.1%	+121.2%	+ 329.4%
	0.1%	0.1%	0.1%	0.2%	0.3%	0.3%			

Notes: * preliminary; (1) normal weekly working time 36 hrs or more; (2) normal weekly working time 1-35 hrs; (3) registered agency workers (überlassene Arbeitnehmer nach AÜG/Workers' Leasing Act) at the end of June according to statistics supplied by the Federal Employment Agency (Bundesanstalt für Arbeit/BA); (4) including roughly 150-160,000 persons on compulsory military/community service; (5) excluding persons on compulsory military/community service; (6) numbers not equal to sum of "temporary" and "permanent" part-time employees due to missing values in data on type of employment contract.

Sources: Federal Statistical Office (Statistisches Bundesamt), European Labour Force Sample Survey 1984 and "Microzensus" 1985/86/87 - special tabulations on behalf of the WZB/AMB; calculations by the authors.

Table 2: **Dynamics of "non-standard" employment in the FRG, 1984/85**

| | Base projected ('000) | Type of employment arrangement, 1985 (% distrib.) | | | | |
| | | Full-time | | Part-time | | Total |
		Per-manent	Tem-porary	Per-manent	Tem-porary	
Total dependent employees (excl. apprentices) in 1985	21,003	78	6	14	2	100
Thereof 1984/85:						
1. Continuously employed with same employer[1]	17,825	82	4	13	1	100
2. First entrants into employment (incl. after completion of apprenticeship[2])	871	67	22	2	8	100
3. Re-entrants into the labour force[3]	1,443	42	17	33	10	100
4. Persons with change of employer[4]	864	80	10	9	2	100
5. Total entries [(2)-(4)]	3,178	59	14	18	9	100

Notes:

(1)   All persons continuously employed in 1984 and 1985 without intermittent change of employer.

(2)   All persons who have classified themselves as "first entrants into employment" at the time of the 1985 survey or who from 1984 to 1985 have changed from apprenticeship into "regular" employment.

(3)   All persons who have classified themselves as "re-entrants" into employment following a longer spell of non-employment and/or were unemployed/not in the labour force at the time of the previous survey.

(4)   All persons with employment in 1984 and 1985 who in 1985 stated to have changed the employer during the previous 12 months.

Source: The "Socio-Economic Panel", Waves I/1984 and II/1985.

III. A closer look at the characteristics of part-time and fixed-term employment

Part-time and fixed-term employment are the most important forms of non-standard wage employment. Before discussing their implications for the worker's employment and life situation, we briefly describe their major features in the Federal Republic of Germany.

1. Forms of part-time employment

The general category of "part-time employment" encompasses a wide spectrum of heterogeneous working time arrangements. This complicates attempts to derive an overall concept of part-time employment. Therefore, when looking at part-timers' personal and job characteristics, we shall distinguish between "regular" and "marginal" (or "casual") part-time employment and compare them both to the patterns observed for full-time employment. Since more than 90% of the part-time labour force consists of women, we shall concentrate our comparison on female employment.

According to the "Socio-Economic Panel", approximately three million women had a part-time job in 1985 and more than two-thirds of them classified their job as "regular" part-time employment, reporting weekly working hours in the range from 20 to 34 hours, with a strong concentration between 20 and 25 hours "normally" worked per week. Thus, regular part-time employment in most cases refers to the classical half-day part-time work. However, almost one in three women part-timers (900,000 persons) classified their job as "marginal" (or "casual") part-time work, implying under twenty hours per week or casual part-time jobs with highly irregular hours.

Time series data computed from the annual German Population Survey tend to support the assumption that marginal part-time employment involving less than fifteen hours per week has increased disproportionately over the past ten to fifteen years [Büchtemann and Schupp, 1988]. The growing concentration of women's part-time employment in the lower range of working hours is also supported by the fact that the overall volume of hours worked by all part-timers did not increase substantially despite the increase in the number of part-time workers [Brinkmann et al., 1986].

2. Personal characteristics of part-timers

Part-time work in Germany is not only almost exclusively female, but is also largely restricted to specific age groups and family situations [Linkert, 1974; Büchtemann, 1989; Schwarz, 1985]. According to the 1984 Socio-Economic Panel, women part-timers are predominantly over thirty years old (annex table A) except for marginal or casual part-timers, among whom there is a larger group of younger women (50%), often employed while studying or engaged in vocational training.

Part-time jobs are predominantly held by married women (82%). However, only half the women in part-time employment and 60% of the marginally employed among them belong to households with at least one child under sixteen years of age. For some older married women, the children may have already left home, so that approximately two-thirds of women with part-time jobs are in this form of employment in connection with or as a result of child-rearing responsibilities [Hofbauer, 1981]. Nevertheless, nearly every fifth female part-timer is single or divorced and thus certainly does not fit the common notion of the married woman who is employed part-time "to bring home an additional income".

Women part-timers, and particularly those with a marginal part-time job, have a significantly lower level of education and training than women employed full-time. One out of three female part-time employees (47% for the marginally employed) does not have any formal vocational qualification (compared to 21% of all women employed full time). This result only partly reflects the higher average age of women part-timers. Nevertheless, among regular part-time workers the majority have completed some type of vocational training.

Men part-timers who, according to the "Mikrozensus", numbered just under 300,000 in 1985, drastically differ in their personal characteristics from both women part-timers and men employed full-time. Their age pattern is far more polarised than that of the female part-time labour force, one out of two being younger than thirty-five years and a substantial number of them (one-third) even still attending school. On the other hand, roughly 17% of the male part-timers are fifty-five years or older, with most of them already receiving pension benefits. Men part-timers are more likely to hold a university degree than their female counterparts (27% against 7%). These differences indicate that men's motives for working reduced schedules differ from those of women; family responsibilities account for a modest fraction of all men part-timers: only one male part-timer in three lives in a household with children under fifteen years of age.

3. Job characteristics of part-timers

Part-time work is concentrated in the service sector and more particularly in low-skilled service industries such as retail trade, cleaning, catering, and other personal services, which alone account for more than 40% of the total female part-time labour force (as compared to 27% of female full-time workers) and for half (49%) of the marginal part-time workers among them. Partly as an effect of this concentration in the service sector, women part-timers work significantly more frequently in small firms (41% in firms with fewer than twenty employees) than women employed full-time (24%). Once again, this applies especially to women in marginal part-time employment, of whom more than half work in firms not employing more than 20 persons.

An above-average number of women part-timers, particularly among those with a marginal part-time job, work as unskilled or semi-skilled blue and white collar workers and perform simple service and administrative jobs. Many of these jobs neither require any specific training nor provide an opportunity for acquiring (additional) skills. Thus, 44% of all women part-timers and 60% of the women with marginal part-time jobs stated that their work required no specific skills or instructions whatsoever. Similarly, 47% of all women part-timers and, again, 60% of those with a marginal part-time job declared that their present job provided no opportunity at all to acquire any further skills.

For women who have had formal vocational training, part-time work often seems to imply a process of losing acquired skills. In 1984, nearly half of these part-time employees no longer worked in the occupational field for which they had been trained (62% of marginal part-time workers). Accordingly, the overwhelming majority of women part-timers (75% as compared to 53% of all women employed full-time) did not expect any occupational advancement for the next two years. However, there is again a significant group of women part-timers who do not fit the previously described type of unqualified part-time work. About one woman in three regular part-timers (roughly 700,000 persons) thought that her job required full vocational training or even a university degree. They were mostly white collar workers in service, administrative, semi-professional and professional jobs.

Men part-timers, too, perform low-level tasks more frequently than their full-time colleagues. On the other hand, they are more often employed in professional occupations like teaching or research, indicating that, if anyone, it is primarily men in highly qualified positions who can afford to reduce their work time [Bielenski and Hegner, 1985; Strümpel et al., 1987; Büchtemann, 1989].

4. Personal characteristics of fixed-term workers

Unlike part-time work, fixed-term employment is concentrated among younger workers in the early period of their occupational careers (annex table B). In 1985 every second worker on a fixed-term employment contract was under thirty years of age, and 16% of them had become gainfully employed for the first time or had transferred from in-plant training (apprenticeship) to their first regular job only since the previous year (compared to only 3% of the employees with permanent work contracts). Many younger fixed-term workers are still in education. In 1985 this was true for almost one fifth of all men and one tenth of all women having fixed-term employment contracts.

This peculiar age pattern is reflected in the family situation of fixed-term workers: almost one in two fixed-term workers (43%), male and female alike, are unmarried. Only 23% of the men and 36% of the women have a family with children under sixteen (compared with 52% of the men and 40% of the women in permanent employment). By contrast, nearly every fifth person in this group of employees still lives with his or her parents (compared with less than 10% among their colleagues with a permanent contract). Consequently, a higher proportion of fixed-term workers (29%) than their permanent colleagues (16%) have not yet completed their vocational training. At the same time a significant share of the former holds a university degree (22% as opposed to 14%). This characteristic of workers with a fixed-term contract is true of both men and women.

5. Job characteristics of fixed-term workers

The jobs held by fixed-term workers show a strongly polarised skill pattern: fixed-term workers are employed as unskilled or semi-skilled blue and white collar workers more frequently (42%) than their colleagues in permanent employment (31%) and more often perform tasks that at best require a short period of initial training (52% against 38%). Fixed-term employment often implies an occupational downgrading of workers who, though they completed formal training, cannot capitalise on it because they are not employed in the field for which they were trained (37% of the fixed-term employees with completed vocational training as opposed to 17% of the permanent employees). On the other hand, fixed-term workers perform tasks that they report as requiring a university degree more frequently than their colleagues with permanent employment contracts.

This highly polarised structure of skills and the relatively low average age of fixed-term personnel may influence their comparatively favorable assessment of their opportunities for occupational advancement: 31% of the men and 16% of the women with fixed-term employment consider occupational advancement to be either certain or probable in the near future (as compared to 23% of the men and 13% of the women with permanent contracts; annex table B).

IV. Is non-standard employment precarious?

Accounting for more than one third of the total labour force, non-standard work can hardly be considered atypical, at least in quantitative terms. However, the terms "atypical" or "non-standard" employment allude primarily to the regulatory structure of most European labour markets, with the "standard" type of permanent, full-time employment as reference point. Consequently, the recent debate about non-standard forms of work has focused largely on their lack of social protection, of regulation by labour law, of social security provisions, and of collectively determined standards. Non-standard forms of employment have been generally regarded as more precarious in terms of both employment security and income maintenance.

1. Legal status and protection of non-standard forms of work

By definition, non-standard forms of work exhibit a series of particularities within the labour market's regulatory framework. Most regulations in the area of labour law, social security, and collective bargaining agreements exclude all forms of work that do not have the legal status of employee, i.e. self-employment, freelancing, and outwork (including family workers). But (dependent) part-time and fixed-term employment in Germany also tend to be directly or indirectly disadvantaged in terms of protective regulations.

A. Part-time work

Part-time employment is directly disadvantaged through both legal and collective regulations, which restrict protection or benefits to jobs above certain weekly working time thresholds. Part-time workers are:

–   excluded from paid sick leave if employed as blue-collar workers for less than ten hours a week or forty-five hours per month (paragraph 1, *Lohnfortzahlungsgesetz*). In 1986, this applied to roughly 170,000 persons or 6% of all part-timers.

–   exempted from compulsory contributions to both National Health Insurance and the Statutory Pension Scheme if their usual working time is less than fifteen hours per week and their monthly gross earnings are below a minimum threshold (currently DM 440). In 1986, this was true of 12% of all part-time workers[4].

–   excluded from the public Unemployment Insurance Scheme, and consequently not entitled to any benefits in case of job loss, if their weekly working time does not exceed seventeen (1986: eighteen) hours [Benner, 1987]. In 1986, this applied to 23% of part-time workers.[5]

In addition, part-timers with working hours below a certain threshold (usually 15 hours per week) are excluded from a number of collective agreements on pay and fringe benefits such as thirteenth salary, holiday allowances and additional paid leave, as well as firm-specific saving and pension schemes [Kurz-Scherf, 1984]. In 1985, about 20% of all female part-timers received none of the most common fringe benefits such as a thirteenth salary, Christmas bonus or holiday allowance (compared to only 3% of female full-time workers). Only a small minority (15%) of the female part-timers is covered by firm-specific pension schemes (compared to 26% of women employed full-time). Collective agreements tend to exclude part-time wage and salary earners from special overtime compensation by restricting the definition of overtime to hours exceeding the full-time work standard, presently between 37 and 40 hours per week. Last but not least, in most cases collectively determined standards and rules governing the distribution of weekly and annual working time do not apply to part-timers, their working time being subject only to individual agreement between employer and employee.

Apart from these types of direct discrimination, part-time workers are indirectly disadvantaged because they are concentrated in small firms, to which a number of protective regulations do not apply (such as protection against unfair dismissal in firms with fewer than six regular employees) and

---

4.   These data refer to all part-timers except civil servants, who generally are not subject to social security contributions. Part-timers who are not obliged to contribute to the National Health Scheme are often covered by the contributions of another family member.

5.   The data refer to all part-timers except civil servants, who due to the system of life-long appointment are generally excluded from both contributions to and benefits from the unemployment insurance system.

which normally do not have a works council to represent workers and employees on the shop-floor.

This brief overview demonstrates that while part-time work is by no means all precarious in terms of legal and collective protection, legal and institutional disadvantages tend to cumulate within certain categories of part-time employment, namely those considered to be more or less marginal because of the low number of weekly working hours involved. While part-timers with a regular part-time job involving twenty hours or more per week suffer only minor disadvantages, marginal part-time workers, especially those falling below the working time threshold of 15 hours per week, face an array of disadvantages and discriminations.

B. Fixed-term work

By definition, workers with fixed-term employment contracts are excluded from all regulations concerning protection from unfair dismissal and redundancy procedures. At the end of its term, the contract expires without the requirement of any notice from the employer, even in cases in which special job-protection regulations (guaranteeing a person's job in case of maternity, compulsory military service, or disability) apply to permanent workers. Moreover, many wage and salary earners on fixed-term contracts are also excluded from collectively bargained fringe benefits and company profit-sharing schemes unless their fixed-term contract exceeds a certain minimum duration, which can range from three to twelve months [Büchtemann and Höland, 1989].

Fixed-term workers tend to be indirectly discriminated against by legal and collective-bargaining regulations that require a minimum length of employment. To qualify for paid sick leave, for example, a worker must have been in his job for at least four weeks with the same employer. Usually, paid leave is granted only after six months of continuous work with the same employer. A minimum of two months is also required for a job to be subject to compulsory social security contributions, shared equally between employer and employee.

In most cases, the extra payments and social security benefits that fixed-term workers could receive depend largely upon the duration of their current contract or, if a person has successive fixed-term engagements with the same employer, upon the total duration of the employment relationship (unless interruptions exceed certain limits, usually four months). According to a survey conducted in 1985 by the Bundesvereinigung der Deutschen Arbeitgeberverbände, 73% of all fixed-term employment contracts in private industry did not exceed six months (thus falling short even of the minimum period required for job protection in the case of a permanent employment contract).[6] As shown by data from the Socio-Economic Panel for 1985, almost 50% of the workers employed on a fixed-term contract at a particular

---

6.   FORSA [1987] found that 25% of all fixed-term contracts did not exceed six months. The data, however, are based on the stock of fixed-term personnel at a given point in time and therefore tend to grossly underestimate the percentage of short-term engagements among all fixed-term contracts concluded during a specific period.

point in time[7] did not receive any fringe benefits like a thirteenth salary, Christmas bonus, or holiday allowance, whereas this was true of only a small minority of the persons who had been working under a permanent contract for the same length of time [Büchtemann and Höland, 1989]. Like marginal part-time work, temporary employment seems to be associated with lower labour costs for the employer.

2. Other dimensions of precariousness

Legal and collective regulation covers only one aspect of the overall life and employment situation of non-standard workers and does not automatically decide its precarious character. The degree of actual material protection and well-being enjoyed by workers is to a large extent determined by the level of their earned income. An employee's private household situation is another important factor, because it affects the individual's standard of living in terms of other household incomes and the needs that the total household income has to satisfy. This, in particular, applies to part-time and casual employees.

The fact that an employment relationship does not come under protection from unfair dismissal or that a person is not insured against unemployment says little in itself about the actual stability of that employment relationship or that person's actual risk of unemployment. An initially fixed-term employment relationship does not necessarily end when the contract expires; it can be transformed into a permanent contract or renewed as a succession of fixed-term relationships. And vice versa a formal permanent employment contract does not guarantee protection from dismissal and the loss of one's job.

The lack of security frequently associated with non-standard employment has implications for the material livelihood of older workers. They depend essentially on the length of time a person has been working in such jobs, how they fit into that person's overall occupational career, and how, if so desired, a worker could achieve the transition to a SER.

In some instances, non-standard forms of employment may correspond better to the specific living situation and working time preferences of a worker than a SER. This could be the case, for example, with students or retired persons, who hold the position as a second job or who are supplementary earners in a household. It might also be the case with persons whose private and family situations restrict their availability on the labour market or who for other reasons, such as leisure preferences or further training, do not want a full-time job.

---

7. This figure, too, underestimates the number of brief, fixed-term employment contracts as a percentage of all such contracts concluded during the year. Consequently, the share of fixed-term workers who receive no fringe benefits must be significantly higher.

3. Part-timers

When part-time work is referred to as precarious, the income situation of part-timers is an important consideration. In the West German debate, however, this consideration is either too narrowly restricted to the dimension of personal earnings or too quickly dismissed by arguing that part-timers are earning that income only "on the side". On the contrary, we think that the income situation of part-timers has to be analysed from both the perspective of personal earnings and the perspective of total household incomes.

A. Personal earned income

In view of the average work volume of women employed part-time, it is not surprising that their wages are strongly concentrated at the lower end of the income scale. According to data from the Socio-Economic Panel, the monthly net earnings of 75% of regular and virtually all marginal female part-timers in 1985 fell into the lowest income quintile (the 20% of all workers with the lowest monthly earnings).

In most cases, these earnings are so low in absolute terms that single-person households could barely make ends meet without other sources of income: in 1985 nearly 80% of all women part-timers had monthly net earnings not exceeding DM 1,000. Approximately one third of all women part-timers (32%) earned even less than DM 540 per month. Only in a few cases (8% of all female part-timers) did net incomes exceed DM 1,500 per month.

Besides the low number of weekly working hours of most part-timers, these figures reflect the low level of qualification of the majority of part-time jobs. Part-timers can at best earn moderately high incomes in more highly qualified positions, but such jobs are the exception.

In a series of recent studies concerning other countries, the differential in overall wages between women part-timers and full-timers has been in part explained as a result of more or less direct wage discrimination against part-timers [Robinson and Wallace, 1981; Ermisch and Wright, 1988; Ehrenberg et al., 1988; Levitan and Conway, 1988]. However, in terms of gross wage per hour, no direct wage discrimination can be found in West Germany between women with a regular part-time job and those with full-time employment [Büchtemann and Schupp, 1988; Schoer, 1986]. But the picture changes when we look at the group of marginal part-timers: after allowing for skill level, we have found their average hourly gross earnings (DM 9.61) to be significantly lower than the earnings of regular part-timers (DM 10.78) and full-time employees (DM 10.86) (annex table A). This wage differential, however, levels off when average net earnings per hour are considered. Because marginal part-timers are frequently exempted from mandatory social security contributions and because of a special 10% flat-rate tax relief for low-income earners (*Lohnsteuerpauschalierung*), the average net hourly wage earned by female marginal part-timers in 1984 (DM 7.92) was slightly higher than that of regular part-timers (DM 7.22). For the marginal part-timer, of course, this short-term advantage in terms of hourly wage is "overcompensated" by the lack of eligibility for social security benefits and, hence, increased income hazards in the medium or long run [Büchtemann and Schupp, 1988].

However, for approximately 75% of all part-timers whose weekly schedules exceed eighteen hours and who, therefore, are subject to mandatory contributions to the Unemployment Insurance Scheme, the principle of equivalence between contributions and benefits means that the level of expected benefits in case of job loss does not guarantee a subsistence level income[8]. If these part-timers lose their jobs and become unemployed, their likely average unemployment compensation would not exceed 37% of the average monthly net earnings of women full-timers. To make ends meet, they require additional sources of income or supplementary public transfers (such as means-tested welfare benefits).

B. Household incomes

The overwhelming majority of female part-timers (80%) live in households with at least one other earner, in most cases a full-time earner. Because of low earnings, part-time work usually requires at least one additional full-time earner in the family in order to assure a sufficient household income. Nevertheless, nearly one in five female part-timers lives in a household without another person receiving a full-time salary. Such instances frequently involve single-person households (33%), single mothers with children (14%), wives of unemployed men (14%) and persons already drawing retirement benefits. In 1984 about half of these part-time households without at least one full-time earner were dependent on additional income from public transfer payments [Büchtemann and Schupp, 1988].

To get an idea of the extent to which other household incomes supplement low earnings from part-time work, we have calculated per capita net household incomes (table 3).

In 1985, the average per capita net household income for women part-timers as a whole was DM 1,300, slightly less than that of all dependent wage and salary earners (DM 1,456). However, there are differences, depending on the type of part-time job and the type of household involved:

–   The average per capita household income of regular women part-timers in both "couple" households[9] (DM 1,570) and family households (DM 1,336) differs only slightly from the corresponding figures for all wage and salary earners in comparable households (DM 1,651 and DM 1,223 respectively). Clearly, regular part-time jobs are frequently held by women with spouses in better-paying jobs (white collar workers or civil servants) [for comparable results, see Stück, 1989].

---

8.   Unemployment benefits do not exceed a maximum of 68% of the former net wages, excluding extra payments.

9.   A "couple" household is defined as a (married) couple without children; a family household, as a three-or-more-person household in which the worker lives with a spouse and at least one child under sixteen years of age.

Table 3:   Average monthly household and per capita income according to working time and
type of household in the Federal Republic of Germany, 1985[1] (in DM)

	All house-holds	family household with children	married couple without child	single parent with children	single person hsehold
Dependent employees total[2]	1,456	1,223	1,651	1,729	1,944
thereof:[3]					
- full-time employees	1,484	1,214	1,674	1,854	2,025
- part-time employees	1,316	1,256	1,526	1,070	1,354
- "regular" part-time	1,416	1,332	1,591	1,114	(1,874)
- "marginal" part-time	1,054	1,039	(901)	(851)	(1,052)
Dependent employees women[4]	1,482	1,296	1,690	1,374	1,751
thereof:[3]					
- full-time employees	1,596	1,342	1,761	1,507	1,883
- part-time employees	1,300	1,267	1,531	1,061	(1,146)
- "regular" part-time	1,381	1,336	1,570	1,099	(1,413)
- "marginal" part-time	1,036	1,051	(1,010)	(827)	(995)

Notes:
(1)   Derived from non-standardised statements of monthly net household income. Per
capita incomes are calculated as follows: monthly net household income divided by
the number of persons living in the household, adults being weighted with a factor
of 1, children under 16 years with a factor of 0.5.
(2)   Base not weighted: 5,369 employees; base extrapolated: 21,410 thousand employees.
(3)   Subjective self-classification as "fully employed", "in regular part-time employment"
or "in marginal or irregular part-time employment".
(4)   Base not weighted: 2,062 employees; base extrapolated: 8,390 thousand employees.
( ) = Values in brackets are based on less than 30 cases.

Source: The "Socio-Economic Panel", Wave I/1984 and Wave II/1985, longitudinal analysis.

–   A different pattern emerges for marginal women part-timers: their
average per capita incomes are conspicuously below the average for all
wage and salary earners in comparable households (40% lower in
couple households, and 15% lower in family households). Besides the
earnings level of marginal women part-timers, those types of jobs are
obviously held more often by persons in households where the
household head also earns a relatively low income.

–   The situation is especially unfavorable for women part-timers living
alone or as a single parent, and again particularly for those with a
marginal part-time job: their average per capita incomes are
approximately 40% below the average for all wage and salary earners
living in households of the same type. This also means that the public
transfer payments drawn simultaneously in most of these cases do not
adequately compensate for low incomes from work.

Just as working in a part-time job requires at least one other income in the household (a reality reflected by the unfavorable income situation of single part-timers), most households with a part-time and a full-time income could not forego the additional income from part-time work without incurring financial difficulties: without the extra income from part-time work, the average per capita income in these households would be lower than in the control group of multi-member households with only one full-time earner [Büchtemann and Schupp, 1988]. Moreover, given the conditions at the time, the results show that part-time work represents an acceptable alternative to full-time employment almost exclusively for married women whose spouse has a full-time job in the middle or higher income categories. For all the other groups, the income from part-time employment is at best a stopgap for dealing with family requirements [Büchtemann and Schupp, 1988; Büchtemann, 1989]. Considering the low level of individual earnings, the frequent lack of social protection, and the relatively low household incomes associated with it, the disproportionate increase in the number of marginal part-time jobs is a serious problem.

C. Job stability and unemployment risks

In the current debate, unions in particular have frequently assumed that part-time employment is used as an employment "buffer" to cushion economic downturns and, therefore, implies high risks of job loss and subsequent unemployment. But the available evidence for West Germany tends to refute this view. The very concentration of part-time jobs in the administrative and service area entails less cyclical fluctuation than for a large number of full-time jobs in production. The only sector in which part-time employment is subject to slight cyclical fluctuations is manufacturing, but only a small minority of part-timers are employed in this sector [Brinkmann and Kohler, 1981].

The notion that part-time work means less stability of employment is also refuted at the micro-level. Although women part-timers frequently have a discontinuous work history[10] and are disproportionately in low-skill jobs, there are on the whole no differences between women full-timers and women part-timers with respect to the length of employment with their current employer (annex table A). According to the Socio-Economic Panel, in 1984 about 60% of both groups had worked for their present employer for at least five years.

Marginal women part-timers, however, showed a significantly higher degree of job instability. Again in 1984, more than half of them (56%) had worked for their current employer for less than five years, and one third (32%) of women working less than fifteen hours per week had been with their employer for less than a year. About one in four marginal women part-timers (24%) had worked for a total of three or more employers

---

10.   According to Hofbauer [1982], this is true for about half of women part-timers. See also Werner [1984].

between 1974 and 1984 (compared to 16% of the full-time and 14% of the regular part-time employees).[11]

Reliable statements about the relative risk of dismissal and unemployment can only be made on the basis of panel data. Such a longitudinal study, started in 1984, shows that women part-timers, even those with a marginal part-time job, were not more frequently unemployed than women working full time (only 4% of both groups were unemployed a year later; annex table A) [Büchtemann, 1989]. These results confirm those from an earlier longitudinal study, according to which women employed part-time in 1978 had neither been more often dismissed by their employers in the subsequent four years (even during the severe recession of 1981), nor did they more frequently experience unemployment than women employed on a full-time basis [Büchtemann, 1983].

Nevertheless, women part-timers have a significantly higher level of employment instability, which stems from their higher frequency of withdrawal from the labour market. Here too, there exist significant differences between regular and marginal women part-timers: among those holding a regular part-time job in 1984, 6% left their jobs temporarily or permanently in the subsequent twelve months, a proportion hardly higher than that among their full-time counterparts (4%); whereas one in six (17%) marginal part-timers did so, thus again reaffirming the highly "fluid" and transitory character of such job arrangements.

These findings are reflected in the workers' subjective perceptions and future anticipations:

–   The share of women part-timers, including marginal women part-timers, who consider their jobs to be relatively secure is just as great as that of women employed full time. In both groups only 7% think it is certain or at least likely that they will (involuntarily) lose their jobs in the next two years.

–   The share of regular women part-timers who are considering quitting their jobs in the next two years (12%) is not much higher than for women with full-time jobs (10%). By contrast, 16% of the marginal women part-timers think it is certain or at least likely that they will withdraw from their jobs within the next two years (annex table A).

Thus, part-timers, whether regular or marginal, do not face higher risks of involuntary job loss and subsequent unemployment. The relatively high degree of employment instability of marginal part-timers, however, requires explanations which take into account the effects of discouragement resulting from their rather unfavorable employment conditions as well as the particular supply side constraints of these workers [Büchtemann, 1989].

---

11.   As the duration of employment with the present employer could only be observed up to the date of the survey, the short average employment duration of marginal part-timers may partly result from the general increase in marginal part-time work in recent years.

D. Working time flexibility

Part-time employment is frequently held to be more "flexible" than full-time work in the sense that it allows a better matching of working hours with short-term variations in labour demand, due to such factors as varying customer demand or unforeseen short-term production fluctuations. Indeed, recent studies have shown part-time work to feature a high degree of working time flexibility. In 1985 more than one in four female part-timers (29% as compared to 20% of women employed full time) reported their daily and weekly working schedules to vary strongly with demand [Büchtemann, 1989].

From the workers' point of view, however, flexibility also implies the possibility of switching between different working time arrangements, say, from full-time to part-time work and vice versa as individual circumstances or working time preferences change over the life cycle. Since part-time work in most cases seems to correspond to specific life situations (motherhood and family obligations), and to presume a particular household pattern (mainly the existence of additional income sources in the household), it is of prime importance to consider the opportunities to return to full-time work when these circumstances no longer apply.

Examining the work histories of part-timers, we found that they experience a high degree of working time mobility. According to the Socio-Economic Panel, some 80% of women part-timers had worked full time in previous years, whereas only 10% of the women presently working full time had worked part time in their work biography – a pattern that applies even within identical age cohorts. Apart from individual preferences, this finding might also indicate that changes from full-time to part-time work are easier than from part-time to full-time because they involve fewer demand-side barriers (such as the higher skill requirements for full-time jobs) than changes in the opposite direction. This interpretation is supported by a recent survey where 20% of all women with part-time work experiences between 1980 and 1985 perceived the lack of opportunities to return to full-time schedules as one of the prime drawbacks of part-time work [Bielenski and Strümpel, 1988].

The greater working time mobility of part-timers compared to full-timers is indicated by a longitudinal perspective as well.[12] According to the Socio-Economic Panel nine out of ten persons (92%) working full time in 1984 were still working full time one year later. Over the same period fewer than one in fifty full-time workers (300,000-350,000) actually changed to part-time work (almost exclusively regular). By contrast, 11% of part-timers switched to full-time schedules in 1984-85, their absolute number (about 370,000), however, not significantly exceeding that of full-timers switching to part-time work during the same time-span.

Again, mobility between working time categories (which does not necessarily imply a change of job or employer) is largely concentrated within the group of marginal part-timers, which shows that marginal part-time work

---

12. The following sections refer to all part-timers opposed to all full-timers.

frequently functions as a "bridge" to regular part-time employment rather than as a "trap" in which workers are involuntarily held for longer periods. By 1985, 33% of the "marginal" part-timers of 1984 (roughly 325,000) had moved into regular part-time jobs, and another 10% (about 100,000) had moved into full-time employment. Only a minority of about 36% (350,000) of the "marginal" part-time labour force of 1984 had stayed in marginal part-time jobs during the twelve-month observation period. This finding reaffirms the highly transient nature of most employment arrangements in this category. By contrast, the working hours of regular part-timers are highly stable, with 75% of them remaining in regular part-time jobs and less than 3% classifying their job as marginal part-time work at the time of the subsequent interview in 1985.

E. Working time preferences of part-timers

Patterns of mobility between different categories of working time arrangements allow no conclusions to what extent part-time work is "involuntary" in the sense that a full-time job is preferred but not found. The question of voluntary versus involuntary part-time work has been dealt with in a series of recent American studies, which have concluded that a considerable part of the recent growth in part-time employment in the United States was due to involuntary part-timers who would prefer working on a full-time basis if suitable full-time jobs could be found [Ehrenberg et al., 1988]. Voluntary part-time work in this context means that supply-side rather than demand-side factors and constraints on the labour market account for the individual's option to work on a part-time basis. For the FRG, evidence from the annual European Labour Force Sample Survey (EEC-LFSS) tends to indicate that only a small fraction of part-timers can be classified as involuntary: in 1986, only 8% (about 250,000 persons) stated that they were working part-time because they had not found a full-time job, a percentage which, however, has shown a moderate increase over recent years [Büchtemann, 1989].

This general picture is largely confirmed by a comparison of actual and preferred working time among part-timers on the basis of information supplied by the Socio-Economic Panel for 1985. On the question about how many hours per week they personally preferred to work, assuming that their income from work would vary accordingly, almost 90% of all part-timers chose working times within the range of what is commonly classified as "part-time" work (i.e. not exceeding thirty-four hours per week). A total of 11% of the part-time labour force (about 350,000 persons) preferred to work full time (thirty-five hours or more per week). The slightly higher share of "involuntary" part-timers revealed by the "Socio-Economic Panel" (11%) as compared to the EEC-LFSS (8%) may be due to the differently worded questions in the two surveys. Given that the vast majority of part-timers seem to work part time on a voluntary basis, it is interesting to note that the desire to work more hours per week is expressed significantly more often (41%) by "marginal" part-timers, out of whom 29% percent would prefer a regular part-time job, and 12% would prefer to work full-time. By contrast, only 10% of those part-timers working between twenty and thirty-four hours per week would prefer to work fewer than twenty hours per week. Regular part-time employment thus clearly emerges as the working time arrangement preferred by the vast majority of part-timers. Involuntary part-time work seems to be largely concentrated in the segment of marginal part-time work, implying that the preferred alternative is not full-time but rather regular part-time work.

With regard to the 11% of the part-time labour force (roughly 350,000 persons) preferring to work full-time, the data available do not allow any conclusions about the extent to which their short working hours reflect constraints inherent in their family situation or demand-side barriers preventing a return to full-time schedules.

F. Part-timers and provision for the future

One of the most serious hazards associated with part-time work is the status of part-timers in the public pension scheme and the relative level of income maintenance they can expect upon reaching retirement age. As stated earlier, a considerable and growing portion of part-timers (12%, or roughly 350,000 persons in 1986) is exempted from mandatory contributions to the Statutory Pension Plan. According to data from West Germany's annual official population survey, 31% of that group had never in their lives paid contributions into the public pension scheme. But even for part-timers who are subject to mandatory contributions, the level of contributions is far below the overall average because of their low average income.

Few conclusions can be drawn regarding the likely pension level of part-timers solely on the basis of their current earned income, because the level of individual benefits drawn from the Statutory Pension Plan is determined essentially by two factors: (i) the overall number of years during which contributions were paid[13] and (ii) the average earned income subject to contributions until retirement age is reached. The level of the benefits to which an individual is entitled is calculated according to a formula based on the assumption that forty years of full-time contributions would amount to a pension providing a standard of living comparable to that enjoyed during the beneficiary's working years [Landenberger, 1985].

Thus, the total employment biography is much more crucial in determining the level of pension benefits than is the level of earnings at a given point in time. Previous studies about income and employment biographies have largely focused on career interruptions rather than on varying patterns of working time during the career. In our analysis (based on data from the Socio-Economic Panel) we have tried to combine both aspects in order to get a rough idea of the impact of part-time work upon a person's provision for the future. The results show that part-time workers' previous work histories deviate from the "standard occupational biography" assumed by the calculation principles of the Statutory Pension Plan:

---

13.   This number includes the years spent in education, military service, maternity, and other life situations during which one is not obliged to pay into the scheme but which count toward the total period that a person is insured.

- Every second woman employed part-time in 1984 had been working part-time for more than six years uninterruptedly.

- About two-thirds of women part-timers – including four-fifths of those older than 45 years – had interrupted their career at least once, the proportion of part-time women who have done so being clearly higher than among women employed full time in all the age groups considered.

Drawing on these data about work histories, we calculated how much of their potential life-time employment (and, hence, their potential years of social security contributions) the respondents had realised up to the time of the survey.[14] These calculations showed that only one in five women part-timers of 1984 had worked three-quarters or more of her potential life-time employment. Almost one out of two women part-timers had worked less than half of her potential life-time employment. In terms of realised employment as a proportion of potential life-time employment, regular women part-timers differ little from marginal women part-timers and younger women among them little from older ones.

For most women with part-time jobs in 1984, such employment was not a short interlude in an otherwise continuous work history of full-time employment. On the contrary, the work histories of most women part-timers are incomplete and riddled with periods of non-employment.

Older women part-timers who had worked less than three-quarters of their potential life-time employment by 1984 are unlikely to catch up by the time they reach retirement age. Younger women part-timers, on the other hand, still have more opportunities for increasing their retirement benefits by accumulating longer periods of full employment in the future. Even so, their future occupational patterns would have to be significantly more continuous and concentrated on full-time employment than those of their older part-time colleagues, in order to fulfill the requirements of a "standard occupational biography" at the time of retirement.

If the previous career patterns are extrapolated into the future – an assumption supported by the higher share of female part-time workers in the older age groups – then one can predict that the retirement benefits paid to most women employed part-time today will be well below the level necessary to maintain an adequate standard of living in old age. Most of the women part-timers of today will be dependent on their spouses' retirement income and, if they are single without dependents, on supplementary public transfer payments. Given the growing instability of marriage as reflected in rising divorce rates, most part-time employment thus must be considered precarious at least in the medium or long term. As the increase in female

---

14.   The potential life-time employment up to 1984 was defined as the number of years since the person was fifteen years old minus the duration of the individual's training, that is, the number of years in which the person concerned could theoretically have been gainfully employed up to the date of the survey. The realized life-time employment up to 1984 is defined as the sum of the years in which the person was actually employed, with years of full employment being weighted with a factor of 1 and years of part-time employment being weighted with a factor of 0.5.

labour force participation is more likely to take the form of part-time than full-time employment, women's economic independence in their old age is not guaranteed, given the principles of the current public pension system [Rolf and Wagner, 1988].

4. Fixed-term workers

By reducing costs of dismissals due to variations in demand, fixed-term job arrangements are seen as a means to reduce labour costs and thus to exert a positive influence on employers' hiring decisions in the economic upturn. However, critics of recent legislative changes facilitating the conclusion of fixed-term contracts (the 1985 Employment Promotion Act/*Beschäftigungsförderungsgesetz*) have argued that these regulative measures have failed to increase the overall level of employment. They have also pointed out that, by offering no job protection, fixed-term contracts encourage employers to revert to a strategy of short-term "hiring-and-firing". Such a strategy entails increased medium-term risks of job loss and unemployment, and eventually results in increased segmentation and competition between unprotected "outsiders" and protected "insiders" in the labour market.

In order to assess the relative precariousness of fixed-term employment arrangements, we have analysed earnings, social security coverage, employment stability, and risk of unemployment over time.

A. Earnings

A look at the distribution of net earnings received by fixed-term workers reveals that they are clustered in the lower income bracket to a far greater extent than one would expect from the skill level of their jobs and to a far greater extent than persons with permanent employment contracts. According to data from the 1985 Socio-Economic Panel, 57% of the approximately 1.5 million fixed-term workers earned less than DM 1,500 net per month, compared with 31% of workers with permanent contracts. Only a small minority of the fixed-term workers in the sample had monthly net earnings exceeding DM 2,000 in 1985, as compared to 42% of all workers with permanent contracts.

These differences exist among people employed full-time as well. Even in that group, 11% of those with fixed-term contracts earned less than DM 1,000 net per month compared to only 3% of those with a permanent contract; only 26% of full-time workers with fixed-term contracts earned more than DM 2,000 compared to 50% of permanent full-time workers. The low income level of many fixed-term workers must be considered in the light of results from the annual official population survey (*Mikrozensus*), according to which, in 1986, earned income was the prime source of living for the overwhelming majority of fixed-term employees (92%). Unlike most marginal part-timers, fixed-term workers are not persons for whom earned income only supplements other (primary) sources of livelihood.

The less favorable overall income situation of fixed-term workers is not fully accounted for by the low average skill level of their jobs or their comparatively low average age:

- Among unskilled and semi-skilled workers, the average gross hourly wages are lower among fixed-term permanent workers. In 1985, a gross hourly wage of less than DM 13 was earned by 74% of the workers with a fixed-term contract as compared to 64% of those with permanent contracts (with a similar differential of 42% against 15% for skilled white-collar employees).

- These wage differentials do not shrink appreciably even when the age variable is held constant: in 1985, 90% of fixed-term workers aged under 30 in unskilled or semi-skilled jobs earned less than DM 13 per hour, which was the case for only 72% of the permanent employees in the same age group and the same type of job.

Apart from the fact that fixed-term workers tend to be concentrated in rather low-paid service jobs, one can assume that the remaining income differential between fixed-term and permanent employees can be accounted for mainly by seniority (length of service). Junior colleagues usually start with collectively bargained minimum wages and are frequently excluded, either explicitly or implicitly, from company profit-sharing schemes and collectively bargained fringe benefits. This has persistent negative effects on workers with a succession of several fixed-term contracts, interrupted by intermittent spells of unemployment, who thus never accumulate enough seniority to qualify for wage increases and fringe benefits. In addition to the income losses incurred during intermittent periods of non-employment, these workers are in danger of losing their link to the income dynamics of their age cohorts in the medium term. Furthermore, fixed-term workers more frequently (12% in 1986) than their permanent counterparts (2%) do not qualify for compulsory contributions to the Statutory Pension Plan.[15] All in all, these results tend to support the assumption that total labour costs associated with some fixed-term job arrangements are distinctly lower than those of permanent job arrangements at the same skill level. For the employer, this can certainly act as an incentive to substitute fixed-term for permanent jobs, at least in the segment of low skill activities entailing minimal fixed costs (i.e. for recruiting and training).

B. Employment stability and unemployment risk

In the continuous debate over employment policy, the alleged higher risk of job loss and unemployment must certainly be regarded as the most serious argument against promoting fixed-term work. This view is supported by recent studies showing that a stable employment history has now become one of the most important selection criteria for firms recruiting labour on

---

15.   People with few weekly working hours and low incomes and people who are employed for up to two months with the same employer are excluded from compulsory contributions to the Statutory Pension Plan and the Public Health System [see Benner, 1987].

the external labour market (the other most important factor being acquired skills) [Windolf and Hohn, 1984]. This implies that persons alternating between successive fixed-term contracts and intermittent spells of unemployment may become the victims of a vicious circle, eventually ending in long-term unemployment [Büchtemann, 1984; Büchtemann and Brasche, 1985; Andress, 1988]. This argument could also be cited against those who claim that fixed-term employment contracts might function as a means to promote the reemployment of persons whose low productivity (in terms of acquired skills) at a given level of labour costs would prevent employers from hiring them on a permanent basis [Schellhaass, 1985].

In order to assess the relative employment stability of fixed-term workers and their proneness to involuntary unemployment, we have looked at three different indicators: their proportion among the registered unemployed; their subjective anticipation of job loss; and their subsequent labour market experience.

(a) Proportion of the registered unemployed
The most commonly used indicator of the unemployment risk faced by fixed-term workers is the relation between the share of persons registering as unemployed after the expiration of their fixed-term contracts in the total inflow into unemployment, and the share of persons holding a fixed-term contract in the total dependent labour force at a given point in time [Rudolph, 1987]. According to the official unemployment records of the Federal Employment Agency (BA), the percentage of persons registering as unemployed after the expiration of a fixed-term contract in the total inflow from wage work into registered unemployment has steadily increased over the past five years, to reach 18.4% in 1987. Compared to the percentage of fixed-term workers among the total dependent labour force at a given point in time (5.6% in March 1987, excluding public servants), the percentage of fixed-term personnel is clearly higher among those registering as unemployed. This suggests that the probability of job loss and subsequent unemployment for them is significantly higher than for permanent employees (table 4).

However, given the considerable structural differences between fixed-term and permanent workers as far as personal and job characteristics are concerned, it would certainly be misleading to infer from these statistics that the type of employment contract has a genuine impact on the relative incidence of job loss and unemployment. Instead, seniority and length of service with the same employer are likely to explain a considerable part of the uneven distribution of dismissals and job loss between fixed-term and permanent workers [Büchtemann, 1983; Büchtemann and Höland, 1989]. Since fixed-term workers usually have a rather brief tenure with their current employer, their high risk of unemployment may result largely from the principle of "last in, first out" applied in both redundancies and individual dismissals. In fact, data for 1987 from the Federal Employment Agency show that 61% of the persons registering as unemployed after a spell of employment came from jobs that had not lasted more than 18 months. The last in, first out principle holds even more for persons registering as

Table 4: Share of workers with a fixed-term employment contract among the dependent labour force and in the inflow into registered unemployment in the Federal Republic of Germany, 1984-1987 (%)

	June/May-June			
	1984	1985	1986	1987
1. % of fixed-term contracts in total dependent labour force (excl. public servants, military personnel and apprentices)				
- Total	4.0	5.6	6.4	5.6[2]
- Male	2.9	5.1	5.5	4.9[2]
- Female	5.6	6.4	7.3	6.5[2]
2. Persons entering unemployment at end of fixed-term contract as % of total in-flow into unemployment from dependent employment (excl. apprenticeship)				
- Total	14.1	16.0	17.4	18.4
- Male	12.2	14.3	16.0	16.6
- Female	16.9	18.3	18.8	21.1
3. "Relative representation" index[1]: (2)/(1)				
- Total	3.53	2.86	2.72	3.29
- Male	4.21	2.80	2.91	3.39
- Female	3.01	2.85	2.58	3.25

Notes:
(1)   "1" indicating an even distribution, values above 1 indicating an over-representation of workers from fixed-term employment in the inflow into unemployment.
(2)   Based on preliminary data from the 1987 "Mikrozensus".

Sources: Employment data, June: EEC-Labour Force Sample Survey 1984 for Germany; "Mikrozensus" 1985/86 (May)/87 (March) – data supplied by the Federal Statistical Office (Statistisches Bundesamt); calculations by the author.
Unemployment flows, May-June: Official Unemployment Insurance Records ("Arbeitslosenstatistik" St 9) 1984/85/86/87 – data supplied by the Federal Employment Agency (Bundesanstalt für Arbeit/BA); calculations by the author.

unemployed after the expiration of a fixed-term contract: for 85% of such persons registering as unemployed in 1986 the last job had not exceeded 18 months in duration, for 46% not even 5 months (table 5).

(b) Anticipated job security
        According to data for 1985 (table 6), only 7% of all wage and salary earners considered their current job to be insecure in the sense that they expected or thought it possible to be laid off or dismissed within two years. The vast majority of workers (92%) regarded job loss as most unlikely or even impossible. However, the share of persons anticipating job loss is markedly higher (14%) among those with less than two years tenure, although most persons even in this group did not expect to be "fired" within two years.
        The picture changes with the type of employment contract held. In 1985, 40% of the fixed-term workers with a tenure of less than two years did

Table 5: Previous job durations of persons registering as unemployed with the Federal Employment Agency by type of termination of last job - FRG, May/June 1986 (%)

| | All persons entering unemployment following dependent employment[1] May/June 1986 | Termination of last job through | | | |
		Dismissal (on employer's initiative	Mutual agreement	Expiration of fixed term contract	Voluntary resignation (on employee's initiative)
Duration of last job:					
up to 5 months	2.8	33.1	16.2	46.1	24.3
6 to 18 months	28.6	27.8	21.2	38.6	23.6
more than 18 months	38.6	39.1	62.6	15.3	53.0
Total	100	100	100	100	100
Number of cases:	58,771	35,250	1,969	10,089	11,463

Note: (1) Including apprenticeship.
Source: Federal Employment Agency (Bundesanstalt für Arbeit/BA), Unemployment Statistics (Arbeitslosenstatistik ST9); tabulations on behalf of the WZB/AMB; calculations by the author.

Table 6: Anticipation of job loss by dependent employees (excl. apprentices, trainees and persons on compulsory military/community service) in the FRG in 1985 according to tenure in the present job and type of employment contract (%)

| | All dependent employees, excl. apprentices, incl. public service | | Workers with less than 2 years of tenure in present job | | Permanent employment contract and less than 2 years of tenure | | Fixed-term employment contract and less than 2 years of tenure | |
	total	private industry*	total	private industry*	total	private industry*	total	private industry*
Anticipation of job loss within 2 years:								
- most certainly	1.6	1.6	5.9	5.8	1.7	2.5	21.4	28.7
- probably	4.9	5.3	8.4	7.0	5.7	5.0	17.3	13.9
- rather unlikely	38.2	44.8	48.2	51.7	52.3	52.9	34.9	39.9
- impossible/ certainly not	55.3	48.3	37.5	35.5	40.3	39.6	26.4	17.5
Total	100	100	100	100	100	100	100	100
No. of cases	5,363	3,755	985	659	531	353	172	83
Projected ('000)	21,394	14,109	3,933	2,544	2,080	1,405	6,840	383

Notes: * excluding public service.
Source: The "Socio-Economic Panel" Waves I/1984 and II/1985, longitudinal analysis.

Table 7: **Employment careers of dependent employees in the FRG, 1985-1987, according to type of employment contract and tenure in 1985 (%)**

	Total dependent employees (excl. public servants and apprentices)	Thereof: contract at date of the 1985 survey		
		Permanent employment contract and tenure with present employer of more than 2 years	Permanent employment contract and tenure with present employer of up to 2 years	Fixed-term employment contract
Labour force status				
In employment, incl. self-employment				
- 1986	90.9	93.5	88.2	76.1
- 1987	88.7	90.7	86.5	75.2
Unemployed/looking for work				
- 1986	2.7	2.1	4.1	4.9
- 1987	3.9	3.6	5.7	3.6
In education/training or compulsory military/ community service				
- 1986	1.6	0.4	1.5	15.6
- 1987	1.7	0.4	1.5	16.4
Other persons not in the labour force				
- 1986	4.8	4.0	6.2	3.4
- 1987	5.7	5.3	6.3	4.8
Labour market experience				
Spring 1985 to December 1986				
- continuously employed	82.8	86.2	72.9	59.9
- at least one spell of unemployment	6.9	5.0	12.9	14.2
- at least temporarily in education/training or compulsory military/ community service (without unemployment spell)	2.8	1.1	4.0	17.6
- other persons (neither continuously employed, nor unemployed, nor temporarily in training/comp. military/ community service)	8.1	7.8	10.2	8.3
Number of cases	4,187	3,201	582	234
Projected ('000)	19,366	14,389	2,609	1,383

Source: The "Socio-Economic Panel", Waves II/1985, III/1986, IV/1987 (tabulations supplied by the German Institute for Economic Research (DIW) on behalf of the WZB/AMB).

expect to lose their current job within two years (as compared to only 8% of the permanent workers with the same length of service). Considering that most fixed-term contracts are concluded for only short periods, however, an explanation seems to be needed for the fact that 60% of all fixed-term workers do *not* expect to lose their jobs in the subsequent two years. The answer may be provided by a recent survey [FORSA, 1987] which showed that, in the autumn of 1987, 32% of all fixed-term workers were expecting to be granted a permanent position, and 22% of them expected to have their contract renewed for another fixed-term period by their current employer. As far as expectations of employees go, fixed-term employment often seems to bear the possibility of being a "bridge" to permanent employment.

(c) Job stability over time

Fixed-term workers experience a high degree of employment instability according to Socio-Economic Panel data for 1985-87 (table 7). At a second interview (in 1986), one out of four workers (24%) holding a fixed-term contract when first interviewed in 1985 was not employed any more, as compared to only 12% of those with permanent contracts and a length of service of less than 2 years. The same pattern recurred in a second follow-up survey in 1987.

The finding that fixed-term workers have a higher degree of employment instability is confirmed when our perspective shifts to their experience on the labour market during the twenty month period between May 1985 and December 1986. In that period 73% of the permanent workers with a length of service under two years in May 1985 had a continuous (i.e. uninterrupted) employment career, but the figure was under 60% for the initially fixed-term workers. The relatively high share of fixed-term workers with an uninterrupted subsequent employment history reflects the fact that a substantial minority of these people [roughly one out of four according to the Bundesvereinigung der Deutschen Arbeit-geberverbände, 1986; see also Rudolph, 1987] are actually given a permanent employment contract on the expiration of their term. As reflected in the subjective expectations of the workers, in many instances fixed-term contracts can thus lead to permanent employment, a circumstance that could, however, partly result from the fact that fixed-term contracts are frequently used by employers as prolonged probationary periods for newly hired personnel.

However, the overall higher employment instability observed for fixed-term workers cannot be explained by higher unemployment: the share of persons experiencing at least one spell of unemployment during the 20 month observation period is virtually the same for both workers recently hired on a fixed-term and those hired on a permanent contract (13-14%). Instead, fixed-term workers undergo vocational training (including university courses) much more frequently than their permanent colleagues with less than two years of length of service (18% and 2%, respectively) or enter compulsory military service (less than 1%) when their fixed-term contract expires, often without any unemployment. Fixed-term job arrangements thus frequently seem to function as an intermediate episode in the transition from school to vocational training.

V. Conclusion

In the preceding sections, non-standard work in the form of both part-time and fixed-term employment has been shown to cover a relatively broad spectrum of different employment arrangements and different life situations. This range makes it difficult to draw general conclusions about the socio-economic implications for the members of the labour force affected. This is all the more true for the extent to which non-standard forms of employment can be regarded as precarious in the sense of seriously endangering the social and economic well-being of the worker in the short, medium, and long run.

Our analysis has shown that non-standard employment is not necessarily associated with above-average risks and hazards. For example, there is little or no precariousness about the situation of a part-timer in a qualified position (only a minority of all part-timers in the FRG) living with a well-paid spouse or partner and working part-time only for a short period within an otherwise continuous full-time career. The same is true of fixed-term workers who receive a permanent employment contract when their fixed-term contract expires.

A quite significant number of non-standard workers and employees, however, face an array of disadvantages. This is especially true for marginal part-timers, who are frequently subjected to unfavorable working conditions and are excluded from a wide range of protective laws and collectively negotiated benefits. Moreover, their total family income is also lower than that received by persons with full-time or regular part-time jobs. The negative impact of this cumulation of risks particularly affects those persons - although a relatively small group - who work in marginal part-time jobs for long periods of time.

Some employment patterns that are not associated with above-average risks in the short term may, however, turn out to be "traps" in the medium or long term. This feature is true for many part-time workers, who appear to have few opportunities for occupational advancement because they are in jobs requiring low skills, and who are likely to qualify only for low-level retirement benefits. Similarly, the significant role that fixed-term contracts play when people enter the employment system does not mean that those people will remain on the labour market, as shown by the greater employment instability of persons who have been with their employer for only a short time. Since employment instability is a characteristic of recently hired personnel, whether fixed-term or permanent, it shows there are precarious sides to standard employment as well. Last but not least, the discussion of the precariousness of non-standard forms of employment should not obscure the fact that under present labour market conditions few "bridges" can be found between unemployment and employment, whether standard or non-standard.

Although not all non-standard employment can be regarded as intrinsically precarious, our results suggest that in the medium term a further growth of such forms of employment is likely to increase social inequalities and labour-market segmentation unless the current framework of welfare-state regulation undergoes some changes. On the other hand, if the life circumstances and the working time preferences expressed by several groups of wage and salary earners [Büchtemann, 1989] are to be taken into account, a policy that defends only the SER cannot be an alternative. The discrimination inherent in the existing social security system, largely based on the standard model of life-long continuous full-time work, is increasingly becoming a problem.

Measures likely to reduce the risks associated with non-standard employment should be considered. For example, the integration of marginal part-timers into the existing social safety net and collective agreements would not only improve the protection of the individual wage and salary earner but also reduce the cost incentive that prompts employers to replace standard forms of employment by non-standard ones. The Public Pension Scheme could be reorganised to ensure a sufficient independent basic livelihood at retirement time for persons with discontinuous employment biographies and long periods of part-time work. Such a change would certainly eliminate a substantial handicap suffered by persons whose occupational trajectories do not conform to the norm.

Opening opportunities within a collectively bargained framework to provide the right to switch from part-time to full-time employment, from full-time to part-time work, or to take leave with a guaranteed job to come back to, could improve the current patterns of part-time work, counteract gender-specific segmentation within the labour market, and at the same time result in a desirable redistribution of work [Büchtemann, 1989].

The socio-political measures outlined above would not only reduce the risks of individual workers involved in non-standard forms of employment but could also counter a general erosion of social welfare standards.

References

Andress, H.-J. (1988): *Recurrent unemployment – The West-German experience: An application of count data models to panel data.* International Conference on Social Science Methodology, Dubrovnik, Yugoslavia, June.

Benner, W. (1987): *Versicherungspflicht und Versicherungsfreiheit in der Krankenversicherung, Rentenversicherung und Arbeitslosenversicherung.* Heidelberg (16th edition).

Bielenski, H.; Hegner, F. (1985): *Flexible Arbeitszeiten: Erfahrungen aus der Praxis.* Frankfurt, Campus.

Bielenski, H.; Strümpel, B. (1988): "Eingeschränkte Erwerbsarbeit bei Frauen und Männern: Fakten – Wünsche – Realisierungschancen", in *Beiträge zur Sozialökonomie der Arbeit* (Berlin), Vol. 15.

Bosch, G. (1986): "Hat das Normalarbeitsverhältnis eine Zukunft?", in *WSI-Mitteilungen* (Cologne), No. 3.

Bosch, G.; Seifert, H. (1984): "Das geplante Beschäftigungsförderungsgesetz – ein arbeitsmarktpolitisches Notstandsgesetz", in *WSI-Mitteilungen* (Cologne), No. 10.

Breidenstein, W. (1987): "Personal des öffentlichen Dienstes am 30. Juni 1986", in *Wirtschaft und Statistik* (Stuttgart), No. 12.

Brinkmann, C.; Kohler, H. (1981): "Am Rande der Erwerbsbeteiligung: Frauen mit geringfügiger, gelegentlicher oder befristeter Arbeit", in Klauder, W.; Kühlewind, G. (eds.): *Probleme der Messung und Vorausschätzung des Frauenerwerbspotentials*, BeitrAB No. 56. Erlangen.

Brinkmann, C.; Kohler, H.; Reyher, L. (1986): "Teilzeitarbeit und Arbeitsvolumen", in *Mitteilungen aus der Arbeitsmarkt- und Berufsforschung* (Stuttgart), No. 3.

Brose, H. G. et al. (1987): *Zeitarbeit – Soziologische Aspekte eines neuen Beschäftigungsverhältnisses*, Zwischenbericht. Marburg, Institut für Soziologie der Universität Marburg.

Büchtemann, C.F. (1983): *Die Bewältigung von Arbeitslosigkeit im zeitlichen Verlauf*, Repräsentative Längsschnittuntersuchung bei Arbeitslosen und Beschäftigten 1978-1982, Bd. 85 der Reihe "Forschungsberichte", hsrg. vom Bundesminister für Arbeit und Sozialordnung. Bonn.

—— (1984): "Zusätzliche Beschäftigung durch befristete Arbeitsverträge?", in *Wirtschaftsdienst* (Hamburg), No. 10.

—— (1987): *Structural change in the labour market and atypical employment: The case of part-time work in the Federal Republic of Germany*. Conference on "Labour Force Surveys as an Employment Policy Instrument", Fontevraud/France, Sep. (mimeo).

—— (1989): "The socio-economics of individual working-time reduction: Empirical evidence for the Federal Republic of Germany", in Buber-Agassi, J.; Heycock, S. (eds.): *The redesign of working time: Promise or threat?*. Berlin.

Büchtemann, C.F.; Brasche, U. (1985): *Recurrent unemployment: Longitudinal evidence for the Federal Republic of Germany*, report prepared on behalf of the OECD, SAMF-discussion paper no. 5-1985. Berlin/Paris/Paderborn.

Büchtemann, C.F.; Burian, K. (1986): "Befristete Beschäftigungsverhältnisse: Ein international-vergleichender Überblick", in *Internationale Chronik zur Arbeitsmarktpolitik* (Berlin), No. 26.

Büchtemann, C.F.; Gout, M. (1988): *Développement et structure du travail "indépendant" en R.F.A.*, report prepared for the Commission of the European Communities and the French Commissariat au Plan. Berlin (mimeo).

Büchtemann, C.F.; Höland, A. (1989): *Befristete Arbeitsverträge nach dem Beschäftigungsförderungsgesetz 1985*, Ergebnisse einer empirischen Untersuchung i.A. des Bundesministers für Arbeit und Sozialordnung. Berlin.

Büchtemann, C.F.; Schupp, J. (1988): *Socio-economic aspects of part-time employment in the Federal Republic of Germany*, Discussion Paper FS I, 88-6. Berlin, Wissenschaftszentrum Berlin für Sozialforschung.

Bundesanstalt für Arbeit (Federal Employment Agency/BA) (1988): "Arbeitsmarktanalyse 1987 anhand ausgewählter Bestands- und Bewegungsdaten", in *Amtliche Nachrichten der Bundesanstalt für Arbeit (ANBA)* (Nuremburg), No. 5.

Bundesvereinigung der Deutschen Arbeitgeberverbände (BDA) (1986): *Auswertung der Umfrage der BDA über die Auswirkungen des Beschäftigungsförderungsgesetzes 1985*, Cologne (mimeo).

Cordova, E. (1986): "From full-time wage employment to atypical employment: A major shift in the evolution of labour relations?" in *International Labour Review* (Geneva, ILO), Vol. 125, No. 6.

Cramer, U. (1986): "Zur Stabilität von Beschäftigung", in *Mitteilungen aus der Arbeitsmarkt- und Berufsforschung* (Stuttgart), No. 2.

Dahrendorf, R. et al. (eds.) (1986): *New forms of work and activity*. Colloquium at Brussels, April 1986. Dublin, European Foundation for the Improvement of Living and Working Conditions.

EEC/Commission of the European Communities (1984): *Geänderter Vorschlag für eine Richtlinie des Rates zur Regelung der Zeitarbeit und der befristeten Arbeitsverträge*, KOM (84) 159 endg., 3 April. Brussels.

Ehrenberg, R.G. et al. (1988): "Part-time employment in the United States", in Hart, R. A. (ed.): *Unemployment, employment and labour utilization*. Boston, Unwin Hyman.

Ermisch, J.; Wright, R.E. (1988): *Women's wages in full- and part-time jobs in Great Britain*, Discussion paper No. 234. London, Centre for Economic Policy Research (CEPR).

FORSA-Analysen (1987): *Ungeschützte und statusgeminderte Arbeitsverhältnisse*. Dortmund.

Hanefeld, U. (1984): "Das Sozio-ökonomische Panel – Eine Längsschnittstudie für die Bundesrepublik Deutschland", in *Vierteljahreshefte zur Wirtschaftsforschung* (Berlin), No. 4.

Hinrichs, K.; Offe, C.; Wiesenthal, H. (eds.) (1982): *Arbeitszeitpolitik. Formen und Folgen einer Neuverteilung der Arbeit*. Frankfurt am Main, Campus.

Hofbauer, H. (1981): "Zur Struktur der Teilzeitarbeit bei Frauen", in Klauder, W.; Kühlewind, G. (eds.): *Probleme der Messung und Vorausschätzung des Frauenerwerbspotentials*, BeitrAB No. 56. Erlangen.

—— (1982): "Ausbildung und Berufsverläufe: Retrospektiv-Analysen des IAB", in Mertens, D. (ed.): *Konzepte der Arbeitsmarkt- und Berufsforschung*, BeitrAB No. 70. Erlangen.

Kurz-Scherf, I. (1984): "Mitbestimmung durch Tarifvertrag", in *WSI-Mitteilungen* (Cologne), No. 3, Mar.

Landenberger, M. (1985): "Aktuelle sozialversicherungsrechtliche Fragen der flexiblen Arbeitszeit und Teilzeitbeschäftigung", in *Zeitschrift für Sozialreform* (Wiesbaden), Nos. 6/7.

Leighton, P. (1986): "Marginal workers" in Lewis R. (ed.): *Labour law in Britain*. Oxford, Basil Blackwell.

Levitan, S.A.; Conway, E.A. (1988): "Part-timers: Living on half rations", in *Challenge* (White Plains, N.Y.), May/June.

Lindley, R.M. (1986): *New forms and new areas of employment growth in France, Germany, Italy, the Netherlands and the UK*, a comparative study on behalf of the Commission of the EEC. University of Warwick.

Linkert, K. (1974): "Die zeitliche Beanspruchung der Frauen durch Erwerbstätigkeit", in *Wirtschaft und Statistik* (Stuttgart), No. 5.

Marchand, O.; Martin-Le-Goff, E. (1987): "Stabilité de l'emploi mais reprise du chômage en 1986", in *Economie et Statistique* (Paris), No. 198.

Merz, J.; Wolff, K. (1988): "Eigenarbeit, Nebenerwerb und Haupterwerb: Versorgungsstrategien privater Haushalte in der Bundesrepublik Deutschland", in *Mitteilungen aus der Arbeitsmarkt- und Berufsforschung* (Stuttgart), No. 2.

Möller, C. (1988): *Flexibel in die Armut: Empirische Untersuchung und theoretische Verortung ungeschützter Arbeitsverhältnisse*. Hamburg.

Mückenberger, U. (1985): "Die Krise des Normalarbeitsverhältnisses", in *Zeitschrift für Sozialreform* (Wiesbaden), Nos. 7/8.

Münstermann, J.; de Gijsel, P. (1981): *Der verschleierte Arbeitsmarkt in ausgewählten Ländern der EG*, Study No. 80/05 on behalf of the Commission of the European Communities. Dortmund/Brussels.

OECD (1986): *Employment outlook, 1986*. Paris.

Puel, H. (1980): "Il y a emploi et emploi", in *Travail et Emploi* (Paris), No. 4.

Robinson, O.; Wallace, J. (1981): "Relative pay and part-time employment in Great Britain", in *Oxford Bulletin of Economics and Statistics*, May.

Rolf, G.; Wagner, G. (1988): "Altersvorsorge von Frauen – Probleme und Reformmöglichkeiten", in *Zeitschrift für Sozialreform* (Stuttgart).

Rudolph, H. (1987): "Befristete Bessschäftigung – ein Überblick", in *Mitteilungen aus der Arbeitsmarkt und Berufsforschung* (Stuttgart), No. 3.

Schellhaass, H.-M. (1985): *Kündigungsschutz und Krise auf dem Arbeitsmarkt*, Referat für die Trierer Tagung des Sozialpolitischen Ausschusses des Vereins für Sozialpolitik am 19./20.9.1985. Technical University of Berlin, Dept. of Economics (mimeo).

Schoer, K. (1986): "Teilzeitbeschäftigung in Großbritannien und in der Bundesrepublik Deutschland", in *WSI-Mitteilungen* (Cologne), No. 1.

Schwarz, K. (1985): "Umfang der Frauenerwerbstätigkeit nach dem Zweiten Weltkrieg – Erwerbsbeteiligung und Arbeitszeiten", in *Zeitschrift für Bevölkerungswissenschaft* (Wiesbaden), No. 2.

Soltwedel, R. (1985): "Tarifrunde 1984: Einstieg in eine andere Arbeitsethik und Arbeitspolitik?", in *Aus Politik und Zeitgeschichte* (Bonn), No. 4, Jan.

Strümpel, B. et al. (1987): *Motive und Konsequenzen einer eingeschränkten Erwerbsarbeit von Männern*, Ergebnisse einer empirischen Untersuchung von Hausmännern, Teilzeitbeschäftigten und ihren Partnerinnen, Forschungsbericht der Forschungsstelle Sozialökonomik der Arbeit. Berlin, Freie Universität.

Stück, H. (1989): "Einkommens – und Freizeitpräferenzen der Angestellten – Ergebnisse einer Befragung im Lande Bremen", in *Arbeitszeit zwischen Wunsch und Wirklichkeit*, Schriftenreihe der Angestelltenkammer Bremen. Bremen.

Walter, N.; Soltwedel, R. (1984): *Gutachten zum Thema Arbeitsmarkt und Zeitarbeit*. Bonn.

Weitzel, G. (1986): *Beschäftigungswirkungen von Existenzgründungen*, IFO-Studien zu Handels- und Dienstleistungsfragen, Vol. 28. Munich.

Werner, J. (1984): *Die Erwerbstätigkeit von Müttern mit Kindern unter 15 Jahren und die Situation der Kinderbetreuung in Baden-Württemberg*, Auswertung einer Zusatzerhebung zum Mikrozensus 1982. Stuttgart.

Windolf, P.; Hohn, H.W. (1984): *Arbeitsmarktchancen in der Krise: Betriebliche Rekrutierung und Soziale Schließung – Eine empirische Untersuchung*. Frankfurt.

Annex Table A: **Patterns of female part-time employment in the FRG, 1984/85**
(% distribution within categories except where indicated)

	All female employees[a]	Fulltime[b]	Part-time all parttime[c]	Part-time regular parttime[d]	Part-time marginal parttime[e]
Number of cases, unweighted	7,976	4,873	3,103	2,197	906
1. Normal working hours per week					
1-10 hrs	5.3	-	13.6	0.2	46.2
11-14 hrs	0.8	-	2.2	0.5	6.3
15-19 hrs	3.1	-	7.9	1.4	23.3
20-25 hrs	18.5	-	47.5	67.4	1.6
26-34 hrs	6.6	-	17.3	23.7	-
35 hrs and more	59.8	97.6	-	-	-
No regular working hrs/ irregular schedule	5.4	2.3	10.2	6.5	19.2
No answer	0.4	0.1	1.6	0.3	3.4
Total	100	100	100	100	100
2. Personal/household situation					
Age in 1984					
16-30 years	33.1	44.8	15.4	12.8	21.5
31-50 years	50.4	40.6	65.2	67.8	59.7
51-60 years	14.3	13.6	15.3	17.3	10.5
60 years and older	2.3	1.0	4.1	2.1	8.4
Marital status					
Not married	24.6	39.1	7.2	4.7	10.9
Married/living with spouse	60.3	46.2	81.5	81.7	83.8
Married/not living with spouse	1.9	2.2	1.5	1.7	1.0
Divorced/widowed	11.5	12.5	9.8	11.8	4.3
Type of household					
Single person	16.5	22.2	7.2	3.5	18.9
Married couple without children	19.7	21.7	17.1	20.4	6.1
Married couple with child(ren)					
- youngest child under 6	5.4	3.3	8.6	7.7	11.5
- youngest child 6-16	21.8	15.3	32.2	29.6	40.4
- youngest child over 16	24.8	24.1	26.0	29.1	15.8
Parent without spouse	2.3	2.3	2.2	2.3	2.2
Unmarried couple	5.2	7.5	1.6	1.8	0.7
Students (in education at university etc.)	4.5	4.1	5.2	2.3	14.6
Vocational training					
Without completed vocational training	25.0	20.7	23.4	30.1	47.1
Completed apprenticeship	39.5	47.3	48.5	49.4	37.6
Other completed vocational training below university degree	26.3	22.3	10.8	13.9	11.6
University degree	9.2	9.7	6.2	6.6	3.6

	All female employees[a]	Full-time[b]	Part-time		
			all part-time[c]	regular part-time[d]	marginal part-time[e]

3. Job characteristics

Skill requirements of job:

No specific skills required	31.2	22.7	43.6	36.8	59.5
On-the-job training	12.2	11.7	13.0	13.6	11.3
Completed vocational training/ special courses etc. required	49.7	57.6	37.9	43.6	26.0
Completed university training required	6.9	7.7	5.6	5.9	3.2
Job is in the same occupation as vocational training for	47.5	55.4	35.5	39.5	27.3
Not in the same job	36.1	30.5	44.4	43.5	44.9
No vocational training received	16.5	14.0	20.0	17.0	27.9
Not in the same job, % of those with vocational training	43.2	35.5	55.6	47.6	62.2

Type of activity

Un-/semiskilled manual job	5.0	5.8	2.9	4.8	2.0
Skilled manual job	7.5	9.1	5.3	5.7	5.0
Technicians/engineers	3.1	3.3	2.8	3.1	2.4
Un-/semiskilled service job	19.6	12.3	29.8	23.1	44.3
Skilled service job	4.9	6.2	3.0	3.3	2.4
Semiprofessional job	11.7	14.0	8.4	10.3	4.2
Professional job	5.0	6.2	3.4	2.7	4.1
Semiskilled sales/admin job	17.8	14.2	22.8	23.4	20.1
Skilled sales/admin job	23.7	26.4	19.8	23.3	13.3
Managerial job	0.2	0.3	-	-	-

Learning on the job

Job frequently involves learning of new skills	25.8	31.1	17.0	19.2	9.6
Job hardly ever/never involves learning of new skills	35.7	28.6	47.4	43.7	60.0

Working time arrangement

Working time varies according to demand/highly flexible schedules	46.4	42.8	52.2	46.8	69.9
Person is member of a union	17.4	22.3	9.3	11.7	1.7

4. Type of establishment

Industry

Sales/services	72.8	17.0	78.2	76.4	82.2
Low skill service industries/ retail	32.1	26.5	41.2	36.9	49.1
Higher skill service industries	34.9	37.1	31.1	33.5	26.7

Size of establishment (no. of employees)

Less than 20	30.5	23.9	40.5	34.7	51.4
20 to 199	28.0	39.6	25.4	24.9	29.1
200 to 1999	19.9	22.0	16.6	21.1	6.8
2000 and more	21.7	24.4	17.5	19.2	12.8

	All fe-male em-ployees[a]	Full-time[b]	Part-time		
			all[c]	regular[d]	marginal[e]
5. Pay, social security and fringe benefits (DM)					
Average monthly gross earnings	1,887	2,351	1,130	1,204	550
Average monthly net earnings	1,225	1,563	764	866	420
Average gross wage per hour	8.87	8.98	8.68	8.66	8.81
Controlled for skill:					
(unskilled/semiskilled workers only)					
Average gross wage per hour	-	10.59	10.36	10.78	9.61
Average net wage per hour	-	7.16	7.40	7.22	7.92
Differential gross-net wage	-	3.43	2.96	3.56	1.69
Differential as % of gross					
wage per hour		(32.4)	(28.6)	(33.0)	(17.6)
Social security contributions					
Contributions to the national					
pension system	86.4	93.0	75.0	87.2	42.9
As % of those employed,					
excl. public servants	91.7	99.9	78.2	92.1	43.6
Covered by special pension					
scheme of firm					
Yes	21.4	25.5	14.8	17.2	2.9
No/do not know	8.5	9.4	7.2	10.1	2.8
Firm does not have pension					
scheme/unknown	70.0	65.0	78.9	72.9	94.3
Fringe benefits					
13th salary	46.2	52.3	36.1	43.5	13.2
14th salary	2.4	3.3	1.1	1.4	-
Xmas allowance	44.1	44.7	43.0	44.4	40.0
Holiday allowance	62.9	68.9	53.0	63.7	23.3
Other benefits	4.8	5.2	4.0	4.8	2.0
None	9.6	3.3	20.0	11.1	44.6
6. Future expectations					
Search for a new job in next 2 years					
Certain/most likely	15.1	15.8	14.1	11.2	23.8
Certainly not	65.4	64.8	66.3	68.9	57.8
Termination of labour market					
participation in next 2 years					
Certain/most likely	10.9	9.6	13.1	12.2	16.3
Certainly not	68.3	72.6	61.2	62.9	55.4
Involuntary job loss in next 2 years					
Certain/most likely	7.4	7.7	6.8	6.5	7.9
Certainly not	54.9	53.7	57.1	51.0	51.6
Professional advancement in next 2 years					
Certain/most likely	12.6	18.0	3.7	3.8	3.1
Certainly not	61.5	53.4	74.9	74.4	76.9
Starting in a different occupation in next 2 years					
Certain/most likely	7.5	7.2	8.2	5.5	16.7
Certainly not	75.5	76.6	73.8	76.0	65.2

	All fe-male em-ployees[a]	Full-time[b]	Part-time		
			all[c]	regular[d]	marginal[e]
7. Subjective work attachment; Job is:					
Of great personal importance	7.5	10.5	2.6	3.1	0.9
Important but must not interfere with other activities	75.9	76.5	75.0	77.6	66.5
Not so important/would give up work if had enough money	16.6	13.0	22.4	19.3	32.6
8. Mobility					
Tenure with present employer					
Up to one year	13.9	12.8	15.4	11.3	25.3
Over one year to 5 years	25.0	25.2	24.5	22.0	30.5
Over 5 years to 10 years	25.6	26.5	24.4	25.4	21.8
Over 10 years to 15 years	18.0	18.0	17.9	21.2	12.1
Over 15 years to 20 years	8.9	7.4	11.2	13.5	4.4
Over 20 years	8.8	10.1	6.8	6.0	6.0
Number of employers 1974-84 as % of those with less than 10 yrs tenure					
Two employers	40.4	46.9	38.3	43.6	30.1
Three or more employers	25.3	27.4	26.6	24.5	29.0
Labour force status in preceding year (1984) as % of female respondents in dependent employment in 1985					
Employed	87.7	90.5	83.6	90.1	62.6
- full time employed	55.4	85.4	7.0	7.5	4.2
- in regular part-time empl't	24.0	4.1	56.0	68.8	14.6
- marginal part-time empl't	8.5	1.0	20.6	13.8	42.8
Not employed	9.5	5.3	16.1	9.4	37.4
- unemployed/looking for work	4.5	4.5	4.5	3.6	7.2
- not looking for work	5.0	0.8	11.6	5.8	30.2
Labour force status in following year (1985) as % of female respondents in dependent employment in 1984					
Employed	90.3	92.4	-	89.9	78.9
- full-time employment	57.6	87.8	-	9.8	7.0
- in regular part-time empl't	27.3	3.9	-	75.7	36.2
- marginal part-time empl't	5.4	0.7	-	4.4	35.7
Not employed	9.5	0.7	-	4.4	35.7
- unemployed/looking for work	3.6	3.7	-	3.4	3.2
- % of those not employed in 1985	37.9	51.4	-	33.7	15.2
Others (in vocational training)	0.2	0.4	-	-	-

Notes: (a) excluding apprentices; (b) subjective self-classification "fully employed".
          (c) self-classification "regular part-time employment" or "marginal or irregular part-time employment"; (d) self-classification "regular part-time employment";
          (e) self-classification "marginal or irregular part-time employment".
Source: "Socio-Economic Panel", Waves I/1984 and II/1985. Due to differing questionnaires some indicators refer to 1984, others 1985. See Büchtemann and Schupp [1988].

Annex Table B: **Patterns of fixed-term employment (excl. trainees/conscripts) in the FRG, 1985 (% distribution within categories)**

	Dependent employees (Total)	Type of employment contract		Thereof: with tenure of up to 2 years	
		Perma-nent	Fixed-term	Perma-nent contract	Fixed-term contract
Number of cases (unweighted)	5,363	4,803	328	531	172
Sex					
Male	60.9	61.3	57.7	58.5	55.1
Female	39.1	38.7	42.3	41.5	44.9
Nationality					
German	91.1	91.5	87.1	90.4	89.0
Non-German	8.9	8.5	12.9	9.6	11.0
Age					
16-24 years	12.6	11.1	31.4	28.0	38.2
25-30 years	15.3	15.3	20.4	24.5	24.3
31-40 years	24.4	24.9	22.2	26.6	21.3
41-50 years	28.2	28.6	18.2	17.7	12.7
51-60 years	16.9	17.8	7.3	2.8	3.5
older than 60 years	2.6	2.3	0.5	0.4	--
Occupational training					
No certified occupat. training	17.5	16.2	29.4	24.0	28.0
Completed apprenticeship	46.5	47.4	35.7	47.7	34.0
Medical/technical vocational (below university level)	18.2	19.1	9.3	15.0	6.9
Training as public servant	3.9	3.9	1.8	0.7	--
Post secondary technical college/university	14.0	13.5	21.8	12.6	31.1
Occupational (professional) status					
Unskilled worker	6.1	5.2	11.2	9.9	11.2
Semi-skilled worker	14.9	14.2	20.5	20.9	17.3
Skilled worker/foreman	21.8	22.6	11.7	17.4	10.3
Employee with simple task	11.6	11.8	10.4	8.9	11.6
Employee with qualified job	22.9	24.0	16.2	8.6	22.6
Highly qualified position	11.4	11.5	11.8	9.4	13.9
Civil servant	11.3	10.6	28.2	1.7	13.0
Working time arrangement (subjective self-classification)					
Full-time	83.8	84.9	75.2	82.0	75.7
Regular part-time	13.2	12.7	17.8	9.8	16.8
Irregular/marginal part-time	3.0	2.4	7.0	8.2	7.5
Contractual weekly working time					
1-14 hours	2.5	2.4	(2.5)	5.8	(3.9)
15-19 hours	1.6	1.6	(0.9)	(1.8)	(1.2)
20-25 hours	7.2	7.2	10.9	5.3	9.0
26-34 hours	2.8	2.8	(2.8)	(3.1)	(1.8)
35 and more hours	77.3	78.3	69.6	73.4	74.8
No specified working time	8.6	17.7	13.3	10.6	9.2

	Dependent employees	Type of employment contract		Thereof: with tenure of up to 2 years	
	(Total)	Perma-nent	Fixed-term	Perma-nent	Fixed-term
Industry					
Manufacturing/construction	41.6	40.7	44.0	51.2	28.5
Trade/services	53.7	54.2	51.2	42.7	63.5
Sector					
Public sector	29.1	28.3	40.3	11.4	40.4
Private sector	70.9	71.7	59.7	88.6	59.6
Size of enterprise (no. of employees)					
Less than 20 employees	19.0	18.8	19.6	28.2	20.3
20 to less than 200	27.0	27.4	23.0	36.5	23.3
200 to less than 2000	23.0	23.3	24.2	20.2	25.1
2000 and more employees	31.2	30.5	33.2	14.8	31.3
Opportunities for acquiring additional skills on the job	32.8	32.8	28.6	39.5	29.7
Future expectations:					
Search for a new job in next 2 years					
Certain	4.7	3.9	16.1	12.9	25.0
Probable	8.1	7.9	13.1	11.3	19.9
Unlikely	20.2	20.5	16.8	32.1	20.6
Certainly not	67.0	67.7	54.0	43.8	35.1
Involuntary job-loss in next 2 years					
Certain	1.6	0.6	13.8	1.7	21.4
Probable	4.9	4.3	12.4	5.7	17.3
Unlikely	38.2	38.6	34.7	52.3	34.9
Certainly not	55.3	56.5	39.1	40.3	26.4
Professional advancement in next 2 years					
Certain	3.0	2.8	5.5	3.7	6.1
Probable	16.7	16.7	19.5	27.6	20.6
Unlikely	29.1	30.2	17.7	31.6	17.9
Certainly not	51.2	50.3	57.3	37.2	55.4
Starting again in a different occupation in the next 2 years:					
Certain	1.7	1.1	10.1	3.2	16.9
Probable	5.2	4.8	10.5	10.7	15.1
Unlikely	16.5	16.3	20.0	24.0	27.6
Certainly not	76.6	77.8	59.4	62.1	40.4
Union member	28.4	28.8	20.3	17.9	12.9
Tenure with present employer:					
Up to 2 years	18.6	15.8	46.4	100	100
More than 2/up to 5 years	18.4	18.0	17.8	--	--
More than 5/up to 10 years	20.9	20.1	8.8	--	--
More than 10/up to 15 years	17.1	17.9	7.8	--	--
More than 15/up to 20 years	9.7	10.3	1.3	--	--
More than 20 years	15.3	16.1	2.8	--	--

Source: The Socio-Economic Panel Study Waves I/1984 and II/1985 - longitudinal analysis.

6 Non-wage work and disguised wage employment in Italy

Francesca Bettio and Paola Villa[1]

I. Introduction

This paper discusses two aspects that, for quantity and quality, distinguish the Italian labour market experience, over the past two decades, from that of other developed countries: the considerable incidence of non-wage labour in total employment and the growth of disguised employment.[2] Our argument is that the two aspects are related via a set of institutional and structural factors that have charted a distinctive evolution of the labour market in Italy.

The first part of the discussion analyses factors and features of non-wage and disguised employment, illustrates the employment forms involved, identifies segments that link those different forms to the specificities of the productive structure, and finally gives an overview and an evaluation. The second part is more descriptive and refers to disguised employment only. Estimates and qualitative information on the overall proportions of disguised employment as well as on its three main components – homeworkers, moonlighters and immigrant workers – are presented and discussed.

II. Analytical presentation of non-wage and disguised employment

1. An analytical premise: Classifying wage versus non-wage employment

The customary classification of wage and non-wage forms of employment in the Italian context may not always be adequate from an economic point of view, but we shall nevertheless use it on the under-

---

1.   University of Salerno and University of Trento.

2.   We have chosen to leave out of the discussion employment in illegal activities, unless the issue bore strict relevance to the arguments put forward.

standing that it represents a convenient terminological escape, rather than a substantive solution.

We shall use the case of homeworking to illustrate our point. Homeworking is clearly defined in legal terms, and precise norms are attached to this legal definition. According to the 1973 law (Law No. 877/1973) a homeworker is:

> ...any person who, under the authority of another person and for remuneration, performs work in his own home or in premises made available for the purpose, with or without the assistance of members of his family, and with the exception of any wage-earning employee or apprentice, for the account of one or more employers, using raw materials or supplies and tools provided by himself or the employer.

A homeworker in the 1973 law is a subordinate worker whose energy is at the disposal of the employer; subordinate work is to be distinguished from autonomous work, where the products of the worker, rather than his direct energy, are available to employers or purchasers. As subordinate work, homeworking is entitled to the guarantees of all wage work in Italy. Employers and employees are obliged to be recorded on special registers that formalise their relationship, and to record their transactions in a "work book". The main difference with wage employment is that pay is on a piece-rate basis, and upon delivery, though rates should be linked to those of inworkers specified by collective agreements.

From an economic point of view, an alternative definition is possible. A homeworker is characterised by little or no initiative in the product market, both with respect to the choice of inputs and outputs, and with respect to the sale of output. This implies economic dependency on the employer who gives out the work, rather than on the final market. On these grounds, homeworking should be viewed as part of the phenomenon of outwork. The whole of outwork, in fact, implies dependency in that the choice of inputs and outputs is made by the main contractor, and payment is by results. The major difference between homeworking and outwork is in the location, for the homeworker works primarily at home. However, this is not a fundamental difference in economic terms; nor is the legal distinction whereby an outworker may employ wage labour, whereas a homeworker may only rely on family labour. In the case of small, family-based subcontractors, the legal distinction between these and homeworkers may well carry little economic relevance.

If the above economic definition of homeworking is accepted, it may extend to groups of workers that the law would classify otherwise. In Italy, it may extend to the category of traditional artisans. From both legal and statistical points of view, artisans are considered autonomous workers, i.e. self-employed. Yet, within the large subcontracting network existing in industry and in services, the economic distinction between an artisan acting as an outworker and a homeworker is often negligible. Main contractors gain from giving out work to artisans, in lieu of registered homeworkers, since they are thus freed from compliance with norms and costs associated with wage employment. The worker, on the other hand, may be indifferent between these two alternative employment statuses. Social security coverage could make a difference. But in Italy, the national health system is currently free for everybody. As for pensions, voluntary contributions to the State on the part of artisans are modest and may even be passed on to the main contractor. This explains why many *de facto* homeworkers register as artisans. Homeworkers may, finally, operate entirely in disguise, i.e. without registering at all. Those who do not work in any official capacity may still be entitled to social security as dependents of family members in official employment. This may be the case of married women or dependent children, particularly vulnerable to the pressure of the main contractor wishing to avoid registration.

To sum up: since economic convenience and legal prescriptions often lead to divergent solutions, it is not surprising that most homeworkers are actually disguised under the official registration of artisans or altogether within the hidden economy. This means that what should be classified as wage work (i.e. homeworking) has collapsed into the category of autonomous work (i.e. non-wage work) on legal grounds, or disappeared from the statistics altogether.[3]

2. Non-wage employment

A labour market feature that sets the Italian experience apart from that of other industrialised countries is the disproportionate weight of non-wage earners in total employment. The 1986 Eurostat figure of 29% for the share of non-wage earners in total employment in Italy is strikingly above the EEC (10 countries) average of 17.3%.

Non-wage earners comprise entrepreneurs and professionals, autonomous workers, and family workers, the two latter categories accounting for the vast majority of this aggregate. The definition of entrepreneurs and professionals is fairly standard, but the other categories need to be closely looked at. Workers are classified as autonomous if they manage a farm, a small industrial enterprise, a shop, a hotel or a bar, provided that they contribute to production with their own manual labour. Workers based at home, but working directly for the consumer and not for a contractor, are also included in this category. Family members assisting other self-employed family members (whether autonomous workers, entrepreneurs or professionals) outside any contractual employment relation are classified as family workers, and included among the self-employed.

The continuing dominance of family enterprises in all sectors of activity is a major factor explaining the strong presence of autonomous workers and family workers within Italian employment. Family enterprises are typically managed by workers falling into the "autonomous" category, whose labour is supplemented by family workers. Their share of wage labour employed is modest, if at all positive.

---

3. The potential ambiguity attached to categories such as wage and non-wage employment should be borne in mind to set statistics in their proper economic perspective.

The fact that Italy is a latecomer to the process of development accounts for the persistence of family based enterprises in many sectors of activity. This traditional productive structure has withstood the pressure of late and rapid development, rather than giving way on a large scale to "modern" forms of productive organisation. However, in the process, family enterprises have evolved, showing considerable capacity to adapt to the requirements of development.

The sectors where family enterprises have retained more than elsewhere their pre-industrial character are agriculture and private services, especially the distributive trades. A substantial share of family workers and a negligible proportion of wage labour is a distinctive feature of these traditional family enterprises. The share of non-wage earners reaches peaks of 63.1% and 57.5% in agriculture and the distributive trades, respectively (tables 1 and 2). Taken together, these two sectors account for 65.7% of non-wage earners in total employment. Agriculture continues to have the highest weight in the structure of non-wage employment, despite a significant post-war decline; and that decline has been substantially compensated by the growth of non-wage employment in the distributive trades.

In industry, far fewer family firms have survived. Those which did evolved considerably in the process, integrating and interacting with large and "modern" industrial concerns. Through this interaction, mature industries like textiles, footwear and light engineering have acquired a capacity for innovation and penetration of foreign markets. It is best to refer to these firms as artisan firms, rather than family firms, bearing in mind that this is a different phenomenon from that of petty commodity production (tailors, ice-cream makers, locksmiths, etc.).

Table 1: Non-wage earners, numbers ('000) and structure, 1986

	Agriculture	Industry	Services	All sectors		
				No.	%	% female
Non-wage earners	1,413	1,162	3,577	6,152	100.0	30.2
- Professionals & entrepreneurs	34	124	592	750	12.2	15.3
- Autonomous workers	1,043	893	2,367	4,303	69.9	23.9
- Family workers	336	146	618	1,100	17.9	64.7
Total employment	2,241	6,821	11,794	20,856		33.1
Share non-wage earners (%)	63.05	17.03	30.30	29.50		

Source: ISTAT, *Rilevazione trimestrale della forza lavoro*. Rome.

Table 2: Share of non-wage earners in total employment in private services, 1985*

Sectors	Total employment ('000)	% share non-wage earners
Trade, hotels and catering	4456.7	57.5
Transport and communication	1261.2	25.1
Banking & finance, insurance	382.5	1.2
Business and personal services	2033.5	34.9
Total private services	8133.9	44.2

Notes: * Private services exclude public administration and private non-marketable services.
Source: ISTAT, *Annuario di contabilità nazionale*. Rome ("occupati presenti").

Primary reliance on family labour is not a necessary feature of artisan firms. They do retain, however, strong links with family networks within a given territory. The typical figure of a non-wage worker in these firms is the artisan, statistically classified as autonomous worker. The incidence of the *artigiani* in total industrial employment is obviously lower than the corresponding figure for autonomous workers in agriculture or in the distributive trades (table 1). Nevertheless, thanks to the *artigiani*, the share of non-wage employment in total industrial employment in Italy is far higher than in other industrial countries: 17% against 9.9% for the EEC (10) average in 1986.

3. Disguised employment: Why and where?

It is commonplace to assume that, in Italy, small scale production equals disguised employment, especially where artisan or family firms are involved. Disguised employment is too pervasive a feature of the Italian labour market to be confined to small firms. For 1986, ISTAT estimates attribute some 20% of the total labour input to GNP to disguised forms of employment. Nevertheless, the common *cliché* tells an important truth. Artisan firms, on one side, and family firms, on the other, typify those sections of the productive structure that are most likely to feed on disguised employment. In fact, a broad correspondence can be instituted between those two types of firm, on the one hand, and the two major segments within the area of disguised employment, on the other. Artisan firms exemplify the kind of production fabric that underpins what may be termed *the novel segment* of disguised employment, or the Italian way to flexibility. Family firms and the family structure sustain what may be termed *the functional segment*. And we would identify a third segment – *the degenerative segment* – which partially overlaps the previous ones without necessarily relating with a specific structure of firms; the term "degenerative" refers, in this case, to the quality of the employment conditions prevailing in this segment. The reasons behind the growth or the persistence of each of these segments differ in each case.

Throughout this paper, the term *disguised employment* is meant to comprise both irregular and hidden employment. Irregular employment refers to employment positions that are only partially recorded or "regularised". Hidden employment refers to positions that get round fiscal and legal norms entirely, and may also fall completely outside the coverage of official statistics.

A. The novel segment: A channel for flexibility

The story about what is, perhaps, the most distinctive segment of disguised employment in Italy is best told with exclusive reference to industry, although its validity is not confined there. It begins with the peculiarities of the institutional framework within which the Italian labour market operates. Throughout the post-war period, labour law and collective bargaining have been shaped by the central concern of strengthening the bargaining power of the weak side in the wage employment relationship. Workers have been granted protection in three key aspects of the wage contract: (i) non-discrimination in access to employment, for which the State has been given the monopoly of the Labour Exchange, and rigid rules have been defined for the selection of workers; (ii) continuity of employment, which is ensured by defining the standard, reference contract as an indefinite duration contract (*contratto a tempo indeterminato*); (iii) security of employment, which is safeguarded by very rigid clauses against individual and collective lay-offs.

During the upsurge of industrial conflicts in the 1970s, the trade union movement succeeded in further limiting the discretionary power of employers within the firm, by imposing rigid controls on all aspects of labour management. The success of trade union action owes a great deal to the enforcement in 1970 of the Workers' Charter, recognizing the rights of union organisation at the workplace. As a result of the combined influence of union action and of labour legislation, the majority of contracts were and remain full-time ones, and of indeterminate duration.

Considerable innovation in labour legislation during the 1980s has begun to undermine, but not yet drastically altered, this picture.[4] Before the new legislation was enacted, existing norms regulating the wage relation allowed limited discretion to employers, if rigidly applied. However, the system of firms as a whole could, and still does, recover discretion and flexibility via two main channels. The first relates to the distinction between small and big firms, based on the threshold of 15 employees. Small firms

---

4.   Up to 1983, contracts specifying a definite time period were allowed only in a limited number of cases (hotels and catering in touristic areas, seasonal work in agriculture, theatre and picture studios). From 1983, the option of temporary contracts has been progressively extended, and currently constitutes the major option for the recruitment of young workers. Moreover, part-time work has been regulated for the first time in 1984 (nevertheless, the actual spread of part-time contracts continues to be very modest). Finally, the rules for selecting workers have also been relaxed in the 1980s.

are exempted from abiding by some of the restrictive clauses mentioned above. They have much greater discretion in the selection of personnel, and are completely free to dismiss workers at short notice, even if the standard, unlimited duration contract applies. Furthermore, since the Workers' Charter is not binding for these firms, direct union controls do not restrict their management of labour. While small firms enjoy considerable flexibility, large firms may acquire some flexibility via small firms by resorting to subcontracting, whenever this is economically viable and technologically feasible. The growth of a vast area of industrial subcontracting has thus been encouraged and has contributed to the expansion of disguised employment.

If the segment of small firms provides flexibility to the entire industrial structure, some small firms do so more than others: artisan firms, i.e. the segment of non-wage industrial employment. An artisan is often an ex-inworker turned outworker. The earnings of skilled workers as employees cannot go beyond a certain threshold: the amount of overtime finds limits within a firm and hourly earnings are independent of the work effort. By turning outworker, the ex-employee is free to choose both pace and hours of work and thus to increase earnings if he chooses to do so. And, in this case, greater freedom for outworkers means flexibility for the system of firms on which they depend.

Most small firms have preferential links with the area of hidden employment. As we have argued with reference to "undeclared" home-working, all firms, large and small, may find it convenient to make use of "hidden" or "irregular" labour. The reason is all the more apparent when the high incidence of social security contributions in Italy, compared to other countries, is added to the rigidities of the institutional framework. Social contributions amounting to between 50 and 60% of pre-tax pay are reason enough for resorting to hidden employment. Small firms find it easier to avoid legal and fiscal controls. Moreover, they operate within those family and community networks that provide contacts between employers and potential disguised labour, and favour an informal management of labour.

The labour force of small firms is often recruited among relatives, if not the entrepreneur's own family. Family links, however distant or indirect, may be conducive to a paternalistic management of labour relations that hinders unionisation and gives rise to irregular forms of remuneration, work schedules, and employment conditions. But family links may provide the necessary personal contacts, and strengthen the complicity between employers and employees when the interest of both converge towards by-passing employment or fiscal norms.[5] Tax evasion prompts a particularly strong convergence of interests. Employees themselves often accept or seek irregular employment in order to avoid income tax, for, in Italy, the *de facto* tax burden on regular employees is very high compared to what the state is willing and able to extract from non-wage labour. But the greater the

---

5.   Some family members may be willing to work "undeclared" if social security coverage is provided by other members in regular employment.

evasion, the heavier the burden that the state will try to impose on incomes that cannot escape controls, i.e. wage-income.

Small firms have thus acquired the role of *trait-d'union* between the unofficial and the emerged industrial and employment structures, and the phenomenon goes beyond the confines of the industrial sector. A successful story within the service sector – that of the "pony express delivery system" - illustrates that the novel segment is well represented outside industry and that large firms also may be involved. The pony express is a quick delivery metropolitan service. Youths on mopeds or motorbikes are typically employed for collection and delivery; irregular employment is the norm, employees often consenting rather than compelled to irregularity. In the span of a decade the service has grown, but regular employment continues to be the exception, outside the administrative occupations.

B. The functional segment

Disguised employment is functional to the economy of traditional family firms for reasons that must be kept distinct from the need to respond to a rigid institutional framework, on the one side, and the growing requirements of flexible specialisation, on the other. Family firms operating within agriculture, tourism, retail trade and personal services provide the best example. The management of labour within such firms has always been highly informal. On account of small size, and uneven or uncertain patterns of work – including seasonality – proper formalisation of occasional employees would entail unbearably high administrative costs to these firms, let alone the extra fiscal and wage costs. A historic example is that of small peasants recruiting wage labourers among relatives or other peasants at harvest time; such recruitment is rarely regularised. Understandably so, for regularisation entails bureaucratic procedures of which the cost in terms of time alone would be disproportionately high. Furthermore, labour needs may vary from day to day, thus further complicating the process of regularisation. Instances of this kind are not confined to traditional, small scale agriculture. They are equally common in urban contexts: corner shops, small restaurants, small transport enterprises and the like. We would also add to the list most professionals' offices: notaries, lawyers, family doctors, accountants, etc., whose work organisation often mirrors that of small family enterprises.

In all these instances, innovative forms of disguised employment may be observed side by side with customary forms. For example, health food shops and restaurants, or fringe bookshops (that in recent years have often grown out of the co-operation of groups of friends) not infrequently survive their initial stages thanks to the highly informal management of labour. In this case, the relevant network is that of friends rather than family members, but the reasons and implications are broadly similar as far as the management of labour is concerned.

Households too buy services on the informal labour market, partly to avoid related administrative costs, and partly to avoid paying social security contributions. Such services are almost exclusively confined to assistance in housework and caring (e.g. baby-sitting, cleaning, etc.). While households may boost the demand for informal employment in most industrialised countries, the inefficiency of the welfare state in Italy has pushed up this tendency to distinctive proportions. Poor nursery provisions, inadequate transport facilities for schoolchildren and lack of home assistance for the elderly are key areas where families substitute for inadequate public provisions, often buying the relevant services on the informal labour market.

C. The degenerative segment

Those specific features of the firm structure which sustain the functional segment of disguised employment may be compatible with favourable terms of employment. By contrast, the degenerative segment feeds on factors, such as pauperisation and underdevelopment, which weaken the bargaining power of labour to the point that degenerative forms of employment are accepted, whatever the location within the productive structure may be. We call "degenerative" those forms where conditions of work and employment fall below socially acceptable minimum standards, or where the nature of the activity is illegal. The two possibilities are not mutually exclusive, and in fact are closely intertwined, especially in the South of the country where they occur more frequently.

Wherever the productive structure offers insufficient employment opportunities, the bargaining power of labour is weak. Workers may experience difficulties to organise themselves within certain sectors, perhaps on account of discontinuity and spatial dispersion of the activity. For example, in Southern Italy harvesters and unskilled construction workers are recruited, paid and supervised by intermediaries – the *caporale* in agriculture, the *capocottimista* in construction – who discretionarily determine terms and conditions of employment, taking advantage of the weakness of labour. Similar phenomena may also be found in backward manufacturing production, i.e. within the area of homeworking.

Lack of adequate employment opportunities has moreover fuelled the growth of the illegal economy, cemented via the family structure. Direct employment in illegal activities (kidnapping, prostitution, drug and extortion rackets, smuggling, etc.) is perforce disguised. Illegal activities feed on an extensive area of disguised employment in related legal activities and child labour is a jack-of-all-trades in this scenario.[6]

4. Disguised employment: Who is where?

In the Italian literature, disguised employment is fitted into categories which are effective for descriptive and statistical purposes, but too composite for analytical purposes: moonlighters, child labour, homeworkers, illegal immigrants, irregular employment, etc. Such categories may

---

6.   Often, outright illegal activities and informal ones combine to form economic sub-systems with a high degree of self-sufficiency and internal synergy. Such economic sub-systems of great complexity are found in urban contexts of the South.

not, in particular, be used to identify a hierarchy based on pay, employment and work conditions. We shall adopt a mixed approach that utilises descriptive categories but places the specific workers in the broad hierarchy defined by the above segments.

On a descriptive level, five categories of disguised employment may be identified: undeclared and under-declared homeworking, fictitious autonomous work, moonlighting, disguised self-employment, irregular and hidden wage employment.

Homeworking: thanks to the success of decentralised production, home-workers have become one of the largest categories of disguised employment (see section III). They comprise predominantly female manual workers in manufacturing, but conditions of employment differ considerably. While in, say, the industrial district of Carpi (Modena), skilled and well paid home-workers for the knitting industry are not infrequent, southern regions still abound with examples of exploitative homeworking, e.g. stitchers of strass on bridal costumes. We would attribute the first case to the novel segment of disguised employment, and the second to the degenerative segment, stressing that this differentiation needs not follow the clear-cut North-South divide, but may be found within the same region or industry.

Fictitious autonomous work: homeworkers may prefer to register as artisans, especially if they are male. This is only one of several examples of *de facto* wage employees legally registering as self-employed in order to evade contributions and taxes, or to increase earnings by increasing the work effort. Within this category, the dominant type in quantitative terms is that of skilled construction workers organised in gangs, informally working as subcontractors, for the completion of a given task (e.g. tiling). Most instances of wage employment disguised as self-employment unmistakably belong to the novel segment.

Moonlighting: in terms of the number of people involved, moonlighting outweighs any other category of disguised employment and, as such, it will be reconsidered in the second part of this paper. Moonlighters hold secondary occupations mainly in the service sector. With reference to the principal occupation, they record the highest frequencies among pro-fessionals, skilled industrial workers and public services employees (they total some 3,160,000).[7] Pay for public employees has generally been lower than in equivalent positions within the private sector; hours of work, on the other hand, have generally been less and the opportunities for overtime more restricted. Thus, both conditions and incentives are there to favour the spread of moonlighting.

Moonlighting is a significant means of entry to disguised employ-ment in industry. On the supply side, skilled or craft workers with a regular full time job elsewhere have been found to work in equivalent occupations for small firms outside their regular schedule. On the demand side, engineering firms are known to resort to moonlighters more frequently than

---

7.   ISTAT, *Annuario di Statistiche del Lavoro*. Rome, 1986.

other industrial branches. In quantitative terms, moonlighters are roughly on a par with undeclared homeworkers within industry.

Since moonlighters primarily aim at supplementing their income from their principal occupation, it is not surprising that far fewer women than men, but far more adults than young, are found among them. Moonlighting is so widespread across the occupational structure that the numbers involved are significant in the novel, the functional, as well as the degenerative segments of disguised employment. The latter segment is, however, comparatively modest, for here would mainly be included multiple job holders whose occupations were all irregular or even illegal.

The blooming of service occupations has generated a steady expansion of moonlighting, which started in the 1970s. Moreover, following recent changes in the tax structure, disguised moonlighting has gradually been encouraged to emerge. As a result of both the increasing trend and a fiscal/statistical effect, official sources (ISTAT, new national accounts estimates) have recorded a growth in moonlighters since the early 1980s.

Disguised self-employment: undeclared young and female family workers have historically been the figures of disguised self-employment in agriculture, services and, to a lesser extent, traditional crafts. The incentive here is greater if declaration entails the loss of some social security benefits. This may, for example, be the case of the wife of an industrial employee who is entitled to family allowances on the grounds of being a housewife and works as helper in, say, the pizzaria of one of her cousins during the season. Disguised family workers are progressively losing relevance, while the recent growth of service employment has enhanced the importance of other types among the self-employed.

Retail trade, small scale transport, personal and professional services contribute to disguised employment with a colourful multiplicity of undeclared self-employed figures. The occupations range from baby-sitter and part-time domestic help[8] to unlicensed car-park attendant, taxi driver and peddler, as well as to apprentice for a profession (lawyers, notaries, accountants, but also secretaries). The typology is highly composite in terms of skills represented, the sex or nationality of the worker, and the work schedule.

Domestic helpers are often adult housewives, working for a limited number of hours in each family. Baby-sitters are traditionally young and female, but often foreign au-pairs. Apprentices for the professions are young males and females, usually working full time for at least several months and paid a symbolic sum, if at all. Unlicensed occupations in retail distribution and in transport services have historically been filled by young and adult males of southern origin. Their numbers were markedly reduced by post-war development, but in recent years illegal immigrants have progressively revived their experience.

---

8. We include domestic helpers, baby-sitters and office cleaners within disguised self-employment, rather than wage employment, on the presumption that the majority work few hours for many customers. Even in legal terms, this justifies inclusion of these cases among the self-employed.

The current wave of foreign immigration from non-EEC countries is an novelty for Italy. It impinges on the rapid increase in living standards within the country and the concomitant tightening of immigration controls by traditional countries of immigration (UK, France, Germany, etc.). The average threshold of acceptance of unrewarding job conditions has gradually risen for Italian nationals, thanks in part to industrial and legal action. Unpleasant or poorly paid occupations thus tend to attract foreign workers. Three reasons explain why the bulk of these occupations occurs in the hidden or irregular labour market. First, work by foreigners is inadequately regulated by existing norms, so that most non-EEC foreign immigrants are clandestines or, if holding a visa, they do not hold a regular work permit. Second, the compensating wage differential, or the costs to obviate the unpleasant features and make these occupations attractive to domestic labour, would be so high as to price them out of the market. Third, the 1980s offer most opportunities for employment in the services, unlike the 1960s when industrial jobs attracted immigrants into European countries. And informal employment is more easily arranged in service occupations.

This is not to deny that, like moonlighters, foreign workers are found across a wide range of activities, from harvesting in agriculture, to night surveillance in industry, to household service, street selling, small scale transport and catering in the services. All available evidence suggests, however, that with the exception of maids and other domestic helpers the largest numbers are to be found among the self-employed in the services and, to a small extent, in construction.

Self-employment as peddlers or unlicensed operators in transport is a solution of last resort in a context of practically non-existent alternative opportunities. Both southerners and foreigners turning to such options should thus be placed in the degenerative segment of disguised employment. The remaining types of disguised self-employment belong to the functional segment since demand for the related services originates from households, family firms, or traditional professions.

Irregular and hidden wage employment: within industry, the two most common practices of under-declared wage labour are: off-books overtime, and delayed registration of the dates of hiring. Off-books overtime is widely resorted to by small firms, but large firms also practise it to some extent. By contrast, delayed recording of hiring is practised almost exclusively by small establishments, for it implies some laxity of administrative and fiscal controls, and becomes profitable when labour turnover is high, i.e. only within firms that can hire and fire freely. Some in-workers go entirely undeclared, thus swelling the ranks of hidden industrial employment. Informal hiring of young school leavers is almost a norm for small industrial and craft firms. The number of young people affected is very high. Outworkers too, as mentioned before, may go undeclared, as is the case with a considerable number of homeworkers.

Family firms in "traditional" services and commerce, tourism and agriculture also follow the practice of hiding or under-declaring employment, or even family labour, if only on account of seasonality and high administrative costs. But when the seasonal pattern is marked, even large firms may follow such a practice. Tourism, in particular, typifies the spread of *irregular* employment outside industry. Here, small and large establishments alike – hotels, restaurants, campings, etc. – customarily under-declare the total number of hours or weeks worked by seasonal employees. Some types of employees may go completely undeclared, young first entrants more than others, as is the case for industry. Retail trade and transport are the next most significant contributor to non-industrial disguised wage employment. More traditional forms are equally common; e.g. vendors in open air markets frequently recruit helpers informally, particularly during market days.

The borderline between hidden and irregular employment may be fluid. Recall the earlier example of the *caporalato* in agriculture and of the *cottimismo* in construction, where terms and conditions of employment are set by the respective intermediaries, who may also transport and supervise the workers. While under the *caporalato* and the *cottimismo* in the South of Italy, most workers go completely undeclared, this is not necessarily the case in Northern Italy. Southern *cottimisti* are disproportionately unskilled and hungry for jobs while in Northern Italy the majority of them are skilled operatives, who not only bargain successfully for high pay rates, but also impose registration of the minimum number of hours necessary for an adequate social security coverage. The northern *cottimisti* behave like the artisans in decentralised industrial production, preferring to increase their total work effort beyond the threshold that regular employees would face, in order to maximise their income. Similar labour practices may pertain to different segments, depending on labour market conditions and the characteristics of workers. Thus, the unskilled *cottimisti* in the South of the country ought to be placed in the degenerative segment, whereas the skilled *cottimisti* working in the North of Italy may be seen as part of the novel segment.

To which degree does disguised wage employment affect the young working population? Not only is informal hiring the main port of entry into employment in small firms for young school leavers, but also child labour is a significant entry to hidden employment. A recent authoritative estimate[9] suggests that there are in the neighbourhood of 500,000 child workers. The phenomenon is especially common in the South of the country, or among southern families migrated to the North. Industry is estimated to take the second biggest share of child labour (25%), after the retail trades (40-50%) [Dallago, 1988].

Child labour is a clear-cut illustration of the degenerative segment of disguised employment. But irregular or hidden employment takes such a variety of forms that entries are numerous for both the functional and the novel segment. Off-books overtime is an illustration of an extensive practice pertaining to the novel segment. Informal hiring of young people by family concerns in the tourist or retail industries unmistakably pertains to the functional segment.

---

9.   CESPE, 1983, cited in Ministero del Lavoro [1985, p. 126].

Finally, the example of the *cottismo*, respectively in Northern and Southern regions, suggests that similar labour practices may pertain to different segments, depending on labour market conditions and the characteristics of workers. For the unskilled *cottimisti* in the South of the country ought to be placed in the degenerative segment, whereas the skilled *cottimisti* working in the North of Italy may be seen as part of the novel segment.

III. Disguised employment: A closer look

1. A quantitative overall evaluation

To date, the most reliable and internally consistent estimate of the level and structure of disguised employment has been provided by the Central Statistical Office (ISTAT).[10] The ISTAT estimate for disguised employment has been elaborated as a cardinal step towards the re-evaluation of GDP, based on the assumption that underestimation of employment in existing labour statistics implies underestimation of GDP. Two sources of information have been used:

(i)   existing official labour statistics – discrepancies between different statistics have been taken to signal the existence of disguised employment;

(ii) *ad hoc* ISTAT surveys (e.g. on household expenditures for house maintenance) and official external sources (e.g. Ministry of Interior information on foreigners).

Man-year labour units have been chosen as units of account on the following grounds:

> Existing sources on the supply of labour (i.e. population census and labour force sample survey) count the number of people employed, or *heads*, and as a rule each head is counted only once and with reference to the principal occupation. ...[This way] the recorded supply of labour neglects secondary occupations. ... Sources on the demand side (i.e. industrial census) ... identify and count, however incompletely, the number of employment *positions* [Mamberti Pedullà et al., 1987].

The latter identifies the number of jobs to be performed in a specified interval and on a specified production site: e.g. the same occupation on weekdays and at the weekend within the same firm counts as two employment positions. Thus,

---

10.   Two previous estimates, based on different methodologies and therefore not directly comparable with the ISTAT one, reached the figures of 3,635,000 disguised workers in 1982 according to CESPE and 3,560,000 in 1983 according to the Labour Ministry [Ministero del Lavoro, 1985]. The methodological appendix presents in more detail the methodology followed by ISTAT.

... the sum of employment positions exceeds that of employed heads, since the first includes multiple jobs held by single heads. But neither the number of employed heads nor that of employment positions measure the quantity of labour effectively employed for national production. Hence, the need to introduce the new concept of 'standard labour units' [SLU] [ibid.].

In order to arrive at SLUs, each employment position is weighted in accordance with its duration, the reference duration being that of full-time year-round employment. For example, 4 full time positions of 3 months each correspond to 1 SLU. The results of the ISTAT re-evaluation for 1986 are shown in table 3 and are listed separately in terms of employment positions and labour units. The sectoral breakdown, currently available only in terms of positions, is summarised in table 4.[11]

Two clarifications must be made. First, owing to intrinsic difficulties, disguised foreign employment has been directly estimated in terms of labour units. For convenience, and following the ISTAT methodology, we have also recorded it in terms of employment positions, the two totals being reported as equal, given that no additional information is available. Second, employment in secondary occupations comprises both disguised and regular jobs. However, the share of the latter is probably negligible: the 1986 ISTAT Labour Force Sample Survey reports only 413,000 holders (heads) of at least one secondary occupation in the course of the year, most of them presumably being regular.

Table 3:   Regular and disguised employment, 1986 ('000)

	Employment positions	Labour units	
	No.	No.	%
Disguised employment			
- wage employment (by nationals)	2,174	1,744	7.66
- self-employment (by nationals)	1,991	1,227	5.39
- foreign employment	604	604	2.65
Regular employment			
- wage employment (nationals,foreigners)	13,263	13,036	57.28
- self-employment (nationals,foreigners)	4,726	4,725	20.76
Empl. in secondary occupations (regular and disguised)	7,088	1,423	6.25
Total employment	29,846	22,759	100.0

Source: ISTAT. See text for details.

11.   The figures reported in tables 3 and 4 had not yet been officially released when the paper was completed. Official figures released since contain some adjustments which do not alter significantly the orders of magnitude reported here, nor our analysis.

Table 4: Regular and disguised employment positions by sector, 1986 ('000)

	Agri-cult-ture	Ind-ust-ry	Cons-truc-tion	Market services			Non-mark. serv.	All sec-tors
				Total	(a)	(b)		
Disguised employment								
- wage employment (by nationals)	723	251	486	665	253	360	49	2174
- self-employment (by nationals)	824	182	134	851	531	291	-	1991
- foreign employment	58	12	42	205	163	2	286	603
Regular employment								
- wage employment (nationals,foreigners)	164	4410	719	4269	1640	1359	3701	13263
- self-employment (nationals,foreigners)	832	581	376	2937	2028	754	-	4726
Secondary employment (regular and disguised)	3986	257	100	2548	1284	573	197	7088
All positions	6587	5693	1857	11475	5899	3339	4233	29845

Notes: (a) distributive trades and repairs.
(b) services to firms, private health, education, entertainment.
Source: ISTAT.

Taking the latter consideration into account, the incidence of disguised over total employment in terms of labour units would reach, according to ISTAT, roughly 22%: 15.7% in principal occupations, plus a little more than 6% in secondary occupations.

Disguised foreign workers contribute 2.7% of total SLUs in the country – a considerable figure given that the process of immigration has just begun. Almost fifty per cent of total foreign employment positions (table 4) are found in non-marketable services where foreign workers are employed as domestic servants, mainly maids in metropolitan areas. An additional third is found in retail trade (peddlers), followed at some distance by other service occupations. Taken together, marketable and non-marketable services account for 81.4% of all foreign disguised employment. The remaining 18.6% is found mainly in agriculture and construction (9.6 and 7% respectively), while foreign employment in industry is negligible (2%) and concentrates on the processing of metals and minerals.

The contribution of moonlighters to total SLUs (6.25%) is more than double that of foreign workers. However, this figure would go down if moonlighting in agriculture were given its proper weight. In fact, agriculture accounts for 56% of total secondary employment positions (table 4). But these positions refer mostly to occasional cultivation for self-consumption by people employed elsewhere, housewives or pensioners who own a piece of land too small to be profitably cultivated otherwise. As such, this component of moonlighting is hardly comparable to the rest and has, in fact, been kept out of our previous analysis. If, on the strength of these considerations, agriculture is excluded, the service sector accounts for 80% of moonlighters, half of these in the distributive trades. This is broadly supportive of our discussion in section II.

Finally the incidence of disguised employment in principal occupations is much higher among the self-employed. The share of disguised in total self-employment ranges between 20 and 30% in all non-agricultural sectors, while it almost reaches 50% in agriculture. This last figure is not surprising given the absolute dominance of family firms in agriculture, and the especially high degree of informality of labour management in this sector.

Disguised employment is less important for wage employment as a whole (14% of labour units) than for self-employment (30%). However, the absolute amount of disguised wage employment exceeds that of disguised self-employment. Besides agriculture, irregular wage employees are particularly strongly represented in the construction industry (40% incidence), followed by the distributive trades. The incidence is comparatively low in manufacturing and, in the light of the preceding discussion, we would identify irregular positions there with those held by young first-time entrants.

2. The three main forms of disguised employment

For obvious reasons the ISTAT estimate of disguised employment highlights the importance of those figures which lend themselves more readily to quantitative investigation. This is the case for moonlighters and foreign labour. No less important is a third group, homeworkers, whose weight is only implicit in the ISTAT reconstruction. All of these categories will be explored in greater detail in the following sections.

A. Homeworking

Homeworking is regulated by law No. 877 of December 1973. A specific employment contract is provided for this form of atypical work, giving homeworkers the status of employees. The norms regulating employment conditions for homeworkers reflect the legislator's explicit wish to put, as far as possible, homeworking and standard wage employment on a par, and to restrict the specificities of homeworking to a minimum (i.e. those relating to the work place, the control over work activity, and the determination of pay). This legislation, as rigid as it is exhaustive, has hardly been applied.

Table 5 summarises available statistical information giving an approximate idea of the quantitative dimension of homeworking in Italy. Regular homeworkers (i.e. employed by a firm, with a regular employment contract, registered at the local Labour Office) total less than 90,000. *De facto* homeworkers registered as artisans and unregistered homeworkers are, of course, excluded.

Table 5: Homeworking in Italy: Estimates and sources

Source	Nature of data	Typology	No. of workers
Ministero del Lavoro, 1985	Ministry of Labour registers	Registered homeworkers (employee status only)	88,644
ISTAT Family Survey, 1983	Occasional survey	Estimate of homeworkers (employee and self-employed)	160,000
ISTAT LF Sample Survey 1983	Regular survey	People who work at home in industry (professionals, self-employed, family workers, wage labour)	482,000
CESPE, 1983	Estimate of homeworkers in hidden economy	Disguised homeworking (in manufacturing)	700,000

Taken together, properly registered homeworkers and those registered as artisans constitute the "emerged" component of the phenomenon to be distinguished from the hidden component. A first rough estimate of "emerged" homeworking was provided by the ad hoc ISTAT Family Survey carried out in 1983, with exclusive reference to manufacturing industry. Although this estimate nearly doubled (160,000) the previous figure recorded on the Ministry of Labour registers, it still probably underestimated self-employed "emerged" homeworkers. This is all the more true for men who prefer to consider themselves as artisans and more frequently register accordingly, both to conform and to reinforce the widespread perception that differences between the sexes are marked in terms of the skill content of homeworking.

One could however argue that, from an economist's point of view, a large number of the people employed in industry who declare "that they work at home" – in the regular ISTAT Labour Force Survey[12] – should be included among actual homeworkers. In this case, total "emerged" homeworking (employees and self-employed) would rise to over 400,000 in industry.

---

12.   In agriculture and services too, the survey reports large numbers of people whose place of work is their home. Nevertheless, while in agriculture family workers dominate, professionals and the self-employed dominate services.

The CESPE – a private research organisation – has put forward for the same year an estimate of hidden homeworking. Despite the rather traditional definition of homeworking adopted there (implying under-estimation of male homeworkers), hidden homeworkers are reported to number 700,000. This last figure should be considered with caution, although it is widely regarded as sufficiently representative.

There is no reason to believe that "irregular" and "hidden" home-working are distributed across industrial sectors differently from regularly registered homeworkers. We may thus refer to the distribution of the latter (table 6) in order to infer that of the former.

Table 6: Registered homeworkers (economically active) by industrial sector, at 31.12.1985

Industrial sector	%
Clothing and knitwear	44.8
Footwear	20.5
Textiles	8.7
Leatherwork	5.3
Metalwork	4.2
Jewelry	2.1
Straw Products	1.4
Wood	1.3
Others	11.7
Total	100.0
(Absolute number)	(88,644)

Source: Ministry of Labour, Rome (unpublished data)

The disproportionate incidence of homeworking in traditional manufacturing industries – textiles, clothing, knitwear and footwear – is clearly brought out by the data. The specificity of the Italian industrial structure in relation to these sectors is twofold: (i) they weigh heavily in manufacturing industry, both in terms of output and in terms of employment; and (ii) they are characterised by a high degree of productive decentral-isation. Both reasons help explain why outworking in general and home-working in particular have flourished in the country.

The vast majority of homeworkers still perform manual and highly labour intensive tasks within traditional manufacturing processes. Home-working is a typical female occupation, both because it is found in sectors characterised by a high degree of feminisation, and because the more labour-intensive stages of the production process are given out, i.e. those where female labour is traditionally employed. The share of male labour is rather small; men are found in a few sectors only, in occupations involving specific skills. In footwear, firms resort to female outworkers for manual sewing and for stitching, which require a large amount of labour, while male outworkers are assigned to hide cutting, which requires far less labour.

Despite the modest share of male homeworkers, their absolute number is significant, though the exact figure is statistically difficult to pinpoint. Moreover, given the rigid sexual division of labour within homeworking, male homeworkers tend to consider themselves – and eventually to register – as artisans.

Homeworking in Italy should not be considered as work of last resort exclusively, despite being feminised and labour-intensive. In fact, it is found in a variety of situations. For example, homeworkers around Lecce (in the South), by and large employed in footwear and clothing, are almost totally part of the submerged economy and are paid subsistence wages or less. In Empoli (near Naples) homeworkers can count on relatively high earnings, but they are paid off-books, with no social insurance. In the area around Milan where the production of ties is concentrated, homeworkers are well paid, with wages comparable to those of inworkers, and employed in conformity with the law. Finally, in Carpi (in Emilia Romagna), where the knitwear industry is well developed, homeworkers have a stable relation with the product market and their total earnings can be substantially higher that those of inworkers, given their higher skills and bargaining power.

B. Moonlighters

Moonlighting is an old practice but in-depth studies suggest that, in Italy, the phenomenon has taken novel and notable proportions since the beginning of the seventies. The extent of multiple job holding is difficult to assess: people who hold secondary jobs have every incentive not to report them. Table 7 summarises available statistical information on the extent of moonlighting – emerged and disguised – in Italy.

For 1986, the ISTAT Labour Force Survey records 413,000 people holding at least one secondary occupation. This figure can be taken to represent the emerged component of the phenomenon as it refers to people declaring that they have held at least a secondary job in the course of the year. This would indicate that 2% of all people employed hold one (or more) regular secondary occupation.

An overall evaluation of the "disguised" component of moonlighting was provided by the Ministry of Labour for 1983. Within the broader estimate of 3,564,000 people in hidden employment, roughly 1,600,000 moonlighters were identified. Under the strong assumption that they all represent regular workers with an undeclared secondary occupation, they would account for 7% of total employment in that year. If this assumption is relaxed, the 7% figure would drop. This estimate is definitely on the conservative side.

In fact, according to the most authoritative *ad hoc* survey funded by CNR,[13] and carried out between 1979 and 1981, the percentage incidence

---

13.   The survey on moonlighting was carried out in six metropolitan areas: Turin, Pisa, Caserta, Catania, Ancona and Bari. See Gallino [1985].

of multiple job holders (in total employment) was then comprised between 15 and 29% in most areas of the country.

Table 7: Moonlighting in Italy – Estimates and sources

Source	Nature of data	Typology	No. ('000)
ISTAT LF Sample Survey, 1986	Regular survey	No. of emerged moonlighters (*heads*) (people who declare to hold at least one secondary occupation)	413 (= 2% of total employment)
Ministero del Lavoro, 1985	Estimate of multiple job holders in disguised employment	No. of disguised moonlighters (*heads*)	1,650 (= 7% of total employment)
CNR research project on moonlighting, 1979-81	Estimate of multiple job holders in 6 areas	No. of moonlighters (*heads*) in the different areas (emerged and disguised)	(between 15 and 29% of total employment)
ISTAT National Accounting Data, 1986, new estimates	Estimate of employment positions	No. of secondary *employment positions* (emerged and disguised)	7,088 (= 23.7% of total positions)
ISTAT National Accounting Data, 1986, new estimates	Estimate of labour units	No. of *labour units* in secondary occupations (emerged and disguised)	1,423 (= 6.25% of total SLUs)

For the same years, the ISTAT figures (LF sample survey) for "emerged" secondary occupations were higher than in 1986, and ranged between 4 and 5%. The comparison between the CNR sources (e.g. disguised and emerged moonlighters) and the ISTAT source (e.g. emerged moonlighters only) would indicate that, at the turn of the 1970s, 10% or more of all people employed held one or more undeclared additional occupation. In other words, at least 10% of the whole employed population in Italy appear to be moonlighters in the narrow sense, i.e. to hold *irregular* or *undeclared* secondary occupations.

This order of magnitude is indirectly confirmed by the ISTAT new estimates in national accounting. Employment in secondary occupations (both regular and disguised) would contribute 23.7% of total employment positions in the country, and 6.25% of total SLUs according to these estimates. It thus seems plausible to infer that the total number of people holding secondary occupations is not too different from that suggested by the CNR survey.

The typical moonlighter is a male employee in his prime, who resorts to moonlighting in order to supplement family income during the critical financial stage of the family life cycle. Skilled craftsmen (among manual workers) and professionals (among non-manual workers) are over-represented within moonlighting. These workers exploit their skills or the professional capacity acquired in their main-regular job (or in previous occupations), offering services in irregular and non-protected activities. Most multiple job holders benefit from a system of guarantees (employment, income, social security, etc.), provided by their main-regular job. Only those workers already covered by the social security system can afford to sell their services on the irregular market and are in demand.

This explains why moonlighters hold their principal occupation mainly in large scale manufacturing and in the public sector, both of which sustain a structured and relatively "protected" labour market. In the CNR survey [Gallino, 1985], the incidence of multiple job holders in total employment of large industrial establishments has been found to average 25%. Among public employees, the corresponding figure varied between 18 and 53% for teachers, 52% for postal workers, 31% for local government employees and 41% for hospital workers.[14]

On the demand side, one of the factors accounting for the increase of moonlighting in the seventies has been the expansion of the subcontracting network within manufacturing. This has multiplied opportunities for industrial employees to informally engage in secondary activities to the benefit of small artisan firms. But it is definitely the growing demand in services that has multiplied opportunities for moonlighting. The demand may come from firms, who need to obtain skilled manual work or professional services at irregular intervals (translations, accounting, legal and tax advisors; exceptional maintenance, etc.); or it may come from households, who could not otherwise satisfy their need for services (electricians, plumbers, carpenters, private tuition, private medical care, etc.).

C. Foreign workers

Immigration from non-EEC countries took on considerable proportions in the late seventies and flows into the country have been increasing since. Until law No. 943 was passed in 1986, most non-EEC immigrant workers (henceforth, foreign workers) were *de facto* irregular, i.e. clandestines or without a regular work permit. The 1986 law has regularised as well as regulated foreign wage labour, but self-employment remains outside the scope of legality for foreign workers. In order to regularise their stay in the country, self-employed immigrants were given the option to register as unemployed. 93,194 foreign workers registered during the first ten months after the law came into force, of which 68%

---

14.   However suggestive these figures may be, they should nevertheless be treated with caution since they refer to local and very limited surveys.

registered as unemployed and 32% as wage employees (table 8). Since most registrations were made quickly, it is unlikely that numbers rose significantly later. Yet they refer to a negligible proportion of all foreign workers estimated to be in the country.

The most reliable non-ISTAT estimates in this respect quote figures ranging from 500,000 to 800,000 for the mid-1980s [Ministero del Lavoro, 1985 and 1988]. Other estimates put forward even higher figures. This suggests that the law has regularised less than 10% of employment positions covered by foreign labour (recall that the majority of foreigners are registered as unemployed). As noted earlier, one reason may be that self-employment has not been considered by the law. A related reason is that foreign workers find preferential employment within the hidden economy.

The 1986 ISTAT figure of 604,000 SLUs for (disguised) foreign labour (table 3) would suggest that the estimates on the higher side are more accurate, since it is reasonable to presume that the number of heads exceeds that of SLUs. However, there is no solid ground on which to compare the estimates from different sources.

**Table 8: Registration of foreign labour – Geographical distribution
(27 January to 27 October 1987)**

	Registration of foreigners		
	as unemployed	total	unempl./total (%)
Valle d'Aosta	49	111	44.1
Piemonte	4,234	5,918	71.5
Lombardia	7,614	14,890	51.1
Trentino A.A.	305	637	47.8
Veneto	2,125	3,473	61.8
Friuli V.G.	890	2,188	40.7
Liguria	4,185	4,866	86.0
Emilia Romagna	3,764	5,869	64.1
Toscana	3,724	6,249	59.6
Umbria	1,459	1,930	75.6
Marche	944	1,590	59.4
Lazio	11,542	15,709	73.4
Abruzzo	778	1,266	61.5
Molise	89	113	78.8
Campania	6,653	8,344	78.7
Puglia	1,910	2,675	71.8
Basilicata	273	332	82.2
Calabria	1,472	1,863	79.0
Sicilia	9,303	12,837	72.4
Sardegna	2,154	2,334	92.3
Total	63,386	93,194	68.0

Source: Campus [forthcoming].

Occupations and sectors where foreign workers are well represented differ notably from one Italian region to the next. In fact, three of the features that have customarily accompanied foreign immigration into industrialised countries are also apparent in Italy, namely, geographical, occupational and ethnic bunching of foreign employment. Each region or area where immigration has been significant is thus associated with a typical set of occupations where foreigners have made inroads. Maids are usually females and Asians. But, while in the regions of Lazio and Campania the majority come from the Philippines and Cape Verde, in North-eastern regions and in Emilia nationals of Cape Verde, Sri Lanka or the Seychelles predominate. Egyptians dominate the catering industry in all regions, but Tunisians, Algerians or others may also work in this trade in specific regions. Work on fishing boats is monopolised by Tunisians and is mainly found in Sicily. Peddlers are mainly Moroccans but they may work alongside Tunisians in Emilia, or Egyptians in Lazio, or Somalians and Eritreans in Lombardia, and so on.

On the quantitative level the geographical distribution of immigrant labour may be assessed on the basis of the data on registration. Although absolute numbers are grossly underestimated, there are no reasons to believe that the degree of underestimation varies considerably across regions. According to these data (table 8), Lombardia, Lazio, Campania and Sicily have witnessed the strongest inflow of foreigners. Taken together, they account for over 55% of total registration in the country. Milan, Rome and Naples – the capitals of three of these regions – absorb an especially large share of foreign workers.

As for the sectoral distribution, we have already commented on the disproportionate importance of service occupations that is indicated by the ISTAT figures on foreign employment. Confirmation comes from data on registrations made in compliance with the 1986 law. The data refer to the occupational distribution of registration in the city of Milan (table 9). The assumption underlying these data is that all registered unemployed were actually working clandestinely in those occupations which they had specified at the time of registration, so that their sectoral distribution would be indicative of their actual distribution in the employment structure.

If all clerical work is included among tertiary occupations, the share of the latter ranges from 58.8% for foreigners registered as unemployed – i.e. for disguised self-employment according to the above assumptions – to 85.7% for foreigners registered as employees. However, the figures for self-employed are bound to be an underestimate. The table reports, in fact, a negligible incidence of foreign employment in the distributive trades. Such is the discrepancy between this latter information and common knowledge confirmed by ISTAT estimates that it is difficult to avoid the conclusion that one of the most visible segments of foreign labour, peddlers, has massively disregarded the legal obligation to register. This is an indication of the degree of caution needed when analysing the scanty information available.

Table 9: Registered foreign labour by sector or occupational category in the city of Milan, 1987 (% distribution)

	Registered as	
	unemployed	employees
Personal services	15.5	18.7
Cleaning and others	17.5	45.8
Professionals, teachers	0.6	5.5
Clerical	17.8	13.1
Industry and crafts	23.5	9.8
Distributive trades	3.7	1.8
Transport	3.7	0.8
Construction	16.2	4.2
Agriculture	1.5	0.3
Total	100.0	100.0

Source: Campus [forthcoming].

IV. Concluding summary

No less than 20% of the total labour input to GDP is supplied under irregular terms of employment or goes entirely undeclared. Disguised employment is especially common among the self-employed who make up as much as 30% of total employment in the country. Distinctively high proportions of disguised and self-employment are not a recent feature of the Italian labour market; nor are they contingent on current trends towards deregulation. To some extent, they are accountable in terms of the resilience of productive networks based on family and artisan firms. These firms have evolved and adapted to a rapid pace of development during the post-war period, rather than given way to large managerial concerns.

The rigidity of labour market institutions has buttressed the viability of these flexible production networks, particularly in the face of the current diversification of product demand. But viability has ultimately been dependent on informality in employment relations and labour management. Inadequate welfare provisions have also fostered informal employment. Families often obviate these inadequacies by buying the relevant services on the informal labour market.

Self-employment and especially disguised employment are so entrenched in the functioning of the Italian labour market, and such an important part of it, that they are bound to form a highly composite picture in terms of workers' employment conditions (e.g. pay, stability, mobility and working conditions). In fact, the association between disguised and secondary employment conditions is not justified within the context of the Italian labour market.

The complexity of the picture has discouraged the existing literature from going beyond descriptive typologies, such as homeworkers, moonlighters, (non-resident) foreign workers, irregular wage employment, and so on.   As an attempt to make a step forward, we have identified three segments within disguised employment – the novel, the functional and the degenerative segments – and outlined the criteria for assigning existing typologies to the relevant segment. In our view, these segments provide an analytical connection between the productive (or social) structure and the (informal) labour market, as well as a broad hierarchy based on overall conditions of employment.

Being so composite, disguised employment could not be exclusively confined to the "disadvantaged" sections of the labour force, or to the "mature" industries. The case of women may serve as an illustration. When decentralised production was discovered in the 1970s, it was believed to have fostered informal employment mainly among women because they constitute a flexible, cheap supply. As the research progressed, it was found that the division of labour among the outworkers (including irregulars) mirrored that of the (regular) inworkers. Within textiles, for example, the cutting was done by men, who registered as artisans even if they acted de facto as homeworkers. Female homeworkers would do the sewing, thus following a very similar pattern to that observed within the firms.

Over the years, the composition of disguised employment has changed. Homeworkers are declining, at least in the North of the country, while moonlighters, foreign labour and young workers appear to be increasing. But, perhaps, young workers have always been a major component of disguised employment. For, unlike other countries, Italy lacks effective institutions that structure and organise the first entry of youth into employment, e.g. the German apprenticeship system. As a result, informal hiring in small concerns often represents the only channel of entry for young workers. In addition, high levels of unemployment over the past and current decades have encouraged attempts by youth to turn to forms of self-employment that frequently border on the informal labour market. The good thing is that such attempts occasionally give rise to innovative enterprises.

If, on the whole, young workers may be penalised in having to resort to or accept irregular forms of employment, moonlighters largely benefit from this possibility. They are, in fact, typified as a male worker in his prime who cumulates the salary from a stable, skilled occupation in a large firm or in the public sector with the earnings from at least one secondary occupation where similar skills are required. The majority of foreign workers – often illegal immigrants – find themselves at the other extreme of the spectrum from moonlighters. This is the case for (foreign) peddlers who eke out a living, if at all, under conditions of severe precariousness.

The important point to stress is that the different components of disguised employment need not compete with each other. In particular, moonlighters do not enter into competition with young workers. Demand for the services of the former exists insofar as they possess skills and experience which they can afford to sell on the informal market. Foreign labour is a more complex case. In many occupations competition with domestic labour should not arise, given that foreigners predominantly hold occupations that would disappear if the only candidates were nationals. However, this is not the case for all occupations. Unlike other European countries (e.g. the UK), where the largest flows of immigrants in the sixties found their way into a tight labour market, Italy still records vast reserves of labour, especially among women. Thus, the recent supply of immigrants faces a slack labour market, too slack to meet even the domestic potential, i.e. the newly emerging supply of women.

Italian women and foreign women may not compete for the same occupations because of differences in aspirations. That is, only female immigrants may be willing to serve as maids. Likewise, Italian women may not currently compete with male foreign labour because of occupational segregation, as well as differences in aspirations. Nevertheless, the urge to find employment might gradually induce foreign male workers to disregard the sexual division of labour. Or, sections of Italian women may be induced to lower their aspirations in order to gain entry into employment.

Methodological appendix

The comparison between sources is a key step in the methodology devised by ISTAT for re-evaluating employment. For simplicity, we refer here to the re-evaluation of employment in the services and in industry. The reference year in this case is 1981, when both the Population Census and the Industrial Census were taken (henceforth PC and IC, respectively). The two Censuses were compared to the Labour Force Sample Survey (LF) for the same year, after the data from the three sources were fully harmonised. The steps outlined below for the comparison were carried out separately for employees and the self-employed, and at the finest possible level of aggregation.

One possible case is that depicted by the diagram below. Employment according to the LF exceeds by the amount *cd* that recorded by the PC, and the latter exceeds employment according to the IC by the amount *bc*.

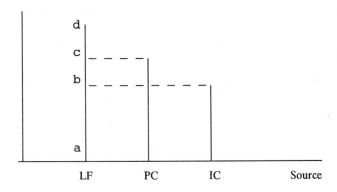

Under the assumption that the IC picks up regular employment positions, the total of the latter was assumed to coincide with that reported by this source, corresponding to segment *ab*. The PC, on the other hand, was assumed to record all those who work full time, under regular or irregular terms of employment. Thus the difference between the PC and the IC, corresponding to segment *bc* in our figure, was assumed to measure full-time, irregular positions. Finally, the difference between the PC and the LF, i.e. segment *cd*, corresponds to those who work on an irregular but also casual or temporary basis.

An alternative case arises when the Industrial Census reports higher figures than the Population Census. In this case, the difference has been taken to indicate multiple employment positions. The final estimate of multiple employment positions required, however, integration with additional estimates based on a large body of information.

Finally, estimation of "irregular" foreign workers required an *ad hoc* procedure. The estimate comprises both illegal immigrants and regular foreign residents working under irregular employment conditions.

References

Abburrà, L. (1987): "Il lavoro del disoccupato", in *Politica ed Economia* (Rome), No. 4.

Albertini, S. (1980): "Il lavoro minorile in provincia di Brescia", in *Economia e Lavoro* (Padua), No. 1-2.

Alvaro, G. (1979): "L'Italia sommersa che non paga le tasse", in *Mondoperaio* (Rome), Feb.

Arlacchi, P. (1983): *La mafia imprenditrice*. Bologna, Il Mulino.

Arena, G. (1983): "Lavoro femminile ed immigrazione dai paesi afro-asiatici a Roma", in *Studi Emigrazione* (Rome), No. 70.

Becchi Collidà, A. (1986): "I giovani a Napoli e l'occupazione", in *Politica ed Economia* (Rome), No. 4.

Brambilla, M. (1984): "I lavoratori stranieri in Italia: decifrare e ricostruire una condizione", in Demerio, D. (ed.): *Immigrazione straniera e interventi formativi*. Milan, Franco Angeli.

Brusco, S.; Solinas, G. (1986): *Mobilità occupazionale e disoccupazione in Emilia*, Materiali di discussione No. 17. University of Modena, Dipartimento di Economia Politica.

Calvanese, F. (1983): "Gli immigrati stranieri in Italia", in *Inchiesta* (Bari), Oct.-Dec.

Calvaruso, C. (1980): "I lavoratori clandestini: verso un nuovo modello di migrazioni internazionali", in *Quaderni di Economia del Lavoro* (Milan), No. 12.

Campus, A. (forthcoming): *Immigrazione straniera e mercato del lavoro, Regione Lombardia*. Milan, Assessorato del Lavoro.

Cetro, R. (1978): "Il lavoro a domicilio a Pomigliano d'Arco", in *Inchiesta* (Bari), No. 33.

CENSIS (1978): *La presenza dei lavoratori stranieri in Italia*. Rome, Censis.

—— (1985): *Dossier "Illecito". L'economico ed il soggettivo nello sviluppo delle attività illecite in Italia*. Rome, Censis.

Collicelli, X. (1988): "Speciale migrazioni. Oltre la residualità", in *Note e Commenti* (Rome), No. 5.

Dallago, B. (1988): *L'economia irregolare*. Milan, Franco Angeli.

Deaglio, M. (1985): *Economia sommersa ed analisi economica*. Turin, Giappichelli.

Faustini, G. (1987): "(Lav)oro nero: la scoperta dell'ISTAT", in *Politica ed Economia* (Rome), No. 4.

FLC Napoli (ed.) (1982): *La camorra e il mercato edilizio.* Naples.

Franchi, M. (1986): "Giovani e occupati: chi assume nell'industria", in *Politica ed Economia* (Rome), No. 5.

Frey, L. (1979a): "Dal lavoro nero alla misurazione del reddito sommerso", *Notiziario CERES di Economia del Lavoro* (Rome), Mar.

—— (1979b): "'Lavoro nero' e politica dell'occupazione in Italia", in Frey et al.: *Studi di statistica e di economia in onore di Libero Lenti.* Milan, Giuffrè.

Gallino, L. (ed.) (1982): *Occupati e bioccupati.* Bologna, Il Mulino.

—— (ed.) (1985): *Il lavoro e il suo doppio. Seconda occupazione e politiche del lavoro in Italia.* Bologna, Il Mulino.

Guiducci, M. (1980): "Il lavoro minorile in provincia di Salerno", in *Economia del Lavoro* (Rome), No. 1-2.

Laino, G. (1984): *Il cavallo di Napoli. I quartieri spagnoli.* Milan, Franco Angeli.

Lungarella, R. (1983): "L'immigrazione straniera in Emilia Romagna. I risultati di una ricerca sui lavoratori egiziani a Reggio Emilia", in *Inchiesta* (Bari), Jan.-Feb.

Mamberti Pedullà, G.; Pascarella, C.; Abbate, C. (1987): *Le nuove stime della 'occupazione presente' in contabilità nazionale. Concetti, metodologia e risultati.* Rome, ISTAT (mimeo).

Mingione, E. (1985): "Marginale e povero: il nuovo immigrato in Italia", in *Politica ed Economia* (Rome), No. 6.

—— (1987): "Lavoro informale e stili di vita nel Mezzogiorno", in *Politica ed Economia* (Rome), No. 5.

—— (1988): *Underground economy and irregular forms of employment: the case of Italy.* Brussels, Commission of the European Communities – Employment, Social Affairs and Education, V/1780/88.

Ministero Dell'Interno (1981): *Conference "Immigrazione Araba in Italia e in Sicilia".* Rome (mimeo).

Ministero Del Lavoro e Della Previdenza Sociale (1985): *La politica occupazionale per il prossimo decennio.* Rome, Poligrafico, 2 Vols.

—— (1988): *Rapporto '88. Lavoro e politiche dell'occupazione in Italia.* Rome, Fondazione Brodolini e CER.

Natale, M. (1983): "Fonti e Metodi di rilevazione della popolazione straniera in Italia", in *Studi Emigrazione* (Rome), No. 71.

Pettenati, P. (1979): "Illegal and unrecorded employment in Italy", in *Economic Notes* (Siena), Vol. 8, No. 1.

Pugliese, E. (1983): "Aspetti dell'economia informale a Napoli", in *Inchiesta* (Bari), No. 59-60.

—— (1985): "Quale lavoro per gli stranieri in Italia", in *Politica ed Economia* (Rome), No. 9.

Reyneri, E. (1984): *Doppio lavoro e città meridionale.* Bologna, Il Mulino.

Rosti, L. (1986): "Imprenditori per scelta, ovvero per necessità", in *Politica ed Economia* (Rome), No. 2.

—— (1987): "L'occupazione indipendente in Italia: Stock e flussi", in *Economia e Lavoro* (Padua), Vol. 21, No. 4.

Rey, G.M. (1985): "Influenza del sommerso sulla formazione del prodotto interno lordo", in Rey et al.: *Il sommerso, realtà ed influenza dell'economia irregolare nella società italiana.* Novara, Europia.

Solinas, G. (1982): "Labour market segmentation and workers' careers: the case of the Italian knitware industry", in *Cambridge Journal of Economics*, Vol. 6, No. 4.

—— (1986): *Mercati del lavoro locali e carriere di lavoro giovanili.* University of Modena, Dipartimento di Economia Politica (mimeo).

Tagliaferri, T. (1980): "Il lavoro minorile in provincia di Milano", in *Economia del Lavoro* (Rome), No. 1-2.

Varesi, P.A.; Villa, P. (1986): *Homeworking in Italy, France and the United Kingdom: Final Report.* Brussels, Commission of the European Communities – Employment, Social Affairs and Education, V/1910/86.

Villa, P. (1986): *The structuring of labour markets: The steel and construction industries in Italy.* Oxford, Clarendon Press.

7 The emergence of atypical employment in the European Community

Danièle Meulders and Bernard Tytgat[1]

A series of forms of employment has developed which differs from so-called "traditional employment" in such diverse respects as duration of contract, working hours, exceptions from wage agreements, etc. This paper, which is essentially descriptive, outlines trends in the EEC, synthesising studies carried out on the basis of a common work plan.[2] It reviews different forms of atypical employment (part-time work, temporary work, work at unusual times, self-employment, sub-contracting and family help, home-working, training courses). For each we consider its definition, assess quantitatively its importance and development – largely on the basis of the EEC Labour Force Survey, 1986 (LFS) – and identify its characteristics at individual, micro-economic and macro-economic levels. Subsequently, we seek to analyse the attitudes adopted by the social partners and public authorities towards such forms of employment.

I. Part-time work

Definitions of part-time work in the EEC countries are fairly similar: the part-time worker is a person who exercises an activity for a duration of time less than the norm. In some cases the latter is specified: 35 hours a week for Portugal, the Federal Republic of Germany and the Netherlands, 40 hours for Spain, 34 hours for Greece and 16 hours for the United Kingdom. In France, between 1975 and 1981, part-time workers were those working less than 30 hours a week; since 1982, they are persons declaring that they exercise their main activity part time.

---

1.   Département d'Economie Appliquée, Université Libre de Bruxelles (DULBEA).

2.   This paper is the synthesis of a study, *Women in atypical employment*, carried out in 1988 for the Commission of the European Communities by a group of experts: M.P. Alcobendas Tirado (Spain), M. Cavouriaris and A. Protopsaltis (Greece), A. Gauvin (France), E. Garnsey (UK), P. Jackson (Ireland), R. Knudsen (Denmark), M. Langkau-Hermann (FRG), D. Meulders and B. Tytgat (Belgium), H. Perista and M. Silva (Portugal), A. Schermer and F. Crutzen (Netherlands) and P. Villa (Italy).

Table 1: Part-time work

	Part-time workers as % of total employment	Women part-time workers as % of total of women employed	Main sectors	Main status
Less than 10%				
Italy	5.02	9.51	0	Employees
Greece	5.78	10.33	0	Self-empl/employees
Portugal	6.04	9.98	0	Self-empl/employees
Ireland	6.14	14.29	6 9	Employees
Luxembourg	6.71	15.69	6 9	Employees
Belgium	9.37	22.64	6 9	Employees
10% to 20%				
France	11.71	23.05	6 9	Employees
F.R. Germany	12.91	29.77	6 9	Employees
Over 20%				
Denmark	23.67	41.88	6 9	Employees
United Kingdom	21.36	44.51	6 9	Employees

Notes: 0 = Agriculture; 6 = Trade; 9 = Other services.
Source: 1986 Labour Force Survey data.

1. Estimates and trends

The proportion of part-time work in total employment has evolved differently in the different countries, irrespective of the percentage of workers working part-time at the beginning of the period under study. In Belgium and Spain, the proportion of these workers doubled between 1975 and 1985, and there was considerable growth also in the Netherlands, the United Kingdom and France, while in the other countries growth (whether negative or positive) has been less spectacular. The situation is similar for growth in the percentage of women workers working part-time: there has been considerable growth in Belgium, the Netherlands, Spain, the United Kingdom and France, with maintenance of the status quo or a decline in the other countries. It would therefore seem that in the first group of countries growth in part-time employment corresponds to an increase in the number of women employed in part-time work.

The situation was as follows in 1986 (table 1): in Denmark and the United Kingdom, over 20% of the labour force was engaged in part-time work, with between 10% and 20% in France and the Federal Republic of Germany and less than 10% in the other countries. There is a constant factor in all cases: percentages are twice as high for women workers.

Both the proportion of women among part-time workers and employment status are correlated with those sectors of activity in which this form of work is concentrated. There are two groups of countries: one where part-time work is relatively important in the primary sector (Greece,

Portugal and to a lesser extent Ireland, Italy and Spain), and one where part-time work is heavily concentrated in services and trade (the Federal Republic of Germany, Belgium, Netherlands, the United Kingdom, Denmark and France). In the first group, men's share of part-time work is higher (dominant in the case of Greece) and independent worker status more widespread. In the second group, women are very much in the majority and wage work dominates. The growth of the proportion of women in part-time employment does not follow the same grouping of countries; there has been an increase in this proportion in Spain, Ireland, the Netherlands and the Federal Republic of Germany, a decrease in Greece, Portugal, Belgium, the United Kingdom and Denmark and no change in Italy. France shows an increase between 1975 and 1985 and a slight decrease between 1985 and 1987.

Although information is fragmentary, several general trends can be identified: (i) the qualifications of part-time workers are lower than those of full-time workers; (ii) the number of hours worked per week has decreased in the Federal Republic of Germany, the Netherlands and Ireland, whereas the percentage of persons working between 0 and 15 hours a week (0 and 18 hours in Ireland) has increased, with the number remaining stable in Belgium;[3] (iii) the percentage of married women among part-time workers is relatively higher in the Federal Republic of Germany, the United Kingdom, Ireland and France. In France, there has been an increase in the proportion of wage-earners among women working part-time.

2. Characteristics of part-time work

From the workers' point of view, the main advantage of part-time work is the possibility of reconciling professional and family life. But this advantage, which is viewed as such mainly by or on behalf of women, is only true if the work itself is not flexible. Moreover, more and more workers - mainly men but also young women – are claiming that they accept part-time work because they have been unable to find full-time work. The disadvantages of this form of employment are a faster pace of work than for full-time workers, a low level of skills required for the work, the fact that it is relatively unsatisfying, an absence of promotion prospects and a lack of contact with colleagues. Another serious disadvantage, which should however be corrected by the public authorities, is inadequate social protection. Although "passive" actions[4] have been undertaken by the authorities in several countries, there remain a considerable number of problems connected with the social protection of part-time workers.

From the firms' point of view, the advantages of this form of work derive from increased flexibility, permitting a better organisation of work, an

---

3.   According to the Labour Force Survey, the mode of the distribution of weekly working hours is between 11 and 20 hours for all countries.

4.   See section VII.3 for a discussion of the distinction between "passive" and "active" policy actions.

increase in hourly productivity, a low level of unionisation and a drop in absenteeism.

It is difficult to evaluate the impact of part-time work at the macro-economic level. It would seem that in Belgium this form of employment is behind the increase in homeworking, which has become apparent since 1983. In the United Kingdom, between 1971 and 1981, the expansion of part-time work was the only source of growth in employment. In Denmark, part-time working has probably permitted an increase in female activity and has had a positive repercussion on public finance. Lastly, in Ireland, increased employment in the public sector has to a large extent been in the form of part-time work.

II. Temporary work

According to the widest definition (the Italian report) "temporary work includes all wage-earning and independent working activities of a non-permanent nature". Temporary work covers a range of employment categories which are not mutually exclusive:

- *Temporary contract work*: The employer and the employee agree that the end of the period of employment is to be determined by objective criteria such as the expiry of a given period or the completion of a task (individual training contracts in an enterprise and make-work schemes for the unemployed form part of this group where they are not permanent in nature). The workers involved are generally wage-earners.

- *Interim employment*: a three-sided relationship exists between an interim employment agency, the temporary worker and the user enterprise. It generally involves wage-earners.

- *Casual work*: This is temporary work characterised by its occasional nature, related to variations in the level of activities in particular sectors (if the person is a wage-earner, he will also come into the category of temporary contract worker). Those involved include both wage-earners and the self-employed.

1. Estimates and trends

Quantitative evaluation runs into many problems and there is a considerable risk of underestimation.

Temporary work in the broad sense of the term: There is no uniform statistical basis in EEC countries, and figures from the 1986 Labour Force Survey (LFS) which correspond to temporary work in the broad sense of the term relate only to wage-earners. However, in Italy, for example, 60% of temporary workers are self-employed.

Table 2: **Temporary work**

Country	Temporary workers as % of total employment	Women temporary workers as % of total of women employed	Main Sectors		
			Women	Men	Total
Italy	3.23	4.84	9 0	5 0	0 9 5 6
Luxembourg	4.02	5.88	9 6	9 6	9 6
France	5.30	5.92	9 6	9 6 5	9 6 5
Belgium	6.76	9.60	9	9	9
United Kingdom	6.19	8.14	9 6	9 6	9 6
Ireland	6.23	10.12	9 6	5 9 6	9 6
Greece	9.36	8.20	9 6	5	5 (3 2)
F.R. Germany	9.71	10.86	9 6	9 6 3	9 6
Denmark	9.98	11.39	9 6	9	9
Portugal	10.08	10.63	4 9	5 4 6	4 9 6

Note: 0 = Agriculture; 3 = Metal working; 4 = Manufacturing; 5 = Construction;
6 = Trade; 9 = Other services.
Source: 1986 Labour Force Survey data.

Fixed-term work: No analysis in terms of quantitative evolution is possible, except for France where, between 1982 and 1987, the percentage of wage-earners on fixed-term contracts increased from 1.7 to 2.7%. This form of employment is concentrated in the service sector and affects women more than men, but the proportion of women seems to be less high than in temporary work overall.

Interim work: Available data relate only to the FRG, Belgium and France. Attention must be drawn to the relatively small numbers involved in this form of employment, which has developed differently in the three countries: a slight increase followed by a stable situation in the FRG, a doubling of the numbers involved in Belgium, an increase between 1975 and 1980 in France followed by a decrease until 1984 and a further increase since 1985. The proportion of women has decreased during the period in all three countries. This form of employment is affecting an increasing number of young men and production workers in Belgium. In the FRG, a considerable number of foreigners are concerned and interim work is markedly seasonal in nature. In France, such work is concentrated among young workers and the unskilled.

Seasonal work: In Denmark this form of employment involves unskilled female workers in the food (fishing) industry, while for men it is concentrated in the building and civil engineering sectors. In Spain, where data are not broken down by sex, seasonal work involves 4.5% of the labour force, mainly in agriculture. In the UK, it is concentrated in the service sector, with 64% of seasonal workers being fairly young, relatively unskilled women. Seasonal workers have the same characteristics as most part-time workers. In Portugal, 66.5% of seasonal workers are women who work in agriculture and services, with men working in the building and civil engineering sectors.

Casual work: Statistics are available for four countries. In Portugal, such work represents 1.2% of those in employment, 42% of casual workers being women, working mainly in agriculture and services. In Spain, casual work concerns a much higher percentage of those in employment – 13.3%, of which 49% are women, with 30% of casual work being in the agricultural sector. In Italy, it covers undeclared workers; this form of employment is decreasing – it represented 4.6% of occupied workers in 1977 and 3.3% in 1985. A decrease in the proportion of women is also apparent, and there has been a decrease for agriculture and an increase for services. Lastly, in Ireland, this form of employment decreased between 1979 and 1984. Women comprise 67.4% of casual and seasonal workers but this percentage seems to be declining, with a considerable decrease in the agricultural sector to the benefit of trade and services, which explains the transition from the seasonal work concept to that of casual work.

2. Characteristics of temporary work

In the vast majority of cases, workers have become temporary workers because they have been unable to find permanent employment. In Denmark, there are two categories of temporary contract workers: (i) highly skilled experts, to be found in both the private and public sectors, and (ii) workers hoping to find an opening for entry into the labour market, even though there is no guarantee of this. Whereas in the first case workers and employers seem to be satisfied, this is not so for workers in the second case. In the UK, temporary contract workers are more skilled than casual and seasonal workers and are more often self-employed.

This type of employment is hardly compatible with family life, given its inherent lack of security. Temporary workers tend to be more ready to put up with difficult working conditions. They often also have a succession of fixed-term contracts with the same employer, interrupted by varying periods of unemployment. They are also at a disadvantage with respect to training and promotion. There is, however, apparently no significant difference in earnings for otherwise similar jobs.

Three problems arise in relation to social protection: (i) no layoff payment; (ii) the obligation to work a minimum number of hours of work per week in order to qualify for sickness and unemployment benefits; (iii) the obligation to have been in employment for a minimum period in order to qualify for sickness and unemployment benefits. The last two problems have already been raised in connection with part-time employment. If enterprises and governments wish to see temporary work develop, it will be essential to review the social legislation applicable to these workers in order for them to be assured of effective social protection.

The use of temporary contracts enables firms to have greater flexibility in controlling employment levels by adapting them more rapidly to output fluctuations. Such adaptability also involves reduced dismissal costs. The risk arising from fluctuations in activity levels is thus shifted onto workers by the use of temporary employment. Moreover, temporary workers are often more productive because they are under a constant threat of losing their employment, which tends to accelerate the rate at which other workers perform in a production line.

The macro-economic impact of temporary contract work is very difficult to evaluate. Simulations with macro-economic models to test the effect of perfect numerical flexibility (i.e. the instant and total adjustment of effective employment to optimal employment for enterprises), carried out in Belgium, show marked differences by sector and time period, with a negative impact on employment since 1975. This negative result is due to weak or nonexistent economic growth, which in the absence of dismissal costs would have encouraged enterprises to reduce employment more than was actually the case. Another macro-economic impact can be measured by the effect on social security expenditure. Two different arguments have been put forward: according to some experts, such expenditures will tend to decrease since temporary workers are not always able to enjoy benefits, while, according to others, expenditures will increase because of the lack of stability in such employment and increasing periods of unemployment.

III. Work involving unsocial, variable and fragmented working hours

Such forms of work result from different ways of organising working time: i.e. shift work, night work, weekend work, variable work schedules (such as staggered arrival, departure and break times), "block" working (typical of Denmark; distinguished from shift work by the greater flexibility of hours or "blocks"), on-call work (in Italy and the Netherlands, where the worker must be available when the enterprise needs him), etc.

1. Estimates and trends

Quantitative analysis is based on the 1986 LFS and comprises an overview of the responses given under the heading: "Normal working hours cannot be provided because hours worked vary considerably from one week to another or from one month to another". As this definition is very broad, the data provided do not allow for any breakdown into forms of employment as above. It can be noted, however, that the numbers involved seem to be relatively small and that there has been no spectacular change. The lack of data makes it difficult to draw any precise conclusions. It may be noted that women are represented less than men, that two main sectors emerge – agriculture, and services and trade – and that self-employment predominates.

Table 3:   **Work involving unsocial and variable hours**

	Such work as % of total employment	Such work as % of female employment	Main Sectors	Main Status
Belgium	2.84	2.32	6	Self-employed
Greece	0.64	0.57	0	Self-employed
France	10.89	8.18	0 9 6	Employees
Ireland	7.53	4.17	0 9 6	Employees
Italy	1.05	0.96	0 6 9	Self-employed
Portugal	3.81	3.09	0 6	Self-employed

Notes: 0 = Agriculture; 6 = Trade; 9 = Other services.
Source: 1986 Labour Force Survey data.

2. Characteristics of work involving unsocial and variable hours

From the worker's point of view, these forms of employment often appear incompatible with family life and may prove to have a harmful effect on health. The Danish expert has pointed out that reduced working time may encourage some workers to participate in more than one "block" (thereby increasing not only their income but also the total duration of their working time, with the negative consequences which the latter implies). The Belgian report, however, points to the fact that these forms of work are sometimes a response to new needs experienced by workers, and permit a better organisation of their family life and leisure activities. Research in France, however, points to the possibility of conflict between the rhythm imposed by non-standard work schedules and social and family organisation of time. In addition, as the social security system was set up in terms of traditional employment, such workers will in some cases be disadvantaged in this respect.

There are two main reasons for enterprises to introduce a more flexible organisation of working time: firstly, to reorganise and, in particular, extend production time in order to make more intensive use of existing capacity; secondly, to adjust a firm's activities to its workload. The Belgian report points out that, to the extent that such arrangements correspond to workers' particular circumstances, there may frequently be less absenteeism and increased output.

IV. Self-employed and family workers

The self-employed worker works on his own account, organises his work himself, owns the means of production and is responsible for production. The family worker is a person working in an enterprise belonging to a relative, generally a spouse. Work is often remunerated not in cash but in kind (board and lodging, etc.).

1. Self-employed workers

The highest percentage of self-employed workers is to be found in Greece, Italy and Portugal, then in Ireland, Belgium and Spain and, lastly, in France, the UK, Luxembourg and Denmark. Special attention should be drawn to two countries: Ireland, where the number of self-employed workers has been halved (due largely to a reduction in the number of agricultural workers); and the UK, where there was an upsurge in such workers in the early 1980s. Developments in the other countries have been much less spectacular: there has been a slight increase in the percentage of self-employed workers in the FRG, Belgium, Spain and Italy and a slight decrease in Denmark, Greece and the Netherlands. The proportion of women has increased overall, except in Denmark and Ireland (where there has been a slight decrease). However, the situation seems to be changing once more in Ireland, where the proportion of women is tending to increase again.

It can be noted in relation to incidence by sector that:

(i) The share of the agricultural sector is decreasing in all countries, but there remains a marked difference between countries where the agricultural sector remains predominant (Ireland 63%, Spain 36.2%, Greece 46.3% and – although data are lacking – probably Portugal) and countries where the agricultural sector is less important – the latter showing evidence of greater dispersion of self-employed workers in other sectors.

Table 4: Self-employed workers

	Self employed workers as % of total employment	Main Sectors	Women self-employed workers as % of women employed
F.R. Germany	4.19	0 6	2.91
Denmark	4.91	0	2.01
Luxembourg	6.04	6 0	5.88
United Kingdom	7.29	5 6	4.57
France	8.40	0 6	4.58
Belgium	13.63	6	10.24
Ireland	17.40	0	5.36
Spain	19.25	0 6	16.19
Portugal	22.65	0	25.06
Italy	22.84	6 0	15.63
Greece	29.71	0 6	16.39

Notes: 0 = Agriculture; 5 = Construction; 6 = Trade.
Source: 1986 Labour Force Survey data

(ii)   In the secondary sector, the construction category is generally the most important (representing on average some 7%).

(iii) The proportion of self-employed workers in the services sector (trade, transport and communications, finance and insurance) is comparable in all countries.

A final observation is called for: the proportion of self-employed workers working over 40 hours a week stands at about 85% in all countries.

The economic crisis has encouraged more people to become self-employed, apparently as an alternative to unemployment (Belgium, Denmark, Spain, Italy). In Italy, this seems the case only for men, women tending to become unemployed when unable to find paid employment.

2. Family workers

With the exception of Greece, there is a general decrease (which is considerable in Portugal and the FRG, and moderate in Belgium, Denmark, Spain, Italy and Ireland) in the numbers of family workers. In the Netherlands, the number of such workers has remained stable. This decrease results to a large extent from the reduction in employment in the agricultural sector. In 1985, this form of employment was most important in Greece (14% of workers), followed by Portugal, Italy and Spain (6-7%), Belgium (4%), the FRG, Denmark, Netherlands and Ireland (3%). The proportion of women decreased, except in Belgium, the Netherlands and Ireland. In this last country this proportion has remains particularly low in comparison to the other countries (52% as opposed to 70-80%).

An analysis of the various sectors of the economy shows that in Belgium, and to a lesser extent in Italy and the Netherlands, the proportion of family workers in the agricultural sector is low. There has been an increase in the share of the tertiary sector in all countries except the FRG. As in the case of the self-employed, the number of hours worked per week is very high.

3. Characteristics of these forms of employment

Self-employment allows some to obtain job satisfaction and others to avoid the threat or the reality of unemployment. This form of employment would seem to be relatively incompatible with family life (a longer working day and the increased risk which such activity entails). The self-employed have less social protection (in Belgium and Ireland) than other workers. In Belgium, they are not entitled to unemployment benefits and receive a lower pension.

Table 5: Family workers

	Family workers as % of total of employment	Main Sectors	Female family workers as % of total women employed
Ireland	2.14	0	3.57
Denmark	2.19	0 6	4.69
F.R. Germany	2.79	0	6.07
Belgium	3.63	6	8.40
France	3.94	0	7.87
Portugal	6.02	0	7.30
Italy	5.17	6	10.09
Spain	6.80	0	14.36
Greece	15.38	0	35.74

Notes: 0 = Agriculture; 6 = Trade.
Source: 1986 Labour Force Survey data

The status of "family worker" would seem to allow women to reconcile their working and family lives with greater ease (in the FRG, Spain and Belgium). In the FRG, 90% of family workers are married. In many cases, economic necessity obliges a wife to contribute to her husband's business. The employment of a married woman as a family worker is assured for as long as the business continues and the marriage lasts. Such women workers are at a particular disadvantage in that they receive no direct wage and are often not registered for social security. In Greece, a family worker may benefit indirectly from social security as a result of family ties with the owner of the enterprise, but provisions concerning working hours are not applicable.   In other countries, such workers have no protection.

At the micro-economic level, the Irish expert considered that lower costs of data-processing equipment would lead to an increased number of self-employed persons in the service sector. The existence of small family sub-contracting businesses means that work can be organised so that members of a family may be employed in them without payment. As a result of this form of employment, such businesses can survive and maintain their particular form of activity.

V. Homeworking

The European Commission report on homeworking in Italy, France and the UK[5] defines homeworking in terms of three dimensions:

---

5.   Fondation Pietro Seveso, *Homeworking in Italy, France and the United Kingdom.* Brussels, EEC V/1910/86, 1986.

(i)   *Place:* the person in question works mainly at home (i.e. outside the premises of the enterprise providing the work);

(ii)   *Dependency (technical and/or economic):* the homeworker works in a situation of dependence for one or more principals and not for the end market;

(iii) *Market standing:* the homeworker can take little or no initiative in relation to the market for the product. This is at the origin of the homeworker's economic dependence.

1. Estimates and trends

Certain characteristics of homeworking are common to several or all the countries. Homeworking is generally concentrated in certain well-defined sectors: manufacturing, ready-to-wear clothing, textiles, leather and wood. As these sectors employ a large number of women workers, the proportion of women homeworkers is very high (90% in the FRG and in Ireland). In some countries, a high percentage of workers are occupied on a part-time basis (in Spain and the UK). This form of employment may be concentrated in areas – often rural areas – where living standards are low (in Ireland, Portugal and Italy). The weight of homeworking in overall employment is marginal (except in the UK) and much of its development occurs illicitly or disguised as self-employment.

Although it is difficult to quantify homeworking, it is possible to identify certain factors which favour its development and others which favour its disappearance. Factors contributing to its decrease include: (i) the economic recession, which in the early 1980s adversely affected the textile, clothing and leather sectors, etc. (in Belgium, homeworking has practically disappeared); (ii) a large proportion of homeworkers have acquired the status of self-employed or craft workers – in this instance the decrease is therefore artificial (this is the case in Belgium and Italy); and (iii) technological innovation and rationalisation of production (Italy). Factors contributing to its increase include: (i) the fact that many workers are unable to find other employment (Portugal); and (ii) the restructuring of enterprises so that permanent employment is converted into homeworking to give employers greater flexibility.

2. Characteristics of homeworking

Although homeworkers often undertake this type of employment because they are unable to find "normal" employment, it can in some cases represent a compromise between the need for extra income and family obligations. However, homeworking is highly exposed to economic fluctuations and relations with the enterprise and other workers are restricted. According to the Danish expert, the individualisation which it causes may tend to weaken collective agreements and levels of unionisation.

In the case of illicit homeworkers, working conditions are more difficult. Such workers often earn less than typical workers belonging to equivalent economic categories (FRG and Ireland). In Spain, however, homeworkers appear to earn as much or more.

The level of social protection for homeworkers is low. This is so in the FRG, Denmark (for women), Ireland, the Netherlands (no protection against dismissal) and Portugal (in practice, they are mainly considered as self-employed workers for social security purposes). When workers are registered for social security purposes (in Belgium, for example), they seldom receive the same level of benefits as other wage earners, since benefits are calculated on the basis of earnings (which are not guaranteed for such workers). In Spain, homeworkers are entitled to the same benefits as other workers. In the Netherlands, their working conditions are regulated by law but in practice the law is not applied. In France, since 1982 homeworkers are no longer covered by certain laws: for example, they are not entitled to any compensation for loss of earnings due to absences for health reasons. Illicit homeworkers are not entitled to any social protection.

Having recourse to homeworking enables enterprises to reduce the cost of plant, social security expenditure and taxation and, in industries of a pronounced seasonal nature, to adapt production more easily. These characteristics are accentuated when workers are "hired" as self-employed persons or illicitly.

VI. In-firm training for young people

In all EEC countries, the alarming increase in unemployment among young people has led to decisions on the part of the public authorities to take steps or to strengthen existing measures to adapt and improve young people's skills.

1. National experiences

In the FRG, young workers between 15 and 25 years of age may participate in either in-firm or, in the case of the unemployed, outside "vocational training activities" and the government has allocated additional funds for further vocational training. In Belgium, measures range from traditional training courses – i.e. ONEm (National Employment Bureau) courses set up in 1976 and compulsory for firms – to sandwich courses, i.e. practical training in an enterprise or, more rarely, in an administration, together with theoretical training organised by the State or by the independent education sector (these are not compulsory for firms). Sandwich courses fall into two categories: courses for young people still in compulsory schooling (up to the age of 18) and courses for those over 18 years of age. The situation in Spain is very similar to that in Belgium. In Greece, the National Employment Agency organises apprenticeships for young people between 15 and 18 years. In most cases apprenticeship is combined with enrollment in a technical training institute. In Ireland, the State provides and finances training for young people under 25 years of age and for unemployed persons, either in training centres or with organisations which have training contracts with the public sector. Such training is not normally in-firm. There are firms which provide in-firm courses but the number of workers involved is not known, nor the objective of the training (reconversion, further training etc). Portugal has a "first employment" category, which is applicable to young people who have completed their secondary education but who have not gone on to higher education. Employers hiring young people on the basis of open-ended contracts are exempted from payment of social security contributions for two years. Prior to such legislation, many of these workers were hired on the basis of short-term contracts, with all the negative consequences of the latter. Italy has introduced three measures: (i) In-firm training: temporary employment of young persons, usually still at school or in training, for the purposes of establishing contact and providing practical training; (ii) Apprenticeship contracts for young people between 15 and 20 years of age (29 years since 1987) recruited to carry out employment which permits them to acquire vocational training (for a maximum of five years); firms must allow participation in training courses; (iii) Training-cum-employment contracts: this is a recent development following increasing criticism of apprenticeship and is for young unemployed persons between 15 and 19 years of age; the enterprise has a dual obligation to provide remuneration and training; contracts are temporary for a maximum duration of 24 months; incentives for firms are greater than with apprenticeship contracts. France has made three types of arrangements: the TUC (community work schemes), sandwich training schemes and apprenticeships. The first two were introduced in 1983 and 1984 respectively while the third is of longer standing.[6]

2. Characteristics of this form of employment

In principle, such arrangements are intended to enable young people to enter the world of work and acquire employment experience and training. The various measures oblige enterprises to provide young workers with training by using their labour in the enterprise itself and by permitting them to undertake theoretical training outside. In practice, however, the situation is very different. In Belgium and Italy, for example, some enterprises use such schemes in order to employ workers to do relatively unskilled work at low cost and on a temporary basis, and in order to recruit on a favourable basis. Certain training schemes have become practically obligatory to gain entrance to an enterprise, even for young people already possessing the required skills. Such young people suffer from two disadvantages: a fixed-term contract and low remuneration. Unskilled persons are frequently given work which provides them with no worthwhile experience. Sandwich courses

---

6.   These are discussed in more detail in chapter 4 – *eds.*

fail to give the best results because enterprises insist on a certain existing skill level, the occupations for which such measures are intended have poor labour market prospects and, as is also the case for training, certain firms use the schemes for their own ends, taking advantage of them to hire cheap labour without offering any training in exchange. In Belgium, such workers are paid at a lower rate than the normal, calculated solely for hours worked on the firm's premises. Similarly, their social security standing is less favorable than that of other workers, as some benefits are proportional to time worked or to earnings. Lastly, training time does not count for pension purposes.

At the micro-economic level, public authorities have offered a series of incentives to enterprises to participate in various experiments: a reduction in social security contributions (in Belgium and in Spain, 75% for courses and 100% for training; in Italy and France, 100% for sandwich courses); the possibility of recruiting personnel "personally" (i.e. by waiving provisions which impose recruitment on the basis of lists established by job centres) among young people having undertaken a period of training in the enterprise (in Italy); by not treating young people on training-cum-employment contracts as paid employees for the application of certain regulations (in Italy). Such incentives are often necessary because, in the short term, the use and training of young workers are not advantageous for enterprises (given their lower productivity and the costs of training), particularly when there is a legal obligation to take on a given number of young workers, which firms may not need.

At the macro-economic level, public authorities have introduced a variety of measures, albeit often not very coordinated. In Belgium, such measures have on the whole failed as they have not encouraged recruitment of young people, nor has their training been improved. Moreover, the network of measures is such that young people of 25 years of age can no longer find ordinary employment. It is estimated that, in Portugal, exemption from social security contributions represents a loss of 1,900,000 escudos and that, in 1985 in France, the cost of the TUC programme amounted to 2,102 million French francs (i.e. 1.2% of the employment policy overall).

VII. Attitudes of social partners and public authorities

These different forms of atypical employment have generated nuanced, even opposing reactions on the part of social partners and public authorities.

1. The attitude of employers

European employers have generally been in favour of the development of atypical forms of employment and have often encouraged them.

The major advantage from the employers' point of view is the increased numerical and organisational flexibility which they allow. The generalisation of atypical employment is related to the introduction of new forms of organisation and work scheduling which are adapted to production constraints. Specific benefits are associated with particular forms of employment, so that, for example, temporary work is seen as a way of adapting the number of employees of an enterprise to its needs, while reducing dismissal costs, and part-time work is seen as a means of reducing unemployment. However, some national differences do exist: Irish employers in general do not regard part-time work favourably, whereas Danish employers only oppose it in industry.

2. The attitude of the trade unions

The trade unions are opposed to the development of atypical work. They have resisted part-time working because they fear that such workers might be exploited and that their interests would differ from those of other categories of workers, thereby weakening trade union authority. They think that workers only accept forms of temporary employment because they are unable to find stable employment. They are also hostile to unsocial, variable and fragmented working hours because of problems of compatibility with family life and because of health risks. Generally, increased flexibility is regarded as a demand put forward by employers to counter trade union demands for reduced working hours (in Belgium, France and Denmark). The Danish expert, however, remarked that a generalised reduction of working hours would necessarily have as a consequence new forms of organisation of working time.

3. The attitude of public authorities

The public authorities have taken a number of initiatives to encourage the development of some forms of atypical work, among which can be noted:

(i)   Modifications in legislation enabling enterprises to introduce new ways of organising labour (by lifting the ban on weekend and night working, etc.) and use of labour in a more flexible manner (by facilitating dismissal, the acceptance of generalised fixed-term contracts, etc.);

(ii)   Incentives aimed at increasing the numbers of self-employed workers (promotion campaigns, tax advantages, loans, etc.);

(iii) A stricter policy vis-à-vis the informal economy;

(iv)   A policy of recruitment of part-time or temporary workers in public services;

(v)   The establishment of forms of employment aimed at offsetting long-term unemployment and unemployment among young people – forms of employment which are highly atypical (fixed-term contracts, lower rates of wages and less social protection, etc).

Such actions can be divided into two categories: those directed at a better protection of "atypical" workers and those aimed at promoting atypical employment. For part-time work, for example:[7]

- *Passive* measures consist in adapting labour and social security legislation in order to extend the legislation applicable to full-time workers to part-time workers. Workers are thus encouraged to accept part-time employment. Such measures have been implemented in the FRG, Belgium, Spain, Ireland and France, and there are also plans in this direction in Greece. Nevertheless, discrimination against part-time workers persists.

- *Active* measures promote part-time working, by introducing it into the public service (Belgium, Ireland, the UK, Portugal and France), by providing financial aid for job-sharing (Belgium and France), by tax exemption (Ireland), or quite simply by legalising and regulating such work (as in Italy for the purpose of reducing unemployment among women), and by increasing possibilities for semi-retirement (France).

One type of action consists of modifying the legal situation for atypical work. In countries where production has a clearly seasonal nature (Italy, Portugal, Spain), for example, temporary work has generally been restricted to specific activities in well defined sectors, but the public authorities are now tending to extend the legislation concerned to all sectors of activity, so that it is no longer conditional upon the seasonal nature of the work. Temporary work is therefore increasingly responding to fluctuations in production, whatever the cause, and is evidence of the increasingly flexible nature of employment. With the exception of Spain, European governments have at the same time relaxed or attempted to relax legislation in order to facilitate the introduction of new working systems with variable hours. In Belgium and France, the governments have achieved this, while in the Netherlands results are still only partial. The development of self-employment has been encouraged by measures such as: financial aid for the long-term unemployed wishing to start their own businesses (in Denmark and Belgium), tax incentives for young people wishing to become self-employed (in Belgium), an advertising campaign to encourage women to set up their own businesses (in Ireland), etc. Finally, as has already been noted, the development of training courses and the recruitment of young people has been carried out on the initiative of the public authorities.

---

7.   Only two countries make no mention of action on the part of public authorities in favour of part-time working during the period: Denmark (where legislation was probably adapted previously) and Greece (where it is at the planning stage).

VIII. Conclusion

The problem of lack of data: Statistics from the different countries have proved to be insufficient to arrive at an accurate understanding and description of atypical employment and its evolution. This lack of precision is due to the fact that the forms of employment in question are not always clearly defined (officially and/or statistically), thereby making it impossible to clearly distinguish one from another.

The development of these forms of employment – description and explanation: the crux of the matter is to ascertain whether atypical employment has a regulating effect on the imbalance of supply and demand on the labour market. Employers are demanding greater flexibility in the use of labour in order to regain a certain competitivity, while workers, in the face of increasing unemployment, have no choice but to accept so-called atypical employment because it is the only type still available to them. The forms taken by atypical employment are not always new. Some of them may be described as traditional (self-employment, sub-contracting, illegal employment), while others are much more sophisticated and innovatory. These are generally the results of efforts on the part of enterprises in their search for greater flexibility and include new forms of organisation of working time (part-time working, temporary work, shift work, night work and weekend work, etc). A predominant role in this process has been played by the public authorities.

Atypical employment and sexual discrimination: Women are considerably over-represented in atypical employment. The development of this employment has facilitated their entry into the labour force, particularly as some of these forms of employment seem to permit combining family life and work more easily. It may be observed, however, that women are more concentrated in forms of work (part-time work, temporary work, homeworking, family work) where remuneration and/or social protection are less than in normal employment, while men in atypical jobs often face working conditions which are harder and may have an adverse effect on health (night work, weekend work, illegal work, self-employment). In addition, as far as men are concerned, more and more young workers, who have not found work, are accepting atypical employment.

Conditions to be observed if these forms of employment are not to lead to marginalisation: The situation of workers vis-à-vis their rights to work, remuneration and social security must be reviewed with a view to eliminating all discrimination and abuse. The present organisation of these three elements is based on a "traditional" labour market structure generally ill-adapted to atypical employment. Measures so far taken by governments in this direction have not been sufficient. In practice, workers are often at a disadvantage because of lower wages, abuse by employers in relation to dismissal, working hours etc., and little or no social security protection with respect to unemployment, retirement, and invalidity.

8 Psychological and sociological perspectives on precarious employment in Belgium

Pierre Salengros, Cécile van de Leemput and Luc Mubikangiey[1]

I. Introduction

Up until the 1970s, wage employment in the private and public sectors and remunerated self-employment constituted the vast majority of contracts between a worker, his activity and its principal. All economic indicators and established industrial and organisational models supported this convenient pattern of integration; moderate unemployment rates and the slow rise in productivity allowed adjustment between micro-economic and macro-economic developments; conventional employment contracts represented a wage and tax equilibrium in the transaction between the worker and his employer.

This is not the place to go back over the genesis of events which have, in the past fifteen years or so, radically altered this equilibrium. Unemployment has increased and its image has changed; the data-processing revolution and all that goes with it has had an impact even on the most isolated workers and has shown that skills previously acquired in another form are no longer appropriate; the cost of in-firm training has proved to be overwhelming for enterprises already faced with the choice of rapid restructuring or closure.

A dual development has taken place at the levels of the enterprise and the worker. The form of the enterprise has changed on the basis of considerations which ten years ago appeared to be self-evident: personnel costs are the most important component of running costs, and technical rationalisation permits more accurate forecasts of production possibilities, taking the state of competition into account. An enterprise can reduce its personnel by thirty to forty per cent and still be functional. In such a context, new workers who hold recent qualifications or a proven capacity for adaptation, must naturally be recruited. However, in the meantime, new forms of employment contract must be found in order to make the transition from the old to the new form of organisation. Creativity is also necessary in the implementation of these contracts, as dismissal costs under typical contracts – in which the wage relationship is formalised and protected for an

---

1.   Laboratoire de Psychologie Industrielle et Commerciale, Université Libre de Bruxelles.

undetermined duration and gives entitlement to a variety of specific or contractual advantages – can force many enterprises to close down.

Today, the worker is faced with individual or collective bargaining, characterised by an imbalance in the traditional exchange between employment and remuneration. Modifications to the contract which binds him to the employer have to be accepted if labour supply exceeds labour demand. However, in the highly mediatised context of the West, cynicism is ill-considered in an employer; forms of employment must therefore be found which, while making it possible to avoid the shortcomings of the old forms, provide the individual, the organisations which may represent him and public opinion with the image of a new professional perspective; this precaution is all the more necessary as most persons are unable to visualise the possibilities of technological evolution and thus forecast which skills will become essential tomorrow to operate the new tools.

New forms of employment contract will sever the employer-employee relationship from advantages from which the employee previously benefited. The most frequently lost advantage will be automatic perenniality of the contract; thus *interim work, temporary work, fixed-term work* – even in situations where indeterminate duration had been the rule hitherto, as in the public service, previously the traditional place of security of employment, in which the status of *special temporary supervisor* (cadre spécial temporaire) is now being used in order to avoid increasing the number of supervisory staff for positions which may only exist temporarily – and *part-time work* which facilitates the adaptation of working time to work requirements.

Various other forms of employment have developed but we will not dwell on them here because attitudes towards them are particularly difficult to analyse. Official recognition of underground forms, such as *undeclared work* or *homeworking* (the two being frequently combined), is the result of unfavourable treatment in working relationships. Those who are made partially or wholly redundant, those who for social or medical reasons stop normal work at an early age, those who take early retirement because of rationalisation or closure of enterprises consider the "moral" contract between a worker and the society (i.e. the firm which employed him as well as society at large) to have been revoked by the latter; they, therefore, consider themselves to be free to seek a new source of income or to supplement a pension which they judge inadequate, without any feeling of guilt or social disapprobation. From specialists in the construction sector to teachers and consultants of all types, there is a whole flexible range of activities which allows greater adaptability in the use of personnel, the declaration of whose employment would only benefit the State, a theoretical being with no real significance.

Common to these new forms of employment is the increased precariousness and the element of instability which they introduce into the life of the worker. The emergence of precarious employment has modified relationships within the enterprise. We will define precarious employment here as any remunerated activity where the worker is placed in a situation of temporary or fixed-term work. In some cases, employment of indeterminate duration may also fall within the framework of precarity because workers remain in such employment for only a short time before moving on to another job which better matches their aspirations. Under such conditions, the backgrounds and training of workers in precarious employment may be highly diversified.

II. Psychological evaluation

1. Perspectives from individual and psychological analysis

Our aim here is not to make an comprehensive and detailed survey of atypical forms of employment or of their statistical or economic incidence. Nor is it to make a differential study of the feelings and motivations associated with these different statuses by the actors involved. Our basic hypothesis can be expressed as follows: the subject himself evaluates the precariousness of his situation whatever his present employment position; atypicality or precariousness may concern only one or all of the dimensions or motivations which characterise his activity. This hypothesis has been, right from the beginning, reinforced by specific case studies. The particularity of such situations goes beyond the question of status; it brings about a differential balance in the evaluation of the past, present or possibly future precariousness of the worker's employment. Methods of analysis taking such diversification into account are therefore necessary.

At the same time, the heading, "psychological and sociological perspectives on precarious employment in Belgium" should be qualified to avoid the impression that the situation in Belgium is particular in respect of workers' motivations towards work. This is certainly not our opinion; the temptation has been great to generalise from the case studies below and present them as being characteristic of European industrial democracies. In actual fact, the analyses undertaken relate to two places: Brussels and Charleroi; they are concentrated on limited, French-speaking population groups with a homogenous cultural level. The generalisation from such experiences seems to us a subject for discussion rather than a statement of fact.

A final comment before going on to the methodology used in our research: the analyses have been undertaken from a microscopic view of the problem of precariousness; they are based on the idea that while macro-economic models are particularly useful statistically, as they tend to maximise the overall benefit derived by a society from the choices it faces, they can be somewhat lacking in relevance when it comes to handling finer dimensions. It is the task of the specialist to ascertain whether a healthy population is the sum of balanced pathologies or whether subjects should be cared for on a differential basis. Our analysis adopts the latter approach through concepts such as the balance between employment and life outside work, or occupational style (already a more operative notion in organisational monographs for example).

2. Methodology of psychological analysis

From the outset, any research into attitudes and feelings of persons in precarious or atypical employment situations comes up against the problem of how to collect information which is relevant, individual and homothetic to experienced reality. This difficulty is a feature of any research where respondents, for whatever reason, tend to give an altered rendering of their evaluation either by exaggerating or minimising it, or by transforming it so that it conforms to one of the social stereotypes.

The methodology adopted was based on the use of formalised questionnaires proposed to populations of individuals in precarious or atypical employment. Bearing in mind our preliminary comments, our choice was oriented towards diversified "targets" and therefore to the study of specific and statistically limited population groups rather than to the analysis of one occupational case-study. This decision naturally had repercussions both on the elaboration of research tools and on the analysis of data collected. Each specific targeting of a population group involved the development of an original tool for the survey (which was prepared by prior interviews and analyses); the form of questionnaire had then to lend itself to analytical processes which as far as possible offset the drawbacks of dealing with small numbers; lastly, samples had to correctly represent the parent populations surveyed.

The choice of an indirect method of survey whereby, once the questionnaire has been prepared, the control over the adequacy of responses as a representation of reality is entirely left to the respondent, is not without consequences on the interviewees' general attitude vis-à-vis their status. While 1973 saw the emergence of general economic difficulties and increasing numbers of workers in atypical and precarious employment, 1968 had seen the appearance of another phenomenon, initially restricted to educational institutions but which quickly spread to factories: the control assumed by individuals over their own future both at their place of work and outside. Because of this evolution, and, it must be admitted, the spread of research undertaken in the industrial field (researchers either found or rediscovered the path to the factory...), it has become increasingly difficult to obtain information unbiased through some mechanism or other. Workers have become witnesses of their working life and act out this role like old hands. Within the framework of this role game, our team tried to elaborate instruments to analyse work on the basis of concepts such as "style", or on the basis of a perspective on employment extended to life outside work [Karnas, 1982; Karnas and Salengros, 1983].

In the case studies presented below, the large majority of questions are precoded, making it possible to obtain firm numerical patterns from the data presented: Likert scales, bipolar scales and classification of items constitute ways of responding to the methodological requirements of our demands. Two mechanisms of interaction between the researcher and the subject were followed on the basis of a general hypothesis. As respondents tend to have control over their reply, they have to be placed in situations where the questioner may control the degree of relevance of their answers (i.e. their conformity with the feelings of the subjects) either through the tool used for the survey and the initial processing or at the stage of the analytical procedures. The technique of classification of items, for example, is well suited to the objective of placing the respondent before choices which, by confronting him with items which are equally attractive, make it difficult for him to manipulate replies. The bipolar scale, deriving from the Osgood differentiator technique, also presents an advantage of this type, at least up to a certain point.

Such scales make it possible to achieve the aims of psychological analysis by means of two specific techniques:

(i) *Typological analysis*, which offers a functional grouping of replies. As a base for the grouping of persons, this technique presents the advantage of focusing on the answers of the subjects and not on *a priori* criteria. Traditional research tends to study the behaviour of averages in relation to *a priori* criteria – for example, socio-economic variables – or to attitudes to given stimuli. However, the results of such studies are often disappointing as such "sociological" variables involve a relatively evident evaluation (replies of "old" and "young" persons, for example, are partially determined by the limitations of the question contents); moreover, some subjects adopt profiles of replies which do not fit into the classical stereotype of the population group to which they belong. Typological analysis aims at grouping subjects as a function of the similarity of their responses by calculating the squared distance between profiles. At the same time, it offers an excellent introduction to the notion of "employment style". All the subjects who present a set of homogenous replies to items may be considered as displaying a style of response of which the details can be analysed through the average replies. The level of individual response is transcended in order to reach the characteristics of broader population groups: thus, where analysis leads to five typological groups, it is reasonable to believe that the survey of a statistically infinite population, using the same questionnaire, would lead to the same groups and thus to five styles or ways of working with respect to the instrument used for the investigation.

(ii) *Factor analysis* makes it possible to study the relationships between subjects (or groups of subjects in the case of typological analysis) and questions. Traditional binary analysis offers the advantage of being able to represent graphically image points of the subjects and image points of the questions at the same time while respecting as far as possible the relationships which unite them. Conventionally, the position of subjects or groups is interpreted in relation to axes or factors defined by the respective position of items, variables or questions.[2]

---

2. A demonstration of the method is to be found in Faverge [1975] and characteristic examples in Karnas [1982] and Karnas and Salengros [1983].

We will illustrate the methodological principles outlined above and show the use of these techniques through three case studies from the tertiary sector.

III. Three case studies on precarious employment

1. Precarious employment in the service sector – the Charleroi region

The Charleroi region has been particularly affected by unemployment because of the age of its enterprises and difficulties in introducing technologically competitive industries. The active population was hitherto mainly comprised of industrial workers but the gradual reduction in their numbers through closures or reorganisation has brought about shifts in employment similar to those found elsewhere: Belgium has seen its industrial population decline from 1,400,000 to 900,000 persons in 15 years, while services in the private sector increased by 120,000 and in the public sector by 200,000 persons. The status of young workers in the tertiary sector is frequently precarious.

Our study covered some seventy persons mainly in medical and paramedical employment in both the public and private sectors.[3] One third of these persons had fixed-term contracts, another third had interim or replacement status, while a sixth had "National Employment Office" status, special temporary supervisor (cadre spécial temporaire), etc. The basic questionnaire was prepared within a fairly original framework: most of the students who conceived this tool of investigation were young adults of whom a majority were experiencing, or feared to experience in the near future, the themes of their analysis. Those themes included:

(i)   Evaluation of the employment situation itself and its connection with personal adjustment outside work;

(ii)   Employers' responsibility for precariousness of employment;

(iii)   Family, social and financial adjustments resulting from precarious status;

(iv)   Projections concerning the future of employment and of the image of the precarious worker in society;

(v)   The comparison of employment-related motivations for both the "established" worker (i.e. a worker benefiting from a contract of unlimited duration) and the "precarious" worker;

(vi)   The socio-economic situation of the respondent and his immediate future prospects (in relation to the time horizon concept, for example, developed in France over the last thirty years).

---

3.   The survey was undertaken by students of the Institut du Travail.

The form of the questionnaire is in line with the principles outlined above; it is divided into three main sections:

- The first section is in the form of a Likert scale of 35 items – i.e. in the form of a series of statements on which the respondent must express agreement or disagreement on a five-point scale. Some questions are general and concern working conditions and the impact of precariousness on employment, while others are more directly addressed to the respondent and involve him or her in the question. In the latter case, questions relate to the perception which the worker has of his or her precariousness and the repercussions of this status inside and outside work.

- The second section comprises two successive classifications relating to the "easy to accept" nature of twelve items such as earnings, working hours and usefulness of the work. One of these classifications reflects the point of view of the precarious worker and the other of the established worker.

- The third section is in the form of a Likert scale of 53 items, subdivided into different sub-themes: employers' responsibility, the worker's future, family and social aspects, the image of precarious work and the financial aspect.

A. The first section of the questionnaire

On the whole, the persons surveyed reject the idea that they are less motivated than other workers; they are equally involved in their work, they take initiatives but they may state that their precarious status is discouraging in the long-term. This is no doubt a sign that these persons defend their position in relation to their involvement in their work and to its short-term influence on their life in general. Divergence of opinion is greater for those items related to the influence of precariousness on working life and outside work, on family and social life. We carried out Student t tests on groups identified in terms of sociological criteria: sex, marital status, type of contract. It was shown that men had greater difficulty in accepting their precarious status; they felt jealous of those in permanent employment, left out and hoped to be appointed indefinitely by taking initiatives. People living as couples also experienced this situation as discouraging, stressful and demotivating in terms of personal involvement in their work. Among the population surveyed, 12% of respondents had a contract of unlimited duration and, although these results must be taken with a certain amount of caution, it would seem that these persons more than the others considered precarious employment to be discouraging in the short and long runs.

We then proceeded to a typological analysis in order to group subjects as a function of proximity of replies, going beyond the gross average ranks obtained. We thus achieved a classification into four groups which were as coherent as possible in terms of opinions on the items proposed.

Two problems were raised:

(i)   Is it possible to use the means of the replies to items by these groups to carry out a structural analysis of the correspondences between groups and items?

(ii)   Can the content of typological groups be characterised with respect to the descriptive variables used in the questionnaire, the functional classification, the type of precarity, etc.?

The reply to the first question can be found by using classical binary analysis, i.e. factor analysis into principal components, making it possible to position the points of one set (for example, of groups of subjects) in relation to the points of another (such as items-motivations). The best way of proceeding is by analysing the position of subject-points in relation to factors arising from the analysis of item-points.

The first two factors selected for the binary analysis explain 86% of the variance. The first factor concerns working life with a pole of job dissatisfaction opposed to a pole of involvement and job satisfaction (see diagram 1). At one end are to be found dissatisfied persons who do not find fulfillment in their work and want to change employment; at the other end are to be found those who are involved in their work, are motivated and hope to be appointed permanently. The second factor concerns the social aspects of precarious employment. At one pole, precarious status is experienced as marginalising, setting the worker apart and interfering with relations with colleagues and superiors. At the other pole, precarious workers try to compensate for the disadvantages of precariousness and the marginalisation which it induces by greater involvement in social activities outside work.

Our second question remains to be answered. We are now able to define the position of each group in relation to factors (items-motivations). However, is it actually possible to characterise them in relation to criteria of identification and *a priori* judgment? We have shown on the diagram the most characteristic indicators of each group. In terms of its relative importance in the sample, it is possible to index each group by its main components. The characteristics of typological groups are as follows in terms of factors derived by classical binary analysis:

–   *Group 1* (23 subjects) for which precarious employment gives rise to permanent stress and long-term discouragement. These persons hope by their initiatives at work to be appointed permanently; they are therefore motivated and as committed as other workers. They do not wish to change employment but hope to be appointed permanently to their present post. In general it is their first contract – a short-term contract. They are well integrated in the enterprise and have not applied elsewhere for employment.

–   *Group 2* (20 subjects) is not under stress from its precarious status. These persons do not intend to change employment. In fact, the precariousness of their employment does not affect their lives nor alter

Diagram 1: **The service sector in the Charleroi region: Grouping of precarious workers in relation to the factors "working life" (horizontal axis) and "social aspects of precarious work" (vertical axis)**

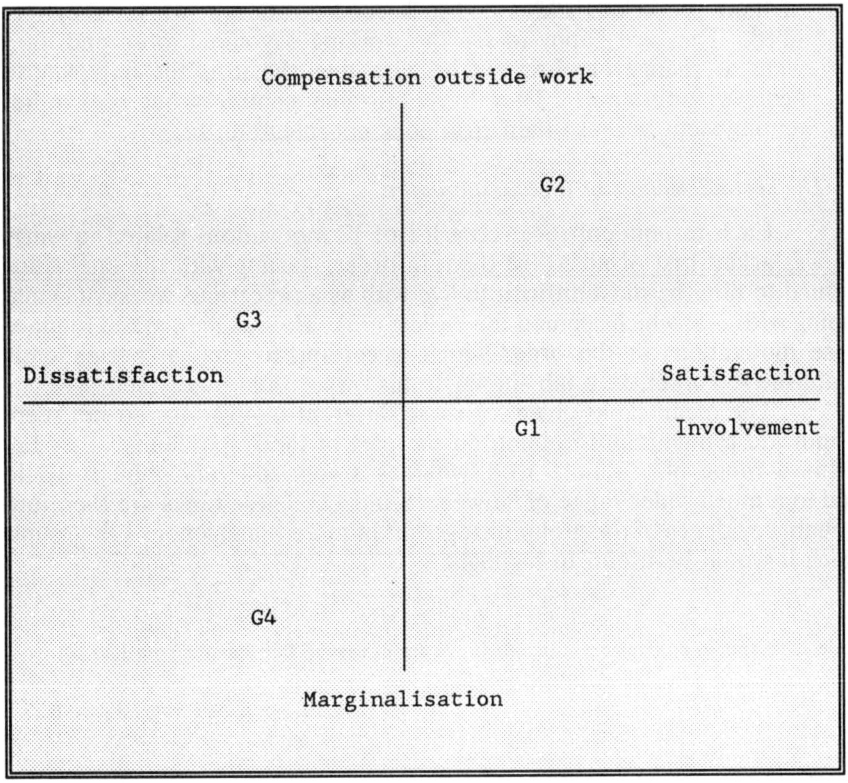

their social habits or working relations. They do not feel marginalised nor do they feel jealous of other workers. This group is particularly made up of unmarried persons and of women on their first contract.

– *Group 3* (13 subjects) is characterised by a general discontentment towards the present job, not because of its precarious nature but because of the work itself. These persons do not think that precarious status interferes with their relations with colleagues and superiors or that it prevents them from taking initiatives or that it is discouraging and demotivating. However, they are happy to see the working day end and would like to change their employment as they see this as the only way to self-fulfillment. They are not invited to meetings in their enterprises even if they hold long-term contracts.

– *Group 4* (8 subjects) considers precarious employment as stressful, discouraging and depressing. Their precarious status seriously interferes with their relations with colleagues and superiors. There are tensions within the working team. These workers feel left out and do not believe that they benefit from the same rights and responsibilities as other workers. They are less involved in long-term projects because of their precarious status and lack concentration at work; they feel tired. They are happy to see the working day come to an end, they want to change employment because they see it as the only way to achieve fulfillment. They have full-time contracts but seek other employment because their firm does not integrate them.

B. *The second section of the questionnaire*

Each respondent received a list of 12 motivations related to work. He was asked first of all to list them in order, starting with the one which seemed to him the most difficult to live with as a precarious worker (1) and ending with that which seemed the easiest (12). He was then asked to place these motivations in the order which, according to him, a "permanently established" worker, in a job similar to his own, would place them.

The mean ranks given for these different motivations do not seem to indicate a unanimous opinion on the part of the respondents: they fall within a range of around 5 to 8, whereas a very coherent opinion would lead to a much wider range of between 1 and 12. These ranks are therefore probably evidence of the grouping together of more homogenous sub-groups, which it would be useful to highlight.

Table 1: Scales of motivation in increasing order of ease of fulfillment (from 1 to 12).

	"Precarious" worker	"Established" worker
1. Relationship with colleagues	8.15	8.22
2. Remuneration	6.05	7.48
3. Working hours	6.72	6.00
4. Physical working conditions	6.13	5.32
5. Work security	4.58	6.17
6. Type of work	6.52	5.80
7. Usefulness of work	7.08	6.91
8. Worker's skills	8.25	6.43
9. Worker's motivations	6.35	5.67
10. Personal choice	5.65	6.02
11. Feeling of belonging	5.75	7.22
12. Relationship with superiors	6.60	6.85

We then applied classical binary analysis to these results; diagrams 2 and 3 show the first two factors of such an analysis. Subsequent typological analysis concerning the classifications "precarious worker" and "established worker" enabled us to group the population studied in socio-economic terms.

In the case of precarious employment (diagram 2), the horizontal factor is typically "relational". It opposes the two "relationship" items to all the others. The vertical factor opposes material motivations (remuneration, working hours etc.) to psychological motivations (worker's motivation, worker's skills, personal choice and feeling of belonging). The positions of the five typological groups can be observed in relation to these two factors: groups G1 and G3 contrast with G2 on the first factor, G3 and, to a lesser extent, G11 contrast with G6 on the second factor. These groups are as follows:

- *Group 1* (13 subjects): this group includes many unmarried persons on full-time contracts, working for the first time for their current employer, who tends to be in the public sector.

- *Group 2* (10 subjects): long-term contracts, part-time, not included in team meetings, tends to be in the private sector.

- *Group 3* (11 subjects): short-term contracts, having already had one or several contracts with the same employer, may benefit from further training and attend team meetings, majority of married persons with children, more particularly in the private sector.

- *Group 6* (17 subjects): short-term contracts, may benefit from further training and may attend meetings, have children, have applied elsewhere.

- *Group 11* (9 subjects): full-time contracts, unmarried, attend team meetings, have generally applied elsewhere.

    Diagram 3, which covers "established" workers, offers a prospective view of our population group in an unstable situation. Interpretation of the horizontal factor remains similar to that for "precarious" employment, mainly opposing the two relational items to all the others. We can thus conclude that this aspect retains an important weight in both employment situations. It is therefore not in this respect that "precarious" employees hope to modify their status. The vertical factor opposes the single item "feeling of belonging" to all the others. There is a marked difference here from the opinion concerning precarious employment: it is as though this item alone counterbalanced all the other material and psychological motivations. Again, the three typological groups studied contrast strongly in relation to the factors: groups G4 and G1 contrast with G2 horizontally, G4 contrasts with G1 vertically. The groups are as follows:

- *Group 1* (18 subjects): precarious contracts, short-term, full-time, in the public sector, mainly unmarried persons.

- *Group 2* (15 subjects): long-term or unlimited contracts, full-time, public sector; mainly men and married persons.

- *Group 4* (21 subjects): many part-time contracts, majority of women, with children, many have previously worked for the same employer, few have applied elsewhere, majority in the private sector.

Diagram 2:   **Grouping of responses concerning precarious workers as a function**
            of relational factors (horizontal axis) and motivations (vertical axis)

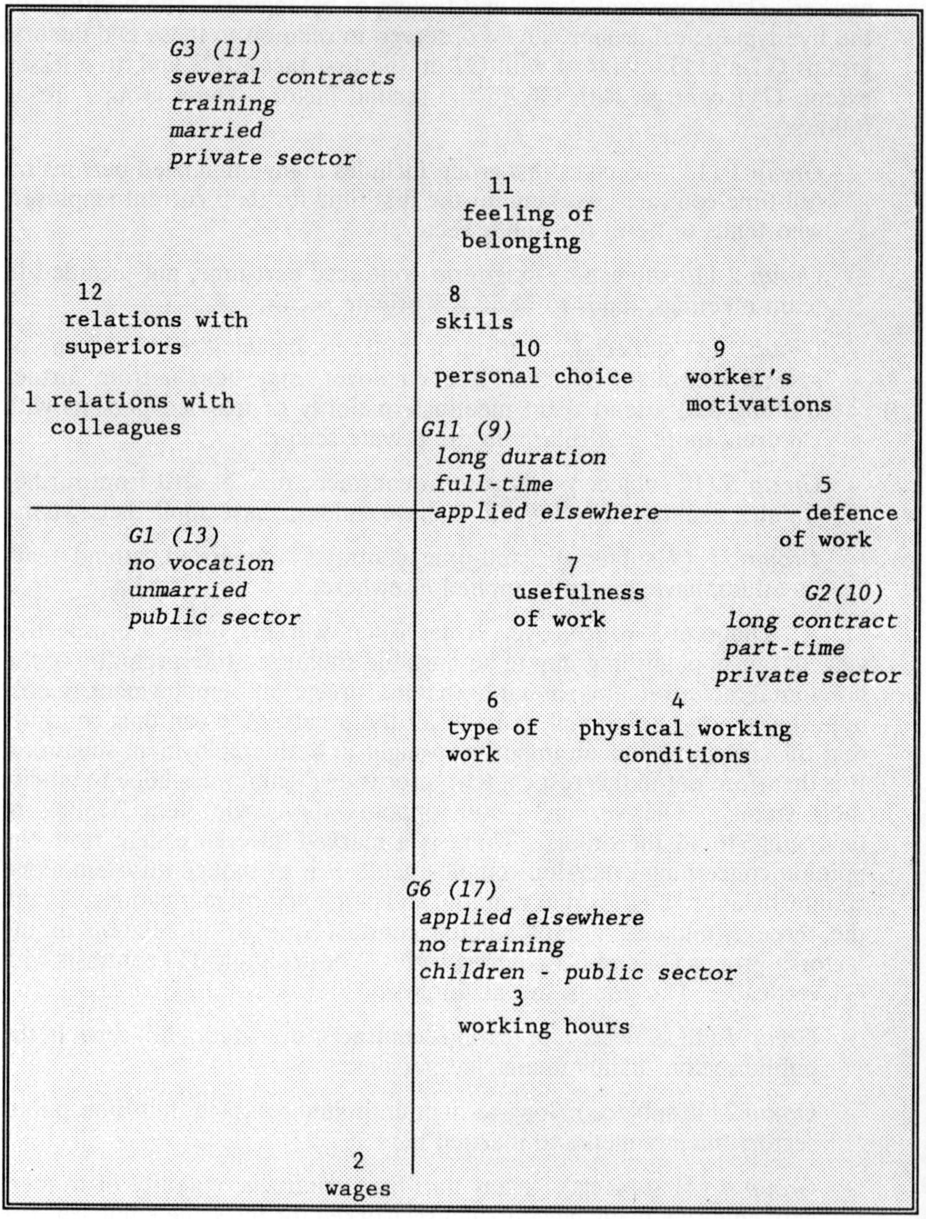

```
        G3 (11)
        several contracts
        training
        married
        private sector
                                11
                                feeling of
                                belonging

    12                          8
    relations with             skills
    superiors                      10              9
                               personal choice   worker's
1 relations with                                 motivations
    colleagues                 G11 (9)
                               long duration
                               full-time                          5
                              ──applied elsewhere──────────── defence
        G1 (13)                                                of work
        no vocation                    7
        unmarried                  usefulness          G2(10)
        public sector              of work             long contract
                                                        part-time
                                                        private sector
                               6              4
                               type of   physical working
                               work          conditions




                           G6 (17)
                           applied elsewhere
                           no training
                           children - public sector
                                   3
                               working hours




                    2
                  wages
```

Diagram 3: Grouping of responses concerning "established" workers as a function of relational factors (horizontal axis) and motivations (vertical axis)

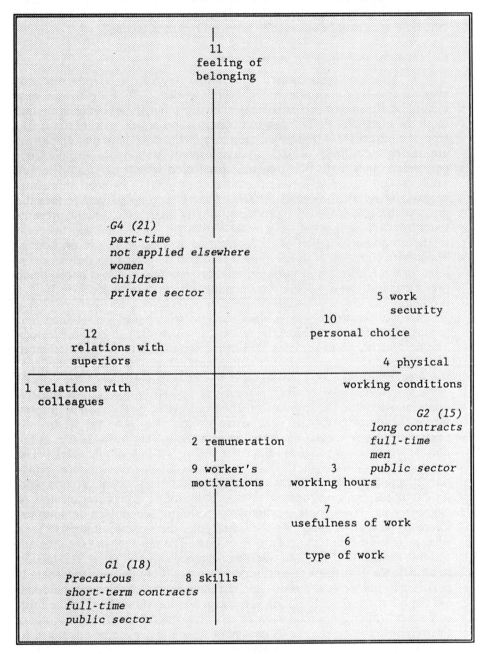

It is possible on the diagram to determine the relationships between factors of opinion on motivations and socio-professional characteristics. Differentiation between the public and private sectors, between full-time and part-time etc., may be informally revealed by these factors.

C. The third section of the questionnaire

All respondents rejected the idea that they form a separate, marginal class, or that they are different from other workers. They are not the only ones to be affected by precariousness of employment. Student t tests applied to all the questions on the basis of differentiation by sex, marital status and type of contract show that: men are more inclined to think that employers are taking advantage of lack of employment stability to exploit their personnel; they state that they are dissatisfied with their social life and would go out more if they had stable employment; women think that precariousness of employment affects all sectors; couples seem to face the greatest difficulties and the precariousness of their employment prevents them from seeing most of their projects through; unmarried persons point to the economic situation of the enterprise as a cause of precariousness. Those with contracts of indeterminate duration think that precariousness is a bar to the fulfillment of most personal projects and that it is not so much precariousness itself as the discouraging effect it provokes which is a problem.

We performed a typological analysis from which we retained four groups, followed by a classical binary analysis which highlighted three factors. The first factor, which explains 53% of the variance, concerns the influence of precariousness of employment on the worker's private life. At one pole, the precariousness of employment interferes with and makes life outside work and social relations very precarious. It put workers in a difficult financial situation and prevents them from realising their plans for the future. Marginalisation therefore exists. At the other pole, the precariousness of employment does not interfere with the worker's private life, as life outside work becomes more important and richer than life at work. The second factor (see diagram 4), which explains 25% of the variance, brings out the search for the causes of precariousness of employment. At one pole, an attempt is made to identify what is "responsible" for precariousness of employment: the political situation, economic conditions, employers' interests, lack of training. At the other pole, there is no attempt to seek what is "to blame" but an acceptance of fate. The third factor (see diagram 5), which explains 22% of the variance, contrasts an attitude of resignation to an attitude of struggle against precariousness. On the one hand, there is passive acceptance of the status and the attitude that nothing can be done. On the other hand, mobilisation is envisaged at individual level in the form of further training, specialisation or of being singled out from the others through better competence. A change of region may even be envisaged to find stable, non-precarious employment.

Diagram 4: Grouping of respondents in relation to the factors "relationship between the precariousness of work and social life" (horizontal axis) and "search for factors responsible for precariousness" (vertical axis)

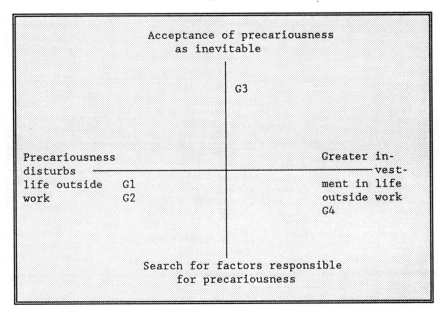

```
                     Acceptance of precariousness
                           as inevitable

                                 |
                                 |
                        G3       |
                                 |
                                 |
                                 |
Precariousness                   |                   Greater in-
disturbs        ─────────────────┼─────────────────  vest-
life outside       G1            |                   ment in life
work               G2            |                   outside work
                                 |                   G4
                                 |
                                 |
                                 |
                     Search for factors responsible
                          for precariousness
```

The typological groups are as follows:

–   *Group 1* (10 subjects) perceives precariousness as a generalised phenomenon with a durable effect on all sectors. Precariousness does not only concern the young and the old. There is no use in undertaking further training or specialising. These persons are resigned to living "like that". Moreover, their status interferes little with their life outside work, it is known to and accepted by their family and friends. Mainly unmarried women are found in this group.

–   *Group 2* (19 subjects) perceives precariousness as an externally determined phenomenon: the political situation, economic conditions and employers' interests. It is therefore a process against which struggle can be envisaged by means of further training, specialisation etc. The precariousness of employment interferes relatively little with the life outside work, it does not hamper plans for the future, it permits a satisfying social life. These persons are mainly women with long-term contracts.

–   *Group 3* (21 subjects). They are often married, quite well integrated in their enterprise; modal replies are less extreme than for other groups. Precariousness is experienced as a lasting phenomenon affecting all sectors of activity and which primarily concerns the young. People feel committed to their work, they are not lacking motivation; there is no passivity in the face of precariousness. However, its influ-

Diagram 5:   Grouping of respondents in relation to the factors "relationship between the
                    precariousness of work and social life" (horizontal axis) and "individual
                    struggle against precariousness" (vertical axis)

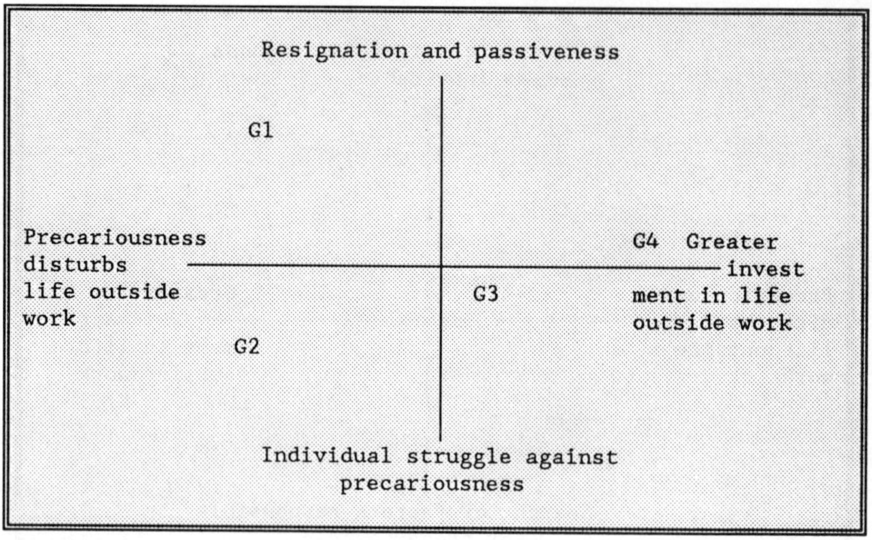

```
                        Resignation and passiveness
                                     |
                                     |
                G1                   |
                                     |
                                     |
 Precariousness                      |                 G4  Greater
 disturbs        ────────────────────┼──────────────────── invest
 life outside                        |    G3             ment in life
 work                                |                   outside work
                G2                   |
                                     |
                                     |
                        Individual struggle against
                              precariousness
```

ence weighs heavily on their financial situation; precariousness
hampers their plans for the future and prevents them from realising
certain investments.

–   *Group 4* (14 subjects) thinks that the precariousness of employment is
     due to political or economic causes and to employers' interests.
     Employers take advantage of the current situation to exploit their
     personnel. These persons are not motivated and do not have the
     energy to withstand precariousness although they state that they are
     not resigned to it. This situation is very difficult to live with at a
     personal level, both from the financial and social points of view.

D. Conclusion of case study 1

     Overall, we have highlighted a defensive form of behaviour whereby
the worker with precarious status is presented as being equally motivated as
other workers and as taking initiatives. Such a worker does not accept the
idea that precariousness can influence his life outside work and rejects the
possibility of being part of a special group, refusing to be marginalised.
However, he shows signs of discouragement in the long term. Concerning
responsibilities outside work, we note that among people forming part of a
couple, men (considered as heads of family) have greater difficulty to face
their precarious state, they feel jealous of other workers, under stress,
discouraged and rejected. Men are also more inclined to think that
employers take advantage of the situation. Two different types of behaviour
have been highlighted among persons who react actively to the precarious-

ness of their employment: either (i) they are happy with their current job and, by taking initiatives and involving themselves, try to set themselves apart and obtain a contract for an indeterminate duration; for them precariousness affects all sectors and is not short-term; nonetheless, it is essential to take action as this status seriously interferes with plans for the future, or (ii) they are not happy with their current job and envisage training, specialising or even changing residence to try to find stable employment. Precariousness is not inevitable, the political and economic situation together with the attitude of employers are responsible. Some of them accept their status, particularly unmarried women; this status does not prevent them from having plans for the future, nor does it interfere with their life outside work. They see the trend towards precariousness as spreading to all sectors; it is therefore no use undergoing training. Some of them show that they are significantly affected, they are under stress, tired and happy to see the working day come to an end. They feel marginalised. They think that employers take advantage of the situation and that the impact of the political and economic situation is quite considerable. These persons are demotivated and do not have the energy to struggle. Such a situation is experienced as difficult both financially and socially.

2. Interim employment in an institutional sector: Teaching

A. Interim employment in education

The interim teacher is a teacher who has not been allocated a post at the beginning of the year and who has registered as a replacement teacher with an appropriate educational system within which he or she wishes to work (State, provincial and communal, or Catholic education). Our research concerned a sample of 66 interim teachers in the Brussels region, working either at primary or secondary level.

The study of how the function of interim teacher is represented is based on three dimensions: motivation, assessment of value and satisfaction. Our questionnaire comprised three sections:

(i) An initial, bipolar questionnaire was prepared in order to assess how the situation of interim teacher was perceived and represented. This questionnaire included 28 pairs of items. The respondent had to place his or her answer on a metric scale (from 1 to 5) linking two statements.

(ii) A second questionnaire in the form of a classification aimed at assessing the contribution of ten factors to the satisfaction which interim teaching status provided.

(iii) A third questionnaire in the form of a composite picture aimed at determining the typical profile of the average interim teacher.

B. Representation of the interim teacher

Generally speaking, over the sample as a whole, we noted that opinions were relatively undifferentiated and did not decisively favour either pole; averages were generally between 2.5 and 3.5. However, convergence on the following items was noted:

- Interim work requires considerable personal investment;
- Interim work calls for considerable flexibility in teaching practice;
- Administrative formalities are considerable.

To study these results more closely, we again used typological analysis. The sample was classified into five typological groups. We noted that those typological groups expressed important differences of opinion which were not revealed by the averages obtained on the basis of socio-logical criteria such as age, sex, etc. We could deduce therefore that there is a perception of interim teaching which does not coincide with membership of a specific sociological group but which stems from a personal perception arising out of opinions and attitudes.

We then went on to perform a classical binary analysis, retaining the first two factors, which explained 69% of the variance (see diagram 6). One factor concerns the concept of constraint-compulsion of the interim function. While its disadvantages are the same for everyone, some persons feel them more strongly than others, depending particularly on what they seek from their employment. On the axis for this factor we situated aspects relating to obligation: interim teaching as an unavoidable path or as the only way to avoid unemployment, the need to have a car, to accept all offers and to establish personal relations through interim employment. Other aspects related to constraint: interim teaching is not inevitable, the acceptance of a post results from a choice and the interim worker expects no more than working relationships. The second factor relates to the concept of job satisfaction, with a positive and a negative pole. On the positive side, satisfaction is high and there is a perception of the work being of value both personally and at the level of integration into the working environment. On the other side, the status is perceived as distressing and dissatisfying.

The characteristics of each typological group as a function of the proximity of replies to the two axes are as follows:

- *Group 1* (17 subjects): fairly satisfied with the job, insisting particularly on the teaching aspect, the work requires considerable personal involvement, colleagues are supportive, the only complaint is about the considerable administrative formalities.

- *Group 2* (17 subjects): happy to be able to teach thanks to their interim status which enable them to embark on a career and avoid unemployment. Ready to accept any offer, which means they require a car. Nonetheless, they are seeking stability as this status is only of interest in the early stages of the career and the obligations arising from the status are considerable. Strong commitment in order to obtain an established post.

Diagram 6:   **Grouping of interim workers in teaching in relation to the factors "constraint-compulsion" (horizontal axis) and "satisfaction/ dissatisfaction (vertical axis)**

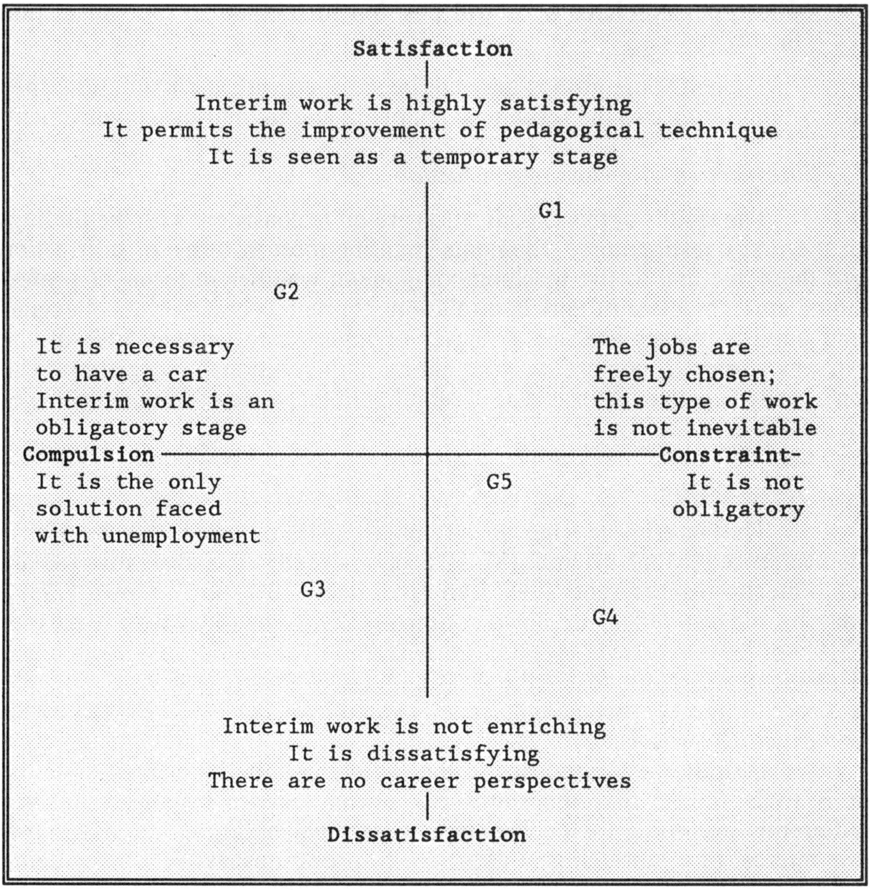

```
                              Satisfaction
                                    |
                 Interim work is highly satisfying
            It permits the improvement of pedagogical technique
                   It is seen as a temporary stage

                                            G1


                        G2

         It is necessary                     The jobs are
         to have a car                       freely chosen;
         Interim work is an                  this type of work
         obligatory stage                    is not inevitable
      Compulsion ——————————————————|——————————————————— Constraint-
         It is the only             G5         It is not
         solution faced                        obligatory
         with unemployment

                        G3
                                    G4


                 Interim work is not enriching
                     It is dissatisfying
              There are no career perspectives
                              |
                        Dissatisfaction
```

–   *Group 3* (12 subjects): they suffer from the interim teacher status, which is considered distressing and a compulsory stopgap measure which is neither enriching nor very satisfying but is the only way for a teacher to avoid unemployment. The persons in this group feel exploited and suffer from the obligations imposed. They experience difficulties of integration.

–   *Group 4* (13 subjects): less investment in the search for employment, interim employment is a choice which is not considered as inevitable in the face of unemployment. The subjects choose from among the interim posts proposed, but they only envisage interim work as a temporary measure and consider it underpaid. They do not believe that the situation offers any career prospects and it is not very enriching.

–   *Group 5* (7 subjects): they accept interim status for lack of other stable employment, consider that interim work offers no career prospects, that it is to be avoided and that administrative formalities are considerable. These persons have a neutral position in relation to the satisfaction factor.

Though some groups may not be satisfied with their situation, they all give importance to the teaching component and to their own involvement.

C. Classification of factors of satisfaction

The results of this classification are quite consistent with the findings of the first questionnaire. Elements counting most in terms of satisfaction are those relating to the teaching component, whether in terms of professional enrichment or of enriched relations through contacts with colleagues and pupils. Wages are not a matter of importance to over 50% of the persons surveyed, nor are working hours or professional recognition. The only really negative factor is that of mobility in the sense of frequent changes of school.

D. Typical portrait

The interim teacher is a woman (87%), young (100%), fairly inexperienced (61%), dynamic (82%), progressive (85%), and creative (83%). The interim teacher rents (79%) an apartment (70%) in the town (79%), may be idealist (48%) or down to earth (52%), may live with a partner (51%) or be unmarried (49%) and may (60%) or may not (40%) own a car. This picture corresponds to the classic image of the teacher embarking on a career, of the energetic beginner, motivated by his or her work and by his or her career prospects.

Despite the limited size of the sample and the lack of information, it is to be noted that the status of interim teacher may be perceived differently according to the individual's personal background; this shows the interest of a more clinical approach to precariousness of employment.

3. Light catering and fast food establishments

We now turn to precarious or atypical employment in the catering sector: light catering and fast-food establishments, snack bars and cafés where turnover of personnel is so rapid that the work can hardly be considered anything but temporary. The type of precarious employment analysed here is strictly speaking formal wage employment which takes place under specific conditions. Several questions come to mind: which population groups are involved in such precarious employment? How do workers feel about their precarious situation? How do they see their future working life and that of their children? Why does precarious employment seem to affect a higher proportion of workers in this sector than in others? We might put forward the following hypotheses: (i) fast food establishments recruit mainly young mobile persons, expected subsequently to seek more stable employment more in line with their training; (ii) employers give more weight to personal characteristics of workers than to schooling and academic skills; (iii) physical fitness is a criterion which facilitates adaptation to work with very varied schedules; (iv) married persons are not often found in the fast food industry.

In view of the specific nature of the different types of catering under consideration, we have approached them separately.

A. Light catering

(a) Methodology

A survey, covering a sample of 80 persons, was carried out. Questions were focused on the respondent's employment history, training, the significant elements of his contract (probationary period, overtime, wages and tips, trade union membership, social security etc.) and on how the subject presents his experience (precariousness, effect on life outside work, further training opportunities, difficulties in the job, and future prospects). 60 replies were statistically processed.

(b) Results

In total, 76% of our population is 25 years of age or under (60% between 21 and 25, 16% under 20) and 20% are between 26 and 35 years of age. 82% are unmarried and 18% married; 86% have no dependents. 83% are Belgian and only 5% are nationals of non-EEC countries. For most of them (60%) this is their first job. Many (75%) have worked in this sector for not more than four years. Few of them have been officially unemployed, 83% have never been registered for employment; most of them have come straight from being students. 73% of them have a secondary school leaving certificate, 36% of whom are university students. In many cases, this job constitutes a temporary break in studying in order to obtain the means to continue. Few of them (15%) have any specific training in the catering or hotel trade.

It should be noted that most contracts (90%) are for an indeterminate duration. However, 83% of respondents were hired on a probationary basis; it is therefore hard to believe that contracts will necessary be renewed, whatever the working schedules offered. 45% of respondents work 40 hours a week and a small majority (17%) work between 10 and 20 hours a week. In some rare cases weekly working hours are as much as 70.

Wages are generally paid in cash (50%) or in cash and in kind (45%). The notion of kind implies no more than compensation in time off or meals. Wages are often paid fortnightly and the workers are usually paid on an hourly basis rather than *pro rata* for sales. In some cases, tips increase their wages: 42% of them keep tips for themselves and 15% have a kitty to be redistributed with kitchen staff or with less fortunate colleagues. Most interviewees prefer team work. In other cases, there is no tipping or if tips are made they are included in the accounts of the establishment. In 98% of cases, the employer assumes responsibility for social security contributions.

Concerning attitudes, we used a questionnaire based on the Likert scale. A number of attitudes were targeted. 57% of respondents considered themselves to be well integrated in their job (the median being 4.3 out of 5). The undetermined duration of the contract in no way troubled 65% of the interviewees, no doubt because they had chosen a situation which they considered from the beginning to be temporary. Their job gave them little feeling of insecurity (57%). A majority (72%) admitted that their work was unrelated to their basic training. We may wonder to what extent such work might enable them to satisfy their aspirations. While they recognised that their aspirations and their work did not match, they accepted this element of frustration because of scarcity of employment in their sector of the labour market. They accepted that their job was neither more nor less satisfying than any other employment available in present economic circumstances.

Working in catering leaves little free time to workers wishing to undertake or continue studying at the same time (68% were of this opinion). Free time was used as leisure time. With regard to the time remaining after work to be with the family, it can be noted, firstly, that few of the respondents were married and, secondly, that the work was experienced as physically tough. The working times and physical tiredness were hardly conducive to family life. 77% of respondents found the work uninteresting from the point of view of schedules and job satisfaction; this is why they would not wish their children to work in the same sector.

Relationships with employers were considered good (25%) or very good (40%). It was no doubt because of the quality of these relations that many workers considered that they could easily negotiate their working hours. Moreover, this flexibility led workers to consider employers as having a positive image of social relations and to view those as satisfactory.

Typological analysis derived from the scale of attitudes reveals four significant groups on the basis of 19 variables. Averages for these so-called typological groups are given in table 2.

The four groups vary in size. From these averages is it possible to carry out a structural analysis which takes into account both variables and groups? To this end we used Classical Binary Analysis 3 [Faverge, 1975; Karnas, 1982]. From this analysis, and bearing in mind the eigenvalues, we retained three main factors:

– The relational factor, particularly relations with employers; it also includes item 2 (feeling disadvantaged compared to other workers), item 4 (relationship between work and training) and item 5 (not wishing to see one's children in precarious employment).

– The second factor includes both integration at work and wages, a factor which involves items 1, 2, 8, 14, 16 and 18.

– The third factor concerns free time and leisure time. It involves items 6 (negatively), 7, 11 and 13.

Characteristic of group 1 are items 1, 5, 9, 12 and 18 and of group 2 items 4, 13, 15 and 19; group 3 is centrally positioned, particularly around items 3, 5, 6, 7, 8, 11 and 17. Groups 1 and 3 give little importance to the relationship with the employer. Insecurity in relation to present work does not preoccupy group 3 subjects.

Table 2: Scale of attitudes of the four typological groups

Variables	G1	G2	G3	G4
1. Integration at work	2.00	1.38	1.38	1.50
2. Disadvantaged by precarious employment	1.21	1.63	1.13	1.50
3. Precariousness as a source of insecurity	1.80	1.70	2.38	1.33
4. Adequacy of work in relation to training	2.07	2.56	2.29	2.50
5. Work corresponds to aspirations	4.07	4.06	4.04	3.50
6. Satisfaction with wages	3.07	2.88	3.58	2.33
7. Wages correspond to work done	1.36	1.88	1.71	1.00
8. Possibility of negotiating work schedules	1.79	1.81	1.96	2.00
9. Job satisfaction	3.21	2.38	2.92	2.00
10. Individual skills used at work	2.36	1.38	2.08	1.00
11. Sufficient time for leisure activities	1.93	1.88	2.00	1.00
12. Sufficient time for training	1.86	1.44	1.71	1.00
13. Precarious employment is a good idea	2.57	2.94	2.42	3.08
14. Could do precarious work all the time	3.21	3.25	3.08	3.00
15. Children could do precarious work	3.93	4.31	4.17	4.17
16. Sufficient time for family	3.07	2.88	3.13	3.50
17. Physically tough work	3.79	3.94	4.21	3.00
18. Psychologically tough work	1.71	1.19	1.50	1.50
19. Relationship with employers	2.29	4.94	3.83	4.33

The plane determined by the first and third factors contrasts the poles "feel disadvantaged vis-à-vis other workers" and insecurity. Group 3 is situated more towards insecurity, psychological tiredness, whereas group 2 is more towards "disadvantaged vis-à-vis other workers". The second and third factors bring groups 1, 2, 3 towards the centre and establish two axes, the first being defined by the pole "leisure time" opposed to "time devoted to the family" and the second by the pole "disadvantaged vis-a-vis other workers" opposed to that of "wages". Items 7 and 11 are opposed to items 16 and 18 on the first axis.

In summary, the study of precariousness has to be indirect, i.e. through questions concerning wages, integration at the place of work, adequacy of hours in relation to external demands and parents' plans for the professional prospects of their children. Whatever the case, none of the respondents wished to remain in their current job for a long time; and the idea that their children may work in the same sector presents little attraction for most parents.

B. Fast food establishments

In this second part, we have focused on the major fast food chains. These enterprises hire students and young people in greater numbers than any other type of catering. Competition is acute; efficiency, profitability and the desire to expand are priorities. We selected for our study *Quick*, *Pizzaland*, *Pizza Hut* and *McDonald*. Having had difficulties in obtaining information from some major chains, we concentrated on those which were more amenable and on employees interviewed outside their place of work.

The chain *Quick*, at the time of our study (June 1988), employed 1,316 persons in 50 different establishments. During the holiday period, it may employ up to 1,500 students. The chain indicated that it offered mainly individually tailored contracts, often involving part-time work (10, 20 or 30 hours a week). The workers acknowledged that the hours were flexible but time initially intended as free time was often used as overtime; this is perceived by workers as detrimental. In *Pizzaland* and *Pizza Hut*, employees mainly work half-time.

In most cases, even before being recruited, the future employee knew that he would not remain in the job for long; this was not because of working conditions, as more often than not he or she was unaware of them at the time of recruitment. Workers are generally paid on an hourly basis; although wages were considered to be insufficient, employees thought it an advantage to be able to do something else outside work. While work was not perceived as being very tiring in *Pizzaland* and *Pizza Hut*, the opposite was more common in *McDonald* and *Quick*. On the whole, whatever the chain, the motto seemed to be "quickly done, well done". During the pre-survey, it was noted that discipline was stricter in *Quick* and *McDonald* than in *Pizzaland* and *Pizza Hut*.

In fast-food, the working population is young. 48% are men and 52% women. The situation of women is not more precarious than that of men. They are more often in the serving area than in the kitchens, where boys are more numerous (68%). Work in the kitchen was not felt to be stressful, but serving was more so. In most cases (76%), workers has been in their job for less than a year. Staff turnover is faster than in other restaurants. It should be noted that this type of distribution chain has developed quite recently. 55% of the young people employed held a secondary school leaving certificate and 21% of them had gone on to higher studies. Most employees (82%) were Belgian and the few workers from outside the EEC were assigned to cleaning and maintenance jobs. Working hours varied greatly; 45% of the personnel was employed half-time and 42% worked less than 20 hours a week. The wage is the main attraction in this type of work. 66% of the workers were satisfied with the average income of BFR 20,000 a month, but none of them wished to make a career in this type of catering.

The pre-survey particularly drew our attention to job satisfaction and feelings about employment stability. To study these attitudes we used a questionnaire on the Likert model. We were only able to question 38 persons. The analysis of these questionnaires led us to retain only those workers from *Pizzaland* and *Pizza Hut* (43% and 57% respectively). They feel less under stress and less closely supervised than workers in other chains; they consider that their work does not involve any risk. They like the product which they serve whereas workers in the other groups do not particularly appreciate the food they serve. Unlike the other groups, they find that workers are not dismissed as easily as is believed. They think that relationships with both customers and fellow-employees are good. In all chains relationships among staff are good but those between workers and employers are better in *Pizzaland* and *Pizza Hut*.

C. Cafés

In this type of establishment, relations between workers and customers tend to be more friendly. Initially, the relationship between customers and serving staff is impersonal, with the use of stereotyped phrases which do not facilitate contact. However, this relationship soon becomes intimate as a result of more personal exchanges between customer and serving staff; the latter quickly becomes the special confidant of various customers. The pre-survey and the questionnaire show that the waiter or waitress often performs a function beyond his or her duties: discussing customers' problems with them, playing the role of priest or public psychologist more than that of waiter. This makes the job more gratifying.

Bipolar questionnaires, each including thirty questions, were completed in cafés in different localities of Brussels. The first dimension to emerge is the attractiveness of the work, grouping together items linked to the notion of monetary income, the quality of life and the quality of social relations. The typological analysis yields five groups:

– *Group 1* gives considerable importance to individual freedom to organise work; the subject organises himself and organises work to make it attractive and interesting. He is involved in his job.

– *Group 2* is rather indifferent to the work and is only interested in its financial aspect.

– *Group 3* is in an intermediate position but is not neutral in that it tends slightly towards the pole of involvement. This group highly values contact with customers and likes the liveliness of the workplace. Satisfaction seems to be more related to the workplace than to the type of work.

– *Group 4* is in a very central position, with an attitude of "no particular involvement" either in relation to work or to the social relations found in these establishments.

– *Group 5* places greater emphasis on the diversity of customers and the variety of social contacts with customers.

A certain homogeneity appears among waiters, no doubt due to the lack of nuance in the questionnaire. But stability in work is closely related to the type of café (local café for example) or to the possibility of organising one's work oneself. The individual's wish to find work yielding job satisfaction, irrespective of chance confidences, and permitting good relationships with customers seems to have considerable importance.

D. Conclusion of case study 3

Our aim was to look at the concerns and motivation of precarious workers in light catering. Most workers acknowledged the precarious aspect of the work, and thought that there was no justification for such a situation: virtually all the respondents viewed this type of work as exclusively temporary; they would remain until they found something better. This work, which is insufficiently gratifying (with some qualification in the case of waiters and waitresses working in local cafés), seems to answer a need in that it leaves time for other activities. The fact also that young people are often sought both in light catering and in fast-food undermines any hopes of working there for a long time. Few people considered this work really suitable for their children. Many envisaged for themselves a future elsewhere. For students employed in this sector, the only reasons for undertaking such work are financial. Those with qualifications are awaiting better times and continue working in the sector while looking for a better job.

While light catering offers fewer possibilities of contacts with customers, in cafés such relations acquire more weight, without which the work would no doubt be even more precarious - which derives not from the decision of the employer but from the worker's wish to find a more agreeable place of employment. Stress is given as a contributory factor of precariousness. In the fast-food industry, as in other light catering establishments, work is undertaken only for a short time and length of service is usually short.

Relations with employers are considered to be good by most of the interviewees, whatever the area or establishment in which they work. This leaves them room to negotiate working hours and thus to be able to devote themselves to other activities outside the workplace. They consider negotiable working hours to be an important component of their job. They see themselves as well integrated in their place of work but few persons spend their free time there.

IV. Overall conclusions

Our evaluation of precarious employment is based on questionnaires completed by persons directly concerned. Replies on our attitude scales did not prove to be homogenous and we therefore went on to identify typological groups and carry out binary analyses. We may conclude that attitudes and feelings towards precariousness of employment vary somewhat according to the population group studied.

In the service sector (case study 1), precariousness is endured less easily than in the other case studies. Respondents are more on the defensive, they are afraid of being marginalised. One group of persons in particular is extremely sensitive to the effect of precariousness of employment, both from the professional and the personal points of view. Such persons nonetheless try to involve themselves in their work and remain motivated in an effort to obtain a contract of unlimited duration.

In teaching, interim status (case study 2) makes personal investment possible from the points of view both of teaching and of social relations (contacts with pupils and colleagues). Interim status is only temporary and the teachers concerned know that there exist long-term possibilities of an established post. While some of them are happy with interim status as a brief compulsory stage prior to permanent appointment, others experience the situation of precariousness as distressing and unrewarding. This factor is to be found in classical binary analysis under the terms of constraint and compulsion although a job satisfaction factor was also identified.

In light catering and fast-food (case study 3), the situation is recognised as being precarious because it is temporary. The work is done for only a short time; it is unusual to find anyone intending to make a career in it. Precariousness stems not from material conditions, nor from work schedules, often negotiable, but more from the personal motivations of workers and their perceptions of their temporary activity. It should be emphasised, however, that many interviewees replied negatively to the direct question of whether they considered work in this sector to be precarious.

References

Alvarez, I.; Bude, J.; Gobin, C.; Waaub, P. (1987): *Cellules d'emploi et environnement de crise*, Research report. Brussels, Université Libre de Bruxelles, Institut de Sociologie.

Cordier, A.; Salengros, P. (n.d.): *Rapport de l'enquête relative à l'image et au fonctionnement de la cellule Verlipack-Recypack*. Brussels, Laboratoire de Psychologie Industrielle et Commerciale et Formation Professionnelle ONEm (mimeo).

Faverge, J.M. (1975): *Méthodes statistiques en psychologie appliquée* (Vol. III). Paris, P.U.F. (2nd edition).

Grootjans, Ch.; Karnas, G. (1981): *Reconversion des travailleurs de Glaverbel — Projet Isolation-Rénovation Charleroi. Les attentes des travailleurs en situation de reconversion*, Research Report. Brussels, I.A.C.T., Laboratory of Industrial and Commercial Psychology (mimeo).

Karnas, G. (1982): "L'analyse binaire classique et le concept de style", in *Le Travail Humain* (Paris), Vol. 45.

Karnas, G.; Salengros, P. (1983): "Quelques exemples de contribution de l'analyse binaire classique au diagnostic en psychologie du travail", in *Le Travail Humain* (Paris), Vol. 46, No. 2.

9 The impact on individuals of precariousness in the United Kingdom labour market

Brendan Burchell[1]

I. Introduction

The effects of precarious work on the psychological health of the individual is a topic that has received almost no attention from psychologists. The study of precarious work has fallen between two traditional concerns of the psychologist, on the one hand unemployment, and on the other processes occurring within the workplace such as job stress, intergroup relations or motivation. Therefore this paper is rather speculative, combining a wide variety of lines of evidence, not all conclusive and occasionally tangential to the main topic under consideration.

Perhaps a further reason why psychologists have so far failed to addressed the topic of precariousness in work is concerned with the complexity of the labour market. Whereas it is relatively straightforward to divide employees from the unemployed and economically inactive, or to study (say) productivity before and after job enrichment programmes, it is less easy to find clear-cut and homogeneous groups of precarious and non-precarious employees, to act as the "experimental" and "control" groups in the normal research design. Indeed, even if such a study were possible, it could be argued that it would be naive in relation to the dynamic nature of the labour market. To be in precarious jobs, that "grey zone" on the edge of the labour market, in most cases involves not only particular character-istics in one's current job but also in one's work history and probable future in the labour market [Pfau, 1988]. It involves either being excluded from access to ladders up the job hierarchy (as is the case with young people), or having been pushed off a career trajectory, usually by involuntary job quits, or (mainly women) domestic interference with labour market activity. The dynamic nature of the labour market is such that, for any one individual, the important question is not so much which stock they are currently a part of, but which flows they have been in, and this eludes any simple study of psychological well-being. This is especially so as psychological health may be a cause as well as an effect of flows within the labour market.

---

1.   Department of Applied Economics and Department of Social and Political Sciences, University of Cambridge, UK.

A further complication is the very diverse nature of different forms of non-standard work. The psychological consequences of these different forms of work will vary widely. The poorly defined terms "precarious" and "non-standard" can cover many situations that have little or nothing in common with each other [Casey, 1988]. This is even more true when considering their potential psychological effects on the individual. For this reason, this paper will discuss two types of non-standard work separately: temporary work and homeworking.

Temporary work, for the purposes of this paper, consists of truly precarious jobs, marked by the insecurity that they place on employees. This category includes short-term jobs, casual work, fixed-term contracts and "quasi self-employment". We restrict the definition in this paper to jobs in which there is not only some real uncertainty about the future but also the potential for this uncertainty to be perilous to the individual. Thus this category excludes many jobs which, although short term in nature, would be considered as good jobs in terms of other criteria such as pay, conditions, status and availability of work; for instance much specialised consultancy work which is, by its very nature, almost always taken on a temporary basis may not be precarious[2].

The second type of non-standard work to be discussed here, homeworking, is work done (usually by women) in the individual's own home. Again there is some imprecision in the definition of this term, but the psychological factors that affect people who work at home (as distinct from people working *from* home [Hakim, 1987]) may affect most home-workers, regardless of other factors.

Part-time work has been considered by others [e.g. Marshall, chapter 2; Rubery, chapter 3] to be a form of precarious or non-standard work. While the psychological impact of part-time working will not be considered explicitly in this paper, many of the psychologically damaging features of temporary work, such as the lower security, would also apply to many part-time jobs in the UK. There is, however, no evidence that part-time workers, on average, are less satisfied with their jobs than other groups of workers [Burchell and Rubery, 1988]. The workers for whom part-time work and dissatisfaction are associated tend to be women who are returning to the labour market after breaks for child-rearing, and have had to take a cut in pay or status compared with the jobs that they held previously. It is the downgrading that is probably more directly responsible for the dissatisfaction rather than the shorter hours *per se*.

As well as considering the psychological effects of non-standard work on the individual, other ways in which the individual is affected will also be considered, albeit briefly. These include the economic, legal and health and safety aspects of the work.

---

2.   Casey [1988], in an attempt to give a typology of temporary jobs in Britain, lists 11 distinct types of temporary work.

II. Precarious work, insecurity and unemployment: The psychological effects of temporary work

This section will combine what little psychological and sociological literature there is directly relating to temporary work and job insecurity with a detailed discussion of theories concerning the psychological effects of unemployment. The latter are relevant for two reasons. Firstly, many of the features of unemployment are similar to the features of temporary work; and secondly, in times of high unemployment a significant proportion of the workforce have careers that alternate between insecure jobs and no jobs, and the effects of job insecurity must be seen in the light of threatened and actual unemployment. Thereafter we present some preliminary findings of a British labour market study that also provides evidence of a strong link between labour market precariousness and psychological health.

A number of studies from different countries using a wide variety of methodologies have all demonstrated the centrality of job security for job satisfaction and psychological health. For instance, in a recent survey of 4,000 American principal wage earners, Dooley, Rook and Catalano [1987] found perceived job security to be the single most important predictor of scores on a checklist of psychological symptoms. Thus feeling insecure in one's job (measured by asking whether respondents expected a change in their employment for the worse, or if anything had happened recently to make them feel less secure in their job) was a highly significant factor in causing symptoms of mild depression in the general population ($\beta = 0.20$, $p < 0.001$). Furthermore, when looking at the risk of an individual being in the top quintile of the sample on their symptom checklist score (a commonly used criterion for potential clinical "cases"), perceived job insecurity was again the most important of all their stress-related predictors, increasing the risk of severe symptoms by a factor of 2.63.

Objective job security was also measured by calculating the extent to which the industrial sector that each individual was working in was contracting or expanding at the time of the interview, the fieldwork period being four years between 1978 and 1982. In a panel design component of the study, 600 of the initial respondents were later re-interviewed, and their change in objective security used in a regression to predict changes in psychological well-being as measured by differences in symptom scores. Although this measurement would clearly have contained a large amount of error variance, because it was at the level of industries rather than firms or individuals, there was nevertheless a highly significant relationship, such that an improvement in the economic prosperity of the worker's industry (whether that industry had changed or not) led to fewer psychological symptoms being reported ($\beta = -0.13$, $p < 0.01$).

Argyle [1972] summarises research that uses a rather different but more direct approach to determine the importance of job security to employees. Research of this kind in both the UK and USA in the 1930s consistently found that employees tended to rate security as the most important aspect of their job. More recent work has found that job security may have dropped from first place, but remains near the top of the list. It is also clearly more important for some groups of workers than others; employees with low incomes and those whose fathers were semi-skilled and unskilled workers were the most concerned about security. Presumably this is largely because those groups of workers are the most likely to be in insecure employment. A further reported effect is that where there is concern about losing one's job, the discontent is likely to spread to all other aspects of one's job. This body of literature seems to point to the conclusion that job security only becomes a major issue when it is threatened. Employees in secure jobs, or in a buoyant economy where they could easily replace their current job with a job of similar status, are less preoccupied with job security than employees under threat of job loss and downgrading.

Qualitative evidence is also available to support this notion of the centrality of security to employees, particularly after they have suffered redundancy or unemployment. Fineman conducted a series of in-depth interviews with white-collar workers who had been unemployed in Britain between 1978 and 1980. They were re-contacted after 6 months, and again in 1985. While there were some differences in the way unemployment was experienced, the overwhelming impression is one of personal crises, whose legacies remain long after re-employment. Many quotes both from those individuals who managed to re-establish their careers, and from those who had to take a job that they considered inferior to the one held before their period of unemployment, emphasise the centrality that job security now had in their lives:-

> "It was bloody hard work being unemployed and this job is worse than my previous one in terms of what I do and job title. But unemployment has left me thinking more about security than the prospects of my job – something that never used to bother me." [Fineman, 1987, pp. 273-274].
> "I constantly think about the vulnerability of my job, at my age, in this recession." [Ibid., p. 227].
> "I suppose I now have to see the security of the job as being more important than the actual work and prospects." [Fineman, 1983, p. 79].

In order to integrate these research findings on job insecurity into some sort of coherent theoretical framework, two of the theories that attempt to account for the serious effects of unemployment on mental health or psychological well-being will be described. Discussion of these theories will also show that they are useful in highlighting when and why precarious forms of employment are likely to have at least some detrimental effects similar to those associated with unemployment. The two theories to be outlined here by no means constitute an exhaustive list of theories to account for the psychological effects of unemployment; they have been selected on the criterion of being applicable to precarious forms of work. What will *not* be discussed here in any detail is the evidence for the detrimental effects of unemployment on psychological and physical health. There is now an abundance of firm evidence from a diverse variety of studies that has proven beyond doubt the direct causal link between unemployment and a number of ill-effects such as psychological ill-health, depression, psychiatric admission, suicide, mortality and loss of self-esteem and confidence [see, for instance, Warr, 1987; Fryer and Payne, 1986].

Theory 1: Warr's vitamin model of employment and psychological health

A recent book by Peter Warr [1987], director of the Social and Applied Psychology Unit at Sheffield University, is a comprehensive synthesis of research, much of it done at his own unit. It is unique in its attempt to synthesise such a large amount of work on both unemployment and occupational psychology into a single, new conceptual framework. Warr's desire to integrate these fields goes back to the beginning of the current resurgence of interest in unemployment; in 1983 he published an article that listed the differences between "good" jobs and "bad" jobs (good and bad for psychological health, that is), and argued that the same psychological features were also important in differentiating between having a job and not having a job, and "good" worklessness and "bad" worklessness.

The conceptual framework that Warr uses both to unite past research and to prescribe where future research should go is his *Vitamin* model. He argues that the way in which the environment affects psychological health is very similar to the way that vitamins are needed for physical health. He then lists nine principal features of the environment that are those metaphorical vitamins:

- Opportunity for control
- Opportunity for skill use
- Externally generated goals
- Variety
- Environmental clarity
- Availability of money
- Physical security
- Opportunity for interpersonal contact
- Valued social position [Warr, 1987, p. 2].

To carry the metaphor further, Warr divides these vitamins into two categories. The first category is similar to vitamins C and E; the effect of having less than a certain threshold value is to leave one vulnerable to illness, but beyond that amount the exact quantity is of no consequence. By contrast, other features of the environment behave in a manner similar to vitamins A and D; there is an optimal dose, and problems may arise if this is either exceeded or not achieved. Variety falls into this latter category: too little leads to boredom, too much can be equally debilitating if it means that no one task can be concentrated on and completed to one's satisfaction.

This model, when applied to the social psychological effects of unemployment, is rather like an elaboration of other well-established theories, such as Jahoda's "latent consequences of employment" [1982]. While Warr is not claiming that each of his nine vitamins has been tested and proven, he does cite an overwhelming number of studies that provide either support for or further understanding of the way in which they may operate.

Theory 2: Fryer and Payne's theory of agency

A very different, and still somewhat controversial, account of unemployment is offered by Fryer and Payne [1984, 1986; Fryer, 1986]. They argue that it is the interruption to the actor's plans and strategies that usually causes the negative psychological consequences of unemployment. Their model of man is as an active agent looking towards the future, rather than Warr's or Jahoda's man who reacts passively to the environment. Their initial evidence for this theory came from very detailed case studies of 11 carefully selected individuals, who were very well adapted to unemployment in most ways (except financially). These individuals had in common an ability to structure and fill their own lives and work towards goals which they set themselves.

Stronger evidence for this theory comes from a study that compared two groups of men from two factories that were facing falling order books. One group was made redundant and the other group was (following union negotiation) being laid off on a rolling basis. The data were collected in a period when the latter group of men, because of the coincidence of lay-off, holidays and maintenance, went for approximately 12 weeks without work. The two groups, redundant and laid-off, were thus both without work, and in most other ways quite similar. The groups differed greatly, though, in their adjustment to worklessness. The laid-off workers planned in advance how they would spend their spare time, for instance decorating their houses, repairing cars, gardening, taking up new sporting activities and going on holidays. They typically bought in the materials that they needed in advance of their lay-off, and were usually successful in carrying out their plans before their return to work. Five weeks after the lay-off these men were, if anything, slightly better in their perceived health than a control group of men who had remained at work in the factory[3].

By contrast, the men who had been forcibly made redundant had considerably worse perceived health. Due to relatively large redundancy payments they certainly did not have immediate financial problems. However, they typically spent a lot of their days watching television and reported feeling bored. When interviewed it was their fear of the uncertainty about their future that these men mentioned frequently as one of their main worries. They did not know whether in a few weeks time they would be working or still unemployed. The researchers concluded that it was the inability to plan for the future that caused the problems for the redundant group. Further evidence for the key role that predictability of the future plays comes from an earlier study in which Payne, Warr and Hartley [1983] found that two-thirds of unemployed men stated that not knowing what was going to happen to them in the future months was a major problem.

What the vitamin and the agency theories have in common is that they see the psychologically damaging effects of unemployment as being

---

3.   It was not being argued by the authors, it should be noted, that this system of lay-offs was necessarily a good long-term solution to a shortage of work. Probably after a while the problems of poverty would bite, and the employees would run out of money and do-it-yourself jobs.

caused by the same processes that affect other aspects of our lives, whether it is a healthy psychological environment or a feeling of security in the future. Where they differ most markedly is in their "model of man". Warr's individual is portrayed as a rather passive organism influenced by environmental forces beyond his or her control, but essential to psychological health and functioning. By contrast, Fryer and Payne's theory emphasises the active role of individuals and the way that they perceive and construct the environment around themselves. A compromise between these two positions is possible: Marsh [1988] has suggested that at least some environmental features are an essential pre-cursor to being able to plan and control one's life in the way that Fryer and Payne's "successfully unemployed" do.

Particularly when viewed through Fryer and Payne's framework, temporary work would now seem to be very similar to unemployment in its disruptive effect on that important human need, the need to be able to plan for, or at the very minimum have some feeling of security over the future. This is illustrated very graphically by another of Fineman's respondents (a graduate) who, after a number of temporary, low-status jobs interspersed with periods of unemployment, found unemployment to be less stressful than the jobs:-

> "I've done absolutely nothing about finding work. Since unemployment my life has been much more pleasant." [Fineman, 1987, p. 273].

Hartley and Fryer [1984] also argue that under many circumstances temporary jobs and under-employment may be more stressful than simple unemployment.

Similarly, some of Warr's "vitamins" would be missing from insecure, temporary jobs. In particular Warr emphasises the need for information about the future under the more general category of environmental clarity. This leads Warr to two tentative conclusions: firstly, that threat of job loss is conceptually similar to other uncertainties about the future, such as uncertainty over chances of future promotion; and secondly, that the need for environmental clarity is one of those vitamins that one can have too much of. In some circumstances, he asserts, some perceived risk about what the future might bring will be beneficial to psychological health, because of the challenge and potential for success that it gives.

The problems with these accounts, though, is that they take individuals at one point in time, either employed or unemployed. How the labour market actually works is that, particularly in times of high unemployment, a significant minority of individuals in the workforce alternate repeatedly between temporary jobs and no jobs. To observe individuals at one point in time and to ignore their history of work and unemployment would fail to capture an understanding of these "precarious careers".

One of the very few empirical studies that does attempt to study insecure *careers* rather than simply insecure *jobs* was conducted in Britain in the early 1970s by Norris [1978a, 1978b]. He identifies the failure to take into account the recurrent nature of unemployment to be a fundamental flaw in both the measurement and consequences of unemployment. He introduces the term "sub-employment" to refer to prolonged periods of unstable employment, and operationally defines as sub-employed any individual who, in the last 12 months, had been unemployed for a total duration of at least one month. This definition should exclude true frictional unemployment, but include those individuals who, although they only show up in the official statistics as short-term unemployed, in fact suffer repeatedly from such spells[4].

The data for this study were drawn from two contrasting local labour markets, one with high unemployment (9.3%) and one with relatively low unemployment (4.1%). Of the total of over 1,300 males interviewed, 12% and 6% respectively of men were found to fall into the sub-employed category. Due to further attrition before a follow-up interview of these sub-employed men, final sample sizes were only 65 and 25.

One interesting feature of the group of men identified as sub-employed was that they were, in many respects, very different in their demographic characteristics from the more commonly studied group of long-term unemployed men. Long-term unemployed men have, in previous surveys, usually been found to be older then their employed counterparts, more prone to physical disabilities and less skilled [e.g. Hill et al., 1973]. Norris found that the differences between the sub-employed men and the rest of the male employees tended to be either small or, in the case of age, in the opposite direction to that usually found for the unemployed. Thus arguments about the lower productivity of unemployed workers cannot be levelled at this group of sub-employed men. This group, though, was much more likely to have suffered compulsory redundancy or dismissal, particularly in the labour market with higher unemployment. Similarly, sub-employed men were much less likely to have taken voluntary job quits than the other employees, and again this trend was even more pronounced in the high unemployment area. This reinforces the notion that it is primarily the nature of the demand side rather than the characteristics of the individual that puts some employees into a cycle of recurrent unemployment and downgrading of skill and status.

Apart from simple statistics on job quits, downgrading and the like, the limits imposed by the small numbers in Norris's samples of sub-employed men prevented any more detailed description of the characteristics of such groups. It must also be remembered that what was at the time of his empirical work a high unemployment area had a level of unemployment that, in the 1980s, would have been below the national average. Norris's most important contribution was his assertion that simply to study individuals during spells of unemployment is to misunderstand the nature of unemployment. Unemployment must rather be studied as part of a career, either representing a crisis point in a career or one of a number of breaks between precarious jobs that prevent the individual from ever climbing out of a downward career path.

---

4.   This operationalisation may seem to be rather loose, but to specify the criteria of sub-employment any more tightly would have, presumably, greatly exacerbated Norris's problem of small numbers of sub-employed men.

It is thus surprising that Norris's work has barely been cited in the 10 years since its publication[5], and the vast majority of social psychological studies of unemployment simply contrast a group of currently unemployed individuals with a control group of employees.

One study that can shed a more direct light on this link between precariousness and psychological health is a recent survey of employees in a British local labour market, Northampton [Burchell and Rubery, 1988]. Northampton is in many ways a typical British labour market. It has moved away from a reliance on its traditional manufacturing industry (footwear) to become a more mixed economy, and has maintained a slightly below-average rate of unemployment throughout the last decade. The data that will be presented here are all derived from a survey of 1,022 twenty to sixty-year-olds in Northampton in 1986.[6]

A multi-stage sampling procedure was used to ensure a representative sample, and a response rate of over 75% was attained. The interview schedule contained a mixture of attitudinal and psychological items as well as numerous details about the respondents' working life, including details of every job held since leaving full time education. A very short version of the GHQ (General Health Questionnaire) was included; the four items with the highest item-whole correlations were selected from the usual 12-item version. This scale measures mild depression by asking questions about, for instance, loss of confidence and an inability to enjoy oneself.

A large number of questions were asked of employees in the sample about their current and predicted future labour market position. In addition, a large amount of detail was collected about each job that they had held since leaving full time education, and the reasons for moves between jobs. Many of these labour market variables are moderately correlated with GHQ scores. Thus a stepwise multiple regression was performed using all of the variables to explore the effects of past, present and perceived future labour market activity on GHQ scores. Table 1 gives the six that were entered (using PIN = 0.01 as the entry criterion), in order of entry.

Clearly, there is a direct link between most or all of the independent variables and the prevalence of labour market precariousness. Unemployment is also often accompanied by a downgrading on re-entry into the labour force [Daniel and Stilgoe, 1977; Norris, 1978b] causing individuals to be less likely to identify their current job as the one that they liked best of all jobs

---

5.   Notable exceptions are a couple of literature reviews by Hartley [1980] and Hartley and Fryer [1984]. In the same vein as Norris, Hartley advocates the study of job insecurity rather than worklessness *per se*.

6.   The data presented here do not allow a full causal analysis of the inter-relationship between labour market experience and psychological health. As with all studies of environmental influences on mental health, the alternative hypothesis that mental health is a factor in selecting the environment must also be confronted. Thus the analyses should not be treated as conclusive proof of a causal relationship between precariousness and psychological ill-health, but rather as strong evidence of where such relationships might lie.

Table 1: Regression weights. Dependent variable, GHQ scores

Variable	ß
Gross hourly pay (log)	-.15
Whether best ever job is current job	-.11
Perceived job security	.11
Perceived chances of better job in next two years	.09
Job choice restricted by household income needs?	.10
Amount of choice when current job selected	.09
R^2 (adj) = 0.09	

that they had held. A fiercer competition for jobs is also likely to lead to less optimism about getting better jobs in the future. Perceptions about the amount of choice over jobs are probably also linked to the level of unemployment.

Thus, from a simple analysis of a sample of employees, two important conclusions can be drawn. Firstly, that good psychological health is related to higher pay, better job security, greater perceived choice over jobs and favourable comparisons with previous jobs. Secondly, many or all of these variables are affected by the rate of unemployment and precariousness in the labour market; thus it is reasonable to predict that as unemployment and precariousness rises, the psychological health of the working population falls.

The problem with this sort of analysis is that it assumes that the effect of each variable is the same for the whole sample. Even many neo-classical labour market economists now accept that the labour market is segmented to some extent, with each sector having very different characteristics. At its simplest, the labour market can be conceived as two sectors, a primary and secondary sector. The primary sector consists of well-paid, skilled workers, the secondary sector of the less skilled, poorly organised labour, whose productivity is not rewarded to the same extent as their counterparts in the primary segment.

One of the problems of studying labour market segments and "non-standard" employment is in defining what exactly we mean by these terms, and how we would select our comparison groups. There are no simple criteria for defining either precariousness or membership of a particular labour market segment; rather both can be thought of as a constellations of variables, or a "syndrome".

In order to divide the very heterogeneous sample of employees into more homogeneous sub-groups (hopefully representing different labour market sectors), a cluster analysis was performed using a large number of labour-market related variables to divide the sample (GHQ scores were not one of the variables used to cluster the sample). Five clusters were thus identified, each very different from the others on a wide variety of variables. While it would be too complex to go into any detail of the results of this analysis, this is a brief description of each of the five groups:

Group 1: "The Primary Segment". This is the largest group (47% of employees in the sample), and by almost all objective criteria, the most advantaged. They are predominantly male (78%), well paid, of high social class and most of their previous job quits have been to get better jobs and have resulted in pay increases.

Group 2: "Stickers". This group (comprising 31% of the sample) is a little older than the others (43 years compared to a sample mean of 38), and predominantly female (62%). They are the most satisfied group with respect to all aspects of their jobs, even though their pay, fringe benefits and skill levels are considerably lower than group 1. They are the least likely to want to change jobs, and see the internal labour market as being more advantageous than all of the other groups.

Group 3: "Female Descenders". Of the 13% of the sample in this group, 96% were female. This group has the highest amount of domestic interference in labour market activity (as measured by working part time, past job quits for domestic reasons, past periods of full-time housework, having to look after children, etc.). They receive the lowest pay, and have had the highest proportion of job changes to same or worse paid jobs. For half of them their last change of job was to a worse paid job than the one that they had held previously.

Group 4: "Young and Mobile Males". This small group (6%) is 80% male. They are, on average, a few years younger than the other groups (mean age 30). They see their chances of getting better jobs as being the highest of all the groups, are most likely to see those jobs as being with other employers, and see the advantage of being an insider as minimal. They are the most likely to have moved to better paid jobs when they changed jobs in the past, but are not the most likely to be currently in their best jobs.

Group 5: "Male Descenders". This group of only 4% of the sample consists of 83% males. They seem to have nothing going for them. They have all had a job change in the past that has involved a drop in the social class rating of their job (as measured by the Cambridge Scale Score), and most have at some time been sacked or made redundant. They are also the most likely to have been unemployed in the past. They stand out most in their current jobs because of their lack of perceived (and presumably actual) job security. As well as being dissatisfied with their job security, they are the most dissatisfied group with their jobs overall. Most of them have been looking for jobs in the last year, and almost all would be keen to change jobs if possible.

When the GHQ scores of each of the five groups were compared there were large, statistically significant ($F[4,575]=7.2$, $p<0.0001$) and predictable differences. In particular, the "male descenders" had the worst psychological health of the five groups, and the two most stable groups (1 and 2) had the best psychological health. Furthermore, a post-hoc test revealed that the GHQ scores of unemployed individuals in the sample were only slightly higher than, and not significantly different from those of cluster 5 (table 2). A simple comparison between the highest and lowest scoring

Table 2: Mean GHQ scores for five clusters of employees and the unemployed in Northampton, 1986

	All		Minus low incomes	
	N*	GHQ score	N	GHQ score
Cluster 1	269	1.62	246	1.61
Cluster 2	176	1.68	143	1.66
Cluster 3	75	1.87	63	1.86
Cluster 4	35	1.78	29	1.80
Cluster 5	22	2.07	19	2.17
Unemployed	144	2.18	66	2.06
All employees	580	1.7	503	1.69

Note: * Apparent inconsistencies in sample size are due to either missing values or the weights used to compensate for sampling error.

clusters reveals that the difference in GHQ scores (0.45) is about the same as the difference between the mean for the employees (taken together) and the mean for the unemployed individuals (0.48).

While the mean GHQ score for the unemployed group is slightly higher than for the group of precariously employed workers, this small difference is reversed (although it is still non-significant) when household income (standardised for household composition) is controlled for. The households of the unemployed respondents had, on average, much lower incomes than those of the employees in cluster 5. If we omit from the model all those cases where the income is less than the median standardised household income received in the unemployed group, the cluster 5 employees have slightly (but not statistically significantly) *worse* GHQ scores than the unemployed. Thus, if the extreme poverty that affects some of the unemployed is left aside, to be unemployed may be no worse than having a job in the precarious or "grey zone" of the labour market.

Unfortunately, though, care must be taken in drawing causal conclusions from a study such as this. The cross-sectional nature of the design gives no indication of the extent to which it may have been individual characteristics such as poor psychological health that lead to the precariousness of these employees in the labour market, rather than the reverse.

III. The economic implications for the temporary worker

The discussion of the psychological consequences of temporary work has so far concentrated solely on the insecurity of such jobs. Another important aspect of temporary work is the reward given for such work, both directly in terms of hourly pay and indirectly in terms of bonuses, holiday entitlement, sick pay, maternity pay, pension entitlements and so on.

A recent survey of 370 British workplaces covering over 300,000 workers, conducted by the Labour Research Department (LRD), collected detailed information about the pay and conditions of temporary workers and, where they existed, permanent employees doing the same jobs [LRD, 1987]. In 62% of firms the basic pay of these two groups was the same; in most of the others temporary workers received a lower hourly rate, but there were some exceptions where they were compensated for their insecurity by receiving higher hourly rates. It is likely, though, that the group of comparison workers, permanent employees doing the same work as temporary workers, are themselves relatively poorly paid. Furthermore, many workers in precarious jobs have undergone an occupational down-grading, so that even though the pay might be comparable for the job, it may be lower than that of permanent workers with comparable skills.

Even where the hourly rate was identical, temporary workers often received less fringe benefits. While about three-quarters of the establishments surveyed would give equal bonuses, shift and holiday pay, equal entitlement to sick pay was given in less than half of the establishments, maternity pay and leave in less than a third and pension entitlement in less than a fifth.

It is interesting to note that, where hourly pay was equivalent for permanent and temporary staff, this rarely developed without union pressure; in 71% of cases it was the result of negotiation. This leads to the conclusion that these figures may, in fact, be favourable estimates of temporary workers' pay. Where there are no permanent employees doing exactly the same work it must be much more difficult for unions to press for parity. It is also likely that, due to the sampling technique of the LRD survey, unionised establishments were heavily over-represented.

Another way to assess the rates of pay of temporary workers is by comparing the hourly rates paid to temporary agency workers with estimates for equivalent jobs in the rest of the workforce. Such a comparison, between the rates paid by Manpower (one of the larger agencies for temporary workers) and LRD's estimates for the workforce as a whole, showed that (with the exception of visual display unit – VDU – operators) the agency rates were lower. The differences were however not large, again suggesting that the principal disadvantage of temporary work is probably the insecurity rather than the basic pay and conditions.

1. Why employ temporary workers?

Different surveys of the reasons employers give for employing temporary staff [LRD, 1987; The Alfred Marks Bureau, 1982, cited in Syrett, 1983] produced rather different results, but there was a consensus that the main reasons were not to undercut pay and undermine working conditions, as has been reported by some unions. More important was the need to provide for seasonal or unpredictable fluctuations in workload, staff holidays, sickness, maternity leave and recruitment delays or problems. A further, perhaps increasing role of temporary contracts is to screen staff before a permanent contract of employment is offered. This was given as a reason by 15% of employers in the Alfred Marks 1982 survey, but interestingly, less than half of this proportion of temporary employees thought that they were being tried out for permanent employment.

One of the reasons that temporary work is not seen as a way to cut costs is that, when the costs of recruitment or agency fees are taken into account, as well as the problem of familiarising temporary employees with practice and standards, temporary workers cost the employer considerably more than permanent staff [Syrett, 1983].

2. Why be a temporary worker?

Reasons given for doing temporary work vary enormously, and include the unavailability of permanent jobs, filling in time between other commitments, students working during vacations, a desire to gain experience or enjoyment of the variety of agency work. However, these reasons are given in response to survey questionnaires, and it is difficult to assess their accuracy. It is asking a lot of any individual to weigh up the combination of structural forces, labour law and their domestic and personal situation that has led them into their current position. The several surveys that have attempted to find out to what extent people choose voluntarily to do temporary work and to what extent they are forced into precarious work by the lack of permanent jobs must thus be treated with caution. A comparison of four such surveys (The Prices and Incomes Board, 1968, The Federation of Personnel Services, 1975, and The Alfred Marks Bureau, 1982, all cited in Syrett [1983]; and the Labour Force Survey, 1984) does show a consistent pattern over time. The proportion of respondents who were doing temporary work because they could not obtain permanent work or who were actively seeking permanent work but doing temporary work until they were successful rose from 13% (1968) through 25% (1975), 33% (1982) to 36% (1984). While these figures are not directly comparable because of differently drawn samples, different phrasing of the question and different response options, the conclusion that might be reached is that, whereas temporary work used to be taken on "voluntarily" in times of almost full employment, in times of high unemployment employees have increasingly been forced into taking temporary jobs due to the lack of alternatives.

3. Health and safety

As a general rule, the Health and Safety Act of 1974 gives equal protection to all employees. The potential problem for temporary workers arises when they are not classed as an employee at their place of work. This may happen either because they are technically self-employed (common in the construction industry) or because their employer is an agency (common, for example, in clerical work). However, legal test-cases have established that, in both cases, the duties of the employer to provide a safe operating environment are the same for non-employees as for employees. What happens in practice may be different though; in the construction industry the Chief Inspector of Factories' 1986 report blamed sub-contracting and non-standard forms of work for a 29% rise in industrial accidents over a four year period. It may also be more difficult for non-employees to obtain compensation when they are injured; the common law duties of employers to employees are more easily established than the duties involved in other employment relationships.

4. Temporary work: Conclusions

Evidence from a variety of sources points to the conclusion that precarious employment is damaging to the psychological well-being of the individual, perhaps to much the same extent as unemployment. Temporary or precarious jobs are often the result of involuntary job quits, and are also associated with other negative labour market experiences such as periods of unemployment or downgrading of skill and status, most of which are also psychologically damaging. The literature on the psychological effects of unemployment suggests that there are many parallels between the effects of unemployment and the effects of precarious employment. In particular, it is the insecurity and inability to plan for the future that makes them both such stressful experiences.

It is these psychological factors that are probably the primary threat to workers in temporary employment. While their economic position is not good, it is not as dire as in some other non-standard forms of work such as homeworking.

IV. Homeworking

Although homeworking is also classed as a form of non-standard work, it has little in common with temporary work in terms of either the psychological problems or the economic factors associated with it. However, as has been argued above, the psychological problems of homeworking may be just as great as those of temporary work, but for very different reasons.

As with the general notion of precarious employment, the definition of homeworkers is not straightforward, and surveys of homeworkers have sometimes used very different definitions and thus computed very different summary statistics. Hakim [1987] used the 1981 Labour Force Survey as a sampling frame and re-interviewed the majority of those who worked at or from home. It was the *from* home group that turned out to be very different from the normal conception of homeworkers. They were predominantly men, unlike traditional homeworkers who are almost exclusively women. In addition, their working environment was much more similar to that of standard employment, as was their average pay. For this reason Hakim and other researchers citing her report have been careful to distinguish the two groups.

Surveys by the Low Pay Unit [Huws, 1984; Bisset and Huws, 1984] have also identified great heterogeneity among homeworkers. One of the main thrusts of their work was to compare two groups of homeworkers, traditional homeworkers and "new" homeworkers taking advantage of advances in new technology and telecommunications to do either computer programming and other highly skilled information technology work or routine office work from home. Although the traditional and new home-workers differed greatly in their pay, in many other ways the new breed of homeworkers were subject to the same disadvantages, such as isolation and insecurity, as traditional homeworkers.

Unlike the evidence on temporary workers, there have been a number of surveys that have looked explicitly at the employment conditions of homeworkers. Unfortunately, though, none of them has given more than a passing mention to the psychological effects of homeworking. A further problem is that much homeworking is done in an atmosphere of secrecy, with both employers and the homeworkers themselves attempting to avoid the scrutiny of the authorities because of fears about tax, national insurance, minimum wage legislation, illegal immigration, work permits and so on. Thus even the most carefully sampled surveys [e.g. Hakim, 1987] may be liable to serious errors in the form of non-response bias. However, a fairly coherent picture is painted by a number of surveys that have been carried out using a wide variety of sampling techniques.

1. The psychological consequences of homeworking

The main threat to the psychological health of the homeworker is probably caused by the isolation of the job. The traditional homeworker typically has only the most minimal of social contact with his or her employer; nine out of ten traditional homeworkers have never visited the employer's place of work [Bisset and Huws, 1984]. Materials and instruc-tions either arrive by post or are delivered by a van-driver. This is one of the main differences between traditional homeworkers and new home-workers, who are much more likely to make regular visits to their colleagues or clients, but both groups have far less social contact through work than virtually any other type of worker. In answer to an open-ended question about the advantages and disadvantages of homeworking, isolation was given as a disadvantage by 60% of new homeworkers, but interestingly, by only 15% of traditional homeworkers[7]. Other writers are unanimous in finding

---

7.   This difference may reflect the comparisons being made by the different groups; the new homeworkers may be comparing their home environment to the office, whereas the traditional homeworkers may be comparing it to staying at home but without the work. The use of different comparison groups makes the interpretation of data such as these potentially misleading.

isolation and loneliness to be a problem [Hakim, 1987; Hope, Kennedy and De Winter, 1976; Allen and Wolkowitz, 1987].

Given that most homeworkers are at home with children, and presumably have spouses with whom they spend time, does not this compensate for the isolation? But social contact within the family is very different from social contact typically found in the workplace, and they serve different purposes emotionally [Jahoda, 1982]. Family relations are, as a rule, much more emotionally charged than relations with other employees. Thus the workplace is a good place for more relaxed, rational appraisal which complements the emotional life of the family. There is also greater diversity in the relations that one has at work, but the people that one dislikes can be missed as much as one's close friends. Thus to miss one's fellow employees is a very different experience from missing, say, one's spouse, but nonetheless just as real. Additional evidence for this link between social isolation at work and job satisfaction has come from studies of conventional workplaces. Hackman and Lawler [1971] found that the extent to which work offered opportunities to "meet individuals whom you would like to develop friendships with" was directly related to job satisfaction. Henderson and Argyle [1985] found that the presence of other employees with whom one's friendship extended outside the workplace significantly reduced current feelings of job stress.

Furthermore, the home environment of many homeworkers is already one that psychologists have found to be conducive to depression. Among the factors found to make women more vulnerable to depression were not having a job outside the home, and having three or more children below the age of 14 [Brown and Harris, 1978]. The additional stress imposed on a woman's daily routine by homeworking may well add to this, although it is also possible that other aspects of the work such as externally generated goals may be psychologically beneficial.

A common defence of homeworking is that it gives the worker far more autonomy than, say, factory work. Homeworkers do not have a supervisor or boss standing over them, so they can pace themselves and take breaks as and when they please. Empirical evidence shows this to be a myth [Allen and Wolkowitz, 1987]. The combination of pressures from employer and domestic responsibilities are very great indeed. The employer can set schedules quite effectively through the times of delivery and collection of work. The pay is almost always calculated strictly on a piecework basis (at a very low rate; see the next section), thus enforcing a very rapid pace of work. As the payment is often not made until the quality of the work has been accepted, it might be more accurate to say that the homeworker has to take on the role of unpaid supervisor as well as worker. Allen and Wolkowitz [1987] and Hope, Kennedy and De Winter [1976] also find that, instead of being a substitute for housework, homeworking is done as well as housework with little help or adjustment of expectations from the husband or other family members to compensate for the dual role of housework and paid employment.

A further threat to the psychological well-being of the homeworker is the insecurity inherent in their jobs. Like most temporary workers, they have little or no comeback against unfair dismissal or rights to compensation for redundancy. In fact, though, the relationship between homeworker and the supplier of work tends to be very stable. Hakim [1987] found that the average length of tenure with the "employer" was slightly longer than for standard employees. But the statistics about tenure and homeworking are probably not known accurately by homeworkers themselves. The fact that they feel insecure is itself enough to cause the associated psychological problems.

The insecurity of the homeworker comes not so much from outright job loss as from having periods with little or no work (and consequently little or no pay) interspersed with periods of intense work. As with many forms of non-standard work, the main benefit for the employer is the passing on of risk from the product market directly to the employees. As was argued above, such insecurity is a major cause of work-related stress and psychological problems.

One might, from a knowledge of the pay and conditions of homeworkers, expect that they would be very dissatisfied with their jobs. This is not the case, though. Bisset and Huws found that a majority of homeworkers, both traditional and new, said that they enjoyed their work. Only 5% of Hakim's sample expressed dissatisfaction with their work; even among her most disadvantaged group of homeworkers, those in manufacturing, only 11% stated that they were dissatisfied with their work. Only one in four women in her sample said that they had to work at home, and one in three said that they had a completely open choice but chose to work at home rather than go out to work.

However, before using this high rate of satisfaction to conclude that all is well with homeworking, a consideration of the literature on job satisfaction suggests that simple, direct questions about job satisfaction generate responses that confound the extent to which an individual is resigned to doing his or her job with true satisfaction based upon some objective criteria of contentment [Agassi, 1979, 1983]. The vast majority of the population state that they are satisfied with their jobs, especially women, even though their jobs are usually objectively less rewarding than men's jobs. If most people consider that they are currently in the best job that they could obtain in view of their circumstances and the jobs on offer, they will be strongly inclined to state that they are satisfied with their job. Given that the belief is still widespread in Britain that mothers of pre-school children should stay at home, and provision of care for pre-school children is scarce and often prohibitively expensive, many women do not even consider employment outside the home as an option while their children are of pre-school age. But instead of being dissatisfied with the poor employment that they are forced into by this combination of economic and social factors, they are satisfied with any job they can get that fits in with these constraints. As Marshall argues in chapter 2, any claims that bad jobs are taken voluntarily should be treated with scepticism for reasons such as these.

There is also probably a certain degree of psychological defence involved in homeworkers justifying their jobs as "real jobs". Researchers often find that homeworkers grossly overestimate their hourly pay by highly selective and biased reports of working time. For instance, Hope, Kennedy and De Winter [1976] gave the example of a woman who reported that she did between 20 and 28 hours machining a week, and got paid between 9 and 10 pounds. After taking into account the considerable amount of time that her husband put into packing her work in the evenings and all of her overheads (electricity, sick pay, rent, etc.) her hourly pay was, they calculated, in the range 18 to 27 pence per hour rather than the 32 to 50 pence implied by her figures. She seemed to almost deliberately ignore all of the hidden costs, and overestimate her real earnings by a factor of almost two.

A better insight into the lot of the homeworker is gained by looking at the advantages and disadvantages that they cite in response to open-ended questions. For traditional homeworkers the four most common advantages of homeworking are childcare (56%[8]), flexibility or convenience (27%), money (15%) and freedom or independence (15%). The most commonly stated disadvantages are low pay (31%), the encroachment on family life or unsociable hours (27%), the lack of sufficient work or job security (21%) and the noise (9%) or dust and dirt (9%). The pattern for the new homeworkers was slightly different. Seventy percent mentioned childcare as the main advantage, followed again by the flexibility or convenience (55%), the way in which homeworking fits in with housework or hobbies (29%) and the absence of commuting (22%). The disadvantages were seen as the isolation (60%), the encroachment on family life or unsociable hours (31%), insufficient work or lack of job security, boring or unsatisfying work and lack of prospects (all 21%).

2. The economic consequences of homeworking

There is no doubt about the very low pay and almost complete lack of other benefits available to homeworkers. At a time when the threshold for low pay was calculated as £2.25 per hour, 76% of the traditional homeworkers earned less than £1 per hour, and 33% earned less than 50 pence per hour. The total range of pay was from 7 pence to £4 per hour [Bisset and Huws, 1984]. Even though some of these workers were in industries where there were legal minimum wages, these may not be applicable to homeworkers if they are "substandard workers". However, Bisset and Huws point out that, given the discrepancies between the minimum wage rates and the earnings of their sample, it is difficult to account for all of this enormous difference through different levels of individual productivity.

The average hourly pay of the new homeworkers (£4.62) did not, on the face of it, seem to be so far removed from the rest of the labour force [Huws, 1984]. However, Huws calculated their hourly rate to be, on average, £2 per hour less than workers of comparable grade and experience

---

8. Due to the open-ended nature of these questions, the actual proportion of individuals giving a particular response is likely to consistently underestimate the actual proportion of individuals who hold that opinion [Belson, 1988].

in the computing industry. Again there was a very large difference between the rates for the best and worst paid workers, from 10 pence to £13.75.

It is beyond the scope of this paper to explore the reasons for the very low rates of pay for homeworkers, but one important consideration that must be borne in mind in assessing the impact of such low pay is that the wages from homeworking usually constitute only a small proportion of the money coming into the household, typically less than 20% [Allen and Wolkowitz, 1987]. Although this is no justification for low pay, it presumably helps to lessen the impact on standards of living. Another important fact, though, is that the partners of homeworkers are often on very low wages themselves, so the wages from homeworking, rather than being used to buy "extras", are often an indispensable part of the household budget for essentials [Allen and Wolkowitz, 1987]. In contrast to this Hakim [1987] finds that much homeworking is intended to help cope with mortgage repayments that had been taken on in the recent past. In both cases, though, the money is important and not just "pin money".

Most homeworkers are either treated as self-employed or, as their wages fall below the threshold for National Insurance payments, the issue of their exact employment status never has to be decided. Where there have been legal cases in which homeworkers have tried to define themselves as employees, they have generally been unsuccessful, as they are deemed to have more autonomy than is normal in an employer-employee relationship (although this is, in practice, questionable). Exceptions have been proven where, for instance, the homeworkers are provided with sewing machines by the supplier of work, even though it was accepted in that case that there was no control over the amount of work that they were expected to do. Even in the rare situations where the homeworker gains the status of employee, part-time workers are often not entitled to the same protection as full-time employees, or they must have worked for the employer for longer to establish those rights. Part-timers who work for less than eight hours per week are hardly protected from dismissal, except on grounds of sex, race or trade-union membership. For workers who average between eight and 16 hours per week, the qualifying period for full employment protection and other entitlements such as maternity leave is five years instead of the usual two years. The combination of these factors means that traditional homeworkers almost never have any entitlement to sick pay, maternity leave, holiday pay or compensation for redundancy or unfair dismissal.

The situation of the "new" homeworkers was better than this, but again not as good as they could have expected in a normal employment relationship. Forty-four percent of them were employees, and the majority of this group was entitled to sick pay, maternity leave, etc. The self-employed new homeworkers were, in most respects, very similar to the traditional homeworkers with no security or other benefits. It was also interesting to note that, although the hourly pay of these two groups was similar, the employees earned considerably more over the year than the self-employed homeworkers. This reflects the greater security of the employees; many of the self-employed homeworkers complained of long spells without any work.

3. Health and safety

As with temporary workers, in theory the Health and Safety at Work Act should apply to homeworking in the same way as for standard forms of work, but in practice this may not be the case. By law, factories putting out work should regularly give the local authority details of homeworkers so that inspection of working conditions can be carried out. In practice this system has never been successfully implemented, and most homeworkers never become known to the inspectors. Similarly, most accidents probably never get reported, so it is difficult to obtain an accurate picture of the actual risks. Surveys have produced inconsistent conclusions on this point. Hakim [1987] concluded that, apart from psychological problems caused by social isolation, there was no evidence that homeworkers suffered more from work-related illness than other workers. Allen and Wolkowitz [1987] are sceptical of this though, giving several examples of women handling solvent-based glue without adequate ventilation, or stocks of material in the home being a fire risk. There has also been some concern about materials or machinery being a danger to children in the household; it is unusual for homeworking to be conducted in a room reserved solely for that purpose. Huws [1984] also points out that, with an increasing awareness of the hazards now associated with clerical work, such as in the use of VDUs, the problems are not limited to manufacturing. Furthermore, without the correct office furniture and regular breaks, the problems may well be worse at home than in the office.

V. Summary and conclusions

While there is relatively little direct evidence on the psychological effects of precarious and non-standard forms of work, the limited evidence available suggests that there is indeed cause for concern.

The primary psychological problem with temporary work is probably the insecurity that it brings. Research on unemployment demonstrates that insecurity and the inability to plan for the future are among the principal causes of the worsening in psychological health that accompanies unemployment. The empirical findings concerning temporary workers suggest that the same problems affect them too, with a similar detrimental effect on their psychological health. The consequences are similar to any stressful situation where the individual does not have good social support: a lowering of general psychological health and an increase in symptoms of mild depression and psychological disorder [Cochrane, 1983].

Homeworkers, as well as suffering psychologically from insecurity, are also subject to social isolation and are barred from the friendships in the workplace that have been shown to be beneficial to psychological health. They also suffer economically due to the extremely low wages that are typical of homeworking.

In theory neither homeworkers nor temporary workers are directly threatened by increased health or safety risk, or are less protected by law.

In practice, because of the difficulties of surveillance, the risks of accidents or harmful environments are probably greater.

Only a minority of either group of workers take on their non-standard jobs "voluntarily". Temporary workers (particularly in times of high unemployment) are forced into precarious jobs through the lack of secure jobs, often following redundancy or dismissal. Homeworkers usually mention childcare and domestic responsibilities as the principal restriction on their choice of jobs.

If these types of non-standard work regimes are to become more widespread, to provide the flexible labour force advocated by industry and the present British Government, it will be at a high cost to the quality of life and psychological well-being of the individuals employed in such jobs.

References

Agassi, J.B. (1979): *Women on the job: The attitudes of women to work*. Mass., Lexington.

—— (1983): *Comparing the work attitudes of women and men*. Mass., Lexington.

Argyle, M. (1972): *The social psychology of work*. Harmondsworth, Pelican.

Allen, S.; Wolkowitz, C. (1987): *Homeworking: Myths and realities*. Basingstoke, Macmillan.

Belson, W.A. (1988): "Major error from two commonly used methods of market and social research", in *The Psychologist*, Vol. 1.

Bisset, L.; Huws, U. (1984): *Sweated labour: Homeworking in Britain today*, Report No. 33. London, Low Pay Unit.

Brown, G.W.; Harris, T. (1978): *Social origins of depression: A study of psychiatric disorder in women*. London, Tavistock.

Burchell, B.J.; Rubery, J. (1988): *Segmented jobs and segmented workers: An empirical investigation into labour market sectors*. International Working Party on Labour Market Segmentation, Xth conference, Porto, Portugal (mimeo).

Casey, B. (1988): *Temporary employment: Practice and policies in Britain*, Policy Studies Institute Report No. 669. London.

Cochrane, R. (1983): *The social creation of mental illness*. London, Longman.

Daniel, W.W.; Stilgoe, E. (1977): *Where are they now? A follow-up of the unemployed*. London, PEP.

Dooley, D.; Rook, K.; Catalano, R. (1987): "Job and non-job stressors and their moderators", in *Journal of Occupational Psychology* (Leicester), Vol. 60.

Fineman, S. (1983): *White collar unemployment: Impact and stress*. Chichester, Wiley.

—— (1987): "Back to employment: Wounds and wisdoms", in Fryer, D.; Ullah, P. (eds): *Unemployed people: Social and psychological perspectives*. Milton Keynes, Open University Press.

Fryer, D.M. (1986): "Employment deprivation and personal agency during unemployment: A critical discussion of Jahoda's explanation of the psychological effects of unemployment", in *Social Behaviour*, Vol. 1.

Fryer, D.M.; Payne, R.L. (1984): "Proactivity in unemployment: Findings and implications", in *Leisure Studies* (London), Vol. 3.

Fryer, D.M.; Payne, R.L. (1986): "Being unemployed: A review of the literature on the psychological experience of unemployment", in Cooper, C.L.; Robertson, I. (eds): *International Review of Industrial and Organisational Psychology,* Vol. 1. London, Wiley.

Hackman, J.R.; Lawler, E.E. (1971): "Employee reactions to job characteristics", in *Journal of Applied Psychology* (Worcester, Mass.), Vol. 55.

Hakim, C. (1987): *Home-based work in Britain*, Research Paper No. 60. London, Department of Employment.

Hartley, J. (1980): "Psychological approaches to unemployment", in *Bulletin of the British Psychological Society* (London), No. 33.

Hartley, J.; Fryer, D. (1984): "The psychology of unemployment: A critical appraisal", in Stephenson, G.M.; Davis, J.H. (eds): *Progress in Applied Social Psychology*, Vol. 2. London, Wiley.

Henderson, M.; Argyle, M. (1985): "Social support by four categories of work colleagues", in *Journal of Occupational Behaviour* (Chichester), No. 6.

Hill, M.J.; Harrison, R.M.; Sargeant, A.V.; Talbot, V. (1973): *Men out of work*. Cambridge, Cambridge University Press.

Hope, E.; Kennedy, M.; De Winter, A. (1976): "Homeworkers in North London", in Barker, D.L.; Allen, S. (eds): *Dependence and exploitation in work and marriage*. London, Longman.

Horrell, S.; Rubery, J.; Burchell, B. (1988): *Unequal jobs or unequal pay?* SCELI working paper. Cambridge, Department of Applied Economics.

Huws, U. (1984): *The new homeworkers: New technology and the changing location of white-collar work*, Report No. 28. London, Low Pay Unit.

Jahoda, M. (1982): *Employment and unemployment: A social-psychological analysis*. Cambridge, Cambridge University Press.

Kelvin, P.; Jarrett, J.E. (1985): *Unemployment: Its social psychological effects*. Cambridge, Cambridge University Press.

Labour Research Department [LRD](1987): *Temporary workers: A negotiator's guide*. London, LRD Publications Ltd.

Marsh, C. (1988): "Unemployment in Britain", in Gallie, D. (ed): *Employment in Britain*. Oxford, Basil Blackwell.

McKenna, S.P.; Fryer, D.M. (1984): "Perceived health during lay-off and early unemployment", in *Occupational Health* (London), No. 36.

McKenna, S.P.; Payne, R.L. (1984): *Measuring the perceived health of unemployed and re-employed men*, Social and Applied Psychology Unit Memo No. 696. Sheffield University.

Norris, G.M. (1978a): "Unemployment, subemployment and personal characteristics: The inadequacies of traditional approaches to unemployment", in *Sociological Review* (Keele), No. 8.

—— (1978b): "Unemployment, subemployment and personal characteristics: Job separation and work histories: The alternative approach", in *Sociological Review* (Keele), No. 8.

Payne, R.L.; Warr, P.B.; Hartley, J. (1983): *Social class and the experience of unemployment*, Social and Applied Psychology Unit Memo No. 549. Sheffield University.

Pfau, B. (1988): *The use of non-standard employment by employers*. International Working Party on Labour Market Segmentation, Xth annual conference, Porto, Portugal (mimeo).

Stewart, A.; Prandy, K.; Blackburn, R.M. (1980): *Social stratification and occupations*. London, Macmillan.

Syrett, M. (1983): *Employing job sharers, part-time and temporary staff*. Plymouth, Latimer Trend.

Warr, P. (1983): "Work, jobs and unemployment", in *Bulletin of the British Psychological Society* (London), No. 36.

—— (1987): *Work, unemployment and mental health*. Oxford, Clarendon Press.

10 Atypical employment and the trade unions in Belgium: The precariousness of strategies

Mateo Alaluf[1]

The recent past, with its rise in unemployment, has been characterised by the propagation of non-standard employment statuses. Most such jobs are in fact "sub-statuses" or precarious forms of employment. These are hybrid positions, giving rise to situations between that of wage-earner and non-wage-earner (e.g. independent wage-earners in manufacturing, construction and services caught in the process of "downsizing"),[2] between that of wage employment and unemployment (e.g. job creating schemes to reduce unemployment) and between that of wage-earning and household activities (voluntary work, home help).

What is the position of Belgian trade unions vis-à-vis these practices which are, at times, criticised as contributing to processes of precariousness and, at times, valued for rehabilitating individual initiative?

It would be a mistake to consider employment as a stable state which generated a specific pattern of trade union behaviour, and which is now being disrupted by instability due to the economic crisis. The wage relationship which is the object of a work or employment contract defines the conditional nature of a worker's participation in an enterprise. By externalising fluctuations in the volume of work outside the production unit, wage-earners bring about the concept of unemployment inherent in the system of wage employment [Salais, Baverez et Reynaud, 1986].

Under such conditions, stability of employment is relative and can be meaningful only in terms of the inherent instability of the wage relationship. There is a limit, therefore, to workers' participation in an enterprise, which is derived from their conditions of employment.

Even if it is not possible to directly identify a strategy or a well-defined trade union point of view on recent developments in the labour market, it is nonetheless possible to formulate a double hypothesis that we shall attempt to substantiate hereafter:

---

1. Institut de Sociologie, Université Libre de Bruxelles.

2. "Downsizing": the process of reducing large units of production to small and medium-sized enterprises.

(i)   Contrary to what is assumed under the dualistic hypothesis [Michon, 1981], the trade union movement tends to consider that the labour market is not subject to an increasingly rigid division between primary and secondary employment [Piore, 1981], but is becoming gradually more precarious overall.

(ii) The trade unions' attitudes towards the extension of precarious jobs not only differ between federations but vary greatly at different levels inside the same organisation. To understand such positions, albeit divergent, it is necessary to consider them within the general programmes for action of trade union organisations.

I. Negotiating levels

In a country where collective labour relations have reached a stage of institutionalisation as elaborate as is the case in Belgium, changes in "employment status" are subject to negotiations between employers and trade unions at different levels: centralised in sectoral or interprofessional collective agreements, in the discussion of specific measures or draft legislation in the National Labour Council (CNT), or decentralised in negotiations within enterprises.

Whatever the level of negotiations, they, on the whole, lead to exceptions from the norm as defined by the standard labour contract (law of 1900), the employment contract (law of 1922), the civil service status or the unemployment regulations. Several studies [for example, Aslin and Oyce, 1987] have revealed two tendencies in Belgium: (i) the increasing number of exceptions, which constitute a "system of exemptions" in order to respond to the flexibility strategies of the employers' organisations; (ii) a fragmentation of the collective bargaining system which gradually tends to focus itself at the enterprise level.

Though this overall trend is currently taking shape, it nonetheless remains limited. Collective Employment Agreement No. 42, concluded through the CNT in 1986, is, on the contrary, an attempt to revert to the traditional system of industrial relations. It reaffirms the predominance of the sector over the enterprise, and thereby puts an end to deregulation in collective relations which is based on the primacy of the enterprise over the sector, as was advocated by the Royal Decree No. 179 of 30th December 1982. Thus, the current "logic of derogations" [Aslin and Oyce, 1987] is increasingly occurring within a traditional sectoral procedure. Despite positions highly favourable to flexibility, employers have accepted the procedures set out in C.C.T. No. 42, which shows their distrust of decentralised bargaining. The breakdown of the traditional bargaining system has not so much resulted in "deregulation" establishing the primacy of the enterprise, as in the transformation of the enterprise. We may very well wonder whether the debate on centralised or decentralised bargaining does not leave out hybrid situations, centred on the region and more adapted to a network of related enterprises, often linked via local sub-contracting [Centre d'Etudes de l'Emploi, 1988].

II. Non-standard forms of employment

While the propagation of non-standard forms of employment status originated with high unemployment levels, it has actually resulted from governmental strategies aimed at reducing unemployment and from the labour management practices of enterprises. In 1987, the public authorities sponsored schemes to provide practical training for young people and to create jobs in the non-commercial sector (targeting the unemployed, temporary special "cadres" [C.S.T], "third work circuits" [T.C.T], subsidised contract workers, etc.) which involved some 110,000 persons [Derroite, 1987].

At the same time, new alternatives in labour management have emerged within firms and have induced an increase in the number of small and medium-sized enterprises, often ephemeral: sub-contracting has been encouraged by new forms of work organisation such as "kan ban" or "just in time"; new workers have been recruited via temporary labour agencies or fixed-term employment contracts; some inworkers have been turned into outworkers, leading to various forms of "downsizing" [Vanheerswynghels, 1981],[3] which illustrates the different ways large conglomerates use small and medium sized enterprises; and finally, there has been greater recourse to part-time work.

In fact, the slight growth in global employment registered over recent years results from an increase in these forms of "special employment".[4] If the standard employment contract defines the terms on which most individuals are employed, it does not apply to new offers of employment which are either part of schemes aimed at reducing unemployment, or part-time positions, or fixed-term jobs, or a combination of these forms.

It should be noted that to varying degrees we find mostly women in non-standard forms of employment; this explains why women's employment is resisting the crisis relatively well. The discrimination against women has gradually shifted from the *work performed* (i.e. the type of task and circumstances) towards the *conditions for employment* (i.e. access to and

---

3.   This "downsizing" can be summarised under four headings:
   - The firm breaks away from a factory or subsidiary, and consequently what was only an establishment becomes an enterprise;
   - The group is transformed into several small and medium enterprises;
   - The firm encourages a number of its employees to become self-employed to continue the same activity;
   - The group participates in the valorisation of a site which it no longer exploits itself.

4.   Over a period of three years (1984-1986), global employment increased from 3,634,711 to 3,697,937 in Belgium, and global wage employment from 2,997,499 to 3,042,777 (source: Ministère de l'Emploi et du Travail). Over the same period, the number of "unemployed working part-time to escape unemployment" increased from 65,400 to 128,300 (source: ONEm).

expulsion from the labour market, occupational status and role)[Maruani, 1987].

The measures adopted by governments to reduce unemployment and encourage a maximum of individuals to take up non-standard employment on the one hand, and the forms of labour management that firms adopt for their "flexibility" strategies on the other, are contributing to the development of unstable and low paid jobs, of "first job" activities more readily accepted by women, young people or immigrants, and which give credence to dualistic labour market theories. Consequently, two essential elements contribute to the internal composition of the trade union movement: unemployment and precarious employment.

III. Issues at stake in the bargaining process

At the various stages of bargaining on employment issues, the employers' objectives can be broadly described as aimed at introducing a "system of exemptions" into the conditions of employment so as to make them more flexible[5], whereas trade unions tend to set up control mechanisms in view of safeguarding social advances related to employment or at least "to limit exemptions by subjecting them to their prior agreement and to wage and time compensations" [Aslin et Oyce, 1987].

While current positions may thus be described in broad terms, in practice they tend to be asserted in a pragmatic and contradictory manner at different levels. Trade unions are first and foremost concerned with reacting on a case-by-case basis to the situations they face in firms and to legislative or institutional developments.

Trade union responses vary according to regions, sectors, local power relations, types of firms, forms of unionisation, etc. By way of illustration, we will restrict ourselves here to indicating shop stewards' responses, statements and comments from metallurgical firms in the Charleroi region. These reactions are the subject of a recent report from the Charleroi Metal Workers' Federation, affiliated to the F.G.T.B. [1988]. All shop stewards point out the threats that the introduction of agency labour, fixed-term contracts and sub-contracting constitute. In a steelworks, for example, following a strike to stop the hiring of temporary agency labour, the latter were replaced by fixed-term contract workers. "The development of sub-contracting", say the trade unionists, "contributes to the process of precariousness in employment since working conditions among sub-contractors are relatively unfavourable to workers". Precariousness for some leads to precariousness for others and gradually as "bad jobs turn good ones

---

5.   On "flexibility", Aslin and Oyce [1987] insist on "the ambiguity of a polymorphous concept which, at a general level, as a universal synonym for 'doing away with rigidities' or 'dismantling social gains', is a word of which the only reality lies in the ideological coherence of the employers' position on which it is based or of the trade union stand challenging that position" (p. 7).

out", we are faced with a "precariousness dynamic" of employment overall. "We accept changes", unionists readily agree, "but security of employment must be the counterpart". Trade union activity must then "socialise change".

In practice, the behaviour of trade unions at firm, sector or interprofessional levels has been characterised by an adaptation to circumstances and pragmatism. However, it is possible to distinguish the main axes underlying the programmes for action of the major trade union confederations and to schematise how both – the *Fédération Générale du Travail de Belgique* (F.G.T.B.) and the *Confédération of Syndicats Chrétiens* (C.S.C) – take into account the employment problems which arise in a context of increasing unemployment.

IV. Trade union positions[6]

Since the end of the war, the F.G.T.B. has gradually built up a programme based on the concepts of democratic planning, reform of economic structures, workers' control, participation at all levels in the discussions on social action, and a policy of social infrastructure. In such a perspective, the preservation and amelioration of the workers' purchasing power as well as a reduction in working time are fundamental. Concomitantly they would enable the workers' lot to improve and contribute to the economic recovery. Exceptional progress in productivity must be matched by parallel improvements in consumption and leisure if we want to avoid duplicating the conditions which gave rise to the crisis of the 1930s. The struggle for better wages and working conditions, and for a reduction in working time, are not in contradiction but are prerequisites for the defence of employment.

In 1974, while the Tindemans I government embarked upon its anti-inflationary policies, the F.G.T.B. placed emphasis on the increase in unemployment. Its programme – which called for a stronger public sector, for an economic recovery based on the preservation of purchasing power and shorter working time – was viewed as the solution favouring employment. At the same time, the Federation requested government and employers to guarantee existing employment levels in order to stop the rise of unemployment.[7]

While these positions were increasingly divergent from those of employers, which were becoming more radical (opposed to shorter working time for the same wages, cuts in social expenditures, change in the system of wage indexation), and with no interprofessional agreement reached between 1975 and 1980, the F.G.T.B. presented, in 1978, a plan for a general

---

6.   Our presentation of trade union programmes is based on the analysis carried out by Alvarez et al. [1987] of the activity reports of the F.G.T.B. and the C.S.C. between 1970 and 1985.

7.   These positions were to be systematised in the "progressive alternative" presented at the 1977 Congress of the F.G.T.B.

reduction in the working week to 36 hours, to come progressively into force and be effective by the end of 1980.

As for the government measures aimed at reducing unemployment, the F.G.T.B. supported the experiments enabling people to return to work (C.M.T., C.S.T., T.C.T. and practical training for young people) but considered them to be only temporary measures to boost demand. It called for the legislation to be adapted so that these new work statuses would benefit from similar rights to those of other employees. It opposed the generalisation of part-time work, considering it to discriminate against women, to induce lower incomes and to be no solution to unemployment. Part-time working must therefore be kept within certain limits.

The principles of a general reduction in working time compensated by additional recruitment, of an improvement in purchasing power and of a selective recovery, as advocated by the F.G.T.B., would no longer be taken into consideration by employers or government. On the contrary, the latter were advocating the extension of part-time work and fixed-term contracts in response to the need for flexibility. In 1983, the implementation by the government of an employment plan (the 5-3-3 plan) allocating a 5% decrease in the total wage bill to financing a 3% reduction in working time and an additional 3% of recruitment would be considered by the trade union as a failure, since only the restrictive part of the plan was implemented without generating any real extra recruitment.

Throughout this period, the F.G.T.B. was presenting its programme as a way out of the economic crisis. It proposed a general reorganisation of taxation and social security as an alternative policy to reach a more equitable distribution of income and to defend social advances. These positions had little impact on reorienting labour relations, which reflected more the radical employers' positions, expressing a need for flexibility and fashionably flavoured with neo-liberalism.

From the late 1960s, the C.S.C. for its part was also advocating economic planning as a means of guaranteeing economic expansion, ensuring a more egalitarian distribution of income, achieving full employment and developing social infrastructure. From the early 1970s, the C.S.C. stressed slower growth and unemployment. It called for the implementation of an active economic policy within the framework of a government-sponsored industrial initiative.

Up to 1974 these two main trade union bodies had developed convergent themes but subsequently the C.S.C. began to diverge. It emphasised the distribution of available employment rather than working time reduction and specific job-creation measures. From 1977, the C.S.C. seemed to take some economic constraints as given and to agree with the need for austerity measures. It acknowledged that the development path of the 1960s, previously considered as a reference, was no longer valid. At its 1985 congress, while advocating solidarity between workers and the multitude of unemployed, it accepted policies of wage moderation and the restoration of public finances, albeit accompanying them with a large number of conditions.

Concerning employment, the C.S.C. at a very early stage called for the creation of a third work circuit besides the private and public sectors. It therefore supported the establishment of government measures to reduce unemployment (C.S.T., T.C.T., training courses) and wanted to propose new employment measures. For this reason it insisted on the importance of the non-commercial sector and the sharing of available work. However, it remained cautious towards the extension of part-time work.

Although the C.S.C. had accepted, subject to reservations, the austerity measures advocated by governments since 1979, it recognised that while such measures enabled firms to improve their competitiveness, they hardly had any favourable effects on the volume of employment. Like the F.G.T.B., the C.S.C. was therefore to be confined to a defensive position focused on social security and the protection of the least privileged.

Thus, for a considerable time span, the programmes of the two major unions had converged, and they had fought many battles on a common front. Since 1974, under the effect of unemployment, of the trade unions' incapacity to make their positions prevail on the reduction of working time and, no doubt, also as a result of the long absence of the socialist parties from government coalitions, their programmes have diverged. Competition between the two unions grew and the elaboration of common claims and actions became increasingly rare at interprofessional, sectoral or firm levels. Beyond these divergences, however, it is possible to identify, in their stands on employment, a base common to both trade union organisations.

V.   Proposal for a typology

At the sectoral and national levels, the trade unions have three means of influencing developments: (i) through their programmes for action they aim to defend employment; (ii) as "social agency" they sit in a vast number of institutions with multi-partite representation (National Labour Council, National Employment Office) and seek to regulate some forms of work (temporary and part-time work, etc.), to limit as much as possible exceptions from the standard forms of employment and to orient general political choices in a direction favourable to employment; (iii) they function as a service, particularly at the legal level where they assume the defence of individual workers in order to prevent case-law from taking a direction unfavourable to workers and as far as possible to avoid social matters being tinged with legal considerations.

Although "trade union responses" are wide-ranging, depending on the level (enterprise, sector, interprofessional) concerned, and are defined pragmatically on a case-by-case basis, we can identify some common points and establish a typology. Trade union demands vis-à-vis employment can be classified as follows:

–   those aimed at orienting general economic choices in a direction favourable to employment;

-   those encouraging employers to invest and therefore create employ-
    ment;

-   those intended to provide the public sector with the means to play an
    active economic role as State-entrepreneur, creating employment;

-   those designed to reduce working time, thereby redistributing available
    employment;

-   those aimed at defending and extending systems of social protection;

-   those aimed at encouraging public authorities to develop programmes
    to reduce unemployment;

-   those aimed at reducing the number of job seekers by keeping them
    off the labour market (increasing the school-leaving age, lowering the
    pension age, early retirement, etc.);

-   those aimed at obtaining social compensation for workers who are
    victims of restructuring or lay-offs.

On the whole, the demands made since 1974 in a period of
redundancies, scarcity of work and rationing of employment [Vincens, 1987]
have pursued a doubly defensive objective: to dissuade employers and public
authorities from declaring redundancies by making dismissal as costly as
possible and, where this is unsuccessful, to obtain compensation for workers
deprived of employment. Thus, the trade union demands have demonstrated
continuity in union practices, but at the same time an adaptation to the
scarcity of employment. There is continuity since two types of occupational
struggle still dominated: wage demands and job protection. Work may be
considered heavy, arduous, dull or degrading for the worker but the job to
which it corresponds will nonetheless be sought after and its precariousness
or loss deplored[8]. A job enables the wage-earner to be remunerated for the
time he spends in an enterprise. To resist such a system, trade unions have
focused their demands on a reduction in working time and wage increases.

Then we can understand the claims of trade unions on all fronts:
shorter working day and week, longer schooling and lower retirement age
aim at reducing the duration of working life by delaying its start, advancing
its end and creating leisure time within; claims related to the rhythm and
rate of work challenge working time itself; wage claims lead to higher
consumption. The struggle "against" work and "for" employment in the trade
union tradition are two facets of the same struggle. The typology presented
above is truly linked to trade union tradition and emphasises the continuity
in its demands.

This brief outline shows how demands for shorter working time go
hand in hand with those for full employment. It is through fighting for
employment and making provision against unemployment that the wage-

---

8.   Decoufle and Maruani [1987] designate *work* as the situation and the conditions in
which work is performed, and *employment* as the same activity considered from the point of
view of the labour market mechanisms.

earner can both tackle work and take advantage of leisure time. The community of workers, transcending market rivalries, strives to assert itself as the subject of social production.

In the current period of crisis and unemployment, new demands result from the fact that the traditional claims procedure is being undermined within its two components: wage claims come up against the refusal of employers and government austerity policies, while claims for shorter working time, instead of being reinforced, are being checked. On the one hand, the existing power relations do not permit a decrease in working time without a decrease in wages and, on the other hand, the increased scarcity of employment makes it unlikely that allegedly rational wage-earners would withdraw voluntarily from the market or readily accept to share available employment [Decoufle and Maruani, 1987]. On the contrary, some categories of workers are involuntarily dismissed from their jobs while others turn to part-time work to escape unemployment. The crisis of collective bargaining reflects these two stumbling blocks. Consequently, the trade union movement, which had institutionalised its bargaining capability through a group of consultative and participative bodies, appears to be pushing against thin air [Grinberg and Tollet, 1983].

VI. Employment "cells" and "funds"

For trade union organisations, the 1975-1985 period was characterised by a set-back in terms of employment and purchasing power, which reflected the gradual erosion of their positions and the weakening of their bargaining power. However, could not we consider some initiatives, such as the "employment cells" (action groups), and in particular the conclusion of the 1986 interprofessional collective agreement and the resumption of collective bargaining, as a resurgence of trade union intervention?

1. Employment "cells"

The first employment "cell" was created in 1977, following the closure of the M.M.R.A. (Rodange Athus Mining and Metalworks) at Athus. Managed jointly by workers and employers, it comprised some 1,500 metal workers. Its objective was essentially to implement the social part of the closing down agreement which aimed to provide workers with a guaranteed income during a minimum period of readjustment (100% of income for the first year, 90% and 80% respectively for the following two years). The reassignment of workers was to be carried out by a company created for this purpose, the S.D.B.L (Luxembourg Basin Diversification Company). The "cell" remained in existence until 1980.

The closure of part of the Glaverbel factory at Gilly led, in 1979, to the signature of a tripartite agreement (employers, trade unions and government) offering workers either individual reassignment with severance payments higher than those specified by law or collective agreements, or admission to a scheme with, as at Athus, a guaranteed income, and skill training appropriate for new jobs to be created through a public sector project for the renovation/insulation of buildings in Charleroi. The ONEm and recurrent education associations linked to trade union organisations were responsible for workers' training during the transitional period. The "cell" started with 220 participants and came to an end in 1981.

 Such "cells" are not institutional alternatives for workers deprived of employment, but palliatives for lost jobs, secured after social struggles aimed mostly at preventing the closure of enterprises. Subsequently, in order to find concrete solutions to the problems faced by the workers involved, the "cells" and their resulting projects resorted to:

(i)   government schemes to reduce unemployment (C.S.T., T.C.T., etc.);

(ii)   the provisions of the Royal Decree of 30th October 1975, modified by the Royal Decree of 27th April 1976, by which a redeployment allowance might be granted to people who, while receiving unemployment benefits, were to undergo vocational training at the ONEm[9];

(iii)   the special loan for the unemployed, in fact too low to cover expenditures incurred in setting up small-scale enterprises.

Without being equally involved in those different projects, the two trade unions are behind the establishment of the "cells", and have played a very active role throughout their existence. Although the organisations do not express the same positions – the C.S.C. and the André Oleffe Foundation consider the cell projects as "alternatives" to the existing types of enterprises, whereas the F.G.T.B. considers them as workers' rearguard actions – it is clear to those concerned that the "cells" constitute merely a makeshift solution and a meagre compensation for the loss of employment. The first employment cell set up resulted from a failure – i.e. the closure of M.M.R.A.; those organised later on have, on the whole, also been established as compensation for damage incurred and have not represented an alternative, pointing to changes for the future [Olivier, 1983a and b; Lemoine, 1987; Alvarez, Bude, Gobin et Waaub, 1987].

The objectives of the different cells and I.L.E.s[10] have changed. Initially, employment creation projects were to be included within the framework of public or mixed initiatives (Athus, Glaverbel); gradually, they became mostly small-craft projects or created forms of self-employment. Thus, from attempts to reconstitute "standard" employment, the cells became instrumental in the processes of precariousness through their resorting to government measures to reduce unemployment and to encourage individual self-employment. As such, they are efforts to escape unemployment by using any available means.

---

9.   This redeployment allowance, paid for a maximum of one year, corresponds to the previous gross salary, but subject to a ceiling (in 1982, the ceiling was BFR 61,008).

10.   I.L.E.: Local Employment Initiatives.

Evaluation of the employment created through the "cells" or I.L.E.s is not easy because the results diverge among individual cases, the information is insufficient and the evaluation criteria are complex [Alvarez et al., 1987]. Any assessment must take into account the fact that the total number of workers involved (some 2,400) is negligible compared to the number of jobs lost. No doubt this explains why the I.L.E. schemes and the employment "cells" receive more attention from the civil servants responsible for unemployment or the researchers studying it than from trade union programmes.

2. Employment "funds"

Following a period in which the conclusion of collective agreements slowed down, the interprofessional agreement reached on 7th November 1986 for the period 1987-1988 may represent a significant turning point in the resumption of free bargaining between trade unions and employers [Beaupain, 1986; Blaise, 1986; Desmarez, 1987].

It should be borne in mind that this agreement consists only of guidelines and recommendations for negotiations in bipartite commissions on the main areas of trade union demands, i.e. employment, purchasing power and shorter working time. The agreement recommends the gradual generalisation of the 38 hour week, pays particular attention to the guaranteed average minimum wage and recommends the allocation of 0.5% of the total wage bill to employment promotion, in particular for young people.

On the basis of this interprofessional agreement, a large number of sectoral agreements have been concluded. Banking, where no compromise has been reached, chemicals and paper are exceptions. In the chemical sector, following the breakdown of negotiations at national level, strikes, often of long duration (five weeks), took place in a number of firms to press for either wage increases or changes in the organisation of work. These conflicts ended with the conclusion of local agreements which granted important wage increases. In the paper sector, following the failure of a bipartite commission, a strike developed in the Turnhout region and ended in a local agreement shortly before the conclusion of a sectoral agreement [Desmarez, 1987].

Concerning employment, 0.5% of the total wage bill has been allocated towards an "employment fund" in many sectors. In most cases, allocation of these funds has been decided within enterprises (replacement of personnel taking early retirement, hiring of new workers, promotion of part-time work, breaks in careers, industrial apprenticeship, training courses for young people...). In some sectors, firms cannot themselves use the resources thereby levied but must transfer them to existing or new funds which support training or employment promotion. In some cases, as for

example in the metalworking sector, part of the resources must be transferred to a joint training fund [Desmarez, 1987].[11]

This interprofessional agreement is not a departure from traditional
practices, except in being exhortative rather than compulsory. The agreement once again focuses on negotiations within the sector, for both its
finalisation and its application, though trade union activity at enterprise and
sub-regional levels plays a significant part in its realisation and implementation.

VII. The trade union as a "social agency"

Already, between the two wars, at the time of the Labour Plan[12],
the socialist trade union movement had attempted to respond to the "crisis
of capitalism" by an alternative intended to constitute a "left wing" way out
of the crisis. After the war, the F.G.T.B. programme of structural reforms[13]
was seen in the same light. Nowadays, with the revival of liberal theses,
trade union proposals again fall within a Keynesian perspective. Programmes of selective reflation, shared by several European left-wing currents
(including the Belgian socialists), which diagnose the lack of profitability as
the basis for the present crisis, attempt to re-initiate a process of accumu-
lation in industrial structures which have become deficient. But the
promotion of more self-centred growth and an investment support policy
implies a reallocation of public expenditures at the expense of social
transfers. While such a policy may constitute a government programme for
socialist parties, it is fraught with danger for trade union organisations. In
particular, if it implies that trade unions abandon the practice of wage-based

---

11.   It should be noted that, in several sectors, besides this 0.5% of the total wage bill,
special measures concern training, early retirement and breaks in careers (in those sectors with
a large proportion of women).

12.   While the socialist movement was considerably weakened by the crisis and suffered a
heavy electoral defeat in 1929, Emile Vandervelde, President of the Belgian Workers' Party,
called in Henri De Man to prepare "a plan for economic action, claim platform and
programme for government action". The Plan aimed at establishing a mixed economy,
enlarging the domestic market to reduce unemployment, and achieving real economic and
social democracy. On the basis of this programme, with strong trade union support, the
socialists participated in the 1935 government and attempted to implement a policy of
economic reflation. The concepts of authoritarian State and national socialism, which were
later defended by De Man and were to bring him to collaborate with the occupying forces,
were to make the Plan, in the words of the historian J. Gotovitch, "the infant prodigy
prematurely lost of Belgian socialism".

13.   Adopted by the F.G.T.B. Congresses of 1954 and 1959. The report to the 1954
extraordinary Congress emphasised nationalisation of the energy sector and was in favour of
a policy of economic reflation. The report, entitled *Holdings et démocratie économique*,
presented to the 1956 extraordinary Congress, considered that financial groups were the main
means by which capitalism dominated the economy. As remedy the F.G.T.B. proposed flexible
planning, taking into account the interests of the whole society.

claims to favour investment, is it not dropping the substance for the shadow? Is it not through wage demands that the trade union movement has imposed itself as an interlocutor, while it is increasingly excluded from investment mechanisms, as the capital restructuring that we are presently witnessing demonstrates?

The weakening of trade unionism in Belgium is not due to a drop in membership, as in France, Great Britain or the United States, but to a lessening of its negotiating capabilities, as witnessed by the decrease in the number of sectoral and interprofessional collective agreements between 1975 and 1985, and the fragmentation of negotiations at the level of the firm. The growing precariousness of employment, and "the questioning of the status of work through the explosion of precarious forms of work" [Grinberg and Tollet, 1983] are certainly at the origin of this weakness.

But should we not see in the resumption of sectoral and interprofessional negotiations in 1986 the result of intentions on the part not only of the trade unions but also of employers' organisations? Indeed, is not the increasing precariousness of employment compromising participatory projects of management as well as the whole ideology of the "enterprise culture"? Why should a worker commit himself to the full for the success of an enterprise project, when he is only a temporary or a part-time worker? Are not projects for participation in management, imported with great acclaim from Japan, related precisely to systems of life-time employment?

Within the enterprises themselves, methods of personnel management, forms of flexibility in production and static wages come up as much against the spontaneous resistance of workers as against the opposition of trade union representatives. Agreements at enterprise level may even contravene the prevailing sectoral or national rules and allow diverse ways of increasing wages. Sometimes, an agreement constitutes a facade hiding another, parallel one so that, in 1984, the C.S.C. itself denounced "black agreements" in firms which were offering workers *de facto* disguised wage increases (luncheon vouchers, professional expenses, profit-sharing, etc.), despite the government's austerity plan. Thus, changes in the organisation of work aimed at introducing multiskilling have been negotiated in exchange for wage increases or employment guarantees.

The crisis of trade unionism, as it has come to be called, is explained by the discrepancy between, on the one hand, the failure of the trade union leadership to successfully negotiate collective agreements, and thus to make proper use of the whole institutional structure set up since the Second World War, and on the other hand, the active militancy of these same trade union organisations derived from their stronghold within enterprises. Trade union activity in enterprises will therefore continue to weigh heavily on sectoral follow-ups to the interprofessional agreement of 1986.

It should be noted that this analysis is completely opposed to that developed by P. Rosanvallon in *La question syndicale* [1988]. He sees the future of trade unions in a role of "social agencies", i.e. quasi-public institutions responsible for social management and regulation at the expense of traditional militant demands. "The emergence of a more utilitarian attitude of workers towards trade unionism, together with the functions of social agency and interface in regulation that trade unions increasingly assume, raise the possibility, in the long term, of the almost total disappearance of regular trade union members"[14] On the contrary, we have tried to demonstrate that the "social agency" function, which was primordial between 1945 and 1975 in providing an outlet for workers' demands, became empty of content with the crisis, only to take shape once more with the surge of action in support of claims since 1986.

In fact, this opposition hides another more fundamental debate. Should the trade union movement, as Rosanvallon proposes, devote itself to "managing a system of differences" and to "social arbitration within the wage-earning population", or on the contrary, should it still remain mainly concerned with the distribution of income between capital and labour? For our wage-earning societies, the prime importance is given, in the first case, to a struggle for classification, whereas in the second case, the social nature of production is contrasted with the private nature of the ownership of the instruments of production. The importance of wage claims and the distrust of work-sharing formulas with no guarantee of income seem evidence enough of the enduring strength of a conception of class in the trade union movement.

In practice, because of the crisis, trade unionism has had to completely reverse its strategic capabilities. Previously, all actions in support of claims were geared to secure advantages in leading sectors with the view of subsequently "pulling up" the weaker ones, whereas now the movement is reversed and the conditions prevailing in lower income sectors seem to spread. Unemployment and the propagation of precarious jobs – not confined to a limited group of sectors – are leading to a general growth of precariousness in employment.

Even though the temptation may be there, the trade union movement cannot fall back only on workers in those enterprises where it is strong. On the contrary, the disappearance of "workers' strongholds" as restructuring takes place compels trade unionism to occupy its traditional territory: the defence of purchasing power and employment. But, it must also be a force for innovation: it must have an economic and social project for society as a whole, besides suggesting alternatives to the closure of enterprises at local level. In the process, the drive towards a greater autonomy of the trade unions with respect to political parties is accelerating while, paradoxically, their demands acquire a more political colouring.

---

14.   For Rosanvallon "the role of trade unionism as a social agency remains fundamental and cannot but increase, whereas its role as actor-protector and representative in the enterprise has to be considerably modified" [p. 110]. Trade unions would then be subsidised for the public functions which they would carry out, thereby confirming "the essentially functional nature of trade unionism" [p. 94]. To the author, such a development seems "inexorable".

VIII. Hesitant practices

The increasing autonomy of trade unionism, apparent over a long period, is less obvious in the short term. Growing unemployment and increasingly precarious employment affect the capabilities of trade unions to put forward proposals and negotiate; its very representativity is being adversely affected. Consequently, the trade union leadership attempts to restore a compromised situation through its relations with political parties and the State. Thus, the C.S.C. gains much from the continuous participation of the Christian Democrat parties in government, while the pressure of the F.G.T.B. for the socialist parties to participate in government after a long period in opposition has been evident. Trade union organisations thereby reap benefits of a "clientelist" type.

The trade union contribution to the systems of parliamentary democracy has constituted "one of the hinges upon which history turns", in the words of Thompson [1963], insofar as politics is no longer the exclusive sphere of an élite or group of professionals. For all that, it must preserve distinctive forms of representation different from those of electoral representation.

Since the crisis, trade unionism has been ineffectual in a number of its actions: in 1974, when it asked for the control of employment in order to stop unemployment from growing, it proved to be unable either to exercise such control itself or to impose it on the State. Later, although trade unions rallied to the need for austerity, the latter did not yield in return any positive effects on employment (see in particular, the 1983 application of the 5-3-3 Plan). Lastly, while trade unions made shorter working time a priority, progress in that field has slowed down.[15] Indeed, at the present time, the three essential elements of the trade union movement have been adversely affected: its effectiveness – in that its claims are no longer satisfied as they used to be in the past, its solidarity – to the extent that unemployment is exacerbating corporatism, and its legitimacy – insofar as its representativity is challenged.

In this context, weakened trade union organisations, though less so in Belgium than in France, Great Britain or the United States for example,[16] attempt to incorporate in their usual claims themes related to the conversion of industrial structures and its social costs, and to a transformation in modes of consumption and in cultural traditions of wage-earners. Thus, the way they have adjusted their demands has been defensive, wavering and often contradictory.

Since the question of sharing the fruits of progress, which lay at the basis of consensus during the years of growth, has been supplanted by austerity measures, the whole system of concertation has been left without

---

15. Despite the strong pressure of claims, reduction in working time has been less in Belgium during the period 1975-1980 than between 1971 and 1975. On this subject, see Alaluf [1982].

16. For details on the recent evolution of trade unionism in market economies, see *Labour and Society*, Vol. 13, No. 2, April 1988.

any hold on reality. It was precisely the frequency of negotiations which provided a rhythm for trade union life and gave coherence to its organisation. Consequently, the crisis of the system of concertation has been at the origin of the crisis of trade unionism in Belgium. Its whole organisation and machinery remain in a way outside the system on which its strength and its structuring have been based. Many of its current representatives have not experienced negotiations in which the trade union obtained tangible results. However, thanks to the organisation of its services, its firm hold in enterprises, the number of its members and its structure, trade unionism has withstood the crisis in Belgium relatively well in comparison to most industrialised market economies.

It is not possible to understand the attitude of trade union organisations in meeting the employment crisis, which conditions their own existence, without relating their concepts and general programmes to their actions specifically aimed at unemployment and precarious jobs. The pragmatic way in which trade unions have responded, on a case-by-case basis, to the initiatives put forward by enterprises or the State (at national, regional or firm levels), also structures a general attitude, a strategy for which we have proposed a typology.

In so far as employment cannot be circumscribed to a restricted sphere of claims, a trade union in its behaviour as a whole, however diversified, cannot evolve a dual vision of the labour market, which requires two different logics governing a stable and an unstable area. Rather, unemployment and labour market segmentation affect a trade union in its entire capability to push demands forward. Its programme, whether through general or specific proposals, then aims at driving the whole economy towards full employment. Consequently, the concepts of a dual market or society are mostly kept for speeches aimed at warning about the dangers society might face, while in practice, trade unionism attempts to respond to the growing general precariousness of employment and working conditions.

Changes in the level, content and form of collective bargaining lead us away from an atomistic conception of society, albeit without reproducing the post-war system of collective negotiation. We wish to stress here the interest of identifying the new forms which seem to emerge from the opposition between centralised and decentralised negotiations, which we have termed "intermediate" in conformity with the work of the *Centre d'Etudes de l'Emploi.*

In our societies, the transformation of work and of the wage relationship attached to it no doubt affect the use and reproduction of the labour force, i.e. the very notion of employment. It is through exceptions and derogations from regular forms of employment that atypical jobs are created. These, however, have not yet become a new norm. Trade union opposition and the resistance of the social canvas constitute their limits, even though the concept of employment has altered since the relationships, of which employment is the expression, have been notably shaken by the crisis, thereby bringing into question the notions of "contract", employer, enterprise and employment policies.

Trade unionism itself is, of course, at the heart of these changes. It contributes both to the reproduction of favourable terms of employment for wage-earners and to the transformation of such terms. In so doing, it is also the product of these changes. In the wavering positions of trade unionism towards the substance of the labour movement, i.e. employment, we perceive that such a movement can only be understood, borrowing Thompson's terminology, as an "active process, which owes as much to agency as to conditioning" [Thompson, 1963].

References

Alaluf, M. (1982): "Réduction du temps de travail et rapport salarial: une inflexion néolibérale?", in *Critique Régionale* (Brussels), No. 8.

Alvarez, I.; Bude, J.; Gobin, C.; Waaub, P. (1987): *Cellules d'emploi et environnement de crise*, Research report, Vol. II. Brussels, Université Libre de Bruxelles, Institut de Sociologie.

Aslin, M.; Oyce, J. (1987): "Flexibilité du temps de travail", in *Courrier Hebdomadaire du C.R.I.S.P.* (Brussels), Nos. 1148 and 1149, Feb.

Beaupain, T. (1986): "L'accord interprofessionnel", in *L'Année Sociale* (Brussels, Institut de Sociologie), No. 2.

Blaise, P. (1986): "L'accord interprofessionnel du 7 novembre 1986", in *Courrier Hebdomadaire du C.R.I.S.P.* (Brussels), Dec.

Caire, G. (1987): "Une forme de régulation des rapports sociaux: la négociation collective", in *Connexions* (Paris), No. 50.

Centre d'Etudes de l'Emploi (1988): "Negociation collective", in *Lettre d'Information du Centre d'Etudes de l'Emploi* (Paris), No. 7, Mar.

Decoufle, A-C.; Maruani, M. (1987): "Pour une sociologie de l'emploi", in *Revue Française des Affaires Sociales* (Paris, La Documentation Française), No. 3.

Derroite, B. (1987): "Contribution des dispositifs C.M.T., C.S.T. et T.C.T. à la résorption du chômage et profils des travailleurs" in *L'Année Sociale* (Brussels, Institut de Sociologie); No. 2.

Desmarez, P. (1987): "Un premier bilan des conventions collectives de travail sectorielles", in *L'Année Sociale* (Brussels, Institut de Sociologie), No. 1.

Fédération Générale du Travail de Belgique [FGTB](1988): *Agir ensemble pour s'engager plus loin*, preparatory working document. Congress of Metallurgists, Charleroi, 27 May.

Grinberg, G.; Tollet, R. (1983): "Le syndicalisme et la crise ou la crise du syndicalisme", in *Courrier Hebdomadaire du C.R.I.S.P.* (Brussels), No. 990.

Labour and Society (Geneva, IILS): Vol. 13, No. 2, Apr. 1988.

Lemoine, A. (1987): "Modèles expérimentaires de formation: trois expériences de cellules de formation reconversion", in *Critique Régionale* (Brussels), No. 15.

Maruani, M. (1987): "Sociologie de l'emploi: une recherche aux frontières de l'entreprise" (IInd Meeting on the Sociology of Work – PIRTTEM: "L'entreprise, catégorie pertinente de la sociologie?"), in *Cahier du LASTREE* (Lille), No. 2.

Michon, F. (1981): *"Une lecture des hypothèses de dualisme du marché du travail"*. Paris, C.N.R.S.-S.E.T., May.

Olivier, M. (1983a): "Premières expériences de cellules de formation-reconversion", in *Critique Régionale* (Brussels), No. 9.

— (1983b): *Courrier Hebdomadaire du C.R.I.S.P.* (Brussels), Nos. 996 and 1011.

— (1984): *Courrier Hebdomadaire du C.R.I.S.P.* (Brussels), No. 1051.

Piore, M. (1981): "Segmentation et marché du travail aux Etats-Unis", in Jallade, J.P. (ed.), *Emploi et chômage en Europe*. Paris, Economica.

Rosanvallon, P. (1988): *La question syndicale*. Paris, Calmann-Levy.

Salais, R.; Bavarez, N.; Reynaud, B. (1986): *L'invention du chômage*. Paris, P.U.F.

Thompson, E.P. (1963): *The making of the English working class*. London, Victor Gollancz.

Vanheerswynghels, A. (1981): "Les formes de P.M.I.'sation des enterprises de garage : attention une P.M.E. peut en cacher une autre", in *Critique Régionale* (Brussels), No. 7.

Vincens, J. (1987): "Politiques d'emploi et rationnement du travail", in Maruani, M.; Reynaud, E. (eds.): *France-Allemagne: Débats sur l'emploi*. Paris, Syros.

11 Non-standard forms of employment in the Federal Republic of Germany: The role and effectiveness of the State

Ulrich Mückenberger[1]

I. Introduction

In the Federal Republic of Germany (FRG), the concepts of a "normal" or "standard" employment relationship (SER) and of "atypical" or "non-standard" forms of employment have been gaining ground surprisingly quickly. Paradoxically, "normality" in employment – as in France [Supiot, 1984] – only began to be discussed when it could no longer be taken for granted, i.e. when it began to show a tendency to disintegrate. De-standardisation made us conscious of the standard which was formerly implicit.

The increase in atypical work has economic, technological, ecological as well as socio-cultural causes which cannot be discussed here. Due to technological developments, the level of employment is no longer closely linked to the overall rate of economic growth, so that it can no longer be taken for granted that all those wishing to work can support themselves and their dependents through "normal" employment. The persistent labour market crisis cannot be resolved through policies solely aimed at boosting growth because of limitations set by the threat to the environment. Even if, after allowance for economic, technological and ecological factors, a return to full employment were conceivable, would it be desirable? The central importance of paid employment in people's lives, in the individual and collective socialisation processes, and thus in determining social (especially gender) roles, is questioned, at least by certain social groups.

The debate about the standard employment relationship (SER) and the influence of the State on "atypical" employment[2] originated from the above developments. For some – especially the more traditional wings of trade unions – the SER remains the crucial reference point for individual and collective reproduction [Bosch, 1986]. Others – progressive wings of unions (e.g. women and advanced white-collar employees), Social Democrats

---

1.   Hochschule für Wirtschaft und Politik, Hamburg.

2.   Which is by no means "atypical" for certain segments of the labour force – to take but one example, women in part-time work.

[Lafontaine, 1988] and the Greens in general – see in the crisis of the SER a chance of re-defining both the place of work within people's lives and the mode of individual and collective production as well as reproduction [Mückenberger, 1985a].

Both positions implicitly or explicitly assume that the traditional form of reproduction among workers can no longer be taken as given. This also holds for some "neo-conservative" positions which favour more flexible patterns of employment not only because of labour cost saving, but because of new needs to adapt working life (and time) to changing social (e.g. family) life [Baden-Württembergische Landesregierung, 1983; Späth, 1985]. This neo-conservative wing is increasingly gaining support among labour law academics [Adomeit, 1985, 1986 and 1987; Rüthers 1985, 1986 and 1988]. At the same time as employers' associations and traditional Conservatism, they put heavy pressure on state agencies and institutions to deregulate and de-standardise working life and conditions. The role of the State with regard to non-standard work results from these different (and partly converging) interests and claims.

This paper looks at the part the SER plays in state intervention in West German industrial relations and social security, and how it affects opportunities for and risks run by workers whose terms of employment depart from the standard employment contract.

II. Recent trends

The FRG's current labour market and social policy was not initiated by the Conservative government elected in 1982, but has certainly been reinforced by it. This policy is centred around concepts such as "increased flexibility in employment relationships", "reduction in labour market rigidities", or more generally "deregulation" and "de-bureaucratisation". Prior to 1982, the social security net had for some years been loosened with a view to reducing budgetary deficits. Most of these cuts affected "marginal" groups, who could not attract publicity or mobilise support. These groups consisted mostly of atypical workers (relying on government help and family allowances in addition to their low wage incomes) and non-employed (unemployed, elderly, handicapped, sick) people receiving transfer income from social insurance [Bieback, 1984 and 1985]. This policy is still being implemented.

Till the end of the Social Democratic-Liberal government (Schmidt/ Genscher), labour legislation remained relatively unchanged though plans to reduce protective labour legislation existed [Zachert, 1984]. During the decline of the Social Democratic-Liberal coalition and the early period of the Conservative-Liberal government (Kohl/Genscher), conservative Christian Democrats and Liberal politicians such as Heimo George, Ernst Albrecht and Otto Graf Lambsdorff launched far-reaching programmes or at least ideas for deregulation in the fields of labour law and social policy [Zachert, 1984; Mückenberger, 1985b]. Since 1982, not a year has gone by without some legal initiative or projects being launched with the aim of weakening the existing system of legal safeguards. The only major conflict over this policy occurred over section 116 of the 1969 Labour Promotion Act (*Arbeitsförderungsgesetz*) – an act affecting all workers (not only non-standard) concerned by a labour dispute within their industry [Benda, 1986; Mückenberger, 1986a and b; Ossenbühl and Richardi, 1987; Seiter, 1987]. Since this conflict, the government, despite the backing of a re-election in 1987, has slowed down the implementation of its initial deregulation plans. But drafts for a total rearrangement of working time and the protection of minorities within shop floor representative committees [Mückenberger, 1985b] are still on the parliamentary agenda and will probably be passed within the current legislative session.

We shall attempt to demonstrate that these State policies contribute to (i) increasing discrimination against non-standard forms of work, and (ii) thereby, in an indirect way, weakening the SER itself, or at least eroding its universality as a labour policy paradigm.

III. Deregulation as the widening of the contractual sphere

In the neoclassical literature [Hayek, 1973 and 1986; Kronberger Kreis, 1987], deregulation often means a process of decreasing or even abolishing constraints which had been set up by previous State intervention (=regulation). This approach identifies regulation with constraint and therefore asks for deregulation in the name of freedom.[3]

But deregulation in the field of labour policy does not lead to the absence of regulation but rather to a type of regulation different from and – from a historical point of view – prior to the type of social legislation which shapes our current welfare systems.[4] A precondition of labour market regulation is the flexibility of labour considered as a commodity. The socio-institutional development of labour "from status to contract" [Sir Henry Maine; in Habermas, 1963] entails the historical process of the "double liberation" [Marx] of labour from both its feudal bonds and from the means of production, and the subsequent legal exchange of labour for wages. The "original" (as opposed to that observed recently) flexibility of labour did have a legal basis (abolition of serfdom, freedom of trade, freedom of contract) but otherwise was free of regulative State intervention (at least in the modern sense – leave aside traditional remnants of the guild system).

This original flexibility of labour was not at all unregulated though, as the neo-conservative theories argue. It was comprehensively regulated by two general principles which legally opened the way to a nearly unlimited entrepreneurial dominance: the freedom to conclude employment contracts (*Arbeitsvertragsfreiheit* – formerly contracts of service – *Dienstvertrag*) and a

---

3. On this, see an interesting critique by Deakin [1988].

4. For a comparison between the FRG and the UK see Mückenberger [1988].

managerial prerogative, the right of employers to direct labour (*Direktionsrecht*).

Regulation in the fields of labour and social policy was not an intrusion of the law into an unregulated area – at the expense of freedom as the neoclassical theory claims. It changed labour market regimes in order to counterbalance the unbearable absence of freedom that the original flexibility of labour brought about. Modern-day regulation of industrial relations did not impose constraints on "free" people. On the contrary, it aimed at making the freedom of workers more effective, whereas under the regime of free contract, freedom had only been "formal".[5]

In the light of this interpretation we can now focus on the notions of "regulation" and "deregulation". The framework is delimited by the contractual regime and the welfare legislation, which together determine the extent of managerial prerogative. Within this framework, regulation means a narrowing of the contractual sphere or "de-contractualisation" – i.e. the individual employment contract is emptied of some of its substance; welfare guarantees granted to workers are institutionalised and legally taken out of the employment contract. In contrast, deregulation means the widening of the contractual sphere or "re-contractualisation" – i.e. a process of shifting back the conditions of employment into the contractual regime and thus bringing them under managerial prerogative. With this approach, deregulation is conceived as a "re-contractualisation" process in those labour policy areas covered by welfare state regulation.

A contractual regime depends more on bargaining and on market power than does a statutory, even mandatory, protective regime. "Re-contractualisation" thus will favour those who have such power and discriminate against those who do not. But workers in non-standard forms of employment are often unorganised and hence lack bargaining power; "re-contractualisation" will therefore weaken their position more than that of the core of workers in standard employment.

IV. Setting up a "standard"

To assess the role of the State with regard to non-standard forms of work, it is necessary first to look more closely at the prior system of regulation, i.e. the welfare regime implemented before the current deregulation started. The tendency towards labour market segmentation and discrimination against non-standard forms of work did not start with the recent deregulatory movement. It was already embedded in the traditional structure on which the German labour regulation policy was built, in the very existence of a standard employment relationship, and in its formal and informal implications and effects. It has only been reinforced and sharpened through the process of deregulation.

---

5.   For the origin of the modern welfare state see Habermas [1981].

1. The area of law and social protection

In the FRG as in most Western countries, labour law and social protection systems encompass people working under an "employment contract", i.e. who are "employees". Nearly all statutory provisions in the fields of labour and social policy can only apply after the "employee test" has been satisfied. The concept of employee is not defined in the legislation but results from adjudication [Wank, 1988]. Employment is identified with "subordinate labour". An employee is a dependent worker whose dependency is not only economic but also "personal".

In the FRG, protective systems have been extended to some groups of non-employees. Some freelance workers, for example, have been allowed to negotiate collective agreements, and qualify for paid leave and other similar provisions. Homeworkers benefit from health and safety, and wage protection provisions. The social insurance system, though generally based on wage-related contributions and thus on employment, has widely been opened to non-employees such as the self-employed, artisans and farmers. However, these extensions are treated as exceptions – i.e. they apply only to the cases and to the extent expressly laid down in the legislation.

The concepts of employment and employee have a selective function besides a protective one. They cover "work" only where it is organised in a very specific form, with "subordinated labour". Obviously, this selective function gains in importance when applied to non-standard forms of work. Even though it is difficult to get exact figures, self-employment (open as well as hidden) is increasing [Paasch, 1987]. "New" (tele-) homework, though not widespread yet, offers a high potential for non-wage work. With such developments, the function of the existing protective systems is certainly more selective than protective.

2. Thresholds as a means of distributing risks

In the FRG, selection within most protective systems is based on quantitative or qualitative thresholds. Provisions apply only if the threshold figures are exceeded – e.g. if a certain minimum size of plant and/or a certain minimum length of service are reached. We can distinguish thresholds concerning persons from those concerning plants. Among the latter, the most important has been size and, of late, also the age of the plant. Plants with five or fewer employees fall outside the coverage of most important protective provisions – such as the Employment Protection Act (*Kündigungsschutzgesetz*) and the Works Councils Act (*Betriebsverfassungsgesetz*). The bigger the plant the more the firm is obliged to disclose information to the employees or the works councils, to inform state agencies in case of mass redundancies, and to set up "participatory" bodies within the organisation (co-determination, *Mitbestimmung*), etc.

The most important thresholds concerning employees are: duration of employment within the enterprise (i.e. seniority in the Anglo-American sense), length of total working life, age, length of weekly working time and income. Employees working less than 10 hours a week are not entitled to sickness payments by the employer (*Lohnfortzahlungsgesetz*); less than 15 hours (and a minimum income) are not mandatorily covered by the Sickness, Old Age and Invalidity Insurance; less than 19 hours do not qualify for the Unemployment benefits. As the whole system of social security in the FRG (as opposed to Sweden for example) is based on mandatory insurance, wage-related contributions and contribution-related benefits, the level of benefits largely depends on continuity, length of employment, hours worked and level of contributions.

Seniority plays an important role in the whole area of job protection. The Employment Protection Act as well as the Works Councils Act favour long-lasting employment not in the strict sense of the "last in – first out" principle but in a more moderate way: other things being equal, he (or she) who has the least seniority is more likely to be selected for redundancy and will qualify for less compensation. This is not just a matter of labour market power, it is also one of state intervention because these selection criteria are defined by law.

Obviously the whole threshold system has much to do with state policies towards non-standard forms of work. In fact many of these thresholds have a mere selective function – i.e. they distribute risks among employees in such a way as to favour standard and discriminate against non-standard work. Women, in particular, suffer from such discrimination at work. On average, women have less continuity in employment, form the bulk of the part-timers, and obviously accumulate criteria which make their labour market position worse than that of the average man.[6] But, to a certain extent, the increasing number of workers on fixed-term contracts and agency or temporary workers also lack protection in important areas.[7]

Some remarkable, if partly hidden, changes have recently taken place in the area of thresholds. Since the 1985 Employment Promotion Act (*Beschäftigungsförderungsgesetz*), part-time workers are no longer counted as full employees in the calculation of the 5-employee threshold. This slight change has served at least two purposes: an additional number of plants fall outside the coverage of the Act, and it gave an incentive to employers to prefer part-time workers. The same 1985 Act allows firms, in operation for less than 4 years and with less than 20 workers, to employ their staff on a fixed-term basis up to two years without any justification (*sachlicher Grund*) being necessary. Here again, thresholds play an important role in the distribution of risks among employees and lead to (or at least legitimise) an increasing amount of non-standard work.

---

6.   For the empirical side of part-time work in the FRG see Büchtemann and Schupp [1986].   10% of the labour force are part-timers of which 95% are women.   [See also Büchtemann and Quack, chapter 5 in this volume – *eds.*].

7.   For estimates of fixed-term contracts (about 8.5%) and agency or temporary workers (about 200,000 or 1% of the labour force, but much higher if illegal agency work included) see Bosch [1987] [and also Büchtemann and Quack, chapter 5 – *eds.*].

3. Substantive regulation and procedural regulation

Apart from the conditions of eligibility for legal protection (employee test, thresholds), regulation divides into two main elements: substantive and procedural regulation [Clegg, 1980]. Substantive regulation means setting minimum (e.g. minimum wage) or maximum (e.g. working hours) standards. Examples of substantive regulation include limits on working hours, exclusion of certain groups of persons from certain employments or jobs, minimum wage regulations, minimum safety standards at the workplace, some degree of protection from dismissal, etc. They may cover specific groups of working people (such as women, young people, the handicapped) or employees as such (e.g. protection from dismissal, working time regulation, safety at the workplace). Historically social regulation within capitalist societies started with such substantive regulation [for the FRG see Blanke et al., 1975; Stolleis, 1976], and it has remained, up to now, of major importance to safeguard the workers' working and the living conditions.

Procedural regulation consists in the establishment of procedures to set standards, to resolve conflicts, etc. Procedural regulation differs from substantive regulation in that it does not set standards which must be adhered to, but regulates who may set such standards, and determines who ensures that they are complied with. Historically, the State has been increasingly active in establishing and/or recognising collective bargaining and dispute solving procedures at enterprise as well as at regional levels. Examples of procedural regulation in the FRG are the Works Councils and the Enterprise Co-Determination Acts[8] and the Collective Agreements Act (*Tarifvertragsgesetz*). Substantive regulation restricts managerial prerogative and freedom at the level of the individual employment contract; in contrast, procedural regulation shifts bargaining competence from individual workers to collective agents, and thus deals with the collective participation of workers in the negotiation of their contracts and in managerial decision making within the firm.

V. Protective and selective functions of the SER

Both substantive and procedural regulations have recently been subject to the same deregulation trends encountered in other industrialised countries. It was suggested earlier that the current tendency towards labour market segmentation and discrimination against non-standard forms of work was not "invented" by the recent deregulation movement but was only reinforced and sharpened through it. It was already embedded in the traditional structure on which the German labour regulation policy was built, in the very existence of a "standard employment relationship", and in its

---

8.   For details see Mückenberger [1986c].

formal and informal implications and effects. Elsewhere [Mückenberger, 1985a], I have outlined the characteristics of the SER which historically resulted from substantive and procedural regulation. That analysis brought to light seven criteria which determine the degree of protection granted to an employment relationship in the German system of industrial relations:

(i)   duration of employment within the firm (i.e. seniority in the anglo-american sense);

(ii)   overall time spent in employment(s);

(iii) age of worker;

(iv)   weekly working hours (full-time vs. part-time);

(v)   work at the plant site (as opposed to outwork such as homeworking, subcontracting etc.);

(vi)   size of plant/enterprise;

(vii) skill level of worker/workplace.

It could be demonstrated that the reference model for the SER is employment which is continuous, long-term, full-time, in a medium sized or large establishment, and requiring a high level of skill. The protective functions of West German industrial relations and state interventions are designed and indeed most efficient for this type of employment relationship. It would be misleading to suggest that the "seniority principle" is enshrined in and dominates West German industrial relations as it does the North American system [Dohse et al., 1982]. Nevertheless, the protective measures based on the SER do exhibit similarities to such a principle in that legal benefits and the relative degree of protection are more or less strictly linked to the length and continuity of employment.

The finding is important in the context of this paper. Besides its protective function, the SER, as the basis for state intervention, also has a selective function. While it offers a degree of protection against the unlimited power of employers to freely dictate the terms of employment and to unilaterally manage labour, this protection is only provided through "discriminating" between different groups of workers, on the basis of whether or not they fulfill the main criterion of length and continuity of service.

This obviously has implications for the role of the State with regard to non-standard employment. Non-standard employment is defined by departures from the SER criteria mentioned above, especially from the criteria of length and continuity of employment. If the basis for benefitting from state protection is the degree to which an employment relationship meets the "standard", it necessarily discriminates against those employment relationships which do not meet that standard. State regulation in the form of a SER thus discloses a tendency towards discrimination against non-standard work.

The selective function of the SER has probably always existed, and is a reason why the SER has always been a normative, partly fictitious, reference model rather than an empirical model for employment. Besides employment relationships which were similar to the standard, there have always been those which were marginal and insecure (day-labour, seasonal and casual work, etc.). There has always been work which, irrespective of its social value, was not performed by wage labour and thus did not enjoy the same degree of protection as the "standard".

Nevertheless the selective function of the SER does not appear to have been equally prominent or problematic throughout history. The strength of better protected groups of workers can, under certain circumstances (economic prosperity) benefit less well protected groups, and so lead to overall social progress – if not to equality. These conditions probably prevailed throughout the development of state intervention during the prosperous years of the Weimar Republic and the in post-war FRG.

However, the discriminatory effect against non-standard employment, built into the German system of industrial relations and state regulation, is now contested. Two divergent trends express the paradox of current welfare state. On the one hand, the loss of prosperity and the rise in mass unemployment seem to have induced a "new inequality" within the welfare state [Leibfried and Tennstedt, 1985]. On the other hand, the welfare state itself, by means of its "egalitarian" cultural and political norms [Mückenberger, Offe and Ostner, 1988] has encouraged those groups of workers traditionally discriminated against, especially women, to articulate claims for equality and against selectivity of protection [Opielka et al., 1987; Heinze et al., 1987; Grottian et al., 1988].

VI. Compensatory policy

During the periods of economic prosperity mentioned above, the State has increasingly implemented compensatory policies to offset inequalities created by the industrial relations system and legislation. This also contributed to the emergence of a new idea of equality. The social insurance and security legislation, in particular, developed in the FRG during the late 1960s and the 1970s [Bieback, 1985], show an interesting ambivalence. This legislation can be seen as strengthening and supporting the dominance and selectivity of the SER, but at the same time as undermining it.

The German Social Insurance Act (*Reichsversicherungsordnung*), for example, links most of an individual's entitlements to the number of years he paid contributions and to the wages he received. In this respect, it merely extends to non-working periods (sickness, unemployment, old age, invalidity, injury at work) the relative position that an individual held in the labour market while he was employed.

Forms of employment which deviate from the SER norm – such as discontinuous employment, reduced earnings due to part-time work or a low skill level – are likely to lead to inadequate provision during periods of non-employment. This has largely contributed to the so-called "new poverty", especially among older women [Riedmüller, 1985].

The other function of the social security system is, of course, to provide a safety-net at times of non-employment. The development and spread of the social security system can be seen as a "de-coupling" [Gorz, 1983] from the SER. As examples we can cite: the widening of the social security net to encompass more workers and their dependents, the principles of full coverage in kind for health and injury through work insurance, the needs-oriented nature of public assistance (*Sozialhilfe*), and all benefits and social services the attribution of which is not based on current or past employment.

While the examination of social security legislation does not seem to question the SER as a guiding principle for state activities, it does show a distinct modification in the principle of selectivity in the distribution of opportunities on which the SER is based. Again this modification has developed most rapidly during the phases of prosperity already mentioned. Habermas identified these modifications as "compensatory". According to his theory, capitalist societies tend to deprive citizens of true participation and decision-making. In order not to lose legitimacy, states and governments – at least in phases of prosperity – try to "buy off" real participation and to substitute for it with social benefits. "Compensatory" social policies in this sense are equivalent to pacification by means of monetary payments [Habermas, 1981].

The effects of those benefit systems, however, seem ambivalent. They have contributed, besides and contrary to a pacifying impact, to a new cultural pattern, to a stronger belief in equality as such – independent of the workers' role and achievement within the labour market and the formal production sphere [Zoll, 1987 and 1988]. This new cultural pattern seems to be a source of legitimacy for new egalitarian claims and movements.

VII. Deregulation within the production area

Since the end of the "prosperity phase" in the FRG, the type of regulation described above has retreated. As early as the middle of the seventies, there was an erosion of the social security rights of some groups of workers and the relaxation of some labour law provisions began to be discussed. With the coming to power of the Conservative-Liberal government in 1982, such discussions were turned into legislative reality. What are the effect of these developments on state attitudes with regard to non-standard work, or in other words on the SER as a guide to state policy? How has the distribution of opportunities and risks brought about by state intervention been affected?

Trivial as it sounds, deregulation means a partial reversal of regulation: the replacement of a regulatory regime by a contractual one (see above: "re-contractualisation").

1. Substantive deregulation

The current tendency towards deregulation is clearly aimed primarily at substantive regulation. The objective is to lower standards which have been achieved through labour legislation and/or adjudication. It is no coincidence that much of the new legislation has dealt first with individual labour law, as this is more concerned with the setting of substantive standards than the law pertaining to collective relationships. The new legislatorial trend facilitates contractual deviations from the SER; thus forms of non-standard work are getting legitimised: those which used to be forbidden or controversial among labour lawyers (such as work with variable working hours, job sharing) as well as those "normalised" through adjudication along the lines of the SER (such as fixed-term contracts).

Two types of legal change can be distinguished: those dealing with the flexibility of employees' status ("external flexibility" in the terminology of Werner Sengenberger [1984]) and those dealing with the flexibility of personnel policy ("internal flexibility").

(a)   In the field of *external flexibility*, the most important new regulations are those making fixed-term contracts easier (1985 Employment Promotion Act; Acts Concerning Fixed-Term Contract at Universities and Concerning Young Doctors in Professional Training). Since the beginning of the 1960s the Federal Labour Court had imposed legal restrictions on fixed-term contracts to prevent employers from evading the existing regulations on unfair dismissal. German case law had hitherto maintained the requirement of a "fair reason" for both the conclusion and the duration of fixed-term contracts. This restriction has largely, if temporarily, been abolished – weakening not only the existing employment security but also the ability of works councils to exercise control. Another section of the 1985 Act, already mentioned, specifies that part-time workers no longer count as full employees for the calculation of the 5-employee threshold. This obviously restricts the scope of mandatory statutory law, and thus opens the way for the job security of the workers concerned to be placed under a contractual regime.

(b)   Flexibility of personnel policy – *internal flexibility* – is intended to be reached through legislation in the fields of working hours, shop closing time, and work on Sundays. Again this legislation aims at replacing the regular working day by a more flexible time regime. The pioneer, so to speak, in this area was the 1984 amendment to the Protection of Young People at Work Act (*Jugendarbeitsschutzgesetz*) which dramatically extended the length of time during which children and young people could be employed. More important still, the Working Hours Bill will eventually put an end to the notion of the "normal working day". For many workers, the 8-hour day (with a 6-day working week) will cease to be part of the daily routine. The working day will be extendable up to 10 hours, provided that the daily average over three calendar months does not exceed 8 hours (in exceptional cases 9) – with Saturday remaining a working day. Thus it will be possible for working hours to be flexibly increased or decreased to fit the needs of the firm, without infringing overtime regulations, and without overtime bonuses to be paid. Of course the forthcoming Act will apply only where no collective agreement on working time exists. Thus a selective effect of the act can be predicted: the well-organised segments of the labour market will stay under the shelter of working time agreements whereas the unorganised segments, not covered by collective bargaining, will suffer most from the new working time flexibility. This certainly will be the case for non-standard forms of employment.

Two provisions of the 1985 Employment Promotion Act should at least be mentioned in the context of internal flexibility. The act legalised various controversial forms of flexible part-time work (job sharing, "work-on-call"). And it made temporary agency work easier by extending the maximal duration of temporary hires from 3 to 6 months. Thus both the intensity and the flexibility of labour utilisation by firms are being increased.

2. Procedural deregulation

The current efforts at deregulation are more ambiguous when aimed at procedural forms of regulation. Recent legislation is characterised by:

(i)   An unmistakable trend to revert to individual contracts. The decision-making prerogative concerning the terms of the employment relation-ship is being transferred to the individual parties to the contract (cf. the new regulation on part-time work and fixed-term contracts).

(ii)   A rise in "permissive legislation". The new acts merely tend to set very general principles, transferring the real decisions on the setting of standards to other bodies. We often have dispositive rather than mandatory law. The Working Hours Bill contains very few substantive regulations but consists mostly of clauses dealing with procedures to be followed in exceptional cases. For example, section 21a of the 1984 Protection of Young People at Work Act empowers various authorities to grant exceptions from legal standards. A unique recent trend: the Church, one of the biggest employers, has expressly been allowed to deviate from important protective standards and, instead, to follow its own rules.

(iii) A tendency towards "particularist" regulation – as opposed to the "universal" character that labour legislation and social security used to have in the past. The best example is the 5-year time limit attached to the validity of two important provisions of the 1985 Employment Promotion Act (fixed-term contracts and temporary agency work). Regulations referring to particular groups of employees (academics, young doctors, young workers and the disabled) point in the same direction. These specific measures allow a selective reaction (both in terms of situations and personnel) to labour market and economic problem areas. Under different political conditions such selective legislation could be protective – i.e. a "positive discrimination" towards groups of workers who are usually discriminated against by "free" market forces. Under the auspices of Neo-Conservatism and neo-classical economic policy, however, selective legislation tends to strengthen market constraints imposed on weaker groups of workers, thus "de-coupling" their legal status from hitherto universal standards.

(iv) A fragmentation of the collective structures for negotiation. The draft amendment to the Works Councils Act will increase the representation of workforce minorities on the Works Councils and their committees, and will ensure separate representation of the senior staff within a firm, thus undermining the relative unity of collective, plant level employee representation. More important is the disputed reformulation of section 116 of the 1969 Work Promotion Act which was adopted in 1986, after a bitter debate [Mückenberger, 1986a and b]. As a result, if workers in an industry are laid off or put on short-time work owing to an industrial dispute in that industry, the risk of not being entitled to unemployment benefits will increase proportionately to how closely trade union demands are integrated across regional boundaries. In this respect, the consequences of the amendment, whether intended or not, will be to decentralise bargaining, as regards both subjects and timing. This decentralisation again could reinforce a tendency towards de-coupling weaker segments of the labour market.

3. Modification of thresholds

In most cases thresholds, as we have already seen, indicate the boundaries of applicability of mandatory substantive law. Changes detrimental to the workers directly open the way to contractual regulation: under conditions of an asymmetric power relationship, as between the two parties to an individual contract of employment, this will obviously hit the employee – the more so, the weaker his or her position in the labour market.

4. Passive deregulation

In the fourth type of regulation – the "employee test" as a precondition for labour and social security eligibility – we nowadays find a type of deregulation which often is not perceived as such. In the cases mentioned earlier, deregulation consisted of the State modifying the existing legislation. Either the standards on which the SER was built were changed ("active direct deregulation"), or re-regulation encouraged the conclusions of contracts deviating from the SER ("active indirect deregulation"). In the context of the "employee test", we also find a "passive deregulation". Due to recent technological and organisational changes in the industrial and service sectors, more and more work traditionally organised as "subordinated labour" (in the sense of the employee test), is being or will be organised as "self-employment". Such self-employment shows an substantial increase. The contracts between self-employed people and the firms for which they work do not come under the regime of labour and social security law but under that of civil and commercial law. In a welfare state, one would expect that such a weakening of existing protective structures would be counterbalanced by an extension in the coverage of labour and social security regulations. Failing to do so would result in an increasing number of (former) employment relationships escaping from legal protection and entering into an unprotected area. This passivity of the State needs to be perceived as a specific form of deregulation: as an omission of protective steps which ought to be taken. Passive deregulation, for at least a major part, is prejudicial to weak segments of the labour market unable to prevent their jobs from sliding into "self-employment".

VIII. Opposite trends in social security law

While recent developments in German labour legislation reflect a partial rejection of the SER as a policy guide, social security reform – as Bieback [1985] has demonstrated – is pointing in an opposite direction. The market-oriented insurance principle is being strengthened [Bieback, 1985; for unemployment insurance Kühl, 1987]. More specifically, the following lines of development have been observed:

(i)   "social income" (redistributed by the welfare state) as an alternative to "market income" (earned by means of wage labour), even on a temporary basis, has been reduced, and access to it has been made more difficult (e.g. the amendments to the Work Promotion Act, the Federal Social Insurance Act, the Family Allowance Act, the Federal Training Promotion Act). This has resulted in an increased pressure on individuals to take up subordinate employment at more regular intervals.

(ii) At the same time predominance of continuity in employment is strengthened, thus favouring those employment relationships which are closer to the standard. Amendments to the Work Promotion Act and the retirement pension law, for example, require longer qualifying periods ("thresholds") for entitlement to benefits. This leads to the exclusion of non-standard forms of employment, in particular of discontinuous work (such as fixed-term employment). The same amendment also extended the qualifying period for benefit entitlement for workers in long-term employment. Thus, unemployment benefits are part of a state-sponsored redistribution in favour of the SER.

(iii) In social security law, universal criteria for granting social security payments have been revised and to a large extent replaced by specific criteria. Social security law has therefore lost much of its general character and increasingly acquired a selective character. A series of social law provisions (disability and invalidity pensions, old age pensions, unemployment benefits, family allowances, training promotion grants) have now made entitlement conditional on need or poverty. A selection process based on subjective criteria of the social administration has become unavoidable. From past experience it is clear that such a selective structure works differently for different social groups, that it systematically discriminates against people who are either out of employment or in a precarious job. At the same time, it directly increases the discretionary power of those authorities who are responsible for distributing these social funds.

(iv) The re-individualisation of some social security benefits is used as a means of modifying recipients' behaviour. A narrower eligibility (in the unemployment insurance system and in the invalidity pension system), a greater stress put on means-testing (in legislation concerning student grants: Training Promotion Act), and a requirement to cover part of the costs (in health insurance) are measures which show that the authorities expect individuals to take over a bigger share in social responsibility, and which invest the authorities with more power of sanction against citizens. The result has been to increasingly tie social security benefits to what Habermas [1981] has termed "inner/internal colonialisation".

IX. Towards the "two-thirds" society

Paradoxically, deregulation comprises both the erosion of the SER, due to the active and passive weakening of labour law, and its re-establishment, due to changes in social security legislation. An increasing segment of the labour market – in non-standard forms of employment – is being excluded from the protective zone surrounding the SER. At the same time the social security system, formerly the obverse of the SER, and as such a major contributor to social redistribution and equality, is rapidly losing this characteristic.

Thus the two areas of state intervention – one weakening the SER and the other strengthening it – contradictory as they may seem, do in fact lead to the same direction. A common feature to both labour and social security laws is a state of tension between, on the one hand, the dominance of selective and hierarchical characteristics of the SER, and on the other, the compensatory tendencies towards social equality. The former element is more accentuated in labour legislation, the latter in social security law. This tension is being resolved at the expense of social equality. The *de facto* and *de jure* validity of the SER is on the decline, but at the same time, social security provisions are more subject to the criteria of precisely this form of standardised employment relationship.

With these trends the question of social solidarity, of course, is more acute. If state redistribution is more selective, the inherent tendency of the labour market to segmentation will increase, and this will have an effect on state intervention itself. The labour market segmentation will be both reproduced and legitimised, induced and strengthened by fragmentation in the social security system and labour law.

In the short run, this situation will be at the expense of persons and groups of people unemployed or in atypical jobs. The social "peace formula" developed during periods of prosperity can be formulated as "the strong will pull the weak up after them". Under present circumstances this formula is losing ground and threatens to be replaced by another: "the strong have let slip the ropes of the weak". This situation provides a basis for currently popular labels such as the "two-thirds" or the "elbow" society.

In the long run, however, an erosion of the SER itself seems to be unavoidable. The wider the grey zone of non-standard employment surrounding the SER, the more the SER loses its universality (even as a guiding principle for social policy) and hence legitimacy. In the current debate the standard is increasingly stigmatised as being a privilege of "job owners" denied to "non-job owners" (Minister of Labour Blüm). Even though this can be regarded as an ideological view, it still underlines the crack in the principle of social equality.

X. Law and reality

The evidence on the effectiveness of the de-standardising activities of the State is sparse. The major question remains whether governmental measures aimed at deregulation have affected the employment behaviour of employers or whether those measures – in a more symbolic than real mode – just strengthened and legitimised behaviour started earlier, independently of government intervention.

The paper certainly implies that state policies have an impact on labour market developments and therefore on status and conditions of non-standard forms of employment. However, this does not mean that state policies should be regarded as the *cause* of segmentation processes in the labour market. Some empirical research on the impact of the 1985 Employment Promotion Act, especially on whether or not it contributed to an increase in fixed-term contracts, has been published and the evaluation of the most important of these research projects – led by Büchtemann – is still under way.[9]

In the last decade, there has been a substantial increase in fixed-term contracts which started in the public service and spread to industry and the service sector. Interestingly enough, in the FRG the percentage of fixed-term employees in relation to the overall workforce rose from 4.2% to 6.8% between 1984 and 1985 – with a significant proportion among part-timers (7.6% to 8.9%) and young workers under 25 years (9.5% to 16.7%).

The Employment Promotion Act was passed in April 1985 and came into force on May 1st. It would be misleading however to conclude that section 1 of this act which made fixed-term contracts easier was the reason for this development. The trend toward fixed-term contracts started much earlier and followed a production logic more than a legal one [Dombois, 1986]. Nevertheless the 1985 act seems to have reinforced the development

---

9.   WZB [1987], comparing the German development with the UK and France; Linne and Voswinkel [1986] and [1987]; Wahsner [1987]; and statistical summary by Bosch [1987].

towards flexibility in employment status. This is particularly true for the first-time entries into the labour market (e.g. youths) or re-entries (e.g. women after child-bearing or child-care periods). In this respect, a real effect of the new legislation on the employment status cannot be denied. Another effect, no less important, of the State's new attitudes towards SER and flexibility is the changes wrought, remarkably quickly, in the "industrial culture". Within only a couple of years the notion of "flexibility" has gained enormous ground with mostly positive connotations. Job stability is no longer regarded as a value *per se*. Unstable non-standard forms of employment are losing their character of "exceptions". Even workers and their representatives begin to increasingly regard them as normal. The best example of this re-evaluation is the fixed-term jobs financed by the unemployment insurance (*Arbeitsbeschaffungsmaßnahmen*). Less than a decade ago, unions and unionised workers strictly opposed this "second-class" form of employment; nowadays the extension of these programs is unanimously demanded.

This change in the industrial culture clearly erodes hard-core opposition to non-standard forms of employment. At the same time it undermines the legitimacy of their counterpart, i.e. the SER. How quickly this process of erosion will spread is hard to predict. A hallmark in future development in this respect will be the year 1990. As has already been mentioned, the provisions of the 1985 Employment Promotion Act concerning fixed-term contracts and temporary agency work are limited in time until 1990. Whether or not these provisions will be freed from time boundaries will be a proper indicator of the degree to which German industrial culture will have adjusted to non-standard employment as a new "normality".

References

Adomeit, K. (1985): *Das Arbeitsrecht und unsere wirtschaftliche Zukunft*. Munich, Beck.

—— (1986): *Gesellschaftsrechtliche Elemente im Arbeitsverhältnis*. Berlin/N.Y., de Gruyter.

—— (1987): *Wen schützt das Arbeitsrecht?* Stuttgart, Bonn aktuell.

Albrecht, E. (1983): "Unser Sozialsystem liegt wie eine Zentnerlast auf der Wirtschaft", in *Handelsblatt* (Dusseldorf), Vol. 27, No. 8.

Auer, P., et al. (eds.) (1987): *Chronik zur Arbeitsmarktpolitik, National 1978-1986, International 1980-1986*, Beiträge zur Arbeitsmarkt- und Berufsforschung 99. Nuremberg, Institut für Arbeitsmarkt- und Berufsforschung.

Baden-Württembergische Landesregierung (ed.) (1983): *Bericht der Kommission "Zukunftsperspektiven gesellschaftlicher Entwicklungen"*. Stuttgart, Nov.

Benda, E. (1986): *Sozialrechtliche Eigentumspositionen im Arbeitskampf*. Baden-Baden, Nomos.

Bieback, K.-J. (1984): "Leistungsabbau und Strukturwandel im Sozialrecht", in *Kritische Justiz* (Baden-Baden), Vol. 17.

—— (1985): "Das Sozialleistungssystem in der Krise", in *Zeitschrift für Sozialreform* (Wiesbaden), Vol. 31.

Blanke, T. et al. (1975): *Kollektives Arbeitsrecht. Quellentexte zur Geschichte des Arbeitsrecht in Deutschland*. Reinbek b. Hamburg, Rowohlt.

Bosch, G. (1986): "Hat das Normalarbeitsverhältnis eine Zukunft?", in *WSI-Mitteilungen* (Cologne), Vol. 39.

—— (1987): "Arbeitsmarkt", in Kittner, M. (ed.): *Gewerkschaftsjahrbuch 1987*. Cologne, Bund.

Büchtemann, C.; Schupp., J. (1986): *Zur Sozioökonomie der Teilzeitbeschäftigung in der Bundesrepublik*, Labour Market Policy Discussion Papers 86-15. Berlin, Wissenschaftszentrum.

Clegg, H. (1980): *The changing system of industrial relations in Great Britain*. Oxford, Blackwell.

Deakin, S. (1988): *The comparative structure of labour law systems: State systems of regulation and the harmonisation of labour standards in the EEC*. International Working Party on Labour Market Segmentation, Xth conference, Porto (mimeo).

Dohse, K., et al. (eds.) (1982): *Statussicherung im Industriebetrieb. Alternative Regelungsansätze im internationalen Vergleich*. Frankfurt/N.Y., Campus.

Dombois, R. (1986): *Betriebliche Beschäftigungspolitik und Arbeitsmarktrisiken*. Bremen, Universität, Zentrale wissenschaftliche Einrichtung "Arbeit und Betrieb".

Feldhoff, J., et al. (1988): *Regulierung – Deregulierung. Steuerungsprobleme der Arbeitsgesellschaft*, Beiträge zur Arbeitsmarkt- und Berufsforschung 119. Nuremberg, Institut für Arbeitsmarkt- und Berufsforschung.

George, H. (1983): *Persönliche Denkanstöße*, Bonn, 13 July (mimeo).

Gorz, A. (1983): *Wege ins Paradies*. Berlin, Rotbuch.

Grottian, P. et al. (1988): *Die Wohlfahrtswende. Der Zauber konservativer Sozialpolitik*. Munich, Beck.

Habermas, J. (1963): *Strukturwandel der Öffentlichkeit*. Neuwied, Luchterhand.

—— (1981): *Theorie des kommunikativen Handelns*, 2 vols. Frankfurt, Suhrkamp.

Hayek, F. A. (1973): *Law, legislation and liberty, Vol. 1: Rules and orders*. London, Routledge & Kegan Paul.

—— (1986): *Recht, Gesetzgebung und Freiheit, Vol. 1: Regeln und Ordnung*. Landsberg, Verlag Neue Industrie, 2nd ed.

Heinze, R.G. et al. (eds.) (1987): *Sozialstaat 2000*. Bonn, Verlag Neue Gesellschaft.

Kronberger Kreis (1987): *Mehr Markt schafft Wohlstand. Konkrete Problemlösungen, Zusammenfassung der Schriften des Kronberger Kreises*, Vol. 2. Stuttgart, Horst Poller.

Kühl, J. (1987): *Beschäftigungspolitik in der Bundesrepublik Deutschland von 1973 bis 1987*, SAMF-Arbeitspapier 1987-5. Paderborn.

Lafontaine, O. (1988): *Die Gesellschaft der Zukunft. Reformpolitik in einer veränderten Welt*. Hamburg, Hoffmann und Campe.

Lambsdorff, O. (1982): *Konzept für eine Politik zur Überwindung der Wachstumsschwäche und zur Bekämpfung der Arbeitslosigkeit*, Sep. (mimeo).

Leibfried, S.; Tennstedt, F. (eds.): *Politik der Armut und die Spaltung der Sozialstaats*. Frankfurt, Suhr-Kamp.

Linne, G.; Voswinkel, S. (1986): "Befristete Arbeitsverhältnisse und das Beschäftigungsförderungsgesetz", in *WSI-Mitteilungen* (Cologne), Vol. 39.

—— (1987): "Personalpolitische Funktionen befristeter Arbeitsverträge und ihre Folgen für die Betroffenen im Betrieb", in *Die Mitbestimmung* (Dusseldorf), No. 40, Oct.

Mückenberger, U. (1985a): "Die Krise des Normalarbeitsverhältnisses", in *Zeitschrift für Sozialreform* (Wiesbaden), Vol. 31.

—— (1985b): "Deregulierendes Arbeitsrecht. Die arbeitsrechtsinitiativen der Regierungs-koalition", in *Kritische Justiz* (Baden-Baden), Vol. 18.

—— (1986a): "§ 116 AFG: Stadien eines Gesetzgebungsprozesses", in *Kritische Justiz* (Baden-Baden), Vol. 19.

—— (1986b): "Die Reprivatisierung der Arbeitskampfffolgen", in *Kritische Justiz* (Baden-Baden), Vol. 19.

—— (1986c): "Labour law and industrial relations", in Jacobi, O. et al. (eds.): *Economic crisis, trade unions and the State*. London, Croom Helm.

Mückenberger, U.; Offe, C.; Ostner, I. (1988): "Das staatlich garantierte Grundeinkommen – ein sozialpolitisches Gebot der Stunde", in *Festschrift für André Gorz*. Berlin, Rotbuch.

Opielka, M. et al. (eds.) (1987): *Die Zukunft des Sozialstaats, Vol. 1: Sozialstaatskrise und Umbaupläne*. Stuttgart, Die Grünen Baden-Württemberg, 3rd ed.

Ossenbühl, F.; Richardi, R. (1987): *Neutralität im Arbeitskampf*. Cologne, Carl Heymanns.

Paasch, U. (1987): "Besser selbständig als abhängig beschäftigt?" in *Die Mitbestimmung* (Dusseldorf), No. 33.

Riedmüller, B. (1985): "Armutspolitik und Familienpolitik. Die Armut der Familie ist die Armut der Frau", in Leibfried, S.; Tennstedt, F. (eds.): *Politik der Armut und die Spaltung der Sozialstaats*. Frankfurt, Suhr-Kamp.

Rüthers, B. (1985): *Die offene Arbeitsgesellschaft. Regeln für soziale Beweglichkeit*. Osnabrück, Fromm.

—— (1986): *Grauzone Arbeitsrechtspolitik*. Osnabrück, Fromm.

—— (1988): "Wandel der Industriegesellschaft – Möglichkeiten und Grenzen des Arbeits-rechts", in Scholz, R.; Hanns Martin Schleyer-Stiftung, (eds.): *Wandel der Arbeitswelt als Herausforderung des Rechts*. Cologne, Bachem.

Seiter, H. (1987): *Staatsneutralität im Arbeitskampf*. Tübingen, Mohr.

Sengenberger, W. (1984): *Zur Flexibilität im Beschäftigungssystem. Ein Vergleich zwischen den USA und der Bundesrepublik Deutschland*, SAMF Arbeitspapier 1984-3. Paderborn.

Späth, L. (1985): *Wende in die Zukunft*. Reinbek b. Hamburg, Rowohlt.

Stolleis, M. (ed.) (1976): *Quellen zur Geschichte des Sozialrecht*. Göttingen, Musterschmidt.

Supiot, A. (1984): "Délégalisation, normalisation et droit du travail", in *Droit Social* (Paris), No. 5, May.

Wahsner, R. (1987): "Zeitverträge in der Praxis – Auswirkungen des Beschäftigungs-förderungsgesetzes", in *Arbeitsrecht im Betrieb*, Vol. 8.

Wank, R. (1988): *Arbeitnehmer und Selbständige*. Munich, Beck.

Wissenschaftszentrum Berlin für Sozialforschung [WZB](1987): "Befristete Beschäftigung. Entwicklungstendenzen im internationalen Vergleich", in *Internationale Chronik zur Arbeitsmarktpolitik* (Berlin), No. 28, Apr.

Zachert, U. (1984): "Hintergründe und Perspektiven der 'Gegenreform im Arbeitsrecht'", in *Kritische Justiz* (Baden-Baden), Vol. 17.

Zapf, W. (1987): *Individualisierung und Sicherheit*. Munich, Beck.

Zoll, R. (ed.) (1987): *"Nicht so wie unsere Eltern!" Hypothesen eines neuen kulturellen Modells*. Universität Bremen, Dec.

—— (1988): *Plädoyer für eine individualistische Gewerkschaft*. Sprockhövel (mimeo).

12 The behaviour of the State and precarious work

Sergio Ricca[1]

I. Introduction

The development of precarious work is increasingly a source of concern not only for the growing numbers of those engaged in such employment, but also for trade unions, researchers and politicians. In particular, government declarations are more often than not opposed to precarious work, yet this opposition is rarely reflected in specific legislative texts or actions.

The attitudes of governments to precarious work can only be adequately assessed through the compilation of a patchwork of provisions taken from a large number of acts and laws, each dealing with a wide variety of subjects, and through a careful scrutiny of current administrative practice. The resulting picture is one of governments which accept precarious work as an inevitable fact of life, and which behave as promoters of precarious work at the same time as they condemn it.

II. The underlying ideology

During the past decade the development of precarious work was not the foremost preoccupation of governments. The aspect of social policy which concerned them more was the persistent growth of unemployment. The best policies were those most likely to reduce unemployment, or at least to halt its growth.

Until the early eighties two schools of thought dominated the political and economic scene of most market economies, each with its own interpretation of and its own solution to the problem of unemployment. The first, of Keynesian inspiration, defended the theory of employment growth through growth of aggregate demand. Increased job creation could be achieved through stimulation of demand for goods and services, together with an investment policy that would permit domestic production to satisfy that demand. For the second school of thought, more closely linked to the neo-classical theory, employment and wages were interdependent variables:

---

1.   International Labour Office, Geneva.

unemployment grew because labour costs were too high. If firms were to both increase employment and remain competitive they had to find a way of reducing the cost of hiring labour.

Market economy countries watched with utmost interest the attempt made by France to apply Keynesian prescriptions in the early eighties. That policy, which was expected to lead to higher growth and therefore to higher employment levels, consisted in increasing minimum wages, in reducing working time with no parallel wage reduction, in boosting employment in the public service, in encouraging public expenditure and in increasing public control of investment through a broad nationalisation programme. Some two years after its inception, France's experience was widely perceived as a relative failure, and this was interpreted as signalling the victory of the competing, neo-classical thesis: that for firms to be able to raise production and hence increase recruitment, they had to become competitive in world markets by reducing production costs, and first of all labour costs.

Growth in precarious work results primarily from the fundamental belief of many governments in the basic validity of the neo-classical theory for economic and employment policies. In this ideological context, the role of the State is to create an environment favourable to technological innovation, to increased participation in international trade, to greater enterprise profitability and to higher labour productivity. Employment policy should be designed to meet these objectives, and in particular should aim at providing, on time and in the right quantities, the new skills needed to respond to technical change and to fiercer competition in world markets. As for those workers who are no longer needed in the production process, they have to be taken care of by the State. Many governments believe that their role is to attempt to retrain and reinsert in the production process as many redundant workers as possible and, for the least able of them, to subsidise their employment and to provide other social safety nets.

Seen in this perspective, precarious work is not so much perceived as a sign of social failure as an improvement over unemployment. A precarious job is better than no job at all. Most public programmes of skill training or recycling and subsidised recruitment are nothing more than the creation of precarious jobs, on the initiative of governments, in their fight against unemployment. Precarious work then appears as a side-effect of what governments believe to be a sound employment policy.

Attempts to analyse government attitudes towards precarious work are complicated because many policy-makers seem to confuse the concepts of precariousness and flexibility. Flexibility can be defined as the aptitude of enterprises to react promptly to market signals, and to rapidly take rational management decisions (e.g. to renew equipment, to alter work organisation, to relocate plants, or to temporarily increase or decrease production). Flexibility has an obvious effect on labour market relations: in so far as it entails hirings and lay-offs, flexibility makes jobs more precarious. To the public authorities, precariousness therefore appears as the price to pay if enterprises are to obtain the managerial flexibility that they need.

III. The State as promoter of precarious work

So governments can be regarded as the initiators of a certain expansion of precarious work. However, precarious work has always been seen as a by-product of policies which aim at higher objectives, such as economic growth and employment growth.

A rapid survey of measures taken in recent years by various European countries in the field of labour legislation and labour relations reveals a willingness of governments to accept precariousness. No government has officially done away with the principle of the minimum wage, or has even attempted to reduce its nominal level. In practice, however, large numbers of youths and other under-privileged workers were hired at a sub-minimum wage level in government-subsidised employment promotion schemes. Officially, these workers were recorded as trainees, not yet entitled to the full rights of workers. The fact remains that many of these "trainees" were asked to perform tasks which otherwise would have been assigned to workers remunerated at least at the minimum wage level. Under the cover of employment promotion schemes, therefore, governments have often introduced the first form of precariousness, which consists in admitting exceptions to the principle of minimum wage entitlement.

One can record countless examples of concrete provisions made by governments in order to introduce increasing doses of flexibility, and therefore of precariousness, into the production system. The declared objective was to regulate new forms of labour relations, but it could as well be labelled disguised legal recognition of precarious work.

Thus, recent years have witnessed the development of measures aiming at defining and regulating fixed-term contracts. Similarly, many new laws and regulations have dealt with labour contracting and the functioning of labour agencies. In several countries, probation periods before a newly-hired worker is entitled to a long-term contract have been extended. In some countries, the procedures to protect workers against abusive dismissal have been relaxed. In others, the maximum duration of a single temporary work contract has been extended, while at the same time the list of situations where temporary work contracts are allowed has been widened or restrictions abolished altogether. In still other cases, recipients of unemployment benefits were allowed to undertake work for wages for a limited number of hours per week without reducing their entitlements. In a number of countries, private firms were allowed to participate in government-financed employment promotion schemes which were initially designed to create jobs of community or social interest. At the same time, some of the conditions for payment of unemployment benefits were changed to the disadvantage of workers, because either the duration of entitlement to benefits after job loss was shortened, or the rates were reduced, or workers were obliged to accept a less skilled or worse paid job than their previous occupation. Thus less favourable unemployment insurance helped increase the vulnerability of workers, and made them, albeit indirectly, more readily available for precarious work. Moreover, statistical definitions were modified in order to encompass new forms of employment, and accounting procedures were often redefined in such a way that the recording of precarious work contributed to reducing unemployment figures.

IV. The State as protector of precarious workers

It is undeniable, at least in market economy countries, that increasing acceptance of precarious work has been accompanied by an attempt to provide precarious workers with social protection, albeit more limited than that offered to more stable or permanent workers. For example, although exemptions from social security contributions were granted to employers in order to stimulate recruitment, this did not undermine the rights of precarious workers to social security benefits (sickness, family allowances, and pensions), as governments took on themselves the onus of paying the employers' contributions. Similarly, a number of measures granted the temporary worker or contract worker the same rights as those recognised for the permanent worker, including paid leave, and in some cases a special allowance (called "precariousness" allowance) paid as a compensation for the inherently precarious character of the job. Other measures were adopted to set up social security schemes for the self-employed or to extend regular social security benefits to the self-employed or to artisans.

The adoption of these measures cannot be fully set to the credit of governments, since the protection granted to precarious workers was quite often the result of hard negotiations or trade union struggles. Sometimes the precarious workers themselves, e.g. temporary workers hired through labour agencies, established unions in order to obtain recognition and better conditions of employment.

V. The State and the misuse of precarious work

Are governments as ready to fight malpractices in the use of precarious work as they are to recognise the usefulness of flexibility in employment? Government attitudes vary a great deal in this respect, and the existing mechanisms to detect and punish malpractices are diverse in their nature and effectiveness. It is true, however, that during the 1980s, labour inspection services have not grown or been strengthened in the same proportion as precarious work has developed, even though it is widely admitted that this form of employment is highly vulnerable to abuse.

Sometimes government failures are a direct consequence of mis-conceived employment promotion schemes. Take, for example, special schemes subsidising first-time recruitment, with a view to facilitating the entry of youths into stable employment. Many of these schemes have no built-in mechanism which would enable public authorities to detect those employers who systematically dismiss new recruits as soon as their entitlement to wage subsidies ends, replacing them with other new labour market entrants.

Sub-contracting is another endless source of abuse to which most governments have not paid sufficient attention. Sub-contracting is undoubtedly the most ingenious means of establishing a link between legal and clandestine enterprises; it also gives rise to forms of precarious work which have increased rapidly. This increase has not been matched by any parallel effort on the part of governments to define and regulate this form of production, nor by any special effort from labour inspection services to detect and punish illegal employment under the cover of sub-contracting.

Agency work has also given rise to spectacular forms of malpractice, even in the countries with the strictest legislation on temporary work. Checking for possible abuse in the millions of hours worked every year by agency labour is no easy task, but governments have not shown much imagination in devising techniques of indirect control over this very special form of triangular labour contract (for example, inducing associations of temporary work agencies to adopt and enforce a code of practice agreed upon with governments). Instead, control continues to rely entirely on the conventional visits of the labour inspector.

Other responses of the public authorities could be interpreted as forms of official recognition, and even legitimation of clandestine employment. Such behaviour is not intended to deny workers any rights to social protection, but the fact remains that when governments decide to include in the Gross National Product goods and services produced in the black economy, they convey the idea that clandestine employment and its malpractices are, after all, a social phenomenon that deserves to be reckoned with.

VI. Precarious work in the public service

The best way to assess government behaviour towards precarious work is to see how the question has been dealt with in public administration. Generalisation is risky, but one can venture to suggest that precariousness has become established and has spread in the personnel management policies adopted by governments in respect of their own employees. Over the course of the last decade, most public services have diversified their staff rules and generated a hierarchy in employment conditions, which can be ranked in terms of the degree of precariousness. At the top of the ladder, one finds the civil servant with tenure, whose post is financed by the government's budget, whose contract has no time limit, and whose career and conditions of employment are defined in the basic public service regulations. Below this status one finds a multiplicity of positions where public sector workers are employed on less favourable conditions: staff holding fixed-term contracts, temporary workers, staff hired under private contracts, or those hired by private contractors working on special government projects. The professional ambition of these workers is not so much to climb from grade to grade within the public service as to gradually progress towards a more secure employment status, and eventually to obtain the full status of a civil servant.

The relative but real growth in precarious public sector employment is due to various reasons: first, the need for flexibility, which is probably as strongly felt in the public as in the private sector; second, a change in the attitudes of public service unions, which increasingly act as if growing precariousness among public sector staff were a normal phenomenon in labour relations and therefore not a priority for union action; and last, but certainly not least, increasingly tight budgetary constraints. Despite recurrent crises, public sector employment has continued to grow in the majority of countries; but it cannot continue to do so indefinitely, unless ways are found to alleviate the financial burden of new recruitment.

VII. Proposals for government action

How should governments behave if they are really interested in curbing precariousness? Some national experiences can help us to think about possible concrete measures.

In certain countries, among them Sweden, a clear distinction is made between precariousness and flexibility. Cultural tradition and labour market constraints have induced Swedish enterprises to accept the primary burden of uncertainty. Sophisticated methods to forecast manpower needs at plant or company levels, the availability of a wide selection of training options (induction, on-the-job, or skill upgrading), a willingness to question and change work organisation or the distribution of duties, as well as the combination of these internal manpower management techniques, all allow firms to readily adjust skill availabilities to changing technical and marketing needs, while keeping the same core staff. When the enterprise is too small, or when all internal manpower management mechanisms are exhausted, public institutions such as training centres or labour exchanges extend the adjustment efforts of individual firms. Only when these adjustment efforts prove inadequate, at both enterprise and labour market levels, are redundant workers channelled towards subsidised employment promotion schemes, or, as the very last resort, granted unemployment benefits. This approach, where the risks of uncertainty are shared between enterprises and government, is certainly the most humane, as it preserves job stability better than any other. But it is doubtless also the most cost-effective for both firms and society at large. Taking into account on the one hand the costs both of inducting new workers into jobs and of high manpower turnover, and on the other the benefits derived from the high performance of well-integrated and motivated workers, one can see that job stability is efficient and that the obstacles to achieving it are more technical and organisational than financial. To resort to the labour market to resolve every problem of skill surplus or shortage may appear to firms as the most expeditious way of managing labour requirements. But it is not the only possible way, and it is by no means the least costly in either human or money terms.

There are cases where governments can play a stabilising role in highly volatile and uncertain labour markets. The legislation on temporary work agencies in the Federal Republic of Germany, for example, requires these agencies to sign fixed-term contracts with the workers they hire, but then allows them to contract these workers out on successive very short term assignments to different user companies. If the worker has no assignment while his contract is in force, he or she is, nevertheless, paid the agreed wage by the agency. This is a clear case of legislation transferring the burden of precariousness from the worker to an agency of which the *raison d'être* is to make profits.

The methods developed for resettlement or relocation of manpower with obsolete skills provide another example of a stabilising role. Some private firms, commonly known as *outplacement* agencies, have specialised in placement techniques which consist in relocating redundant workers into other skills or different jobs available in other enterprises. These techniques have the advantage of imparting a totally new character to dismissals: lay-offs are converted from a traumatic personal experience into technical transfers of people and skills to the jobs and enterprises where they are most needed. There is no reason why public employment services could not follow suit and adapt, on the scale of the whole society, the outplacement techniques that private firms are already implementing at the level of individual enterprises.

In general, it is the role of governments to become sensitive and make enterprises sensitive to the cost (financial as well as social) of precariousness. Recent research on the behaviour of trainees shows that the better integrated the trainees in an entrepreneurial project, and the more easily they can identify their own output and its contribution to overall production objectives, the more they are motivated to learn, and the greater the effectiveness of training. These motivating and hence efficient approaches to training are not compatible with precariousness. On the contrary, effective training requires workers to identify with their workplace, and this in turn implies a need for a stable working environment.

Finally, it is the role of governments to show determination in fighting abuses of precarious work. Employment promotion policies are too often (and wrongly) conceived at the expense of work stability or workers' protection. But job creation and workers' protection should not be contradictory goals. As precarious work becomes more widespread, the enforcement of legislation on employment conditions becomes more difficult. This suggests that in so far as job promotion schemes may lead to greater precariousness, government employment policies should be coupled with measures to strengthen labour inspection services; all too often the tendency nowadays is the reverse. Labour inspection not only deserves more physical and financial resources as precariousness increases, but it also requires special research efforts to design new methods for the inspection of vulnerable forms of work such as homeworking, or sub-contracted work in very small firms.

The seminar: Non-standard and precarious forms of work

held at the Université Libre de Bruxelles
26-28 September, 1988.

I. A synthesis: André Houyoux[1]

After three days of presentations and debates it would have been desirable to achieve an ideal form of synthesis, a packaging for a series of models stretching from the general to the specific: starting from a general model of the economy, and continuing with a model of the functioning of the state and one of worker behaviour and response. But too many unknowns limit our understanding of both structural and conjunctural variables, to say nothing of the differences of perception and of values among researchers and actors. The conclusion therefore has to be more modest, and is limited to a stock-taking of key factors, chosen because of their historical importance, because they highlight the influence of new forms of work or the contribution of atypical work to labour market regulation, or because they bring out interactions which merit further research.

Two facts emerged clearly from the seminar:

(i)   The actors concerned, operating in a complex and multi-facetted environment, show contradictory adjustments and ambiguous patterns of behaviour. This is true of the State, of enterprises, of workers and of trade unions.

(ii) Many of the processes involved are treated in a bipolar fashion. The solutions adopted are close to one or other of the poles, resulting in a bimodal pattern of solutions inconsistent with both optimisation and convergence.

1. The new pattern of regulation of the economy

A number of actors and variables participate at this level: the State, enterprises, trade unions, workers, the unemployed, jobs. In the following paragraphs an account is given of the part played by each. But other factors play a role which is no less important for being less visible:

---

1.   Institut du Travail, Université Libre de Bruxelles.

- demographic variables, in that population size and age structure have effects on diverse aspects of the economy and the labour market;

- education systems, along with their bureaucratic structures, their standard solutions and their adaptation to different groups of the population;

- the extent and growth of inequality, with its cumulative socio-economic consequences;

- the changing patterns of productivity in the heterogeneous service sector;

- the effects of growing international competition, among industrialised and developing countries alike.

2. New forms of work

Part-time work has historically been common in agriculture, and more widely under exceptional circumstances. Its current spread seems in some countries to respond to high unemployment, but it is also found in economies with full employment, such as Switzerland.

Economic development involves diverse processes, and depending on circumstances may exploit existing structures in new ways. Thus, in Italy the family is transformed into an entrepreneur while the artisan becomes a sub-contractor. But new forms of organisation may also be involved:

- the externalisation of certain enterprise functions towards the self-employed and the tertiary sector;

- a growing importance of production processes aimed at overall quality;

- multiple methods of sub-contracting and a corresponding reduction in stocks;

- the modification of standard patterns of working time in existing sectors and the emergence of new working time requirements in the tertiary sector (phased shifts or part-time work, etc.).

3. The State

For the moment, most Western European governments adhere to the neo-classical vision of the labour market. A minimal social protection is accorded to atypical work, but with a certain hypocrisy – it is interesting to note the weakness of labour inspection and the corresponding lacunae in control. Moreover, the State is an important employer of precarious workers, under the cover of many different statuses.

In this ambiguous situation, government action to limit precarious work is difficult; it is not facilitated by the lack of a policy aimed at sharing the burden of precariousness with enterprises. The outcome is restricted to a few specific, fragmented actions aimed at stabilising the situation. Indeed, the numerous formulas aimed at new forms of work testify to the symbolic nature of political action by their very multiplicity. Moreover, the state seems to prefer to use precariousness as a (negative) incentive, as much in relation to its own employees (whence the utility of a degree of precarity) as in relation to the unemployed (variation in the level of benefits and coverage); one can question the validity of such an approach. One should however also note that there have been attempts to create alternative routes towards valid careers, and significant support for the functional modernisation of enterprises through training activities. One absolute priority for the State is clear: to improve the evaluation of actions in this field in order to limit, as far as possible, undesirable side-effects.

4. Enterprises

The usual formulation, nowadays stereotyped, of enterprise concerns refers to quantitative flexibility, labour costs and the individualisation of pay. Enterprises have introduced numerous process and product innovations, and some have initiated new research into the interaction between the organisation and its work force. In some sectors there is unwillingness to acknowledge the implications in terms of personnel policies. Enterprises use standard work in parallel with atypical forms of work with a view to increasing flexibility, and there is increased creation of internal labour markets.

Among other relevant phenomena, one should note a certain propensity for enterprises to profit from the use of one or other government formula for labour market insertion. But it is also true that knowledge is lacking on how enterprises take decisions in an unstable environment, and the consequences for production organisation. More also needs to be known about the externalisation of certain functions to other enterprises or to self-employed workers; in particular, the development of various types of service enterprise is far from adequately understood.

5. Trade unions

One can interpret trade union actions as a means to protect the core of workers in the expectation of a probable return to full employment. Trade unions are integrated into the global economic system in very different ways from one country to another; but in giving priority to a normative role they are generally following an established historical pattern. One should note their difficulties in adopting new and innovative approaches and in obtaining an operational foothold in the complex tertiary trade system.

Trade unions participate in the regulation of new forms of work with positions which vary from opposition to negotiation. The variability of these attitudes reveals the uncertainty of the objectives of trade union intervention at both micro- and macro-economic levels.

6. Workers

Economic and sociological categorisations based on age, sex and educational level are increasingly needed to characterise workers. Groups such as youth and women are disproportionately represented in atypical work. Rather than to submit to categorisations based on sociological variables, it seems interesting to build up a psychological categorisation in which a typology of workers is based on their perception of their status. This implies the use of new survey instruments (with multi-disciplinary contents) and the identification of socio-economic reference points to permit accurate classification.

In a labour market which is more and more diversified, the management by individuals of their careers becomes more difficult: to establish the "bridges", avoid the "traps" and maintain a dynamic perspective requires motivational "vitamins". The interaction between the working environment and the individual increasingly demands training and learning trajectories which take account of the specificities of each worker; hence the importance of the use by the enterprise of its own internal labour market.

The experience of training for new qualifications highlights the need for a very active role for those being trained. The generalisation of labour force participation of spouses creates the need for households to develop strategies for the use of their available labour, with the compromises and new combinations which this implies.

7. The unemployed

For a large proportion of youths, unemployment is virtually a buffer for school leavers; the various institutional forms of work or training which provide temporary escape from unemployment should be considered in similar terms. It is necessary to know better the life and the perceptions of those who are unemployed or pseudo-unemployed, if we consider that good mental health conditions re-entry into professional life.

8. Jobs

In new organisations, the nature of jobs is modified in a variety of ways:

- each job becomes more and more an integral part of the production process as a whole, with an increase in responsibilities;
- jobs incorporate not only production activities but also prevention and recycling;
- jobs tend to become more multi-functional;
- in the light of the above, both horizontal and vertical communications between jobs are essential.

This situation contrasts with that of precarious jobs, with their shortcomings and their impacts on their temporary holders. One can also raise questions about the status of homeworking and about the need for its humanisation. The heterogeneity of jobs raises the problem of the application of ergonomics: should it refer to specific jobs or do these conditions justify a use of ergonomics at the level of the system as a whole?

II. Summaries of further papers presented at the seminar

Eberhard Köhler: "New forms of work and activity: Development and first results of a research programme of the European Foundation for the Improvement of Living and Working Conditions".

Some of the findings of current research on new forms of work, sponsored by the European Foundation for the Improvement of Living and Working Conditions are summarised in this paper. After briefly reviewing some of the categories of atypical work, it focusses on telework and telehomework. It was found that while there is fairly high potential for telework, the actual incidence remains small. The paper examines the design of working environments for teleworkers, and reviews compatibilities between telework and domestic roles, notably of women. Some implications for labour law and social security are suggested. For further details of this research programme see Dahrendorf, R.; Köhler, E.; Piotet, F. (eds.): *New forms of work and activity*. Luxembourg, Office of Official Publications of the European Community, 1986.

Michel Magrez: "Les nouvelles formes juridiques du travail salarié en Belgique" (New forms of wage work in Belgium from a juridical perspective).

The author reviews the new forms of contractual flexibility in Belgium, with particular reference to temporary work and part-time work, examining the Belgian legislation in detail. He notes the extension of new contractual forms to job creation programmes for the unemployed, and suggests that the outcome has been to undermine former conceptions of labour relations and to pose new problems of social justice.

Bertrand Schwartz: "Rôle et efficacité de l'Etat face aux problèmes du travail atypique" (Role and effectiveness of the State in dealing with problems of non-standard work).

The effectiveness of State-sponsored "alternating" or "sandwich" training schemes, in which work and training alternate, as a way of combatting the precariousness and vulnerability of jobs, are examined here. The author describes in particular two schemes in which he was involved in France in the mid-1980s. One of the objectives was to mould the occupational and training content to the needs of the individuals concerned, creating "new qualifications". The author argues that the schemes were rather successful as a means of occupational integration. They also provided a means of increasing communication and participation within enterprises, while leading to significant quality improvements.

Diane-Gabrielle Tremblay: "Innovation technologique et différenciation des formes d'emploi" (Technological innovation and differentiation in forms of employment).

The theme of this paper is to examine the links between atypical forms of work, internal labour markets (within enterprises) and technological innovation, mainly in a North American context. The forces generating internal labour markets and their structures are reviewed, including the relationship with technology and production organisation. This model is then used to examine the link between the growth of atypical forms of employment and enterprise strategies in the face of accelerating technological change.

III. Participants in the seminar.

M. Alaluf, Institut de Sociologie, Université Libre de Bruxelles.

M. Aseglio, Ministère de l'Emploi et du Travail, Brussels.

A. Bronstein, International Labour Organisation, Geneva.

C. Büchtemann, Wissenschaftszentrum, Berlin.

B. Burchell, Department of Applied Economics, University of Cambridge.

G. Caire, Centre de Recherches en Sciences Sociales du Travail, Sceaux, France.

G. Fonteneau, International Labour Organisation, Brussels.

A. Godart, Institut du Travail, Université Libre de Bruxelles.

A. Houyoux, Institut du Travail, Université Libre de Bruxelles.

G. Karnas, Faculté des Sciences Psychologiques et Pédagogiques, Université Libre de Bruxelles.

J. Jackson, Commission of the European Communities, Brussels.

E. Köhler, European Foundation for the Improvement of Living and Working Conditions, Dublin.

M. Magrez, Institut du Travail, Université Libre de Bruxelles.

A. Marshall, International Institute for Labour Studies, Geneva.

D. Meulders, Département d'Economie Appliquée, Université Libre de Bruxelles.

F. Michon, Séminaire d'Economie du Travail, Université de Paris I.

L. Mubikangiey, Faculté des Sciences Psychologiques et Pédagogiques, Université Libre de Bruxelles.

U. Mückenberger, Hochschule für Wirtschaft und Politik, Hamburg.

R. Plasman, Département d'Economie Appliquée, Université Libre de Bruxelles.

S. Quack, Wissenschaftszentrum, Berlin.

S. Ricca, International Labour Organisation, Geneva.

G. Rodgers, International Institute for Labour Studies, Geneva.

J. Rubery, Department of Applied Economics, University of Cambridge.

P. Salengros, Institut du Travail, Université Libre de Bruxelles.

B. Schwartz, chargé de mission auprès du Gouvernement, Paris.

Song Magrez, Institut du Travail, Université Libre de Bruxelles.

D. Tremblay, Télé Université, Montreal.

C. van de Leemput, Faculté des Sciences Psychologiques et Pédagogiques, Université Libre de Bruxelles.

N. van Gils, Ministère des Affaires Etrangères, Brussels.

E. Verborgh, European Foundation for the Improvement of Living and Working Conditions, Dublin.

P. Villa, University of Trento, Italy.

S. Wolf, Office National de l'Emploi, Brussels.